D1126674

From Dominance to Disappearance

From

Domina

to

Disapp

nce

earance

The Indians of Texas
and the Near Southwest, 1786–1859

F. TODD SMITH

UNIVERSITY OF NEBRASKA PRESS · LINCOLN & LONDON

© 2005 by the
Board of Regents of the
University of Nebraska
All rights reserved
Manufactured in the
United States of America

Library of Congress
Cataloging-in-Publication
Data
Smith, F. Todd (Foster Todd), 1957–
From dominance to disappearance :
the Indians of Texas and the near
Southwest, 1786–1859 / F. Todd Smith.
p. cm.
Includes bibliographical references and index.
ISBN-13: 978-0-8032-4313-2 (cloth : alk. paper)
ISBN-10: 0-8032-4313-8 (cloth : alk. paper)
1. Indians of North America—Texas—His-
tory—Sources.   2. Indians of North America
—Texas—Wars.   3. Indians of North America
—Texas—Government relations.   4. Texas—
History—Sources.   5. Texas—Politics and gov-
ernment.   6. Texas—Race relations.   I. Title.
E78.T4S65 2005   976.004′97–dc22
2005008683

Designed by R. W. Boeche.
Printed by Thomson-Shore, Inc.

For Sophie, Minou, Toby, and Allie

Contents

Maps

Preface

In October 1785 three chiefs, representing the Eastern Comanches, or Kotsotekas, entered into a peace treaty with the governor of Spanish Texas at a meeting held in San Antonio. The agreement, which both parties had been negotiating off and on for thirteen years, was a watershed moment on the Southern Plains. The Comanche Treaty was the last in a series of 1785 agreements in which the Spaniards in Texas, following more than three decades of war, established peace with a group of formerly hostile tribes, known as the Norteños. The treaties proved successful since the Indians and the Spaniards maintained relative peace in Texas for the next twenty-five years, until relations were disrupted by the movement for Mexican independence and the ensuing arrival of American colonists from the United States.

Until the late twentieth century few people were aware of the momentous agreements that had been reached two hundred years before. In 1975, however, the publication of Elizabeth A. H. John's *Storms Brewed in Other Men's Worlds: The Confrontation of Indians, Spanish, and French in the Southwest, 1540–1795*, dramatically changed the way people perceived relations between Indians and Euroamericans in Texas. Prior to *Storms Brewed*, an enormous narrative history that climaxed with the 1785 Spanish-Comanche accord, the few studies of the region's Native Americans tended to neglect the colonial era entirely. They also portrayed the Indians as savage barbarians who presented an obstacle to civilization, which the American settlers were forced to heroically overcome in the nineteenth century. For example, one of the period's most respected works, Rupert N. Richardson's 1933 study, bore the title *The Comanche Barrier to South Plains Settlement: A Century and a Half of Savage Resistance to the Advancing White Frontier*, and only ten of two hundred pages dealt with the era prior to the Americans' entrance into Texas.[1]

John's monumental effort focused exclusively on the colonial era and stressed the central role the various Indian tribes played in the Euroamerican settlement of the region between the Red River in Louisiana and the Rio Grande in New Mexico. *Storms Brewed* presented the Native Americans as rational beings who followed their own material interests in dealing with the

Spanish and French newcomers. Using archival sources, John showed how the Indians closely interacted with the Euroamericans, forging advantageous military and trading alliances with whichever power they felt had the most to offer. The work expertly delineated the various tribes, pointing out that most of the region's Indians did not primarily hunt buffalo from horseback, as a majority of movie-fed students believed (and still do), but that some were sedentary agriculturalists, while others hunted and fished near the Gulf Coast. In the quarter of a century since the publication of Storms Brewed, all worthwhile scholarly studies of the colonial Southwest, no matter how focused on the Euroamerican settlement of the region, have had to consider the importance of the area's Indians.[2]

John's book also launched a series of monographs on the individual Indian tribes of Texas and Louisiana, which traced their histories into the nineteenth century and beyond. A majority of the works focused on the numerous Comanches, the classic buffalo hunting tribe of the region.[3] Fewer studies looked at the Lipan Apaches and the Tonkawas, other tribes that primarily rode horses and hunted game.[4] A number of books examined the history of the settled, farming Caddoan-speakers from the precolumbian era up to the late twentieth century.[5] A few scholars studied the coastal Karankawas and finally succeeded in demonstrating that they were not primarily cannibals, as most Texas schoolchildren have traditionally been taught.[6] Histories of the Cherokees, Delawares, Shawnees, and Alabama-Coushattas, tribes that immigrated to the region in the late eighteenth and early nineteenth centuries, were also written.[7] Of all the area's Indians, scholars neglected only the Atakapas, a group of people that hunted and fished near the Texas and Louisiana coasts.[8] These works successfully overcame the triumphalist nature of the regions' Native American historiography by matching the quality of the sophisticated studies of Indians that had already been completed for the Northeast, Southeast, and Great Lakes regions of the United States.

Despite the recent multitude of individual tribal studies, only a few scholars have followed John's example of producing a general history of all of the region's Indians and their relations with Euroamericans. William B. Gannett's 1984 doctoral dissertation examined the conflict between the various tribes and the American settlers of Texas during the period of Mexican independence and the Lone Star Republic.[9] This work was hampered, however, by the fact that the author did not consult any Spanish language sources and that he dealt with the Indians by location rather than as a whole. More interesting was Howard Meredith's 1995 book, which traced the movements and cultures of the various tribes that were placed on reservations in the Indian Territory—present day Oklahoma—during the late nineteenth century.[10]

Using traditional native dances as a metaphor for the relationship between Southern Plains tribes and Euroamericans, Meredith's book concentrated on the Indians' dealings with the federal government in the twentieth century and neglected the many groups of the region that did not end up in southwestern Oklahoma. Three years after the publication of Meredith's work, David La Vere produced the first complete overview of Texas's Indian tribes in a forty-six page introduction to his edited work of native oral histories that the Works Progress Administration gathered during the Great Depression.[11] La Vere succinctly traced the history of the various tribes from precolumbian times to the 1930s, paying particular attention to how the Indians' material culture evolved following the arrival of the Euroamericans. This book was followed in 1999 by Gary Anderson's revolutionary study of the Indian economy of the Southwest between the beginnings of Spanish settlement in the late sixteenth century and the advent of the Americans' domination of the area in the early 1800s.[12] Through the innovative use of a wide variety of archival sources, Anderson persuasively demonstrated how many tribes altered their lifestyles following the Spanish and French intrusion in order to forge a thriving exchange-based economy relatively independent of the Euroamerican newcomers. Finally, in 2004 La Vere built upon his previous short essay by using secondary works and published primary sources to produce an excellent book-length history of the Texas Indians from their arrival in the region to the present.[13]

Although the past quarter of a century has witnessed a profusion of scholarly studies of the region's Native Americans that have greatly altered and made clearer our understanding of the various groups' experiences in Texas, no author has yet taken up John's unstated challenge of producing a successor to Storms Brewed, a detailed narrative history that would trace the tribes' interactions with Euroamericans from the establishment of peace at the signing of the Comanche Treaty to the Indians' expulsion from the state just prior to the Civil War. During this period of three quarters of a century, the Native Americans continued to play a very important role in the area. For the first half of the era the Indians maintained a numerical superiority over the Euroamericans that allowed them to influence the region's economic, military, and diplomatic affairs to a heretofore unrecognized degree. Although the fortunes of the various tribes declined rapidly following Texas independence, the Indians were not the barriers to civilization that previous scholars have described, but were a race of people desperately trying to survive in the face of overwhelming hostility. By the end of the period almost all of the few remaining Indians were forcibly driven from Texas.

This book, then, attempts to fill the void in the literature by being a worth-while successor to Storms Brewed and, thus, examines the relations between the Indian tribes and the various Euroamerican groups in Texas and the Near Southwest from 1786 to 1859. In order to maintain clarity, however, this work is more limited geographically than *Storms Brewed*. Many readers have complained that John's book, by going back and forth from New Mexico to Texas and Louisiana over a period of two and a half centuries, was confusing and nearly impossible to follow. Actually, the respective colonies' Indian affairs bore very little relationship with one another and, therefore, *Storms Brewed* was actually two separate books rolled into one. This study concentrates on Texas and a region I call—with apologies to Dan Flores—the Near Southwest, an area bordered on the east by the Red River, on the west by the Llano Estacado, on the south by the Nueces River, and on the north by the Canadian River. Throughout the period encompassed by this book, events in this zone—which traverses the political boundaries of Texas, Louisiana, and the Indian Territory—impacted all the area's tribes while having little if no effect on the Native Americans in New Mexico.

I also decided to begin this book a decade earlier than the conclusion of *Storms Brewed*, which ended, for little apparent reason, with the agreement reached between Spain and the United States in the 1795 Treaty of San Lorenzo. In reality, John's study built toward the agreement reached in San Antonio in October 1785—and one concluded a few months later between the Western Comanches and the Spaniards in New Mexico—and terminated soon thereafter. In part, this was a consequence of the fact that the English language translation of the Béxar Archives (the most important original unpublished source for colonial Texas) abruptly ends in 1789. As a result, few of the above-discussed works deal in any significant way with Indian-Euroamerican relations in the thirty-year period between the last decade of the eighteenth century and the American colonization of Texas in the 1820s, when English sources again become plentiful. Therefore, the histories of important tribes such as the Lipan Apaches, Tonkawas, Karankawas, and Atakapas, remain incomplete due to the continued scholarly neglect of the Spanish and French sources of the period. One of the most important contributions I hope to make with this book, then, is to fill the gaping hole that remains in the studies of Native Americans in Texas and Louisiana from around 1790 to 1825 or so. Therefore, I have thoroughly examined original microfilmed copies of the Béxar Archives from 1789 to 1836, as well as other contemporary Spanish language sources held at the Center for American History at the University of Texas. In addition, I have traveled to Seville, Spain, to look at the most important source for Spanish Louisiana, the Papeles Procedentes de Cuba, which contains, for the most part, French language documents held in the Archivo General de Indias.

Through the use of these unpublished archival sources, most of the contemporary published material, as well as the new wave of studies that have appeared over the last quarter of a century, I have attempted to produce a detailed narrative history that provides a clearer and deeper understanding of the nature of the Native Americans' dealings in the Near Southwest with Spaniards, Frenchmen, Mexicans, and Americans during an era of great transition. This work pays particular attention to the Indians' population, for I believe that one of the most important keys to the tribes' success or failure was their numbers in relation to the region's Euroamericans. Simply put, the Native Americans maintained their dominance in Texas and the Near Southwest only as long as they outnumbered the Hispanics, French, and Americans in their midst. I have also maintained a focus on the various tribes' locations and trading and military alliances, for the Indians played a very important role in the diplomatic affairs of the region well into the nineteenth century. Even after the general decline of the Native Americans following Texas independence, the different tribes followed widely disparate paths as they vainly attempted to maintain their position in the state. Unlike what most people today presently believe, not all of the Indians fought the Euroamerican settlers of Texas; in fact, most tried to reach an accommodation with the Texans that would have allowed them to peacefully remain in what they considered to be their traditional homeland. Unfortunately, Texan antipathy to the Native Americans was so intense that the state's citizens were not satisfied until only but a handful of Indians were driven from its borders. This book, then, narrates the story, formerly only told in piecemeal, of the Indians of Texas and the Near Southwest from the late eighteenth century to the middle nineteenth century, a period that began with the Native Americans dominating the region but ended with their disappearance from it altogether.

Special thanks must be given to four people, in particular, who helped me produce this book. Three of them are friends and colleagues, as well as being among the foremost experts on colonial and antebellum Texas. Mike Campbell, Don Chipman (now retired), and Gregg Cantrell (now at Texas Christian University) all read the manuscript and corrected errors I had made concerning the non-Indian Near Southwest, as well as providing important suggestions that greatly improved the original manuscript. The fourth person is my wife, Sophie Burton, who received a Fulbright Award in 2002 to conduct research in Spain on her own dissertation, and allowed me to tag along with her to Seville. Not only did she help me translate the documents I found in the Archivo General de Indias, she also read this manuscript countless times. I now have to repay the debt by doing the same for her. I can hardly wait!

From Dominance to Disappearance

1. Dominance

The Indians of Texas and
the Near Southwest to 1786

For as long as fifteen thousand years the descendents of people who migrated from Asia dominated the area now known as Texas. These first Texans, who came to be known as Indians, adapted to the various changes in climate that occurred during the fifteen or so millennia and established successful and complex cultures in the different regions they settled. Diverse groups of people, speaking numerous languages, adopted various methods that allowed them to survive, raise families, establish religious beliefs, and pass their knowledge on to succeeding generations. Some raised food crops in fertile river valleys, while others hunted animals and gathered wild fruits and nuts along the Gulf Coast and west into the interior. The various tribes arranged themselves advantageously; some moved about in small groups and others remained sedentary in populous towns. Although warfare was not uncommon, it was rarely destructive. In fact, many of the Texas Indians cooperated with one another and established extensive trade networks among themselves and with others of different regions. All embraced various creation myths and engendered beliefs about what occurred following death. By AD 1500 the Indians of Texas and the surrounding area to the north and east—the Near Southwest—were prosperous and thriving.[1]

The situation began to change in the sixteenth century with the arrival of Europeans in North America. The newcomers and the native Texans first came into contact with each other in the early sixteenth century when the Spanish explorers Alvar Núñez Cabeza de Vaca, Francisco Coronado, and Luis de Moscoso separately traversed regions of the Near Southwest between the years 1528 and 1542. Although it would be another century and a half before the Spaniards permanently settled in Texas and the French in Louisiana, these initial forays, together with the Spanish colonization of New Mexico in the early seventeenth century, brought two things to the Indians that would change their lives dramatically: disease and horses. Disease started to ravage the native population of Texas shortly after initial contact, long before the Spanish and French reestablished direct contact with indigenous peoples in the late seventeenth century. Many Texas tribes adjusted well to horses, however, and had incorporated them into their culture before the Europeans returned, thus greatly increasing their ability to hunt buffalo and to wage war. By the time the Spanish and French intruders did come back, the natives had adapted to the changes wrought by both disease and horses and remained the dominant force in Texas and the Near Southwest.[2]

Disease began to affect the Indians of the region almost immediately following the Spanish arrival on the mainland. Because of their isolation from the Eastern Hemisphere the natives of America lacked immunity to the sicknesses that had developed across the ocean. European diseases with the ability to diffuse in advance of direct transmission, such as typhus, plague, and smallpox, caused great population loss and cultural disruption among the tribes of Texas. Epidemics of smallpox, measles, and cholera decreased population fertility, and sporadic infections killed those who were born between outbreaks. Some tribes lost as much as 95 percent of their population. Following the introduction of European diseases into the region in the early sixteenth century, at least eight recorded epidemic "events" occurred in the Near Southwest over the course of the next two hundred years.[3]

These epidemics caused some tribes to disappear, while others were forced to change their lifestyle in response to the population loss. Because of the great demographic and economic changes brought on by the European presence in North America, remaining tribal groups often altered themselves culturally to forge unity with other bands in a process known as ethnogenesis. Threatened tribes created new communities tied together by intermarriage, adaptation of language, and the emergence of a new culture, effectively reinventing themselves in order to adapt to the new reality. Over time almost all of the Indian groups in the region went through the process of ethnogenesis in order to adjust to a growing European population presence.[4]

Tribes living near the Gulf Coast of Texas were the first to be affected by the foreign diseases. By 1680, on the eve of the European return, the population of the Karankawas, who lived along the Gulf Coast of Texas from Galveston Bay to Corpus Christi Bay, had been reduced to about eight thousand individuals. During colonial times the larger Karankawan cultural entity consisted of five principle tribes tied together by language and culture. The Cocos were the most northeastern group, living primarily along the lower reaches of the Brazos and the Colorado rivers. The Carancaguases made their camps southwest of the Cocos, around Matagorda Bay.[5] The Cujanes were located near San Antonio Bay, along the lower San Antonio and Guadalupe rivers, while the Coapites lived eastward near Aransas Bay. The southernmost Karankawa tribe, the Copanes, roamed the area between Copano Bay and the mouth of the Nueces River.[6]

The five tribes shared the same Karankawan language and had similar manners and customs. The Karankawas were unusually tall; men frequently attained statures approaching six feet and were noted for their strong and robust physiques. Like most Texas Indians, the Karankawas painted and tattooed their bodies and also pierced the nipples of each breast and the lower lip with small pieces of cane. To ward off mosquitoes they often smeared their bodies with a mixture of dirt and alligator or shark grease. Karankawa men usually went naked, or wore just a deerskin breechclout; the women wore skirts of Spanish moss or animal skin that reached to the knees.[7]

Although many natives died as a result of the epidemics, and some bands were forced to join with others to offset population losses, the Karankawas still maintained a hunting and gathering lifestyle throughout the European invasion. The Karankawa method of subsistence dictated that the members of the five different tribes arrange themselves into groups of only about five hundred people. As with most nomadic tribes, each group was a separate political entity. Leadership was divided between a civil chief, usually a tribal elder, and a war chief, a younger man probably appointed by the civil chief. The bands spent the fall and winter along the shoreline and the estuaries of the Texas Gulf Coast, where they fished and hunted deer. In the spring the Karankawas divided into smaller bands of about fifty people and moved inland to establish camps along the rivers and creeks that emptied into the coastal bays. In these prairie riverine camps, located no more than thirty miles from the shore, the Karankawa women and children spent the summer collecting the fruits of various plants such as mustang grape, prickly pear cactus, and Texas persimmon, and the men hunted buffalo and deer. The Karankawan bands relocated when the local resources had been exhausted, usually after a few weeks at the camp. To facilitate mobility, the Karankawas lived in portable wigwams that consisted of a willow pole frame covered with animal skins and rush mats, structures large enough to accommodate seven or eight people. The Karankawas, like other nomads, kept their tools and other material possessions to a simple minimum, and like the other native Texas tribes they used stone tools and weapons before the permanent arrival of the Europeans. They crafted light baskets and pottery, lining both with asphaltum, a natural tar substance found on Gulf Coast beaches. Their principal means of transportation was a dugout canoe made by hollowing out the trunk of a large tree. Each canoe was large enough to carry an entire family and their household goods and was excellent for short voyages across the shallow, placid waters of lagoons and inlets.[8]

In the interior, to the south of the Karankawas, resided a group consisting of as many as six hundred different bands that is now collectively known as the Coahuiltecans. The numerous bands of Coahuiltecans seasonally migrated throughout one of the harshest regions of North America, eking out a marginal existence by collecting nuts and fruits, mainly prickly pear cactus and pecans. The men also hunted deer, and tribal members captured small reptiles. Constantly on the move, the Coahuiltecans constructed low, circular huts by placing reed mats and hides over bent saplings. The only container the Coahuiltecans had was either a woven bag or a flexible basket. Spending most of the year under the hot Texas sun, Coahuiltecan men were nude much of the time, and the women wore deerskin skirts. Like the more successful Karankawas, the Coahuiltecans formed small bands of patrilineal kin groups led by a headman with limited authority. European diseases caused great displacement among the impoverished Coahuiltecans. By the end of the seventeenth century, perhaps as few as twenty thousand roamed throughout the entire sweep of southern Texas and northeastern Mexico.[9]

Another hunting and gathering group residing near the Gulf Coast was the Atakapas. Even though by the beginning of the eighteenth century they were less numerous than the Coahuiltecans, the Atakapas were more prosperous than the people living in the interior. The six thousand or so Atakapan-speakers consisted of four principal tribes: the Atacapas, Akokisas, Bidais, and Deadoses. The Atacapas and Akokisas lived near the sea and depended primarily upon gathering, hunting, and fishing for subsistence. The Akokisas roamed the area around Galveston Bay and the lower Trinity River; the Atacapas lived to the east along the lower reaches of the Neches and Sabine rivers. The Bidais and Deadoses lived farther upland, between the Trinity and the Neches, and practiced small-scale agriculture while hunting deer, bear, and occasionally buffalo.[10]

Although the Atakapas, particularly the Bidais and Deadoses, lived in relatively permanent villages, they were divided into separate bands, each led by a headman. In the summer the Atakapas lived in conical dwellings constructed of poles interwoven with vines; in winter they lived in bearskin tents. They manufactured pottery and cane baskets and also used skin pouches as containers. Physically, the Atakapas were short, dark, and stout. They dressed in skimpy animal skins and adorned their bodies with tattoos. Reflecting their close relationship with the sea, the Atakapas believed that they had emerged from the ocean in large oyster shells and had survived a large deluge by moving upland.[11]

Although the introduction of European diseases affected the Gulf Coast Indians, the epidemics caused the greatest disruption between the two sedentary, agricultural tribes of the Near Southwest, the Caddoan-speaking Caddos and Wichitas. The huge population losses forced them to greatly constrict their farming boundaries and to rearrange the ways in which they constructed their villages. The Caddos lived on the western edge of the Eastern Woodlands in permanent villages that originally had stretched from the Trinity River north to the Arkansas. Their forest homeland allowed them to be the most productive farmers of Texas, and the surplus food raised in the Caddo fields led to the development of a sophisticated political and religious system dominated by a hereditary elite. A well-defined hierarchy, led by a chief known as the *caddi*, exercised political power at the individual tribal level. A religious leader, called the *xinesi*, presided over several communities that supported him materially and treated him with great reverence.[12]

Agriculture determined the arrangement of the Caddo living quarters. They lived in scattered dwellings in the midst of their fields, all of which were grouped around a central village where the elites lived. Temple mounds dominated the villages that served as ceremonial centers. Several families—about twenty people—occupied each Caddo house, well-constructed dwellings made of grass and reeds resembling a haystack. Although both men and women planted corn, beans, squash, and watermelon in the spring, during the summer men hunted for deer, bear, and small game in the surrounding forest, and the women collected wild fruits and nuts. After harvesting the crops in the fall, the men went on extensive winter hunts, sometimes heading west to stalk buffalo. Expert craftsmen fashioned quality bows made of the pliable wood of the Osage orange and also some of the finest pottery in North America. The Caddos traded these items, in addition to salt and food products, north to the great mound-building chiefdom and population center at Cahokia and west to the Pueblo villages of New Mexico. Living at the crossroads of four major trails where the Eastern Woodlands met the Great Plains, the Caddos relied heavily on trade.[13]

Extreme drought, which began around 1350, combined with the introduction of European diseases two centuries later, forced the Caddos to forsake the construction of temple mound complexes, abandon the Arkansas River Valley, and move south. By the late seventeenth century, the Caddo population dropped from perhaps as many as 250,000 to as low as 15,000. The Caddos had by this time formed three loose confederacies, still dominated by the political-religious elite. The Kadohadacho confederacy, located near the bend of the Red River, consisted of four tribes. Farther downstream three tribes composed the least populous of the three confederacies, the Natchitoches. To the west, along the upper reaches of the Neches and Angelina rivers in east Texas, the largest confederacy, the Hasinais, consisted of nine major tribes. Two independent Caddoan-speaking tribes, the Aises and the Adaes, lived between the Hasinais and the Natchitoches.[14]

The Caddos' linguistic kinsmen, the Wichitas, lived on the eastern edge of the Great Plains in the Arkansas River Valley. The cultural differences between the two tribes arose primarily because the Wichitas lived on the prairie and consequently relied much more on buffalo hunting than the Caddos, who lived in the forest. To maximize their productive capabilities, the Wichitas adopted a semisedentary lifestyle. In the spring and summer, they lived in fixed, extended villages near their well-kept fields. The Wichitas spaced their grass lodges—which were very similar to the Caddo dwellings—at about fifty-foot intervals, and between them built open-sided edifices to dry and store meat and food. Being prudent, the Wichitas made sure they had good supplies of preserved food to see them through hard times. One of their most important staple items was dried pumpkin, which Wichita women prepared by cutting the hulls into long, narrow strips and weaving them into easily stored and transportable mats. In the fall, after the crops had been harvested, dried, and stored in underground pits, the entire tribe headed west to the prairies for the annual winter hunt. During this period, when the men hunted among huge buffalo herds, Wichita families lived in portable tepees made of skins. On the hunt, women skinned the buffalo and smoked the meat; on returning to their village in the spring, they tanned the hides and fashioned them into blankets and robes. Women also made earthenware pots and other cooking utensils, as well as deerskin and wolfskin pouches for storage.[15]

To facilitate their farming and hunting lifestyle, the Wichitas arranged themselves in numerous independent villages that often stretched for miles. Each village was headed by a principal chief and a subordinate, both chosen by the men on the basis of physical prowess and leadership abilities. The chief's power was not absolute, however, and the warriors could remove him at any time. A council of the entire tribe, including women, debated important matters. Solutions to problems were reached by consensus, and dissenters were free to join other villages rather than adhere to decisions they opposed. The egalitarian nature of the Wichita political system stands in marked contrast to the hierarchical system of the Caddos. The Wichita religious system also differed from that of the Caddos in that it did not revolve around an authority figure such as the xinesi. Instead, various shamanistic societies, open to anyone who cared to join, paid homage to the important deities by performing certain ceremonies and dances.[16]

While the Wichita differed culturally from their linguistic kinsmen the Caddos, they shared a susceptibility to disease; by the end of the seventeenth century the Wichita population had plummeted by more than 90 percent. The great population loss forced the 20,000 remaining Wichitas to change the manner in which they set up their villages. Instead of living in loosely arranged settlements of thatched houses scattered across several miles, the Wichitas shifted to compact villages located in close proximity to other towns. They also built ditches and stockades around their villages for defensive purposes. By 1700 the Wichitas had begun a southward migration that continued well into the eighteenth century.

The Kichais were the southernmost of the five Wichita tribes, living along the Red River in present Lamar County, Texas. North of the Kichais were the Tawakonis, whose villages were on the Arkansas River south of present-day Tulsa. The Iscanis and the Guichitas established towns upstream on the Arkansas at the mouth of Deer Creek. The Taovayas, which became the largest Wichita group, lived to the northeast in twin villages on the Verdigris River.[17]

The Texas Indians were forced to adapt not only to disease but also to horses. The Spaniards brought horses to New Mexico in the early 1600s, and by the end of the century the Indians of the region had acquired many of the animals either by seizing runaways or by poaching them from the newcomers. The horse, which flourished in the open, arid country, added to the hunting abilities of the natives, increasing their range and ease of travel. Horses quickly became a commodity in the villages of most of the tribes, an item that brought wealth and power to the owners. By the time the Europeans returned to the Near Southwest in the early eighteenth century, most of the Texas Indians— including some newcomers—had to some extent incorporated the horse into daily life. In fact, a few tribes completely changed their mode of living because of the possibilities afforded by the Old World animal.[18]

The Athabascan-speaking Apaches were the first Texas tribe to successfully adapt to the horse. They had emigrated from Canada to the plains of New Mexico and west Texas during the thirteenth century. The buffalo-hunting Apaches were divided into small, nomadic bands of a few hundred people, with each band led by a chief who gained his position through displays of bravery and wisdom. The role of chief, however, was mostly advisory as the Apaches had no mechanism for enforcing authority beyond the use of peer pressure. They lived in portable buffalo-skin tepees and dressed skins to use for clothing. The Apaches quickly entered into trading arrangements with the various Pueblo villages of New Mexico, providing them with buffalo products such as dried meat and skins in return for corn, beans, blankets, pottery, and turquoise. The Spanish conquest of New Mexico in the late sixteenth century upset this profitable arrangement as the Spaniards exacted heavy tax burdens on the Pueblos. The Spaniards also brought disease, which caused the number of Indians in the region to decline by two-thirds. Although the Apaches were, for the most part, spared the worst of the diseases, the declining population of the Pueblo villages robbed them of their major source of an essential dietary

element. Therefore, many of the Apaches on the Great Plains began to establish *rancherías*, where they built huts and tended their own patches of corn and
beans.[19]

By the middle of the seventeenth century, the Apaches had come into contact
with Spanish horses. Mimicking the Spaniards and the Pueblos, the Apaches
mounted horses and found that they greatly added to their hunting success.
Horses also increased the Apaches' range and raiding efficiency, and the tribe
obtained even more Spanish animals through forays along the entire northern frontier of New Spain. Apache warriors also acquired horses by trading
with the Spaniards in New Mexico for Indian slaves. The decimation of the
Pueblo people made the Spaniards desperate for manpower, and they sought
other Indians to be used as slaves, even though Indian bondage was officially
illegal in the Spanish empire. One Apache tribe, the Lipans, took advantage
of this situation and moved eastward into central Texas, where they raided
other tribes. The Lipans captured Indian slaves and sold them for Spanish
horses in the underground market that had been established in New Mexico
by Spanish smugglers. The raiding not only allowed Lipan warriors to add
to their possessions, it also afforded them honor and status, conferrals that
depended upon success in battle.[20]

The Lipan Apaches, whose near monopoly of the possession of horses
allowed them to dominate the prairies of Texas during the latter decades
of the seventeenth century, were actually an amalgamation of peoples from
different tribes. The success of the Lipan Apaches after their acquisition of
the horse drew other shattered groups toward them and their way of life.
Various Apache groups combined with Coahuiltecan bands from the lower
Rio Grande, and with the tribe known as the Jumanos—already a product
of ethnogenesis—to form the Lipans. The Lipan Apaches numbered around
five thousand individuals as a whole. The tribe's new power, however, forced
other Indians to acquire horses and challenge Apache control. By 1680, on the
eve of Spanish and French settlement, the tribes of the Near Southwest that
had been victimized by the Lipan Apache slave-raids, like the Wichitas and
Caddos, had incorporated the horse into their cultures through trade, theft, or
seizure of runaways. Along the Gulf Coast, the Karankawas, Coahuiltecans,
and Atakapas adopted horses to a much lesser extent than the other tribes.[21]

The Apaches' success also attracted tribes from outside the area, most importantly the Shoshonean Comanches, whose adoption of the horse eventually
made them the dominant tribe of the region. The Comanches emerged from
the Rocky Mountains and immigrated to the southern Plains in the late seventeenth century. In this new region they learned the art of horsemanship, and by
the early 1700s they had successfully wrested control of the High Plains from

the Lipans, who were driven deeper into central Texas. The Comanches used their horses to hunt buffalo, whose products provided for most of their needs. They ate buffalo meat, used easily portable buffalo-skin tepees for shelter, and utilized buffalo skins for clothes and blankets.[22]

Clearly, the Comanche lifestyle revolved around the acquisition of the horse and pursuit of the buffalo. Their nomadism caused the Comanches to adopt a fluid structure, allowing band size and leadership to change with necessity. The knowledge that all of the twenty thousand or so Comanche individuals were one of the *nuhmuhnuh*, or "people," allowed them to forge tight bonds and at the same time maintain an extremely flexible system. The Comanches divided into small bands, each led by a peace chief chosen on the basis of his leadership abilities. His authority was limited to internal matters, and he could only give advice. A council of men sought to reach a consensus on important matters. If anyone disagreed with a decision, they were free to join another group.[23]

While peace chiefs and their councils provided direction for the internal workings of the group, war chiefs led the warriors in actions that defined what it meant to be a Comanche male: hunting, fighting, and thieving. Comanche success depended on the ability to obtain horses—often through theft—in order to hunt buffalo. The best way for a Comanche man to obtain wealth, honor, and status was through warfare and the plundering of horses from the enemy. Horses were a medium of exchange to the Comanches; an individual could obtain women, weapons, and other necessities of life through ownership of horses. The most successful warriors obtained status through their actions and attracted other followers into battle, leading to the acquisition of more horses and increased opportunities for a prestigious standing in the band. Comanche men gained glory by dying in battle, but death at the hands of the enemy also demanded the vengeance of the living, which only escalated the constant raiding and plundering. Due to the heightened importance of warfare, Comanche men formed military societies that reinforced the martial ethos of the tribe. Ultimately, this aggressive behavior allowed the Comanches to become the paramount tribe in Texas.[24]

The Tonkawas, in addition to the Lipan Apaches and the Comanches, also came to orient their culture toward nomadism lived primarily on horseback. By the late seventeenth century the Tonkawan cultural group began the process of ethnogenesis when a number of ethnic groups who roamed the southern Plains between the middle Rio Grande and the middle Arkansas River came together as a result of changes wrought by the European intrusion. Ultimately, the tribe consisted of the Tonkawan-speaking Tancagues and Mayeyes as well as the intermingled Coahuiltecan Ervipiames and Caddoan Yojuanes. Pressured by the Lipan Apaches from the west, the 5,000 Tonkawas moved their range eastward to the Post Oak Savannah region, bordered by the Hill Country and the Piney Woods, between the Colorado and Trinity rivers.[25]

Like other nomadic tribes, the Tonkawas lived in politically autonomous bands, headed by separate civil and war chiefs. Reflecting the diverse origins of the tribe, Tonkawan society was divided into thirteen matrilineal clans. Individual membership in the clans cut across band divisions and bound the tribe together. Unlike the Apaches and Comanches, the Tonkawas hunted deer more than buffalo and added small mammals, birds, reptiles, fish, and shellfish to their diets. In addition to game, the Tonkawas also ate a large assortment of plant foods, including herbs, roots, fruits, and seeds. Rather than living in buffalo-skin tepees, the Tonkawas constructed small, conical huts covered with brush or hides. The tribal members had few baskets and mats and obtained pottery from other tribes. Animal skins provided the scant clothing worn by Tonkawa men and women. Males wore earrings, necklaces, and other ornaments of shell, bone, and feathers, and both males and females tattooed their bodies.[26]

By the late seventeenth century about one hundred thousand Indians lived in Texas and the Near Southwest. Some hunted buffalo on horseback, others employed the horse to hunt yet subsisted primarily on farm products, and others lived by hunting small game and gathering fruits and nuts. Two new European groups, the French and the Spanish, also settled in the region in the late seventeenth and early eighteenth centuries. The French came to Louisiana and the Lower Mississippi Valley hoping to establish a colony of settlers and slaves that would profit through trade and the development of cash crops. The Spaniards occupied Texas with soldiers, priests, and only a few settlers, with the goals of preventing the French from expanding farther southwestward into their territory and of converting the natives to Christianity. Although both empires would fall short of attaining their goals, the dominant Indians of the region proved far more receptive to French trade than to Spanish religion.

In the final decades of the seventeenth century, two groups of Indians—the Karankawas and the Hasinais—rebuffed the first French and Spanish efforts to settle in Texas. In spite of these failures, representatives of the two countries returned in the early eighteenth century to stay. France and Spain had previously been enemies, but in 1700 the Bourbon grandson of France's King Louis XIV, Philip V, ascended the throne of Spain, and the two nations became cautious allies for the greater part of the century. Each allowed the other to settle Louisiana and Texas, respectively, without threat of invasion or conquest. In fact, the French actually helped the Spaniards reoccupy east Texas so that they would be nearer to Louisiana. In the hope of establishing trade with New

Spain, a French Canadian, Louis Juchereau de St. Denis, founded the post of
Natchitoches on the Louisiana-Texas frontier in 1714. In spite of St. Denis's
assistance and the alliance with France, the Spaniards jealously maintained
their mercantile system and ultimately forbade legal French trade in their
colonies.[27]

Although the French were barred from establishing legitimate trade with
New Spain, the Indians permitted them to settle in their midst, this time because of the firearms and manufactured goods the Gallic interlopers provided.
Guns, balls, and powder were the most important items the French sold to
the natives. Weapons allowed the Indians to hunt more efficiently and also
enhanced their military prowess. In return for their trade goods, the French
wanted, among other things, buffalo skins, deerskins, and bear's fat. The Indians had traditionally obtained these items for their own use, and guns made
it easier for the tribesmen to be successful while hunting. The competition
for trade, coupled with the French desire for Indian slaves, highly militarized
the Near Southwest, and it became essential for the tribes to acquire weapons
for defense. The French also supplied steel hatchets, tomahawks, and hunting
knives, all greatly superior to the stone weapons used in the past. The Indians
also desired other European manufactured goods to replace or enhance native-
produced items. Hide apparel gave way to cotton, linen, or woolen clothing
and blankets. Laborsaving devices such as scissors, awls, screws, and flints
for starting fires were an improvement over stone tools. The French also provided the Indians with vanity items such as beads, combs, vermillion, mirrors,
copper bracelets, and strips of scarlet colored cloth.[28]

The Indians' need for these goods opened the door for French settlement.
By 1718 the French had established New Orleans as the capital of Louisiana, a
colony that encompassed the entire Lower Mississippi Valley and also included
the Gulf Coast east to Spanish Florida. Originally managed by several joint-
stock companies, the Louisiana colonists hoped to turn a profit by raising
crops and trading with the natives. French settlers established plantations
along the Mississippi River and its tributaries and had African slaves shipped
in to work their tobacco and indigo fields. French traders also traveled to the
interior regions and arranged commercial alliances with the various Indian
tribes. For numerous reasons—the lack of a truly valuable cash crop, the
poor health of the settlers, and warfare with some of the natives—the joint-
stock companies failed, and in 1731 management of the colony reverted to the
Crown. For the most part, immigration to Louisiana from Africa and France
came to an end at this point. By 1737, however, nearly 2,500 Frenchmen and
4,500 slaves lived in the French colony.[29]

Although Louisiana had failed to make money for its stockholders, Natchitoches had succeeded in becoming the main funnel through which trade goods flowed from French Louisiana into Texas and the Near Southwest. Following St. Denis's failed attempt to introduce French goods into New Spain, the French Canadian had turned to the Caddo tribes to assist him in forming trading partnerships with the Indians of the region. By 1731, in addition to Natchitoches, the Caddos had allowed the French to establish trading posts at the Yatasi village on Bayou Pierre about fifty miles northwest of town, and at the Kadohadacho village just above the bend of the Red River. From these posts, French traders circumvented the limited Spanish presence in east Texas to barter with many other tribes, most particularly the Hasinais and the Wichitas. While the French trade enriched the Caddos, living in close proximity to the Europeans continued the population decline. By midcentury the Kadohadacho confederacy had been reduced from four tribes to two, the Hasinais dropped from nine to four, and only the Yatasis and Natchitoches remained of the third group. Population loss combined with the increase in economic activities designed to attain French goods also caused the Caddos to do away with the religious position of the xinesi.[30]

To gain greater access to French trade goods and to escape the attacks from their Siouan Osage enemies to the northeast, the Wichitas continued the southward migration they had begun in the previous century. By the 1750s the Tawakonis and Iscanis had moved from the Arkansas Valley to form villages near the Kichais in the area between the Sabine and Red rivers in east Texas. The Taovayas, along with the Guichitas and a few Iscanis, established the most important Wichita settlement at a place that would be one of the landmark villages of the southern Plains for the next half century. The excellent site they chose was on the Red River just west of the thin sliver of forest known as the Western Cross Timbers. On the north bank of the river, in present-day Jefferson County, Oklahoma, the Taovayas constructed an impressive fort with a twelve-foot-high stockade, surrounded by a deep trench. French traders flocked to the villages (which was the farthest point upstream that could be reached by boat) to exchange goods with the tribes, who they referred to as the Panis Piques, or Pricked Pawnees, because of their tattoos. The Panis Piques also cemented a very profitable alliance with the Comanches who lived to the west, and the Taovayas, Guichitas, and Iscanis established themselves as middlemen in the lucrative trade between the Comanches and the French. Comanches provided the Panis Piques with buffalo skins in return for a portion of the French goods the three Wichita tribes were receiving. The Panis Piques also supplied the nomadic Comanches with agricultural products from their fields, including the transportable mats the women wove from dried pumpkins. The

Comanches not only became trading partners of the Panis Piques, the two tribes also formed a military alliance aimed at the Lipan Apaches and the Osages. Whereas the Osages were well supplied with weapons from other French traders, the Lipans increasingly found themselves outgunned by the Comanches and Wichitas. Therefore, the two tribes constantly preyed upon the Apaches for slaves, selling mainly women and children to French traders who distributed them throughout Louisiana and the West Indies.[31]

Through their trading partnership, the natives and the French in Natchitoches developed particularly close ties. The two groups entered each other's settlements with great ease, and the Louisiana-Texas frontier truly became a "middle ground," where people from both cultures met, lived, and worked on equal terms. Indians traveled to the French village of Natchitoches to trade, drink, or meet with officials, including St. Denis, the commandant of the post. Each year, usually in the fall or spring, many Indian chiefs—mainly Caddos or Wichitas—went downstream to receive annual gifts. Five hundred Natchitoches Indians lived nearby and provided the settlers with much-needed food and supplies. Bonds became so intimate that the Natchitoches chief, La Tete Platte (Flathead), chose to be baptized. He was buried among the French upon his death in 1755. Although not common, occasionally Frenchmen married natives under the auspices of the Catholic Church. For instance, Charles Dumont married a Natchitoches woman named Angelique, while Jean Baptiste Brevel married Anne, of the Kadohadacho tribe. Other Frenchmen developed liaisons with Indian women when they visited the native villages to trade.[32]

The commercial partnership established by the Indians and French of the region was crucial to their respective economic successes. The trade stretched across the Atlantic Ocean to France where craftsmen produced the manufactured goods the Indians desired. The trade merchandise was then shipped to New Orleans where merchants purchased the goods, transferred them to smaller boats, and sent the items upriver to traders in Natchitoches. The traders, in turn, hired *engagés* to accompany them into the Indian villages in late autumn. The Indians, following the completion of their winter hunts, returned to the villages in the spring to exchange peltries for trade goods, which the Frenchmen would then take back to Natchitoches. Once the Red River attained high enough water levels—usually by April—the merchants sent the furs downstream to New Orleans and the cycle would begin anew for the following year. By 1766, at the end of the French period, most of the six hundred or so people who lived in Natchitoches—including 269 African slaves—were indirectly involved in some portion of the Indian trade. Although the French also planted tobacco and raised livestock, they were just as dependent on the trade as their Indian partners.[33]

The Spaniards in New Spain weakly responded to the French settlement of Louisiana by occupying Texas with priests and soldiers, and a few settlers. In an effort to forestall any further French incursions, the Spaniards chose to try and win the Indians' allegiance for their Crown by converting them to Christianity. Thus, Franciscan missionaries rather than settlers and traders spearheaded the Spanish efforts in Texas. The priests idealistically hoped to go forth with only a few soldiers for protection and seek out those Indians who wished to accept the Christian faith. The tribes would then, in Spanish terms, be "reduced" to mission life and made to "congregate" around a church built in an Indian village for religious instruction. Spanish soldiers constructed a presidio nearby to protect the priests and the local tribe from enemies. Royal regulations prevented the priests and soldiers from forcing the natives to convert or from providing them with weapons. The missionaries were only allowed to distribute items of "civilization" such as livestock, clothes, and agricultural tools. The priests wanted to teach the natives the Spanish lifestyle in order to transform them into productive subjects of the Spanish Crown who would also serve as bulwarks against foreign invasion. Although the idealistic program of the Franciscans attracted a few converts in Texas, most of the region's natives responded with indifference, and, in some cases, with hostility.[34]

By 1731 the Spaniards had anchored Texas at three vital points: the Louisiana-Texas frontier, Matagorda Bay, and San Antonio. In a futile attempt to monitor French activities, the Spanish established the Texas capital at Los Adaes, about fifteen miles west of Natchitoches, near the Adaes Indian town. A presidio, manned by sixty undersupplied soldiers, protected a mission the Franciscan priests founded for the natives. The priests maintained two other missions in east Texas: one stood at the Ais Indian village, west of the Sabine River near present St. Augustine; the other was located among the Nacogdoches tribe, a member of the Hasinai confederacy. Along the lower reaches of the Guadalupe River, the Spaniards founded the mission-presidial complex known as La Bahía to protect Matagorda Bay and to attract Coahuiltecan and Karankawa Indians. Forty soldiers were stationed at La Bahía, which would be relocated to the lower San Antonio River in 1749. Although Los Adaes was the capital of Texas, San Antonio was the largest and most important establishment in Texas. Forty-four soldiers were stationed on the banks of the San Antonio River, in a presidio that protected five missions established for the Coahuiltecan tribes. Fifteen families from the Canary Islands became Texas's first civilian settlers when they founded the villa of San Fernando de Béxar among the San Antonio missions and presidio in 1731. The Isleño immigration, however, did little to counter the numbers of French and Indians in the region as they raised the total Spanish population of Texas to only a little over five hundred people.[35]

Actually, it would have mattered little how many Spaniards were sent to Texas because only a few of the Indians responded to the Franciscans' invitation. Well supplied with French goods, no Hasinai, Ais, or Adaes Indian ever agreed to live in either of the three missions in east Texas. In 1744 the governor of Texas noted that Mission Nacogdoches had one priest and two soldiers, "but it does not and never has had one Indian reduced to mission [life]." Two decades later a visitor found that the missionary "had not one Indian to whom he could minister, nor had there been one during more than the forty years of this mission's existence." In 1768 a Franciscan priest regretfully concluded that "there is no hope, not even a remote one, of the reduction and congregation" of any of the east Texas tribes. Although a few Karankawas were initially attracted to the mission at La Bahía, they abandoned it in 1723 after killing the Spanish commander of the presidio. In addition to detesting the regimentation of mission life, the Karankawas were uncomfortable with the site of the mission: it had shifted farther inland in 1726 and 1749 and was located outside their familiar coastal environment.[36]

The Coahuiltecans were the only Indian group of the region attracted to the Franciscans' inducements. Poverty and pressure from Lipan Apache raiders combined to cause the Coahuiltecans to seek refuge in the missions at San Antonio and La Bahía. These missions, particularly the ones at San Antonio, greatly improved the economic well-being of the Coahuiltecans because the priests taught the Indians how to divert water from the San Antonio River to irrigate their newly established fields. Very quickly the mission Indians produced enough corn, beans, and other vegetables to supply not only themselves but also to sell to the nearby soldiers and settlers. Cattle herds offered a second food source for the Coahuiltecans, and each mission established an outlying ranch some distance from the establishment where herders tended the animals. The Indians also learned how to weave, and they began to produce cotton and woolen clothes and blankets.[37]

Despite the economic success of the missions, the Coahuiltecan population declined throughout the eighteenth century. The Franciscans housed the heretofore nomads in closely concentrated quarters, which exacerbated the spread of epidemic diseases. Infant mortality rates were high under such conditions. The amount of work the Indians were expected to perform was far greater than what hunters and gatherers normally expended and, as a consequence, the Indians often ran away. Therefore, priests and soldiers used force to keep the natives in the fields. Given the high child mortality rate and the continued problem with runaways, the population at the missions could not sustain itself. To maintain them, the priests had to continually recruit more Coahuiltecans. By the middle of the century, however, very few Coahuiltecans survived outside the church walls of San Antonio and La Bahía, and the numbers at the missions continued to fall.[38]

While the Coahuiltecan population declined, the number of cattle, horses, and mules in the mission ranches—as well as those of the settlers at San Antonio—increased dramatically. An intense period of drought in the first two decades of the eighteenth century had caused the great buffalo herds to disappear from the region south of the San Antonio River, just as the Spaniards settled in Texas. Their cattle thrived in the absence of the buffalo, which were kept from returning to the area by the spread of mesquite. Whereas buffalo refused to forage on mesquite, Spanish cattle and horses fattened up on the plant and their population grew inordinately. By the 1760s at least twenty thousand head of cattle roamed the open ranges between San Antonio and La Bahía. Actually, the numerous Spanish livestock affected the Texas Indians much more than the few Spaniards ever did. Some Indian groups raided the Spanish cattle herds to replace the buffalo as a food source; others poached horses to enrich their own herds or to sell to the French in Louisiana who were desperate for mounts. Nonetheless, the Franciscans continued to hope that some of these Indians could be reduced to mission life.[39]

The availability of Spanish livestock, combined with the effects of disease and Lipan Apache pressure, caused members of a number of different tribes—mainly Tonkawas, Atakapas, and Karankawas—to come together in a community located in the middle Brazos River Valley. From this settlement, which the Spaniards called Ranchería Grande, men stole livestock from the nearby Spanish ranches. The Indians consumed the beef, but exchanged the horses with Hasinai, Bidai, Akokisa, and Coco traders who, in turn, dealt them to Frenchmen in Louisiana. The success of Ranchería Grande, however, attracted even more Apache raiders. In the hope of gaining protection from the Lipans, the Indians on the Brazos requested that the Spanish authorities establish a mission for them in 1745. The Spaniards responded by erecting three missions and a presidio along the San Gabriel River in 1748–49. The three missions grouped the Indians on the basis of tribal and linguistic similarities. One mission contained the Tonkawan Ervipiames, Mayeyes, and Yojuanes; another congregated Atakapan Akokisas, Bidais, and Deadoses; a third mission sheltered the Karankawan Cocos and Carancaguases. Lipan warriors attacked the missions almost immediately after their opening, making it apparent to the tribesmen that the Spaniards could not offer any meaningful protection from the Apaches. Most of the Indians left the San Gabriel missions soon thereafter; the Atakapas and Karankawas moved south toward the coast, while the

Tonkawas relocated to the northeast to gain greater access to French Louisiana. The Spaniards finally abandoned the empty establishments in 1756.[40]

The Franciscans persisted in trying to induce Indians to settle among them, despite the failure on the San Gabriel. In 1754 they established a new mission for the Karankawas, Nuestra Señora del Rosario, about four miles up the San Antonio River from the settlement at La Bahía. All of the Karankawan tribes occasionally visited the station to receive food and gifts, and two hundred or so actually agreed to be baptized in the first fifteen years of its existence. Most of the time, however, the Karankawas avoided Mission Rosario, preferring to remain near the coast. Nonetheless, Franciscan priests maintained the station in hope of attracting converts. The Franciscans had even less success with the mission they founded for the Bidais and Akokisas near the mouth of the Trinity River in 1756. No Indians settled at the mission, which was situated in a malarial lowland with unpotable water. The Spaniards abandoned the station after fourteen useless years.[41]

The most spectacular missionary failure, and the one that best illuminates the weakness of the Spanish position in Texas, was the Franciscan effort to bring Christianity to the Lipan Apaches. The Apaches had begun making raids upon San Antonio to steal livestock almost as soon as the town was founded in 1718. For the next three decades the Lipans and Spaniards fought occasionally as the Indians sporadically assaulted the missions and civilian settlements, to which the presidial soldiers responded with punitive expeditions. By 1749, however, incessant Comanche and Wichita slave raiding—made much more effective by the increased availability of French firearms—forced the beleaguered Apaches to negotiate a peace treaty at San Antonio, and their conduct toward the Béxar community improved accordingly. The slaving expeditions, though, increased in the 1750s as Tonkawas and Caddos joined with the Comanches and Wichitas to plunder the Lipans. The raids induced the Apaches to ask their ally to establish a mission and presidio in their country in hope of gaining protection from their enemies, whom the Spaniards grouped together under the name of Norteños. The Spaniards responded by constructing a mission-presidial complex for the Apaches on the San Saba River northwest of San Antonio in 1757.[42]

Although the Lipans desired Spanish military protection, they had no intention of being reduced to mission life or accepting Christianity. While a few Apaches visited the mission as they passed through the area on their way north to hunt buffalo, none agreed to give up their nomadic lifestyle and settle down. The Norteños, meanwhile, believed that the mission would provide the Lipans with a safe refuge from which to make retaliatory attacks. Therefore, in March 1758, 2,000 Norteño warriors, half of whom were carrying French guns, gathered near the mission on the San Saba. They planned to kill any Lipan they encountered and to frighten the rest of the tribe from ever returning. The Norteños, led by a fully armed Comanche chief dressed in a French army officer's uniform, surrounded the mission and forced the priests to let them inside the walls. When the native force found there were no Apaches present, they turned on the Spaniards, killing eight (including two priests, one of whom they decapitated), and set fire to the mission.[43]

The brutal attack caused the Spanish to seek retribution against the Norteños. In August 1759, Colonel Diego Ortiz Parrilla led an expedition consisting of 360 Spanish troops and 176 Indian allies—130 Lipan Apaches and forty-six Coahuiltecans—out from the San Saba. Two months later Ortiz Parrilla's troops attacked the Norteños at the Taovaya village on the Red River. The well-armed natives outnumbered the Spanish-Indian force, however, and Ortiz Parrilla's men could not penetrate the Taovayas' palisaded village, over which flew a French flag. The stunned Spanish colonel was forced to retreat to the San Saba River after suffering fifty-two casualties. Realizing that the Apaches feared coming to the area, in 1762 the Franciscans abandoned the mission and constructed two others for the Lipans, jointly known as El Cañon, on the headwaters of the Nueces River. The Indians avoided these missions as well, and the Spaniards discontinued them and the presidio on the San Saba nine years later.[44]

By the 1760s the region's Indians had endured having Europeans in their midst for over half a century, and almost all had come to prefer the French and their manufactured goods over the Spaniards and their religion. Nonetheless, in 1763 the Indians lost their French ally when, as a result of the defeat in the Seven Years' War, France ceded Louisiana to Spain and turned over their possessions east of the Mississippi River to Great Britain. It became crucial to the natives of the Near Southwest, as well as to the merchants who remained in Louisiana, that Spain continue the liberal French trading policies with the Indians and not adopt the Franciscan methods that had been so ineffectual in Texas. Without weapons, the Texas Indians—in particular, the Norteños, who were seen as enemies of Spain—would be at the mercy of the Osage Indians who lived in present-day Missouri and Arkansas and had access to British traders, now poised on the east bank of the Mississippi River. Other traders, mainly Frenchmen, simply crossed the river illegally and ascended the Arkansas River to provide the Osages with weapons and manufactured goods in exchange for furs, as well as for horses and Indian slaves plundered from the Texas tribes. The Osages particularly targeted the Caddos and Wichitas on their raids. Unable to defend themselves adequately, the Tawakonis and

Kichais retreated southward during the decade, establishing settlements in the Brazos and Trinity river valleys.[45]

Ultimately, Spain would adopt a modified form of the French trading policies, make peace with their heretofore Norteño enemies, and abandon, for the most part, the missionary efforts among the tribes. The Spaniards, however, put these policies into effect in a piecemeal fashion that took nearly two decades to complete. Matters were complicated by the fact that Spain administered Louisiana and Texas separately; the Captaincy-General of Havana controlled Louisiana, and Texas remained under the jurisdiction of the Viceroyalty of New Spain in Mexico City. In 1769, Louisiana governor Alejandro O'Reilly initiated a reformed Spanish Indian policy in his colony. After reviewing past events, Governor O'Reilly realized that the only way to win the allegiance of the Indians was to forgo missionary efforts and to follow French methods. Tribes that had been French allies, however, would now have to pledge an oath of fidelity to Spain. In return, the Spanish government would provide the tribe with annual presents and would designate distinguished leaders as chiefs, dignified by decoration with great and small medals. Although O'Reilly utilized French trading policies, he made significant modifications. Instead of being free to trade any items to any French trader who arrived at their villages, under the new policy the Indians could deal only with licensed traders, who were closely supervised by the government. The Indians were also forbidden to deal in Indian slaves and livestock, since Indian slave trade was open to abuse and dealing in livestock promoted theft from fellow Spaniards in Texas. Despite the alterations of the French trade methods, the Indians of the region would find them acceptable, and eventually the Spaniards in Texas would adopt the same guidelines.[46]

Among the tribes subject to the reformed policy was a group of newcomers to the Near Southwest. These newcomers were emigrants from the French Gulf Coast—an area delivered to Great Britain at the end of the Seven Years' War—who had been victimized by English slave raiders from South Carolina and did not want to live under British rule. The tribes—Apalaches, Biloxis, Pascagoulas, Taensas, and a few others—shared a similar culture; they were sedentary agriculturalists who supplemented their farm produce by hunting for wild game in the forest. All of the tribes, except the Siouan Biloxis, were of Muskhogean language stock, but differences in dialect caused the various groups to adopt a pidgin grammar, called Mobilian Jargon, that served as a lingua franca. Living near the French towns of Biloxi and Mobile they had, in a similar fashion to the Natchitoches Indians, developed a pattern of close interaction with the colonists. They regularly provisioned the French towns with venison, corn, and other supplies. Women sold herbs, foodstuffs, and baskets to the French, and men earned wages by rowing pirogues and carrying trade merchandise. The Apalaches, having already accepted Catholicism while living near a Franciscan mission in Spanish Florida, insisted that a priest live in their town. The other tribes, however, did not accept the Christian faith.[47]

These tribes began to cross into Louisiana following the transfer of the French Gulf Coast to the British in 1763. The French administrator of the colony—the Spanish did not take actual possession until 1766—allowed the Indians to settle near Rapides Post, a small village on the Red River, located midway between Natchitoches and the Mississippi River. The Frenchman welcomed the tribes, noting that they could give assistance to the boats heading upriver to Natchitoches, as well as providing foodstuffs for the city of New Orleans. The first group to arrive at Rapides, the Apalaches, had established a village there by the beginning of 1764. During the following decade, the other tribes joined the Apalaches and settled on the banks of the Red River, as well as on nearby Bayou Bouef, a stream flowing south directly to the Gulf of Mexico. By 1773 the one hundred or so Indians living near Rapides outnumbered the small French population by two to one. The Indians established farms and successfully began raising livestock. The tribes once again maintained close ties with the local Europeans; the Apalaches even used the Catholic priest at Natchitoches to baptize their children, whose godparents were often leading citizens of the old French town.[48]

Creek and Choctaw refugees from east of the Mississippi also relocated to the Rapides district. The Alabamas, a Creek tribe, lived near the junction of the Coosa and Talapoosa rivers, near present-day Montgomery, in the eighteenth century. Another Creek tribe, the Coushattas, were associated with the Alabamas and resided in nearby villages. After the conclusion of the Seven Years' War a group of Alabamas abandoned the area, moved to Louisiana, and established a village on the Red River above Rapides Post. A Choctaw group, called the Yowanis, lived north of Lake Pontchartrain before 1763, but moved to the Rapides district soon thereafter and settled on Bayou Bouef. As with the other tribes, the Alabamas and the Yowanis planted crops, raised livestock, and exchanged peltries for manufactured goods with the local French traders.[49]

The emigrant Indians established close ties with the Red River's dominant tribe, the Caddos, who were the first group originally living west of the Mississippi to transfer their allegiance from the French to the Spanish. In early 1770, representatives of the four remaining Red River Caddo tribes met in Natchitoches with Athanase de Mézières, the newly appointed commandant. De Mézières was a Frenchman who had lived in Natchitoches since the 1740s and was a widower of the daughter of the town's founder, St. Denis. He had traded with all of the Caddo tribes and had advised Governor O'Reilly to adopt French methods of dealing with the Indians. In April, in front of de Mézières and the town's leading citizens, the Natchitoches, Yatasis, Petit Caddos, and Kadohadachos established formal ties with Spain in return for receiving annual presents and having licensed traders stationed at their villages. Their chiefs, most notably Tinhioüen of the Kadohadachos and Cocay of the Yatasis, received the high distinction of being designated medal chiefs by de Mézières. As a result of the agreement, well-established French traders from Natchitoches returned to the Caddo villages, and the commerce, which remained highly important to both groups, resumed once again.[50]

Although de Mézières also reached agreements with other Norteño tribes such as the Hasinais and the Wichitas, in addition to the Tonkawas and Atakapas, whole-scale Spanish reforms in Texas greatly complicated relations between the Indians and the Euroamericans of the colony. In 1767 the energetic reformist-minded king of Spain, Charles III, sent the Marqués de Rubí to Texas to inspect the situation there and make recommendations for improvements. As a result of Rubí's report, the king issued the Regulation of 1772, a document designed to dramatically transform the way Spain administered Texas. Realizing that most of the province's Indians had not responded to the ministrations of the Franciscan priests, the new rules mandated the adoption of the system Spain employed in Louisiana, that of dealing with the Indians through trade and gifts. Therefore, the Regulation of 1772 called for the abandonment of all missions and presidios in Texas, except those at San Antonio and La Bahía. Now that the French threat from Louisiana was gone, the king saw no need to maintain the capital at Los Adaes, and it, along with the few hundred settlers who lived there, was moved to San Antonio. The king also forced the Franciscans to abandon the three useless missions in east Texas. In addition, the regulations called for making peace with the Norteños at the expense of breaking the alliance with the Apaches. Departing from past policy, the king also authorized Spanish troops to launch active, offensive campaigns against enemy tribes such as the Lipans.[51]

Although the Spaniards followed the king's orders and abandoned the missions and presidios in east Texas the year after the orders were issued, it took much longer to complete the peace process with the Norteños and to initiate warfare against the Apaches. Spanish administrators in Mexico were unable to forget the massacre on the San Saba River and had doubts about the sincerity of the Norteños' desire to make peace. Viceregal officials blocked any attempts to provide the Indians of Texas with trade goods and also blocked de Mèzières's efforts to negotiate a treaty with the Comanches. Things began to change in 1776 when viceregal control over Indian affairs in Texas was superseded by the creation of the Interior Provinces. This new administrative unit, which consisted of all of the northern provinces of New Spain (including Texas, but not Louisiana), was detached from the jurisdiction of the viceroy and brought under the control of a commandant general who reported directly to the king. Free to deal with the Indians as he pleased, in 1778 the commandant general authorized de Mézières to establish peace and trade with the Norteños in order to launch a campaign, in conjunction with Spanish troops, against the Lipan Apaches. The following year, however, Charles III vetoed the plan because of Spain's entry in the struggle against Great Britain that had risen out of the American War of Independence. It would not be until 1783, following the end of the war, that the Norteños and the Spaniards resumed their peacemaking efforts.[52]

In the meantime, the Indians of Texas found other sources of European manufactured goods to supplement the meager amounts provided by the Spaniards. The Wichitas gained access to British goods through their fellow Caddoan speakers, the Skidi Pawnees, who lived on the Missouri River. The Skidis established commercial ties with British traders from Illinois who supplied the Pawnees with arms and ammunition in return for horses. The Wichitas eagerly entered into this trade, using the Skidis as middlemen, and resumed their raids upon the horse herds of San Antonio and La Bahía. In addition, illegal French traders bypassed Natchitoches and entered the Panis Piques villages by traveling up the Arkansas and crossing overland to the Red River. Comanches traveled to the Wichita villages to exchange goods with the traders.[53]

The Indians of coastal Texas obtained trade goods from British ships that entered the rivers and bays to exchange items with the Karankawas and Atakapas. In fact, the Spanish abandonment of east Texas actually made it easier for these tribes to deal with illegal traders. In 1772 the Spanish commander of the presidio at La Bahía encountered a group of Cocos, Carancaguases, and Bidais near the mouth of the Brazos River hunting deer for British traders. At the mouth of the Trinity River the Spaniard met some Cocos, Akokisas, Atacapas, and Bidais awaiting the arrival of British traders who provided them with arms, ammunition, and other goods, in return for deerskins and Spanish horses and mules. These Indians also established commercial alliances with illegal French traders from Natchitoches as well as Opelousas and Attakapas, Euroamerican posts recently established in southwestern Louisiana.[54]

The Lipan Apaches were the only tribe in Texas without direct access to European traders. Although the Spaniards failed to conclude the alliance with the Norteños in the 1770s, Spanish policy makers strove to isolate the Apaches. The Lipans desperately needed weapons to defend themselves for they were still subject to Norteño raiders seizing horses. Despite the Spanish attempts at isolation, however, the Lipans entered into a commercial alliance with the Karankawas and Atakapas who had access to the illegal British and French traders. Like the other Indians of Texas, the Apaches preyed upon the Spanish horse herds in order to gain merchandise for trade with their Indian partners.[55]

As the number of tribes receiving European manufactured goods increased, the number of Indians residing in the few remaining missions declined. In fact, the Regulation of 1772's focus on dealing with Indians through secular means rather than spiritual had pointed toward the demise of the Franciscan missions altogether. By the 1780s the six Coahuiltecan missions (five in San Antonio and one at La Bahía) contained few Indians, and those that remained had become well-instructed Christians. Many other Coahuiltecans had been absorbed into the Hispanic communities through marriage or work. As a result, in the following decade, Spanish officials began the process of secularizing the San Antonio missions by converting them into parishes and placing them under the control of secular priests who ministered to Christians rather than trying to convert pagans. Although the Franciscans maintained control over the mission at La Bahía for years, very few Coahuiltecans remained within its walls.[56]

By the mid-1770s Karankawas rarely visited Mission Rosario. In 1778 a group of Karankawas, led by a Coapite apostate named José María, massacred a group of Spanish sailors who had landed in Matagorda Bay. Emboldened by their success, the Karankawas then attacked the mission. The Spanish commander at La Bahía responded by assembling a force of 167 men to punish the attackers, but the Karankawas used their knowledge of the marshy lowlands to successfully avoid their pursuers. Although the Spanish authorities proposed an elaborate plan for a war of extermination against the Karankawas, it was never carried out. The few Karankawas living near Mission Rosario abandoned the area completely, and in 1781 the Franciscans closed the station and transferred all the church ornaments and cattle to the missionaries at La Bahía.[57]

Thus, following a century of close contact with the French and Spanish intruders, the natives of Texas and the Near Southwest had successfully forced the Spaniards to give up their efforts to convert them to Christianity and to adopt the European lifestyle. The various tribes had also compelled the Spaniards to provide them with the weapons and trade goods they desired. When the legal Spanish trade faltered, as it often did in the late eighteenth century, the Indians could turn to other sources to obtain the necessary items. Disease, however, remained a problem for the natives of the region, and their population had continued to decline during the 1700s. In 1777–78 a smallpox epidemic spread through the area and seriously reduced the number of people in all the tribes. In spite of the sickness, the Indians of Texas and the Near Southwest still outnumbered the Euroamericans and remained the dominant force in the area.

By the end of the American War of Independence in 1783, the Euroamerican and Afroamerican population of Louisiana, including West Florida (reconquered by Spain during the war), stood at 30,000 people, of whom just under half were free. Most of the settlers and their slaves lived along the banks of the Mississippi River, and their presence in the Red River Valley remained slight. Only about one hundred people (three-fourths French and one-fourth slave) lived at Rapides. The settlers planted corn and other vegetables and also raised horses and cattle. Despite losing as many as forty individuals during the epidemic of 1777–78, the three hundred or so Indians residing near the post not only outnumbered the settlers and slaves, they also had many more head of livestock. The 150 Pascagoulas that lived on the Red River were the most numerous of the area's Indians. Mingomita, medal chief, led the tribe, which owned two hundred horses and thirty head of cattle. About thirty Apalaches resided in a village close to the Pascagoulas. Their chief, Denis, owned thirty horses and one hundred head of cattle, while the rest of the tribe had another one hundred horses and fifty cows. At least thirty Alabamas and twenty-five Taensas lived nearby on the Red River. The Yowani Choctaws and the Biloxis resided in settlements along Bayou Boeuf. The sixty or so Indians were said "to have many horses." Although the settlers complained occasionally that the Indians stole their livestock, the tribes at Rapides maintained friendly relations with the local French population and the commandant of the post, Valentin Layssard. In addition to raising livestock, the tribes grew foodstuffs, hunted deer, and exchanged peltries for manufactured goods with French traders, who occasionally provided the Indians with illegal rum. Ties between the Rapides Indians and Spanish officials were close enough that in 1784 Louisiana governor Esteban Miró asked the Yowanis, Pascagoulas, and Biloxis to help track a maroon community of slaves residing near Lake Borgne. Although the tribesmen were willing to assist, the runaways (including their leader, San Malo) were captured before the Indians could join their pursuers.[58]

While the emigrant Indians dominated Rapides Post, the growth of Natchitoches following the Spanish accession of Louisiana threatened the welfare of the nearby Caddoan allies. In the late eighteenth century Natchitoches was the only Euroamerican settlement in the Near Southwest that had a larger population than the surrounding natives. Despite the best intentions of the local French settlers, their increase had a deleterious effect on the local Adaes, Natchitoches, and Yatasi tribes; disease caused their decimation, they ceded their lands to the Euroamericans, and they turned to alcohol in despair. By

The Louisiana-Texas frontier, late eighteenth century

1785 the town's population had grown to about 1,300 people, of whom just under half were free. Trade with the Indians continued to dominate the town's economy. During the 1770s, a little over one hundred men—twenty-five natives of Louisiana or Canada, thirty natives of France, and forty-seven of unknown French origin—signed contracts in Natchitoches that enabled them to legally carry out commerce with the natives. Many others entered Texas illegally to trade. Despite the importance of the Indian trade, the cash crop of tobacco became increasingly significant as the Spanish government heavily promoted its development. By 1791, eighty-three of the town's 175 households engaged in tobacco cultivation, raising more than 700,000 pounds. To work their fields, the tobacco planters brought in more slaves, easily accessible from English and French sources. Over half (101) of the households owned slaves; eight planters owned twenty or more bondsmen. Raising cattle and horses to sell downriver was yet another way to earn a living in Natchitoches. Most settlers raised livestock, and by 1787 the townspeople owned over 2,700 head of cattle and 1,000 horses.[59]

The expansion of the tobacco plantations and ranches occurred at the expense of the traditional Indian allies who lived near Natchitoches. In 1778 Tsaoua Camté, either a Natchitoches or a Yatasi Indian, sold a large tract of land upstream from the French town, to Manuel Trichel and his mother-in-law, Magdeleine Grappe. Trichel and Grappe family members were veterans of the Indian trade, but they began raising livestock on their newly acquired land. Eventually, enough ranchers were attracted to the area that it became known as the settlement of Campti. In 1780 Hyamoc, medal chief of the Natchitoches tribe, sold land containing twenty arpents frontage to another trader, Jean Baptiste Laberry. Soon thereafter, Laberry made the transformation from Indian trader to tobacco planter. By 1790 he owned twenty-eight slaves, making him the fourth largest slave owner in town, and raised 23,000 pounds of tobacco. In 1787 the Yatasis sold land at their village to Paul Bouet Laffitte, a trader who had established a ranch nearby on Bayou Pierre earlier in the decade. By the end of the 1780s Laffitte had 350 cattle and seventy horses on his ranch.[60]

Living in close proximity to the Euroamerican settlers around Natchitoches proved deadly to the local Caddoan tribes. Their numbers had already declined dramatically before the epidemic of 1777–78 reduced the tribes even further. By the early 1780s only about fifty Adaes, led by medal chief Quemsy, survived in their old village fifteen miles west of Natchitoches. About the same number of Natchitoches Indians remained in their village, now located on the Red River, six miles above the old French town. Cocay, medal chief of the Yatasis, had perished in the recent epidemic and was succeeded by his brother-in-law, who died soon thereafter. Only about seventy-five Yatasis remained on Bayou Pierre. In addition to raising crops and hunting, the desperate Indians sought to make ends meet by doing odd jobs for the inhabitants, such as rowing boats or carrying goods on horseback. Often, they used their pay to obtain liquor in the many cabarets in town. Occasionally, the natives were forced to seek other means to get drunk. In 1785 Adaes chief Quemsy paid for drinks in a tavern with his Spanish medal. The post's commandant returned the medal to Quemsy, making "him know the grave mistake he had committed," and fined the cabaret owner. Unfortunately, the three tribes' example of misery set an undesirable precedent that almost all of the tribes of the region would ultimately be forced to follow.[61]

The 1,500 or so Caddos, the other group of Indians living in the jurisdiction of Louisiana, remained powerful despite losing perhaps a third of their population during the epidemic of 1777–78. The Kadohadachos lived in their ancient homeland near the bend of the Red River, about two hundred miles above the French town. A series of logjams, known as the Great Raft, which greatly impeded river traffic, prevented Euroamerican settlement above Campti and protected the tribe from the intrusion that plagued the Indians who lived downstream. Medal chief Tinhioüen, who was said to be "held in very high esteem by all" the tribes of the region, continued to lead the Kadohadachos. Tinhioüen also had influence over his downstream kin, the Petit Caddos, who lived on the Red River about eighty miles below the Kadohadachos. Despite the close relationship both tribes maintained with French traders, the better-armed Osages continued to wage a damaging war against them. In the spring of 1781 the Osages attacked the two tribes and stole almost all of their horses. As a result, Tinhioüen demanded protection and more arms from Spanish officials, who were helpless to prevent the Osage raids. Finally, in 1785 Governor Miró mediated a peace between the Osages and the Kadohadachos. In May the headmen of both tribes traveled to New Orleans for a formal conference held in the presence of the town's notable citizens. Although Tinhioüen doubted the good faith of his Osage counterpart, Governor Miró assured the Kadohadacho caddi that the Spaniards would guarantee the peace between the Caddos and their enemy. Not entirely convinced, Tinhioüen nonetheless agreed to the settlement, which promised to benefit Louisiana traders and the Indians of the region by allowing trade to flow freely without fear of Osage disruption. It remained to be seen, however, how long the Osages would keep the peace, and how the Spaniards would respond if it was broken.[62]

Following the war with Great Britain, Spanish officials in Texas, including Governor Domingo Cabello, also hoped to establish peace through trade with the Indians—most notably the Comanches and Wichitas—and to isolate the Lipan Apaches. Only in this manner would the relatively few Spaniards in the colony be free to maintain their livestock herds without the constant fear of Indian attack. By 1783 the Euroamerican population of Spanish Texas had risen to only about 2,500 individuals, concentrated in three settlements. The capital, San Antonio, was the largest of the Texas towns. The presidio counted about three hundred soldiers and their dependents, while the civilian population stood at 1,200 men, women, and children in three hundred or so households. Most of the settlers, known as Tejanos, were Hispanics from the northern frontier of Mexico; one-third of the household heads were natives of Béxar and another third were from nearby frontier areas. About six hundred people, two-thirds being civilians, lived at La Bahía. Another four hundred or so people resided at the civilian village of Nacogdoches, established in 1778 by settlers of Los Adaes who had been forced to abandon east Texas five years before. Due to the lack of economic opportunities in Texas, most of the civilians raised food crops and livestock. Only a few ranchers bothered to round up unbranded cattle and drive them to market in Louisiana or Coahuila. Countless head of cattle and horses continued to roam on the open range between San Antonio and La Bahía, providing Indian warriors with tempting targets.[63]

With few Hispanics concentrated in three small settlements, the numerous Indians of Texas were free to roam throughout the region. By the early 1780s the Lipan Apaches, pressured by continuing Norteño raids, had moved to the region south and east of San Antonio. As with the other Texas tribes, the Lipans had suffered from disease; epidemics of smallpox and diphtheria simultaneously struck in the fall of 1780 and plagued the Apaches for several years thereafter. Perhaps as many as 2,500 Apaches lived in villages located mainly in the Nueces River Valley. Desperate for more weapons and trade goods than their Atakapan and Karankawan allies could supply, Lipan leaders sought a commercial alliance with the Tonkawas. The epidemic of 1777–78 particularly ravaged the Tonkawas, causing the four tribes to merge into one, led by El Mocho (The Maimed). The chief, so named because he had lost an ear in battle, was actually born a Lipan who had come to live among the Tonkawas. Although El Mocho accepted Governor Cabello's designation as medal chief in 1779, he defied the Spaniard's wish that the Tonkawas obey his authority and settle in a permanent village. Instead, the 1,500 or so Tonkawas continued to roam the area between the middle Brazos and Trinity rivers.[64]

El Mocho disregarded Cabello's desire to keep the Tonkawas away from the Lipan Apaches. In 1782 he invited the Karankawa and Atakapa tribes of southeastern Texas to join with his tribe and hold a trading fair with the Lipans. The Cocos were the Karankawan tribe El Mocho most hoped would meet with the Apaches. The five hundred or so Cocos had continued their move northeastward—begun in the 1730s when they joined Ranchería Grande—to merge with the Tonkawan Mayeyes. Roaming the coastal areas between the Colorado and Trinity rivers, the Cocos separated themselves from the other 2,500 Karankawas, who were centered near the mouth of the San Antonio River. Chief José María had used his successful attack on Mission Rosario in 1778 to unite the heretofore autonomous Carancaguases, Cujanes, Coapites, and Copanes into a more cohesive political unit. These Karankawas were relatively isolated from Louisiana traders, but the Cocos and the remaining Ataka-pas, about five hundred Bidais and Akokisas living along the lower reaches

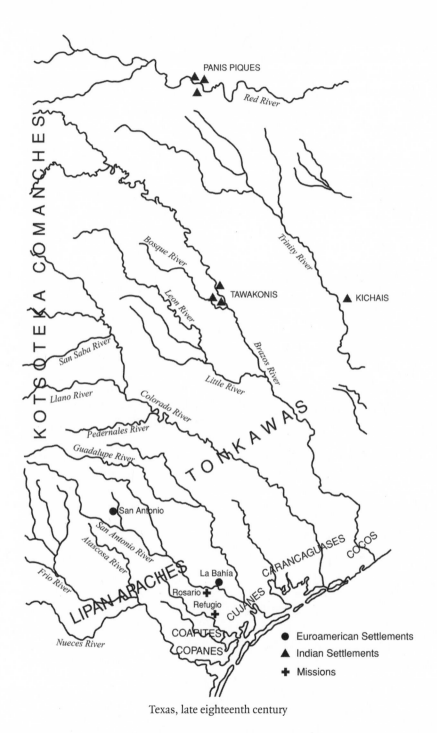

PANIS PIQUES

Red River

KOTSOTEKA COMANCHES

Bosque River

Trinity River

Leon River

TAWAKONIS

KICHAIS

Brazos River

San Saba River

Little River

Llano River

Colorado River

Pedernales River

TONKAWAS

Guadalupe River

San Antonio

San Antonio River

Atascosa River

CARANCAGUASES

COCOS

Frio River

La Bahía

Rosario ✝

LIPAN APACHES

Refugio ✝

CUJANES

COAPITES

● Euroamerican Settlements

Nueces River

COPANES

▲ Indian Settlements

✝ Missions

Texas, late eighteenth century

of the Trinity River, continued to provide peltries, horses, and cattle to the Frenchmen in exchange for weapons and manufactured goods.[65]

El Mocho also invited members of the Hasinai Confederacy to attend the trade fair with the Apaches. Although the Hasinais had previously been enemies of the Lipans, their access to European goods provided them with a profitable opportunity to act as middlemen in the trade with the Apaches. In fact, the availability of manufactured goods had increased since the establishment of Nacogdoches in 1778. The commandant of the Internal Provinces had appointed the town's founder, Antonio Gil Ibarvo, as lieutenant general of Nacogdoches and ordered him to establish Texas's first Indian trading post there. Gil Ibarvo named Joseph María Armant, a Frenchman from Natchitoches, as legal trader for all the tribes of Texas, including the Hasinais. Despite their easy access to trade goods, the Hasinais' proximity to Nacogdoches increased their susceptibility to disease, and the epidemic of 1777–78 reduced the four remaining tribes to about 1,500 people. The Nabedaches, the westernmost Hasinai tribe, lived on San Pedro Creek near its junction with the Neches River. The Hainais, led by medal chief Balthazar Bigotes, resided on the Angelina River twenty miles east of the Nabedaches, while the Nacogdoches lived about fifteen miles north of the Spanish town. Disease prompted the Nadaco chief, Kyaanadouche, to relocate his people farther away from Nacogdoches; they moved northward from the upper reaches of the Angelina River to the waters of the Sabine. The Aises, a Caddoan-speaking tribe not considered a part of the Hasinais, lived thirty miles east of Nacogdoches and had about two hundred members.[66]

About three hundred Karankawas, Atakapas, and Hasinais responded to El Mocho's proposition and, along with six hundred Tonkawas, met 2,000 Apaches on the Guadalupe River in November 1782. The Apaches (Lipans, as well as Mescalero and Natagé Apaches who lived farther west) brought 3,000 stolen horses with them to trade. The tribes of east Texas disappointed the Apaches, however, for they only brought 270 guns to exchange. In any event, the trade fair ended in disarray as a Norteño war party forced its dissolution in December. Desperate Spanish officials, threatened by the possible alliance of the Apaches and the eastern tribes, took the extreme step of ordering the assassination of El Mocho, which the commandant of La Bahía carried out in July 1784. This bold move frightened the Tonkawas, many of whom had never been comfortable with El Mocho's overtures with their heretofore enemies, the Apaches. Therefore, in 1785 the Tonkawas made peace with Governor Cabello and agreed, in return for a wide variety of trade goods, to establish a permanent village on the Navasota River and to end the arms trade with the Lipans. Although the Hasinais, Karankawas, and Atakapas maintained their ties to the Lipans, breaking the alliance with the Tonkawas went a long way toward completing the Spanish goal of isolating the Apaches in Texas.[67]

A treaty between the two main Norteño tribes—the Comanches and the Wichitas—and the Spaniards, however, remained the key to a lasting peace in Texas. The Comanches were, by far, the largest and most powerful of the tribes in the province. By the late eighteenth century, the Comanches had developed two major divisions: the Yamparicas, who lived in a region stretching from eastern New Mexico northward across the Arkansas River, and the Kotsotekas, who roamed throughout Texas, west of the Hill Country and Cross Timbers, between the Arkansas and Colorado rivers. Each was comprised of different bands, tied together through kin, language, and culture. Although the Comanches, living far from Euroamerican settlements, had generally been spared the ravages of epidemic disease, smallpox had spread to the Eastern Comanches in the early 1780s. Still, the Kotsotekas, at ten thousand or so members, had four times as many people as the Spaniards in Texas. They lived in ten to fifteen rancherías, each headed by a civil chief. Of these, Camisa de Hierro (Iron Shirt) and Cabeza Rapada (Shaved Head) had risen to prominence. Kotsoteka Comanche leaders entered into negotiations with de Mézières in 1778 and had expressed a desire to make peace with Texas. Misunderstandings ensued between the Comanches and the Spaniards as raids and counterattacks marred relations during the war with Great Britain. Lack of trade goods, combined with the smallpox epidemic of 1781, caused the Kotsotekas to seek peace and trade with Texas, especially when they realized the Spaniards sought to mount a campaign against the Lipan Apaches.[68]

The Wichitas remained the Comanches' greatest commercial and military ally. During the 1770s disease reduced their population by a third, while Osage attacks forced the tribes to consolidate and continue their southward migration. The Panis Piques, with 2,500 individuals, were the largest of the three Wichita groups. Although the Guichitas and Iscanis still lived in the fortified villages on both banks of the Red River, the Taovayas had become the dominant tribe of the three, and their name became synonymous with Panis Piques. Some Guichitas and Iscanis moved south to join with the 1,500 or so Tawakonis, who lived in two villages on the Brazos River, near present-day Waco. The central location of the Tawakoni villages allowed one of their chiefs, Quiscat, to emerge and become one of the leading Indians in Texas, a role he would fill beyond the turn of the century. Osage pressure combined with disease to divide the third Wichita tribe, the Kichais. The main body of the Kichais, consisting of about two hundred people, moved to the Red River and settled in a village near the Petit Caddos, about one hundred miles north of Natchitoches. Their chief, Brazo Quebrado (Broken Arm), died in the epidemic of 1777–78 and was succeeded by his son, Nicotaouenanan. Another 150 Kichais settled just east of the Trinity River, in present-day Houston County, Texas. Unlike the Comanches, the Wichitas had made peace with Spain, but they had not had much contact with their nominal ally since the death of de Mézières in 1779 and the beginning of Spanish involvement in the war against Great Britain. The Wichitas eagerly looked forward to the resumption of legal trade following the war and, like the Comanches, sought an alliance with the Spaniards aimed at the Lipan Apaches.[69]

Negotiations between the Norteños and Texas officials began in 1784 when Governor Cabello sent Natchitoches trader Jean Baptiste Bousquet, to the Taovaya village in order to confirm their ties to the Spaniards and hopefully begin talks with the Comanches. Bousquet found one Spaniard and two Frenchmen, including blacksmith Pierre Vial, living in the village and convinced them to accompany himself and the Taovaya chief back to San Antonio, where the alliance between the Panis Piques and Spain was renewed. In June 1785, the Wichita tribes cemented the deal by traveling to Nacogdoches to receive their annual presents. After pardoning Vial for the crime of living illegally among Indians, Governor Cabello ordered him to return to the Taovaya village to negotiate a treaty with the Comanches. Vial entered the Panis Pique town in August 1785, and met with twelve principal Comanche chiefs a few weeks later. Following a round of negotiations, all the Comanche headmen agreed to peace. Three chiefs returned to San Antonio with Vial, and in October the Spaniards and Comanches finally reached the accord that both had been trying to achieve for a decade. Each party agreed to refrain from fighting the other, and the Spaniards promised to distribute annual gifts and send traders to the Comanche villages. Most important, the Comanches were encouraged to continue their attacks upon the Apaches.[70]

Thus, by the end of 1785, most of the Indians of Texas and the Near Southwest had worked out a very favorable arrangement with their Spanish allies. They succeeded in resisting the Franciscan effort to convert them to Christianity and, to a great extent, they maintained their traditional lifestyles. The Indians also had forced the Spaniards to provide them with European weapons and manufactured goods in the manner of their former French allies. Although disease had greatly reduced their population, the Indians of the region still outnumbered the Euroamericans. It remained to be seen, however, if the natives could maintain their dominance throughout the rest of the eighteenth century and into the next.

2. Tenuous Coexistence
The Indians and Spain, 1786 to 1803

Relations between the Spaniards and the Indians of Texas and the Near Southwest stabilized somewhat following the agreements reached in 1785. During the final years of the eighteenth century, warfare between the groups was kept to a minimum, the Spanish-Norteño alliance subdued the enemy Lipan Apaches, and even the hostile Karankawas reached an understanding with the Spaniards. However, a great many problems constantly threatened the peace, issues not completely solved by December 1803, when Spain's nominal control over the area was disrupted by the United States' acquisition of Louisiana.

The Indian tribes of Texas and the Near Southwest had entered into peace treaties with the Spaniards for two reasons: to acquire trade goods and to obtain protection from their enemies. The Spanish in the region failed the Indians on both accounts. Chronic shortages of trade goods—exacerbated by the European wars of the 1790s—constantly hampered the Spanish effort to maintain the Indians' fidelity through trade. Therefore, the various tribes sought and developed alternative sources of goods, mainly through American traders from the United States and illicit French traders from Louisiana. The Indians' ability to obtain trade items elsewhere only served to lessen their ties to the Spaniards and to provide incentive for poaching Tejano livestock. This led to friction between the Indians and the Tejanos, which only increased as the turn of the century approached. Spain's inability to provide the Indians a respite from the attacks of enemy tribes also served to intensify the tensions between the Spaniards and their allies. Hostile tribes, such as the Osages and Choctaws, resided between the Indians of the Louisiana-Texas frontier and the American traders east of the Mississippi River, and had easy access to ample supplies of guns and ammunition. The Spaniards proved wholly incapable of curbing these well-armed tribes, who invaded the region in order to steal horses from the local Indians and to take control of the rich hunting grounds that still existed west of the Red River. This pressure, combined with an influx of Euroamerican immigrants into Louisiana, caused the Indians of that colony to begin a westward movement in the 1790s that would continue well into the following century. Nonetheless, by the time the United States took control of

Louisiana in late 1803, many of the Indians in Texas and the Near Southwest eagerly looked forward to establishing a relationship with the Americans in defiance of their weak Spanish allies.

At first, the Comanche-Spanish alliance seemed to be a great success. Within a month of the establishment of peace in October 1785, a succession of Eastern Comanche groups visited their new Spanish allies in San Antonio to celebrate the treaty. Two Kotsoteka warriors met with Governor Cabello in late November, while a Comanche man and his wife came to Béxar during the Christmas celebrations. As the new year began, a delegation of twenty-two Kotsotekas, led by one of the chiefs who had previously negotiated the treaty with Cabello, arrived to eat and smoke with the governor. The Comanche leader informed the Spaniard that the two most important chiefs, Cabeza Rapada and Camisa de Hierro, had been informed of the treaty and had given their approval. Finally, in February 1786, Cabeza Rapada's brother entered San Antonio with twenty-five tribesmen and assured Cabello that the chief was happy about the peace and was looking forward to meeting the governor in person later that spring.[1]

Both groups, however, realized that talk was cheap and that the Spanish ability to adequately provide their Indian allies with trade goods would be the key to maintaining the peace in Texas and the Near Southwest. During each of the Comanche visits to San Antonio during the winter of 1785–86, Governor Cabello was all too aware that he did not have enough gifts for his guests, nor was there adequate housing for their stay. In order to remedy the latter problem, the Spaniards erected a structure, about 144 feet long by 15 feet wide, partitioned into four 36-foot rooms, near the San Antonio dwelling of the local Indian interpreter, Frenchman André Courbière. Finished in July 1786, the structure furnished pleasant lodging for the steady stream of Comanches and other Indian groups that visited Béxar to receive gifts over the next quarter of a century. The months of September and October 1798 provide a representative view of the numbers of Indians from the various tribes that arrived in San Antonio; during that two-month period, over 450 Indians took advantage of the governor's hospitality, including 183 Lipan Apaches, 169 Comanches, sixty-eight Tawakonis, twenty-one Hainais and Bidais, and fourteen Tonkawas.[2]

Keeping all of these Indians well supplied with gifts and trade goods, though, proved to be a difficult task for the Spaniards. Items still had to be transported from Europe to New Orleans, and then up the Red River to be deposited at Rapides and Natchitoches. From both towns, traders took the goods to barter with the tribes considered to be within the jurisdiction of Louisiana, namely the various groups located at Rapides, as well as the Caddoan speakers living near Natchitoches and farther upstream. Goods for the Indians of Texas, however, had to be transported overland to the trading post at Nacogdoches, where Joseph María Armant, the French merchant from Natchitoches, had been granted a monopoly as the colony's official trader. All of the Texas Indians, except the Comanches, were expected to travel to Nacogdoches to receive their annual presents. In addition, Armant sent traders, mostly Frenchmen from Louisiana, to the various Indian villages. Other goods and presents were sent to San Antonio for the governor to distribute as the annual gifts for the Comanches, in addition to providing Indian visitors with items each time they arrived. While this was the Spanish plan for dealing with the Indians of Louisiana and Texas, the Spaniards found it almost impossible to obtain enough goods to adequately supply their Indian allies. The colonies of Texas and Louisiana were located at the extremities of a global empire that Spain could barely maintain even during peacetime. Following the outbreak of the wars of the French Revolution in 1793, the ties between Spain and her colonies in America were almost completely severed. As a result, the legal flow of Indian trade items to the Louisiana-Texas frontier, light during the best of times, slowed to a trickle. An ample supply of illegal goods, however, existed among the American traders east of the Mississippi River, and the Indians of the Near Southwest defied their Spanish allies by eagerly tapping into these sources. Since the Americans desired horses in addition to furs, the illicit trade caused the Indians to resume their raids on Tejano livestock in San Antonio and La Bahía.

Trade that the Spaniards maintained for the Comanches proved to be the most successful of any in the Near Southwest. Aware of its great importance, Spanish officials awarded the Comanche commerce the highest priority and strove to keep the tribe well supplied with goods and presents. In August 1786, the first shipment of goods destined for the Comanches arrived in San Antonio from Natchitoches. It consisted of thirty-seven boxes of imported European goods as well as 474 bundles of tobacco. From this stock, Governor Cabello hoped to deliver gifts to Kotsoteka chiefs Cabeza Rapada and Camisa de Hierro. As it turned out, however, both were killed soon thereafter. Lipan warriors (in conjunction with Mescalero Apaches) dispatched Cabeza Rapada in an engagement on the Pecos River, while Spanish soldiers from New Mexico mistakenly killed Camisa de Hierro. Although no single Kotsoteka Comanche had sufficient prestige, power, or authority to warrant the status of principal chief following the deaths of these two, men such as Sofais, Zoquiné, Yzazat, Chihuahua, and Sargento emerged as important leaders in the last decade of the eighteenth century. Spanish governors in San Antonio showered these dignitaries and other visiting Comanche notables with weapons, metal goods, and cloth, as well as with medals, flags, and staffs. Numerous Comanches traveled to Béxar following the establishment of peace; between 1794 and 1803, for example, the Spaniards entertained more than 4,200 Kotsotekas at San Antonio. Comanches also exchanged buffalo goods with traders sent out from Santa Fe and Taos, as the Yamparicas had entered into a treaty with the Spaniards of New Mexico in early 1786. To maintain the peace and the flow of trade goods, Kotsoteka chiefs strove to prevent their young men from raiding Tejano ranches in order to gain wealth and prestige. Although they were only partially successful, the Comanche leaders often paid restitution for their warriors' transgressions and, for the most part, the tribe maintained the all-important peace with the Spaniards of Texas and New Mexico for the better part of a decade.[3]

The Spaniards had a more difficult time providing the other Texas Indians with trade goods, and relations with the non–Comanche Norteños, in particular, suffered as a result. Despite the initial shipment of items from Louisiana, Armant quickly fell deeply into debt and was unable to acquire an ample supply of merchandise for the Indians. The lack of goods displeased the Tonkawas, who had consented to take up farming and to establish a permanent village on the Navasota River. In October 1787, Armant sent a trader, Cristóbal Equix, to the Tonkawa village to barter with the tribesmen. Equix did not provide the chief with an adequate present. Accordingly, the Tonkawa warriors relieved him of his meager supplies, savagely beat him, and drove him from their village. Soon thereafter, the Tonkawas defied the Spaniards and abandoned their agricultural experiment on the Navasota, choosing to relocate their rancherías southwestward to the Colorado River. While a few young Tonkawa men left the new villages to raid Spanish horse herds, tribal leaders maintained a tentative peace, allowing large Tonkawan groups to visit San Antonio in the summer and fall of 1788.[4]

The Wichitas maintained a similarly tenuous relationship with the Spaniards. Desirous of obtaining horses to exchange with illegal traders, Taovaya warriors stole from the Tejano herds at San Antonio in September 1786. Emboldened by their success, they tried again later in the month, but the Spaniards had set out sentinels, who wounded one raider and killed another. The Taovayas returned to their Red River village vowing to avenge their dead. As a result, seventeen young Guichitas and Taovayas set out to attack San Antonio in December. The raid went awry, and the Spaniards at Béxar captured all but two of the men. Rather than overreact to the Panis Pique raid, the new Spanish governor, Rafael Martínez Pacheco, calmly informed the prisoners that he wanted to establish a lasting peace with the Wichitas. Therefore, the governor released two captives, telling them to return home and invite the Taovaya chiefs to discuss the situation in San Antonio. Upon receiving Martínez Pacheco's invitation, in March 1787 a group of Taovaya headmen entered Béxar and agreed to observe a permanent peace with the Spaniards. The governor rewarded the Taovayas with gifts and allowed the prisoners to return home with their chiefs. The agreement lessened the tension between the Wichitas and the Spaniards, and throughout the summer representatives of each Wichita tribe, including the Kichais, traveled to San Antonio to meet the new governor and receive presents. The visits culminated in September, when seventy-three Tawakonis, Taovayas, and Iscanis met with Martínez Pacheco to reaffirm the peace.[5]

Within a year, however, young Taovaya warriors threatened the accord between the Wichitas and Spaniards. In November 1788, twenty-three Taovayas made off with a herd of horses and mules from San Antonio. Spanish troops caught up with the culprits just north of the Guadalupe River and took seven of them into custody. Back in San Antonio, the leader of the Taovaya war party begged Governor Martínez Pacheco to release him so that he could return to his village and retrieve the stolen animals. The governor, as he had done before, gave in to the plea, swayed by the Taovaya's promise that his people "would live in constant peace" in the future. The man kept his word and returned to San Antonio on December 21 with a few stolen animals, as well as thirty-two Taovaya men, including four notables. The leaders swore that they were still friends of the Spaniards and gave Martínez Pacheco permission to kill the Taovaya prisoners. The governor magnanimously answered that since he loved the Taovayas he would not execute the offenders and allowed them their freedom. In return, one of the four headmen ordered his brother to remain in San Antonio to serve as mediator in case any other Taovaya warriors were caught stealing Spanish livestock. This arrangement remained in place until March 1789, when the brother returned to his village.[6]

Norteño relations with officials in Texas soon soured again due to the Spaniards' failure to provide presents and trade goods. Because of a drought that reduced river water levels and hence impeded travel, in 1789 the annual Indian gifts never arrived in Texas. Disgusted by finding nothing for him at Nacogdoches, the Kichai chief haughtily returned his medal to Lieutenant Governor Ibarvo in August 1789. Wichita and Hasinai warriors traveled to San Antonio throughout the year, complaining bitterly to Martínez Pacheco about the lack of goods. The governor could do nothing but scrape together some form of gift in order to "partially console" his guests upon their departure. Desperate for trade items, the Indians visited Natchitoches and tried to persuade Commandant Louis de Blanc to send them traders from Louisiana. They told de Blanc (the grandson of the town's founder, St. Denis) that the shortages in Texas had reduced them to "dire necessity" and they were "consequently ready to commit evil actions." When matters failed to improve in 1790, annoyed Wichita and Hasinai warriors once again expressed their disappointment to Commandant de Blanc in Natchitoches. The tribesmen stated that the Spaniards had abandoned them and left them without traders. Therefore, they were no longer obliged to keep the peace, especially since they were actually better off when they were at war with the Spaniards, given that they "never lacked horses and mules to steal."[7]

Manuel Muñoz, who became governor of Texas in the summer of 1790, quickly realized that Armant did not have the means to provide enough trade goods to the Norteños. Therefore, he revoked Armant's trading monopoly and granted permission for independent traders, mainly Spaniards, to visit the various Indian villages. This new system did not fare much better because the Indians preferred French traders. For example, Muñoz assigned Francisco Durán and Francisco Travieso to Chief Quiscat's Tawakoni villages on the Brazos. Travieso immediately alienated the tribe by cheating them, burning down one of their houses, and shooting a Tawakoni man to death. In April 1793, Muñoz sent a Spanish troop to the Tawakoni villages to arrest Travieso, but tensions remained high well into the following year. In February 1794, another Spaniard set fire to a Tawakoni house and made off with six horses, while two months later, a Tawakoni man killed a Spaniard he thought had stolen his horse. Further violence was avoided only through the mediation of Chief Quiscat. Despite his effort to maintain the peace, the Tawakoni chief informed Muñoz that he was dissatisfied with the mean character of the traders that the governor had sent him.[8]

As a result of the bad situation in Texas, Quiscat and Hainai chief Sánchez, traveled to Natchitoches in July 1794 to complain, once again, to Commandant de Blanc. They told the Frenchman that, although they had made peace with the Spaniards of Texas in order to receive traders in their villages, they had actually been deprived of goods "in such a way that currently they are in the most major misery." They begged de Blanc to send them traders from Louisiana but he refused. Instead, de Blanc informed Muñoz of the visit, prompting the Texas governor to send a new trader, Juan José Bueno, to the Tawakonis in June 1795. Within eight months of his arrival, however, Quiscat had quarreled with Bueno, culminating in the Tawakonis' seizure all of his merchandise. Lieutenant Governor Bernardo Fernández ultimately forced the angry Quiscat to return the goods. Most of the other Norteño tribes experienced similar unsatisfactory relations with the traders provided by Governor Muñoz.[9]

To remedy the situation, Texas officials granted exclusive rights to the Indian trade to two Irishmen from Pennsylvania, William Barr and Samuel Davenport.

In 1798 the two men, naturalized citizens of New Spain, set up shop in Nacogdoches and sent traders to the various Indian villages. Although the firm of Barr and Davenport did increase the volume of trade goods being distributed to the Indians of Texas, the problems persisted. The Tonkawas immediately complained about their trader and demanded that Barr and Davenport remove him and send another. The Hasinais received two traders who initially supplied them with goods on credit. These men were soon forced to quit when the Hasinais never paid them back in full. Barr and Davenport responded by giving Cabezón, the Nacogdoches chief, goods on credit, with the expectation that he would supply the various tribes and collect payment. Although Cabezón distributed the goods, he never fully repaid the firm.[10]

While the Texas Indians were pleased with the increase in trade goods that resulted from the Barr and Davenport monopoly, most of the tribes had already developed ties with illicit traders and continued to jealously guard these crucial sources of goods. The number of these traders increased during the last years of the eighteenth century as Americans from east of the Mississippi River flocked across the border into Spanish territory. Since these traders desired horses in addition to furs, their entrance into Texas only exacerbated the uneasy relationship between the Indians and the Spaniards, for they prompted the natives to poach mounts from the Spanish herds near San Antonio and La Bahía. As early as August 1786, illegal traders headed up the Red River to encourage the Panis Piques to steal horses from San Antonio. Beginning in the 1790s, Americans from mount-poor Mississippi traveled to the Texas plains to capture horses from among the huge wild herds that roamed near the Wichita villages. The first of these Americans to cross into Spanish lands, Philip Nolan, legally entered Texas from Natchez in 1791 with a passport obtained from the governor of Louisiana. Nolan established relations with the Wichitas and realized that, in addition to obtaining mustangs in Texas, he might supplement his income by providing the desperate tribes with trade goods. Nolan again received a passport to make legal trips to Texas in 1794 and 1797, and on both occasions he conducted illicit commerce with the Wichitas.[11]

While Nolan entered Texas legally, other Americans crossed the Mississippi to trade with the Indians without Spanish approval. In early 1794, a blacksmith from Philadelphia, John Calvert, established a forge at the Taovaya village where he repaired weapons and made knives and lances. Six Americans, along with a black slave, traveled to Quiscat's village on the Brazos in order to barter with the Tawakonis. Other illegal traders came from Louisiana; in June 1794, a Natchitoches Frenchman illegally entered the Panis Pique villages and developed a "great commerce" with them, while others went among the

Tawakonis. Although the Spaniards pressured the Taovayas into removing the French trader, Calvert remained there until the fall of 1795 when a Spanish patrol apprehended him. Encouraged by a group of Frenchmen who arrived in their rancherías with powder and balls, Tonkawa warriors assaulted Spaniards on the road to Nacogdoches and stole their horse herd. The Norteños also developed trade with other Indian tribes that had access to American goods. By the end of 1796, all of the Wichita tribes, as well as the Tonkawas, had begun trading with the Skidi Pawnees, who were obtaining goods and weapons from Americans who illegally entered their villages on the Kansas River.[12]

Southeastern Texas was also open to illicit trade from Louisiana, and the Atakapas and Karankawas maintained their ties with Frenchmen from the southwestern Louisiana posts. Although the Spaniards successfully forced the Tonkawas to break their trade ties with the Lipan Indians, the Bidais, Akokisas, and Cocos continued to act as middlemen between the Apaches and the Louisiana traders. In 1791 and 1792, officials from the Internal Provinces wrote to the governor of Louisiana begging him to prevent inhabitants of his jurisdiction from "bringing guns, powder, and ball through Opelousas and Attakapas to the nations" of Texas. The Spaniards were unable to halt the trade, and by late 1792 Americans had begun to develop ties with the Indians as well. In November, a man named Pete Martin led three Americans from Opelousas to the lower Trinity River, where they exchanged goods with the Bidais. The illicit trade continued unabated, and in 1794, Texas governor Muñoz was forced to reiterate the plea to the Baron de Carondolet, Spanish governor of Louisiana. Despite official prohibitions, the Indians of southeastern Texas were able to maintain the trade with Louisiana throughout the rest of the eighteenth century and beyond. As with the Norteños, the Atakapas and Karankawas also developed trade with eastern tribes, such as the Choctaws, who provided them with metal goods and weapons in return for horses and hides.[13]

Although the Spaniards were unable to provide the Texas Indians with an adequate amount of trade goods, they successfully reinforced the alliance with the Norteños by prosecuting a war against the two groups' common enemy, the Lipan Apaches. Ultimately, the Spanish-Norteño alliance defeated and isolated the Lipans, who were forced to abandon Texas and retreat south of the Rio Grande. Governor Cabello initiated the attacks on the Apaches immediately following the celebration of peace with the Comanches in October 1785, by encouraging the throngs of Kotsoteka visitors to make war on the Lipans. The Texas governor also exhorted other tribes to attack the Lipans; in January 1786, a group of Taovayas, Guichitas, and Tawakonis met with Cabello in San

Antonio. Cabello stressed the importance of unity and then sent the Wichitas, along with a few visiting Comanches, on an unsuccessful campaign against the Apaches. In the spring, the governor sent Miguel Peres, a Tonkawa man who had been kidnapped by Lipans and then raised by Tejanos in Béxar, on a mission to encourage his people to fight against their erstwhile Apache friends. Peres traveled to the Tonkawa village on the Navasota and transmitted Cabello's message. As the entire Tonkawa village met to discuss Cabello's request, two hundred Tawakonis, led by Chief Quiscat's son Quisquichace, arrived and invited them to assist in an attack on the Lipans. As a result, 150 Tonkawas joined the Tawakonis in surprising an Apache ranchería near the Colorado River on the morning of May 22. In a battle that raged for eight hours, the attackers routed the Lipans, killing thirty men and capturing most of their six hundred horses. When the survivors informed the rest of the Lipans of the attack, the entire tribe retreated to the Atascosa River, just south of San Antonio.[14]

Desperately seeking some sort of deal with the Spaniards, the dispirited Lipans chose Zapato Sas as their leader. On June 24, 1786, he and twenty Lipans traveled to San Antonio to negotiate with Governor Cabello. The Indians asked Cabello to take the Lipans under his protection and to officially acknowledge Zapato Sas as the chief of the tribe. Zapato Sas promised that if the Spaniards sent them traders, he would locate the Lipans wherever the governor desired and would prevent his warriors from stealing Spanish horses and cattle. Cabello, plotting to set the Apaches up for a decisive blow from the Norteños, temporized by telling Zapato Sas that he needed permission from his superiors in Mexico before granting his requests. In the meantime, the Spanish governor demanded that the Lipans move their rancherías from the Atascosa to the headwaters of the Frio River, near the abandoned mission on the San Saba, and await the response from Mexico.[15]

Although Zapato Sas told Cabello that he would follow his orders, he realized (as did the governor) that relocating the Lipans to the upper Frio would only make it that much easier for the Norteños to attack and destroy them. With their backs against the wall, the Apaches resisted and were able to thwart the Spanish desire for their annihilation. Desperate for weapons, 150 Lipans succeeded in bypassing the Tonkawas and visited the Bidais in order to secure French guns. At about the same time, Kotsoteka leadership was thrown into disarray by the deaths of Cabeza Rapada and Camisa de Hierro, and the Eastern Comanches were unable to mount an offensive against the Lipans. Taovaya raids on San Antonio, which soured relations between the Wichitas and the Spaniards, also saved the Apaches from Norteño attacks. Free from fear of a joint Norteño-Spanish campaign, Zapato Sas and the Lipans remained on the

Atascosa River throughout the remainder of the year, living off the numerous herds of wild cattle that ranged nearby.[16]

By the beginning of 1787 the Lipans had an ally in the governor's palace at San Antonio when Martínez Pacheco replaced Cabello as governor on December 3, 1786. The new governor, a veteran soldier who had spent more than three decades in Texas dealing with the Indians, was certain that his experience allowed him a better understanding of the situation than other Spaniards. Therefore, he immediately reversed the policy of his predecessor and promoted peace between the Apaches and the Norteños. When a group of Lipans visited San Antonio soon after Martínez Pacheco took office, the new governor greeted them warmly and showered the Apaches with gifts. In order to receive more presents, as well as protection from Spanish soldiers, the opportunistic Lipans took advantage of Martínez Pacheco's favorable inclinations and informed him that they were now willing to congregate at the San Antonio missions. The naive governor eagerly accepted the Lipan proposal and began to make arrangements for their arrival, which never happened. Although a few small groups of Apaches visited the San Antonio missions for short periods of time in the spring, most remained in their rancherías on the Atascosa. By March only one Lipan woman, on the verge of death, had been baptized in Béxar.[17]

Soon thereafter, Comanche and Wichita warriors resumed their attacks upon the Lipan Apaches, despite Martínez Pacheco's desire for peace between the groups. On three separate occasions in December 1787, Norteño warriors successfully raided Lipan rancherías, temporarily located to the northwest of San Antonio in order for the Apaches to make their winter buffalo hunt. First, men associated with Comanche captain Gordo Cojo (Fat Cripple) stole horses and killed a few Lipans in an attack near the old Spanish presidio on the San Saba River. Another group of Comanches killed seven Lipans and kidnapped three women in a second raid. Finally, Tawakoni, Taovaya, and Guichita men followed up these attacks by descending upon Zapato Sas's village on the Frio River, making off with all six hundred of the Apaches' horses. Reeling from the attacks, most of the Lipans retreated south of Béxar and settled on the Atascosa River, near its confluence with the Frio, in the spring of 1788. They remained there throughout the summer without attacking any Spaniards or killing any Tejano cattle.[18]

The inability of the Lipan leaders to keep their young men from poaching livestock from the ranches near San Antonio, however, caused the Spanish leadership to turn against the Apaches in 1789. In February, Lipan warriors stole eight mules and a mare from a Saltillo resident traveling to Béxar. Although Zapato Sas returned the stolen livestock to Governor Martínez Pacheco soon thereafter, another band of Lipans took five cows and a young bull from a San Antonio ranch in June. Once again, the Lipan chiefs forced the robbers to return the cattle and compensate the owner with the payment of five horses and a deerskin. In August, though, a group of Lipans left the Atascosa to join the Mescalero Apaches on the San Saba River. West of San Antonio, the Lipans killed an old Tejano settler and stole eighteen horses from his ranch on the Medina River. As the Lipan party continued westward, they killed five more Spaniards encountered on the road. Fearing reprisals from the troops in San Antonio, most of the Lipans abandoned their rancherías on the Atascosa and joined with the Mescaleros.[19]

The Lipan hostilities induced Juan de Ugalde, commandant of the Eastern Interior Provinces, to mount an offensive against the Apaches. Ugalde, who had never been comfortable with Martínez Pacheco's peace policy and had previously campaigned against the Mescaleros in the Big Bend region, gathered Spanish troops at Monclova in late 1789 and headed north to find the Apaches. Two hundred Comanches, led by Sofais and Zoquiné, joined Ugalde's force, which reached the abandoned presidio on the San Saba in mid-December. Ugalde sent Sofais and a Spanish escort to San Antonio to ask Martínez Pacheco for reinforcements of troops and ammunition. The governor responded by sending eleven soldiers and fifty-two volunteers along with as many cartridges as he could find to Ugalde, who had also been joined by a group of Wichita and Tonkawa warriors.[20]

As Ugalde's Spanish-Norteño force searched for the Apaches, six Lipan warriors entered San Antonio to observe the actions of their onetime friend, Martínez Pacheco. On the morning of December 29, the Lipans snuck into the governor's bedroom unannounced. Surprised but calm, Martínez Pacheco offered the intruders some tobacco as he dressed. He suggested that they join him for a meal in the kitchen from where he signaled a soldier on the patio to call the guard and to send twelve men. When the soldiers appeared, the frightened Lipans drew knives and made a desperate effort to fight their way out of the room. In the ensuing struggle, all six Lipans were killed, one by the aged governor himself, while only one Spanish soldier was seriously wounded. Although it is unclear exactly what the Lipans had in mind by visiting the governor, Martínez Pacheco insisted they had come to assassinate him and collect information on the Spanish campaign. The governor proudly claimed that he had saved Ugalde's army from being discovered by the Apaches. In any event, on January 9, 1790, the undetected Spanish-Norteño force surprised a large Mescalero-Lipan ranchería on Soledad Creek, a small tributary of the Medina River. The Apaches resisted for several hours, but finding themselves surrounded and outnumbered, they made a desperate dash and succeeded in breaking through the line of attackers. Despite their flight, about sixty Apaches died, including two chiefs, and the Spaniards captured a large number of women and children. The attackers also took nearly eight hundred horses from the Lipans and Mescaleros.[21]

Following the rout on Soledad Creek, the wounded Lipans separated from the Mescaleros and retreated southeast of San Antonio, establishing rancherías between the Nueces and the Colorado rivers. From their new settlements, the Lipans pursued a double-sided policy: Lipan warriors robbed Spanish settlements to obtain livestock to trade with their Bidai, Akokisa, and Coco allies; at the same time they entered into peace negotiations with the Spaniards. Although the Lipans did make a few raids upon ranches near San Antonio and La Bahía, for the most part they concentrated their efforts on Spanish settlements along the Rio Grande. Between March and July 1790, Lipan warriors killed twenty-five Spaniards in the towns of Laredo, Revilla, and Mier, while stealing the incredible number of 447 mules, 1,850 horses, 117 head of cattle, and 3,756 goats. Using their gains, the Apaches traveled to southeastern Texas to exchange livestock for arms and ammunition with the Atakapas and Karankawas. In September 1790, Lipan warriors went to the Akokisa village to barter; later in the year, chiefs Canoso (White Hair) and Zapato Sas purchased over three hundred rifles from their Indian trading partners.[22]

At the same time that some Lipans were obtaining horses and arming themselves, various chiefs met with Spanish leaders to ask for peace. In April and May 1790, chiefs Agá and Canoso, as well as a lesser captain named Cabezón, separately traveled to San Antonio to meet with Governor Martínez Pacheco. All three apologized for past hostilities but stated that they now desired a peaceful relationship with the Spaniards. Before Martínez Pacheco could work out an agreement with the Lipans, Manuel Muñoz replaced him as governor of Texas. In August, Agá met with the new governor and informed him that captains Canoso, Zapato Sas, Chiquito (Little Boy), and José Lombreña had sent him to inquire about a peace settlement. Muñoz, taking into consideration the recent Lipan raids in the Rio Grande Valley, refused to enter into an agreement with Chief Agá. Instead, the Spanish governor met with various visiting parties of Norteños, distributing gifts and inciting them to continue their hostilities against the Lipans. As a result, in December 1790, Comanche, Wichita, and Tonkawa warriors attacked Chief Canoso's ranchería on the Colorado River, killing ten Lipans and making off with most of the tribe's horse herd.[23]

This successful Norteño attack caused Lipan captain José Antonio to travel to Mexico and negotiate directly with Pedro Nava, newly appointed commandant of the Eastern Interior Provinces. On February 8, 1791, the two leaders met in the town of San Fernando de Austria and agreed to keep the peace. In the settlement, the Lipans consented to maintain their rancherías south of the Atascosa River, keep their distance from Spanish presidios, refrain from stealing Spanish livestock, and stop trading with the Atakapas and Cocos. In return, the Spaniards agreed to provide the Apaches with traders and allow them to enter Spanish towns and trade buffalo skins with the residents. In addition, the Spaniards consented to try and keep the Norteños from attacking the Lipan rancherías. As a result of the peace accord, most of the Lipans had moved their settlements south of the Atascosa by May 1791.[24]

This peace proved to be short-lived. Lipan chief Canoso not only refused to abandon his ranchería on the lower Colorado River, but in April 1791 he also met with Akokisa traders to exchange livestock and arms. On May 1, Chief José Lombreña traveled to Coahuila with six men and women to meet with Commandant Nava in Santa Rosa to celebrate the peace. Instead, an argument ensued between the Lipans and the Spaniards, and one of the Apache men stabbed Nava twice in the shoulder. The knife, however, did not penetrate deeply, and the commandant was able to shoot his assailant to death. Attempting to flee, the desperate Lipans killed two Spanish soldiers and wounded seven others before a group of townspeople dispatched all seven Apaches. Informed of the incident, Governor Muñoz gathered a group of Spanish troops, accompanied by Wichita, Tonkawa, and Comanche warriors, and sent them westward from San Antonio in search of Lipans. On May 22, the Spanish-Norteño force surprised a Lipan ranchería on the San Saba River. Although the Apaches from a nearby village forced the attackers to retreat, the Norteños still made off with two hundred horses. Throughout the rest of the year, Comanche, Taovaya, and Tonkawa warriors—well supplied with Spanish weapons—continued to raid Lipan settlements. Zapato Sas responded by crossing the Rio Grande and attacking the Spanish settlement of Reynosa in February 1792. Spanish detachments pursued the Indians into Texas and killed the Lipan chief along with fifteen of his warriors.[25]

In the wake of the demise of José Lombreña and Zapato Sas, Lipan chiefs Canoso, Chiquito, and Moreno (Dark Hair) emerged as leaders of the remaining Apache groups in Texas, and the three men began to seriously pursue a peace policy. In July 1792, Chief Canoso and 148 Lipans met with Juan Cortés, commander of La Bahía, and promised to keep the peace with the Spaniards. Receiving no response from Spanish officials, Canoso returned to La Bahía in September with 118 Lipans to request peace again. Informed of Canoso's plea, Governor Muñoz directed Cortés to tell the Lipan chief that his people must return stolen livestock and refrain from future thefts before peace could be considered. Instead of replying immediately, Chief Canoso and the Lipans met with a party of Bidais, who directed the Apaches to the lower Trinity River where four Americans had illegally established a temporary trading post. Now well armed, the Lipans headed west of San Antonio for their winter buffalo hunt before retiring to the Atascosa River in the spring of 1793. Finally, in April, Canoso, Chiquito, and Moreno formalized a peace with Governor Muñoz in San Antonio in which they agreed to stop stealing livestock in return for being granted the right to exchange buffalo skins for metal goods at various Spanish settlements. The three chiefs also consented to forsake their trade with the southeastern Texas tribes as long as the Spaniards promised to pressure the Norteños to keep the peace with the Lipans.[26]

Although the Apaches occasionally broke the terms of the treaty over the next few years, the Spaniards also proved incapable of protecting the Lipans from the Norteños. For the most part, however, the April 1793 treaty would successfully maintain the peace between the Lipans and Spaniards for the rest of the eighteenth century. The Lipans continued to conduct buffalo hunts west of San Antonio in the late spring and fall and traveled to Béxar three or four times a year to sell the hides and receive presents from the governor. Nevertheless, Norteño raiders constantly harassed the tribe, forcing the three Lipan chiefs to move their rancherías southward toward the Rio Grande in the late 1790s. In March 1798, Comanche warriors stole most of Canoso's horse herd, inducing his band of Lipans to cross south the Rio Grande, where they settled south of Laredo. The other two Lipan groups joined their fellow tribesmen later in the month. In January 1799, all three Lipan bands chose Chiquito as their spokesman, and he entered into a treaty of peace, similar to the April 1793 agreement, with the governor of Nuevo Santander. Chief Chiquito agreed that the Lipans would establish their rancherías below Laredo, between the Rio Grande and the Salado River. However, they reserved the right to hunt north of the Rio Grande, all the way to the Nueces. Despite these territorial limitations, the Lipan chiefs continued to travel to San Antonio each year to obtain their annual gifts from the governor of Texas. Although the Lipans had been forced to abandon Texas by the end of the 1700s, they would return north of the Rio Grande and play an important role in Texas affairs during the first half of the nineteenth century.[27]

Just as relations between the Lipan Apaches and the Spaniards stabilized by the end of the century, the Karankawas also ended their hostility to the Euroamerican intruders. At first, however, both sides, mindful of Coapite chief José María's 1778 successful attack on Mission Rosario, maintained their enmity. On July 3, 1786, a detachment of Spanish troops from La Bahía engaged thirteen Karankawas, wounding and apprehending one, whom they took to the presidial guardhouse, where he died ten days later. Three weeks later, a party of Karankawas retaliated by stealing twenty-three horses from a ranch near San Antonio, killing a Spanish boy as they fled. Captain Luis Cazorla, the longtime commander of La Bahía who detested the Karankawas, sent troops down the San Antonio River to seek the assailants. Near the mouth of the river, a group of Karankawas surprised the Spaniards in their camp, killing one soldier and stealing blankets and other items before safely retreating in their canoes. [28]

Instead of escalating the war, the peace-minded governor of Texas, Martínez Pacheco, sent emissaries to the coast in March 1787 to find José María and begin negotiations. In response, José María arrived in San Antonio on June 26 with nine members of the Coapite, Cujane, and Carancaguase tribes. The governor welcomed the party "with every kindness and attention" before an assembly of the town's presidial officers. The Karankawas remained in San Antonio for two weeks, during which time Martínez Pacheco showered them with gifts and had their weapons repaired. A grateful José María agreed to meet with the parish priest in order to make his confession and receive communion. The Coapite chief also submitted to Martínez Pacheco's request that he try to convince the rest of the Karankawas to abandon the coast and return to the defunct Mission Rosario. Well intentioned, José María and his party left Béxar with an accompanying troop of Spanish soldiers and a Spanish engineer who had orders to map the region. [29]

Not all the Karankawas, however, were as eager as José María to establish friendly relations with the Spaniards. After guiding the engineer through the maze of bays and inlets along the coast, the Coapite chief agreed to return with the troops to San Antonio. Other members of his party, including his wife, opposed his decision and the Indians began fighting among themselves. During the struggle, a Karankawa man shot and killed a Spanish sergeant. The other Karankawas then drove off the other soldiers and mutilated the dead man's body, severing his right arm at the elbow and his left at the wrist. They also scalped him, mutilated his testicles, and left the sergeant hanging from a tree by his feet before retreating with José María to a barrier island. [30]

Although the Spaniards discussed exacting revenge upon the attackers, they took no action until early 1789, when a group of Karankawas killed three La Bahía residents and kidnapped a boy while they were stealing cattle. In response, on February 8 a troop of seventy-five Spanish soldiers, along with sixteen Tejanos and four mission Indians, left La Bahía with an artillery piece in search of the Karankawas. A few days later the force found a Karankawa village containing three hundred people near the junction of the Guadalupe and San Antonio rivers. The Spaniards fired their cannon into the camp, killing ten and wounding many others. The Karankawas hastily abandoned the bloody scene amid "the cries and clamors" of the men and women, leaving behind 8,000 iron-tipped arrows.[31]

By the end of the 1780s the continued warfare with the Spaniards had begun to weigh heavily upon the Karankawan groups. The situation was becoming particularly dangerous now that the innocuous Coahuiltecans had disappeared from the region, thus depriving the Karankawas of a buffer from threatening Apache and Comanche raiders, with whom they had always been at war. Rather than maintaining hostilities on two fronts, a few Karankawan bands began to seek an accommodation with the Spaniards, especially after the Franciscan missionary, José Mariano Reyes, reestablished Mission Rosario in late 1789. Suffering from a recent outbreak of disease that killed Coapite chief José María, in November 1789, Copane and Cujane representatives met with new La Bahía commander, Captain Manuel de Espadas, to inform him of their wish to return to the mission. However, before they could actually reenter Mission Rosario, some Carancaguases wounded a Spanish soldier from La Bahía on December 7. Sixteen Spanish troopers headed down the San Antonio River from the presidio in pursuit of the attackers. The Spaniards encountered a canoe filled with four Carancaguases and convinced the Indians to lead them to their village. The Carancaguases apologized to the Spaniards for wounding the soldier and agreed to send a few tribesmen to La Bahía to further discuss matters with Captain Espadas. On December 28, Capitán Grande, the sixty-year-old chief of the Carancaguases, arrived with sixteen men and asked to meet with Martínez Pacheco. On February 15, 1790, he, along with Copane leaders Manuel Alegre and Balthazar, and Cujane chief José Luis, entered San Antonio and told the governor of their desire to return to Mission Rosario.[32]

Martínez Pacheco happily gave them permission to enter the mission, and by May 1790, fifty-three Karankawas lived at Rosario, including the Carancaguase chief. Hoping to receive food and gifts, the Karankawa population rose to 134 by the beginning of the summer. The Indians were soon disappointed, for the priests had hardly enough food for themselves, much less the neophytes. Due to a prolonged drought, there was no corn and, although plenty of cattle ranged near the mission, constant Apache and Comanche raiding prevented the Karankawas from gathering many for slaughter. Father Reyes was all too aware that the Karankawas only wanted food, for he informed the governor "that for these neophytes the Gospel enters through the mouth, not through the ears," and that it was an "illusion" to think that the Karankawas would come "from the coast to work for a living." The Indians ran afoul of Father Reyes in other ways as well. Manuel Alegre angered the priests by "living licentiously" with the daughter of Capitán Grande, claiming that he "would rather die than" marry her as they wished. As a result, Alegre and a few other tribesmen abandoned the mission in late spring, helping themselves to six mules and five horses from a nearby Spanish ranch as they left. Others followed his lead, and by July 1790, only thirty-nine Karankawas remained. In September another eleven left Rosario and, following Alegre's precedent, took twelve horses with them. [33]

Although the Karankawas continued to desire peace with the Spaniards, they mainly wanted to have a station located in their territory from which they could draw food and protection when necessary, and Mission Rosario proved too far from the coast for their comfort. The Indians soon made the Spaniards realize this fact, and within a few years the Franciscans established a mission in the middle of Karankawan territory. Two enterprising Franciscans, Father Manuel Julio de Silva and José Mariano de la Garza, set in motion the chain of events that led to the founding of the new Karankawan station when they arrived at the nearly empty Mission Rosario in February 1791. They encouraged the few tribesmen at the mission to visit their kinsmen and invite them back for a meeting. As a result, on March 31 a Carancaguase chief named Fresada Pinta (Spotted Blanket) came to Mission Rosario and, impressed with the reception afforded him by the priests, promised to return within ten days to guide the Franciscans to his village. Fresada Pinta arrived eight days later with twenty-four companions and on April 10 set out with Silva and Garza for the coast. A few days later, eighty-six Carancaguases welcomed the two Franciscans into their village near the mouth of the Lavaca River. After spending a pleasant couple of days with the Carancaguases, the priests were escorted southwest-ward to Copano Bay, where they visited a Copane village of sixty-five people, led by a chief named Llano Grande (Great Plain). Silva and Garza distributed sugar, biscuits, and tobacco at both towns and invited the tribesmen to return to Mission Rosario. The Karankawas politely agreed, but only a few actually joined the Franciscans when they made their way back to La Bahía a few days later. [34]

Encouraged by the trip despite its meager results, Father Garza returned to the Copane village in June 1791. Once again, Llano Grande cordially welcomed the priest into his village and listened to his ministrations. Garza distributed gifts to the tribesmen and then exhorted them to return to Mission Rosario, reminding the Copanes that they had agreed to visit once before. A Copane leader clearly informed the Franciscan of his people's desire when he warned Garza not to deceive himself. The Copane man said, "we do not want to go to the mission. We will do nobody harm, we will go our own way, and let the Spanish come also to our country, with the assurance that we will receive them as friends; but we do not want to leave our country. If you want to, put a mission here on the coast for us. We will gather in it, all of us who are Christians, and we will bring with us all the heathens that are on the coast from the mouth of the Nueces to the Colorado River, . . . If you put a mission [at the mouth of the Guadalupe] for us, then you can say that the whole coast is yours."[35]

Believing he understood the true wishes of the Karankawas for the first time, Father Garza (guided by Fresada Pinta) traveled to the confluence of the Guadalupe and the San Antonio rivers to inspect the recommended site for the mission. The Franciscan liked what he saw, reported the Karankawan request to his superiors, and received the viceroy's approval for the mission, called Nuestra Señora del Refugio, on December 31, 1791. Eagerly anticipating the mission's opening, 208 Karankawas from the villages of Fresada Pinta and Llano Grande had assembled near the mouth of the Guadalupe by May 1792. Although an Apache raid dispersed the gathering late in the year, 138 Karankawas had returned to the site when Father Mariano Velasco formally founded Mission Refugio in February 1793.[36]

The Karankawas, whose only interest in the mission was as a source of food, were quickly frustrated by the meager rations offered by the Spaniards. Within a month twenty-three tribesmen left for the coast. The rest of the Indians stood idly by and watched as the Spanish soldiers began building a stockade. When Father Velasco urged them to assist the soldiers, a few men took up their bows and arrows and threatened the priest. Another Karankawa stole Velasco's horse and wounded a Spanish muleteer as he rode away from the mission. An outbreak of disease at Refugio killed a few tribesmen and only ninety Karankawas remained at the mission by the beginning of summer. In late June 1793, all but twenty-four of the Indians left Refugio to harvest prickly pear cactus. Matters failed to improve over the course of the following year, and by the spring of 1794 only Llano Grande's son and his wife remained at Mission Refugio. On June 4 an angry and disappointed Fresada Pinta broke into the mission with a group of followers and ransacked the storehouse and priests' quarters. They drank wine kept for Mass, stole sugar and chocolate, and killed two milk cows and a calf before leaving.[37]

With the mission all but destroyed, the Franciscans relocated the settlement to what they hoped was a healthier spot on the west side of the Guadalupe River, unpromisingly called Rancho de los Mosquitos. Fresada Pinta and his warriors appeared at the new mission in August 1794 and threatened to destroy it as well. A Spanish officer bravely confronted the Carancaguase chief and forced him to back down. Fresada Pinta, however, informed the soldier that he and his people "never did and never would want mission life, but that they desired to live in peace with the Spaniards." Although most Karankawas agreed with this sentiment, Chief Llano Grande, who witnessed the exchange, assured the Spaniards that his band of Copanes would settle at a well-located mission. Rancho de los Mosquitos proved inadequate and, following the death of Llano Grande in November 1794, the mission was relocated for the final time in January 1795 southward to a site on Mission River, near present-day Refugio. Forty-three Copanes were present for its formal establishment.[38]

The new mission site of Refugio proved more inviting to the Karankawas than the previous two, especially after Spanish troops delivered 350 or so head of cattle to the mission ranch in May 1795. Spanish officials also strove to make sure the corn supply at the mission never faltered. As a result of the ample food, eighty-two Karankawas had gathered at Mission Refugio by October. Twenty-six tribesmen, however, left the mission to spend the winter on the coast. Their departure set a pattern for many other Karankawas to follow, particularly now that peaceful relations with the Spaniards had, for the most part, been established. While only a few Indians spent the entire year at Mission Refugio, many incorporated the settlement into their way of life as yet another source of sustenance. Most tribesmen spent the period from October through March fishing in large camps along the coast. In the spring the Karankawas dispersed into smaller groups and moved into the interior to collect prickly pear cactus and hunt deer. Some tribesmen visited Mission Refugio as they made their way to and from the inland prairies in March and October. A few, finding life at the mission not too distasteful, remained at Refugio through the summer. Although the Spanish officials and Franciscan priests disapproved of this casual approach to mission life, they realized that the station promoted friendly relations and strove to keep Refugio well-supplied with food and to provide adequate protection from the Comanches and Apaches.[39]

In the meantime, a group of about one hundred Cocos and Carancaguases arrived at Mission Rosario in early 1794 and asked to settle at that station. These Indians had been members of the Karankawan groups (mainly Cocos) that had previously moved inland to live among the Bidais and Akokisas between the Colorado and Trinity rivers. Therefore, they did not mind that Mission Rosario was located so far from the coast. The priest at Rosario, Father José Francisco Jáudenes, allowed them to stay at the establishment until September 1794, when sickness forced him to close the station and travel to San Antonio for treatment. Father Jáudenes reopened Mission Rosario two years later, and by October 1796 one hundred or so Karankawas were living there under the guidance of Carancaguase chief Manuel Zertuche and Pedro José, leader of the Cocos. By the beginning of the summer of 1797 the meager resources at the mission no longer adequately fed the neophytes, prompting Spanish officials to try to convince the Karankawas to relocate to the old missions in San Antonio. Zertuche and Pedro José refused, claiming that Béxar was too far from the coast and too near the Comanches. As a result, in June 1797 the forty-six Carancaguases and fifty-one Cocos were allowed to join the seventy-five Karankawas living at Mission Refugio.[40]

The 172 Karankawas soon strained the resources of Mission Refugio. Comanche raiders exacerbated the situation by driving off two herds of cattle from the mission ranch in October. Intimidated by the Comanches, more Karankawas than usual abandoned the mission in the fall and headed for the coast. In January 1798, most of the Carancaguases and Cocos from Rosario also left the mission. Finally, in March, the few remaining Karankawas left Mission Refugio, sardonically informing the priests to "let the Rosario Indians eat all the cattle," for they did not plan on returning. Although many Karankawas did come back to Refugio before the end of the year, most of the Rosario Indians stayed away until the summer of 1799. Other Karankawan parties continued to visit the mission at times for food and, as they became increasingly familiar with the Spaniards over the years, more and more neophytes remained at Refugio for longer periods. In 1804 for example, at least 224 Karankawas spent some time at Mission Refugio. Although most Karankawas actually avoided the Franciscan priests, by the end of the period a peaceful understanding finally existed between the tribe and the Spaniards in Texas.[41]

Relations with the Lipans and Karankawas improved, but the alliance between the Comanches, Wichitas, and Spaniards was sorely tested at the end of the eighteenth century. The Spanish inability to provide trade goods, combined with the intercession of illegal American traders, induced many Comanche and Wichita warriors to renew their efforts to steal horses from San Antonio and La Bahía. Pushed to the wall by constant raids, the Spaniards ultimately resorted to force in an effort to curb the incursions. Although most of the Comanche leaders tried to restrain their young men to maintain the peace, a group of young Wichita headmen emerged who proved eager to defy the Spaniards. As a result, by the time the United States acquired Louisiana in late 1803, relations between the Wichitas and the Spaniards were at their worst point in nearly three decades.

The Comanche and Wichita raids began in earnest in the middle of the 1790s. Tribesmen, who often traveled through San Antonio on their way to attack the Lipan Apaches, casually stole horses from among the Spanish herds in passing. In September 1796, a group of prominent Béxar citizens protested to Governor Muñoz, claiming that Comanche and Wichita thefts of horses and cattle were becoming unbearable. While Muñoz recommended patience and moderation so as not to upset the Norteño alliance, the new governor of Coahuila, Antonio Cordero, responded aggressively to the raiders. In February

1797, Governor Cordero sent troops in pursuit of Kotsoteka warriors who had stolen three hundred head of cattle from a mission near the Presidio del Rio Grande. The soldiers followed the Comanches to the headwaters of the San Saba River where they overtook the raiders and forced them to return most of the cattle. Unsatisfied, Cordero sent Lieutenant Antonio Toledo to the San Saba to demand that the Comanche chiefs living in the area keep firmer controls on their young men. Despite the protests, Comanche raids continued; in April 1798, two Kotsoteka parties poached horses from herds near the Presidio del Rio Grande. Governor Cordero sent Spanish troops after both groups, but neither was able to overtake the retreating Comanches. As result of the continuing thefts, Commandant General Nava instructed Governor Muñoz to impress upon visiting Comanche and Wichita chiefs that the Spaniards would henceforth hold them responsible for the actions of their young warriors. Unless they were restrained effectively, the Spaniards would retaliate with force, and would discontinue the distribution of gifts.[42]

The Spaniards implemented the new assertive policy following a Kotsoteka Comanche raid upon the presidial horse herd at Laredo in March 1799. The commander of the post, José Ramón Bustamante, pursued the Comanches with forty-five troops, guided by six Apaches from the newly established Lipan rancherías near Laredo. The Spanish-Apache force caught up with the Comanches on the Nueces River and attacked, killing two while badly wounding seven. Bustamante's troops also captured four Comanche men and one woman, who were taken back to Laredo in chains. In three separate incidents, which occurred the following month, Spanish troops in San Antonio captured and incarcerated sixteen Kotsoteka raiders. Governor Muñoz outraged the Comanche warriors by publicly whipping three of the men. On April 23, the Comanche prisoners responded by starting a fire in the jail that allowed seven men to escape. The governor freed another four of the young men soon thereafter, but five Comanches remained in the Béxar jail until August. Although the principal Comanche captains sent messages to the new Texas governor, Juan Bautista Elguézabal, offering to discuss the situation in San Antonio, they assured the official that they did not want to upset the peace just because of the punishment and jailing of a few young men. The matter was settled early the following year as Kotsoteka captains Sofais and Zoquiné had friendly visits with Governor Elguézabal at Béxar.[43]

In the meantime, the new combative policy resulted in the outbreak of violence between the Spaniards and the Wichitas. This was due, in part, to a smallpox epidemic that swept through the area and killed a "great number" of Wichita tribal members. As a result of the sickness, two aggressively anti-Spanish chiefs emerged as leaders of Panis Pique tribes: Eriascoc of the

Taovayas and Awahakei of the Iscanis. Both chiefs considered the Spaniards to be undependable and untrustworthy and were disappointed in the alliance that netted them few trade effects and scant protection from enemies such as the Osages. Therefore, following Eriascoc's accession as Taovaya medal chief in July 1799, Panis Pique warriors stood up to a troop of Spanish soldiers that tried to thwart the tribes' exchange of goods with a party of Cherokees and Chickasaws that had come to their villages from east of the Mississippi River. Inspired by the Panis Piques, the following summer a group of Tawakonis defied their peace-minded chief, Quiscat, and killed a resident of La Bahía while stealing horses. In response, Spanish troops, accompanied by Lipan auxiliaries, pursued the Tawakonis, killing two. Although the Tawakonis were enraged by the Spanish use of the enemy Apaches, Chief Quiscat chose to maintain the peace and sent a captain named Tambor (Drum) to meet with Governor Elguézabal and assure him of his tribe's friendly intentions.[44]

Spanish officials, however, soon angered all of the Norteños with their efforts to stop the incursion of American traders into Texas. In October 1800, Philip Nolan, whose activities over the past decade had raised the suspicions of the Spaniards, illegally entered Texas with thirty or so Americans. Nolan's well-armed force established a camp on a tributary of the Brazos River, upstream from the Tawakoni villages, where they erected a small fortification, including some corrals, and began rounding up wild horses. On March 21, 1801, Spanish troops from Nacogdoches located the camp and attempted to arrest Nolan's party. When the Americans resisted, the Spaniards killed Nolan and captured most of his band of mustangers who were later tried and imprisoned in Chihuahua. However, a few of Nolan's men escaped and returned to Mississippi, intent on returning to Texas to trade with the Wichitas and capture horses. While the Spaniards annoyed the Wichitas by disrupting their illicit relationship with Nolan, they enraged the Kadohadachos and Hasinais by arresting Bayou Pierre resident and trader, Paul Bouet Laffitte, for helping Nolan's compatriots escape. The Kadohadacho chief, as well as Nadaco and Nacogdoches principals, demanded that Nacogdoches commandant José María Guadiana release their longtime friend. Due to the vociferous Caddo complaints, Guadiana set Laffitte free, giving the Frenchman a month's time to leave Texas.[45]

Following the death of Nolan, Kotsoteka Comanche raiders threatened the peace in Texas. In June 1801, a Comanche party poached livestock from a San Antonio resident, but two of the warriors were killed by Spanish troops that chased them to the Guadalupe River. Seeking revenge, Kotsoteka men dispatched a La Bahía resident, and then killed a Spanish soldier and wounded another from a troop that was sent in pursuit. Matters reached the boiling point in the autumn of 1801, when unidentified Spaniards obtained vengeance by killing two Yamparica Comanches as they made their way to San Antonio. One of the Yamparicas was the son of Chief Blanco who immediately put out a call for war to his Kotsoteka kinsmen. Although some Comanches sympathized with Chief Blanco, the leading chiefs rejected his solicitation and even opposed him. Sofais and Yzazat moved their rancherías to the Llano River so that they could monitor developments in the enemy camps and keep Governor Elguézabal informed. Despite the Kotsoteka efforts to maintain the peace, a Yamparica party exacted vengeance in April 1802 by killing a San Antonio resident who was hunting with a group of men on the Blanco River. The hunters, in turn, took revenge on a lone Comanche they encountered on the way back to town; they killed the man, scalped him, and delivered their trophy to Governor Elguézabal.[46]

When news of this murder reached the Kotsoteka villages, one group threatened to attack the Spaniards in Texas as well as the rancherías of Sofais and Yzazat. War was avoided, however, when peaceful Yamparica leaders from New Mexico announced at a general meeting of Comanche headmen that they opposed war on the grounds that it would result in the loss of the benefits of peace with the Spaniards. The Yamparicas convinced Chief Blanco to forget his differences with the Texans, and Kotsoteka chief Chihuahua suggested that the Comanches form a police force to ensure compliance with the treaties. In the fall of 1802 the Comanches sent emissaries to Governor Elguézabal to inform him of the tribe's decision to maintain the peace.[47]

Although the Comanches desired peace, in early 1803 hostilities broke out between the Spaniards and Wichitas that threatened to spill over to the Kotsotekas. In February, a combined Taovaya-Guichita force stole horses from herds outside San Antonio. Fifty-one Spanish troops caught up with the thieves and killed nine as they returned to their villages. Enraged by what they considered an excessive use of force, the Panis Piques called upon their fellow Wichitas, as well as their Comanche allies, to assist them in obtaining retribution. Once again, Kotsoteka leaders rejected the call to war, and chiefs Chihuahua and Yzazat traveled to San Antonio in March to reiterate their desire for peace to Governor Elguézabal. To ensure the Kotsotekas' commitment to the alliance, Coahuila governor Cordero met with Chihuahua, Yzazat, and Sargento in Monclova later that year and agreed to their request for a resident trader at their villages.[48]

While Comanche and Spanish leaders successfully avoided war, Wichita warriors remained determined to exact revenge for the killing of nine of their tribesmen. In the spring of 1803, a party of one hundred Taovayas and Guichitas set out from their villages on the Red River intent on killing and robbing residents of San Antonio. A group of Spaniards, however, detected the Panis Piques on the outskirts of town, and Spanish troops intercepted them before they could do any damage. In July a group of young Tawakoni men raided Spanish herds near San Antonio. A Spanish troop pursued and killed one Tawakoni man while reclaiming the livestock. Finally, in October, Taovaya warriors gained a bit of satisfaction by killing two Tejano residents of Nacogdoches.[49]

Ultimately, the war between the Wichitas and the Spaniards had a detrimental effect upon Spanish-Comanche relations as well. In August 1803, Spanish troops searching for Taovayas near San Antonio encountered twenty-eight Kotsoteka Comanches, led by El Sordo (The Deaf One). The Spaniards recognized that several of the Comanches' horses were from San Antonio and the troop forced El Sordo and his party to return to town. In Béxar, the Spaniards placed twenty-six Comanches under arrest; two members of the group were charged with the murder of a citizen who had recently been killed by unidentified Indians. Although the two men denied having committed the murder, they admitted that they had stolen Spanish horses. In October, Chief Chihuahua returned from Monclova and negotiated a settlement of the tense situation. He chastised the prisoners and promised to punish future criminals, even by death, if necessary. Governor Elguézabal responded by releasing all the prisoners except the two horse thieves, who everyone agreed should serve the jail term for theft. Two months later the governor released both of the Comanche men. War had been averted between the Comanches and Spaniards, yet many Kotsoteka warriors sided with their Wichita allies and felt no great compunction to maintain the peace in Texas. On the eve of the American accession of Louisiana, relations between the Norteños and the Spaniards of Texas had reached their lowest point since peace had been achieved in 1785.[50]

While the Indians of western Louisiana—the Caddoans and the various groups at Rapides—had dealt with the Spaniards for a much shorter time than the natives in Texas, relations between the two groups were peaceful, but troubled, throughout the last years of the 1700s. Although the problems of trade shortages were not as grave in Louisiana as they were in Texas, the Indians still defied their Spanish allies and obtained goods from illicit traders, including Americans from east of the Mississippi River. More disturbing to the Indians than the lack of trade was the Spanish inability to protect them from marauding invaders such as the Osages and the Choctaws. The Spanish weakness convinced the Louisiana tribes that the Spaniards were highly undependable partners. However, the Indians' longstanding friendship with the French residents of Louisiana, combined with the fact that they were greatly outnumbered by the

Euroamericans of the colony, inhibited their ability to use force against their supposed allies. Unlike in Texas, where the Euroamerican numbers remained about the same during the period, western Louisiana experienced population growth that brought immense pressure upon the beleaguered Indians. Rather than fight, the Indians began a westward movement that would ultimately lead them out of Louisiana and into Texas early in the following century.

Unlike in Texas, the Louisiana tribes were relatively well supplied from the Spanish posts of Natchitoches and Rapides. Nonetheless, the Indians living along the Red River flouted their Spanish allies and augmented their income by dealing with illegal traders. Many illicit merchants who bartered with the various tribes came from the recently established Spanish post on the Ouachita River in northeastern Louisiana, located near present-day Monroe. As early as 1787, a Ouachita trader named Louis Lepinet illegally developed commerce with Chief Tinhioüen and his Kadohadachos that greatly angered the traders from Natchitoches, because the Kadohadachos owed them furs that Lepinet acquired instead. In 1791, Americans from east of the Mississippi River began passing through Ouachita Post on their way to the Kadohadachos. Not only did they cut into the Natchitoches trade, they also plied the Indians with alcohol. Frenchmen also continued to barter with the Caddos; in 1793, Gaspard Filibert traveled from Ouachita Post to the Kadohadachos and spent nearly the entire year at the village. By 1789, Ouachita traders were also ranging to Rapides Post, where they bartered with the local tribes. In 1796, illegal traders established camps near Rapides and encouraged the Indians, through the distribution of alcohol, to steal livestock from the local ranches. Following the lead of Philip Nolan, American residents from Natchez began traveling to the Kadohadacho villages to acquire horses in 1798.[51]

Despite the liberal amounts of legal and illegal trade entering into the Louisiana Indian villages, the tribes of the Near Southwest were constantly short of arms and ammunition, especially compared to their better-equipped enemies to the east. The main threat to peace continued to be the Osages, who not only had access to legally authorized Spanish traders but also received numerous supplies of weapons from American traders residing east of the Mississippi River. Prodded by these men and their desire for horses and furs, the Osages resumed their raids upon the Indians of Texas and Louisiana—despite their recent treaty with the Kadohadachos—in early 1786. Although the Osage attacks affected most of the tribes on the Louisiana-Texas frontier, they harmed the Kadohadachos the worst, ultimately causing them to merge with the Petit Caddos and relocate their villages in an attempt to escape the onslaught that their Spanish allies were helpless to contain.

The Osages renewed their assaults in March 1786 by attacking Kadohadacho hunters in the wilderness; in addition to having their horses and furs stolen, two Kadohadachos were killed and two were wounded. The following month Osage warriors invaded the Kadohadacho and Kichai villages on the Red River. The marauders kill four Kichais and also destroyed the product of the hunt in both villages by ripping apart deerskins and buffalo tongues and tipping over pots of bear oil. This violence not only wounded the Indian tribes, it also did serious economic damage to the French merchants and traders of Natchitoches. Osage warriors continued their onslaught in the summer of 1786; one group invaded Texas and killed two Spaniards and two Nabedache Indians, while another band stole horses from the Kadohadachos, who pursued them for two days before recovering the herd following a fierce battle. During the fight, one Kadohadacho and two Osages were killed.[52]

Following the attacks, Kadohadacho caddi Tinhioüen traveled to Natchitoches to complain to the commandant of the post, Pierre Rousseau. Enraged at the lack of protection from the Spaniards, Tinhioüen returned a ribbon—now coated with blood—that Miró had given him in New Orleans the previous year when the Louisiana governor had mediated the peace between Tinhioüen's tribe and the Osages. The Kadohadacho chief now demanded aid from Governor Miró, who he claimed had promised it if the Osages broke the peace. Miró responded by temporarily denying the Osages legal traders, while also discussing the possibility of a punitive expedition against them.[53]

Ultimately, the Spaniards took no military action against the Osages, and the tribe's right to trade resumed soon thereafter. However, Spanish officials discussed the idea of supplying the Kadohadachos with enough arms to allow them to attack the Osages. New Natchitoches commandant, Louis de Blanc, reported that the Hasinais, as well as the Taovayas and the Tawakonis, were prepared to wage war on the Osages at the request of the "great chief" of the Kadohadachos. Although the order was given to supply the Kadohadachos and their allies with arms and ammunition, no attack was forthcoming. In September 1787, Kadohadacho and Petit Caddo leaders arrived at Natchitoches and met with José de la Peña, a local Spanish official. When the Spaniard berated the tribe for failing to launch the proposed campaign, Tinhioüen explained that "at present it would be impossible for him to attack the Osages because the number of his nation is very inferior to theirs." The Kadohadacho chief, however, promised to try to do them as much harm as possible.[54]

Whatever harm he did proved to be ineffectual. The following year the Kadohadachos gave in to Osage pressure and moved their village downstream nearly halfway between the old village and the Petit Caddos. At the same time, the Red River Kichais threatened to leave the area and join with their brethren in Texas, who lived on the Trinity. Both Caddo tribes strongly opposed the Kichais' relocation because they would lose a valuable ally against the Osages. In response, Tinhioüen, along with the leaders of the Petit Caddos, led a party of Kichai headmen down to Natchitoches in August 1788, where Commandant de Blanc helped convince the Kichais to remain in the area. The two Caddo tribes persuaded·the Kichai chief, Nicotaouenanan, to move his village to a site about twenty miles above the Petit Caddos by consenting to give the Kichais their annual gifts for the present year.[55]

Convincing the Kichais to remain on the Red River proved to be Tinhioüen's final official act, for the great Kadohadacho caddi passed away in the summer of 1789. On September 30, 1789, de Blanc held a formal ceremony at Natchitoches to recognize a man named Bicheda as the new Kadohadacho chief. Bicheda was given a large medal, a uniform, a banner, and thirty jugs of brandy to celebrate the appointment. Unfortunately, Bicheda had no better success with the Osages than his predecessor. Although an army of seven hundred Comanches and Wichitas successfully assaulted the Osages in the fall of 1789, this did nothing to stop the tribe's continued attacks on the Kadohadachos. In February 1790, Osage warriors killed a few Kadohadachos, as well as a French resident of Natchitoches, "whom they cut to pieces and scalped." Since the Kadohadachos were "being persecuted incessantly by their enemies," Bicheda, only five months after becoming chief, moved his tribe downstream again to take refuge in the Petit Caddo village. The tribes lived together in the same town, but they maintained their own distinct political identity for a few more years. In April 1792, Commandant de Blanc awarded Cachaux, "the most capable Indian that I have ever known," the large medal as chief of the Petit Caddos. One of Cachaux's headmen, Dioktau, was named the small medal chief by the Natchitoches commandant.[56]

Direct Osage attacks upon the Kadohadachos declined following the unification with the Petit Caddos, yet they continued to assault Indian and French hunters above Natchitoches in the valleys of the Red and Ouachita rivers. In the summer of 1791, Osage warriors killed a Natchitoches resident, Zachary Martin, while he was hunting in the prairies along the Red. In 1792, Commandant de Blanc complained that while an abundance of game existed between the Kadohadacho and Panis Pique villages, the post of Natchitoches was "deprived of these provisions by the treacherous Osages who constantly wage war upon us in this region as well as upon our Indian allies." De Blanc begged Louisiana governor Carondolet to prevent St. Louis traders from dealing with the Osages. Although Carondolet put forth a plan to deny the Osages traders, arm all of the allied Indian nations, and surround the tribe to "finish them once and for all," the Spaniards disappointed the natives on the Louisiana-Texas frontier by failing to implement the project. Instead, a group of Comanches took it upon themselves to attack the Osages without Spanish support, and completed a very successful campaign in which they killed eighty enemy tribesmen.[57]

Osage hostilities in the Near Southwest dwindled over the next few years as internal dissension divided the tribe, and St. Louis traders successfully applied economic pressure on them to maintain the peace. In the wake of the Osages, however, appeared a new threat to the Indians of the Louisiana-Texas frontier, the Choctaws. Ironically, Spanish officials had encouraged bands of Choctaws—with whom Spain had signed a treaty of protection in 1784—to expand west of the Mississippi to act as a deterrent to the raiding Osages. Instead, numerous groups of well-armed Choctaws invaded the Near Southwest around 1790, attacking Indian and Euroamerican settlements alike while trying to take control of the rich hunting grounds between Natchitoches and Nacogdoches. By 1792, Natchitoches commandant de Blanc was complaining that the Choctaws "come in great numbers and cause me a great deal of trouble by their thefts of horses and cattle," which they then delivered to American traders east of the Mississippi. In May 1792, three parties of Choctaws arrived in Natchitoches and aggressively strode around the town as they made their way from tavern to tavern. Once drunk, the Choctaws acted with "great insolence," beating their breasts and "declaring themselves entirely to the [Americans], scorning the Spanish." For the next decade or so, the Spaniards were unable to control the American-supplied Choctaws, who intensified their violent raids in the region as the eighteenth century came to a close.[58]

Hostilities between the Choctaws and Indians of the Louisiana-Texas frontier broke out in the summer of 1792 when Adaes and Ais tribesmen clashed with the eastern invaders near the Sabine River. In the fighting, three Choctaws died and seven Adaes and Aises, including one woman and a child, lost their lives. In response to the constant Choctaw incursions, the Adaes Indians assembled warriors from the surrounding tribes in preparation for full-scale war. Learning of the Adaes' actions, Governor Carondolet stepped in and ordered de Blanc to negotiate a treaty between the two groups that would allow the Choctaws access to hunting grounds in Texas. Although warfare was prevented for the time being, the Natchitoches commandant reported that none of the Indians on the Louisiana-Texas frontier agreed to let the Choctaws hunt in their territory. Due to this aggressive stance, the Choctaws refrained from traveling west of the Red River for the next couple of years.[59]

In May 1794, however, the Choctaws resumed their hostilities in the Near Southwest by crossing the Mississippi and threatening the Pascagoula village on the Red River. They then passed into Texas, where they killed a Hainai man near Nacogdoches. The following year, five Choctaws invaded the Kadohadacho village and killed a man and a woman. Already angered, the Kadohadachos became incensed when a Choctaw named Outabé led a group of warriors into a tribal hunting camp. The Choctaws shot Kadohadacho chief Bicheda in the thumb, killed his nephew, and stole all the furs and horses in the camp. In response, chiefs Bicheda, Cachaux, and Dioktau informed Commandant de Blanc that they wanted the Spaniards to render them justice by delivering the head of Outabé. They warned that, unless this was done, vengeance would be extracted from the first Choctaws they encountered. Informed of the matter, Governor Carondolet ordered Jean Delavillebeuvre, Spanish commissioner for the Choctaws, to force the tribe to punish the guilty parties and give "complete satisfaction to the Caddos by cutting off the heads of the murderers." The Choctaws ignored the feeble Spanish pressure and did nothing to Outabé. Once again, the Indians had been made all too aware of the impotence of their Spanish allies. That awareness turned to incredulity in the following year when Governor Carondolet tried to form an impossible alliance, aimed at the Choctaws, between the tribes of the Louisiana-Texas frontier and their long-time enemies, the Osages. The Indians, led by the Kadohadachos, dismissed the alliance as preposterous since the Osages "have made peace and always have broken their word."[60]

The Choctaws continued their incursions in the Red River Valley in 1796, attacking Euroamericans as well as Indians. François Grappe, the Kadohadacho interpreter, had horses stolen from his Campti ranch in July by a band of Choctaws, who went on to rob other settlers and kill two Kadohadacho tribesmen. The raiders then traveled to Texas, where they committed atrocities among the Aises, Bidais, and Tonkawas. In response, Kadohadacho chief Bicheda and Sánchez, leader of the Hainais, formed a troop among the east Texas tribes and killed two of the retreating Choctaws. Seeking retribution, in November a band of Choctaws killed three Adaes Indians near Bayou Pierre, just north of Natchitoches. Choctaw attacks continued unabated in 1797. In February, Choctaw hunters in Texas killed eight Hainais, including women and children. Choctaw outrages were capped off in the summer, when they killed Petit Caddo chief Cachaux, who was replaced as big medal chief by a man named Tervanin.[61]

Carondolet's replacement as governor of Louisiana, Manuel Gayoso de Lemos, desperately tried to arrange a peace settlement between the Choctaws and the tribes of the Near Southwest. As a result, in October 1797, Kadohadacho chief Bicheda acted as spokesman for a group of tribes living near Rapides—the Taensas, Apalaches, Biloxis, and Alabamas—in a meeting held with the Choctaws in Natchitoches. Rapides commandant Layssard mediated the two-day conference in which the Kadohadacho and Choctaw chiefs exchanged white flags as symbols of a truce. Bicheda then promised to make peace in the spring, provided the Choctaws committed no more hostile acts. On his part, the Choctaw spokesman promised to treat any of his tribesmen who caused trouble along the Louisiana-Texas frontier as renegades, and therefore, would not seek revenge if they were killed by the Kadohadachos or their allies.[62]

Although many Choctaw men abided by the peace treaty throughout the winter and spring, by the summer of 1798 hostile warriors had once again invaded the Near Southwest. In August a band of Choctaws killed a Kadohadacho man and stole furs and goods from a Ouachita Post trader. In response, Bicheda gathered warriors from most of the Caddoan tribes on the Louisiana-Texas frontier and caught up with an encampment of Choctaws near Rapides. Commandant Layssard, however, enraged the Caddoans by preventing them from attacking the Choctaws when he stepped between the groups and fired his weapon in the air. Three months later Choctaw warriors ranged west to Nacogdoches and pillaged Gil Ibarvo's cabin, while stealing and killing cattle from other residents of the town. Hostile incursions continued unabated over the next few years; in January 1800, the Kadohadachos killed two Choctaw warriors and wounded two others who attacked their village with thirty other tribesmen. Six months later a band of Choctaws raided the ranch of a Nacogdoches resident and bound him hand and foot before driving away his cattle. As they made their way back to their villages, the Choctaws killed and beheaded two Ais Indians. The continuing Choctaw incursions caused the Red River Kichais to abandon their village, located upstream from the Kadohadachos, and join with their kinsmen on the Trinity River in Texas. Soon thereafter, the Kadohadachos and Petit Caddos relocated their settlements, taking refuge on Caddo Lake, about thirty-five miles west of the main branch of the Red River. The Spanish inability to check the Osages and the Choctaws had forced the Kadohadachos to move their villages three times in twelve years.[63]

Most of the other tribes in Louisiana were also forced to relocate their settlements during the period. The problem, however, was not hostile Indian attacks, but increased pressure due to the influx of Euroamerican immigrants. The small Caddoan-speaking tribes living near Natchitoches continued to decline in the final years of the eighteenth century, and survived only by combining their forces with their linguistic kinsmen. As the Euroamerican and slave population at Natchitoches increased by 42 percent during the period—from around 1,300 people in 1785 to 1,850 in 1803—the small number of Indians in the region declined accordingly. By 1787 the Natchitoches and Yatasi numbers had dwindled so much that Commandant de Blanc remarked that they did not "deserve to be included any longer among the recipients of presents." Less than fifty Yatasis remained in their village on Bayou Pierre, near the ranch of Paul Bouet Lafitte. In the late 1780s a Nacogdoches tribesman named Antonio married into the Yatasis and emerged as their leader, albeit without the Spanish recognition of medal chief. The Natchitoches medal chief, Hyamoc, died in 1790, but Commandant de Blanc refused to designate his son, Datze, as the official chief "since this nation is almost finished." Like many of the Indian men living near Natchitoches, Datze succumbed to alcohol and often fought with the French inhabitants of the town. In an effort to improve their situation, the thirty or so remaining Natchitoches Indians sold their lands, located only six miles above the French town, and moved about twenty miles farther up the Red River, where they established a village and planted crops. As with the Yatasis and the Natchitoches, Spanish officials also declined to designate any Adaes warrior as medal chief following the death of their leader, Quemsy, in the late 1780s. Like the Natchitoches tribe, the few remaining Adaes moved farther away from the town of Natchitoches and settled near the Yatasis on a small tributary of Bayou Pierre.[64]

Although the Euroamerican and slave population at Rapides increased fivefold—from about one hundred to 550 people—the Indian numbers also rose, as tribesmen continued to cross the Mississippi River to settle with their kinsmen in Spanish Louisiana. By 1796 about two hundred Apalaches, Taensas, and Alabamas lived in contiguous settlements on the Red River, about twenty miles above Rapides. All three tribes maintained a close relationship with the settlers of Natchitoches and Rapides, and were said to be "highly esteemed by the French inhabitants." The tribes impressed their neighbors by successfully raising crops, tending livestock, and by adopting Euroamerican dress. Some tribesmen even engaged in cash crop cultivation; in 1791, eight Indians raised 12,200 pounds of tobacco on their lands upstream from Rapides. In addition, many Taensas, living in close proximity to the Christian Apalaches since 1763, adopted Catholicism as well. Between 1792 and 1799, local priests baptized forty-five members of both tribes, with Natchitoches citizens often acting as godparents. Both Etienne, the Apalache chief, and Louis, the Taensa chief, claimed to be Catholics. In fact, Chief Louis met with Bishop Luis Peñalver y Cárdenas when he visited Rapides in 1796 and informed the priest, in French, that tribesmen from both villages sought baptism and confirmation. As a result, the bishop baptized six children and one man, while confirming ten others. In 1800, a small party of Coushattas, led by Chief Soulier Rouge (Red Shoes), crossed the Mississippi River to join with their close Alabama associates at the Red River settlements.[65]

The groups living near the few French settlers above Rapides experienced few problems with the inhabitants, but by the early-1790s other tribes in the area began to feel the pressure from the recent immigrants, many of them Americans from east of the Mississippi River. These tribes included the 170 Pascagoulas that lived on the Red River, as well as the three hundred Yowani Choctaws and Biloxis that resided on Bayou Boeuf. Although all of the Indians engaged in agriculture and raised cattle and horses, illegal traders, using alcohol as bait, induced some Pascagoulas to steal mounts from the local settlers. The Pascagoula men often went on drunken sprees in which they sold everything they owned in return for wine and rum. Left with nothing, the Pascagoulas then killed the settlers' cattle and hogs in order to survive.[66]

As a result of the settlers' complaints, Governor Carondolet tried to force the Pascagoulas to move northeast from the Red River to an empty region on remote Catahoula Lake. Instead, on April 9, 1795, the Pascagoulas sold their lands to a longtime French inhabitant of the region for $250 and moved to Bayou Bouef, where they established a village between the Biloxis and the Yowanis. Matters did not improve on Bayou Bouef because the three tribes were soon besieged by American immigrants, some of whom traded with the Indians while others desired their lands. Bowing to pressure, in October 1797 the Yowanis sold 2,600 acres of land on both sides of the bayou to John Maguire for $200 in goods. The land sale, however, only encouraged other Americans to settle in the region and the Indians soon complained to Commandant Layssard that the immigrants' cattle were destroying their cornfields. Although Layssard ran some of the Americans out of the area, by the turn of the century the settlers were crowding the Indians, and all three of the tribes were deeply indebted to various traders. In 1800 alone thirty-three American men, most with families, settled in the Rapides district and began to raise cotton.[67]

A couple of traders, Alexander Fulton and William Miller, formed a firm whose actions were representative of the American shift of interests from engaging in commerce with Indians as merchants to acquiring their land as speculators. In October 1800, the Spanish governor of Louisiana granted Fulton and Miller the exclusive rights to the Indian trade of Rapides district. The traders allowed the Indians extensive lines of credit and within a year or so, all the tribes had run up huge debts. Fulton and Miller quickly realized that obtaining the Indians' land in order to sell it to American cotton farmers would be greatly more profitable than continuing the undependable trade. Therefore, on May 14, 1802, Fulton and Miller forced the indebted Yowanis to sell them the rest of their lands for $3,724, all of which was immediately taken and distributed to the tribe's debtors. On the same day, Pascagoula chief Chiquacha and de Blanc, son of Biloxi chief Tygre, sold their tribes' lands to Fulton and Miller for $1,500 worth of goods. Unlike the Yowanis, the Pascagoulas and Biloxis actually kept a bit of the payment for their land. In all,

Fulton and Miller claimed approximately 41,284 acres of land on Bayou Bouef as a result of these purchases.[68]

Following the sale, the Biloxis remained near Bayou Bouef on a small parcel of land granted to them by Fulton and Miller. On the one hand the Pascagoulas returned to the Red River and settled just above the Apalache village. The Yowani Choctaws, on the other hand, began a westward movement toward Texas that ultimately all of the Louisiana Indians would be forced to follow. The Yowanis moved to a prairie, located between the Red and the Sabine, about forty miles southwest of Natchitoches, where they established a village, planted fields, put up fences, and raised cattle. At about the same time, Soulier Rouge led a party of Coushattas from the Red River to the east bank of the Sabine, about eighty miles south of Natchitoches. Another group of Coushattas, led by Chief Pia Mingo, joined their kinsmen on the Sabine soon thereafter, bringing the total number of tribal members living in the village to about six hundred. By the end of 1803, the Coushattas, along with the Alabamas, Yowanis, and Biloxis, were crossing into Texas to hunt and obtain horses. It would not be long before many of these tribes actually settled in Texas.[69]

In the face of the Osage, Choctaw, and Euroamerican pressure, a Kadohadacho caddi, Dehahuit, emerged to become a strong spokesman for, and a defender of, many of the Indians living along the Louisiana-Texas frontier. Like their fellow Caddoan-speaking Wichitas, the Kadohadachos and the Petit Caddos were seriously affected by the outbreak of smallpox around the turn of the century. The epidemic killed perhaps a third of the tribal members, including Kadohadacho chief Bicheda and Petit Caddo chief Tervanin. In early 1801, the two tribes united under the leadership of Dehahuit, Bicheda's nephew. The new Kadohadacho caddi was described by observers as being "a very fine looking man," who was a remarkably "shrewd and sensible fellow." Dehahuit immediately began to establish his role as the leader of all the tribes on the Louisiana-Texas frontier. Upon informing Natchitoches commandant Felix Trudeau that he had become chief of the Kadohadachos in January 1801, he demanded uniforms for himself and the Yatasi and Natchitoches leaders, as well as "a few small gifts" for his dependents in Texas, the four Hasinai tribes and the Kichais. As a result of Dehahuit's actions, the Kadohadachos were said to be predominant over all the Caddo tribes, "who look up to them as fathers, visit and intermarry among them, and join them in all their wars." Soon thereafter, Dehahuit began to use his influence on behalf of the tribes living near Rapides, who, by the time the United States gained possession of Louisiana in late 1803, had come to recognize the Kadohadacho chief "as superior." For the following three decades, Dehahuit would provide the Indians on the Louisiana-Texas frontier with inspired leadership through extremely trying times.[70]

Over the course of the period between 1786 and 1803, the Indians of the Near Southwest maintained a tenuous existence with the Spaniards who governed Texas and Louisiana. On the one hand, following initial hostilities, the Lipan Apaches and the Karankawas established a peaceful relationship with the Spaniards. On the other hand, some members of the tribes that had made peace with Texas in 1785, the Comanches and the Wichitas, began to turn away from their Spanish allies around the turn of the century as increasing contact with American traders encouraged them to steal livestock from San Antonio and La Bahía. While the various tribes in Louisiana remained friendly with the French officials who governed the colony in the name of Spain, the lack of protection offered them against the enemy Osages and Choctaws, as well as from encroaching land-hungry settlers, disgusted them. Continued population loss, due to outbreaks of disease, exacerbated the Indians' situation. Although relations between the Spaniards and the Indians of Texas and the Near Southwest had generally stabilized during the final years of the eighteenth century, the various tribes certainly realized that their Spanish allies did not have firm control over the region and that the Spanish weakness could easily be exploited. The United States' acquisition of Louisiana in 1803 would further undermine the Spanish position in Texas and provide some of the Indians with an excellent opportunity to improve their situation. Leaders such as Dehahuit would eagerly respond to the creation of an international boundary within their midst and manipulate the tensions between the United States and Spain in such a manner to gain the most benefits for the Indians who remained dominant in the area.

3. Contested Boundaries
The Indians, Spain, and the United States, 1804 to 1810

The transfer of Louisiana to the United States in December 1803 affected the Indian tribes of Texas and the Near Southwest in various ways over the next decade. The emigrant groups that had abandoned Florida for Louisiana following the British accession in 1763 found their Rapides-area villages threatened once more by land-hungry people of English descent. As a result, most of the tribesmen living near the town—the Apalaches, Taensas, Alabamas, Coushattas, Yowani Choctaws, Pascagoulas, and Biloxis—immigrated to southeastern Texas within five years of the Louisiana Purchase. Not only did the region's natives—the Aises, Bidais, and Akokisas—greet the emigrants as potential allies against the rampaging Choctaws, the Spaniards of the colony welcomed them in hope of preventing American encroachment into the unpopulated area. The Karankawas, Tonkawas, and Lipan Apaches who lived in south central Texas at a great distance from the United States were relatively untouched by the Louisiana Purchase and continued to maintain their lukewarm relationship with the Spaniards. Although a few Karankawas submitted to mission life, most of the tribesmen acted in the manner of the Tonkawas and Lipans and had little to do with Euroamericans at all.

The Caddos, Wichitas, and Comanches, meanwhile, found themselves in the middle of a boundary dispute between Spain and the United States, which brought them into repeated contact with determined suitors from both sides desperate to win their allegiance in case of the outbreak of war. The Caddos and Wichitas, already dissatisfied with their Spanish alliance, eagerly looked toward the Americans and sought to manipulate the situation to gain commercial benefits from the young republic's numerous traders who entered their villages. By the end of the period, both groups had been won over by representatives of the United States and were ready to come to the assistance of their new ally if called upon. Most of the Kotsoteka Comanches, who maintained their rancherías on the buffalo plains of west central Texas far from easy access to American trade, continued to honor their peace treaty with the Spaniards in the immediate aftermath of the Louisiana Purchase. Increasingly, however, American merchants drew some Comanche groups into their trade orbit by offering better and cheaper goods than their Spanish competitors. Although Kotsoteka leadership tried to bring the recalcitrants in line, by 1810 rebellious warriors threatened the heretofore reliable Spanish-Comanche alliance.

The Indian tribes that had migrated to the area around Rapides in the 1760s had done so to escape the British subjects who settled in Florida after the Seven Years' War. Forty years after moving to Spanish territory, these tribes once again found themselves threatened by Angloamericans following the United States' purchase of Louisiana in 1803. The Indians' fear of the land-hungry settlers induced most of the tribesmen living below Natchitoches to relocate within half a decade. As a result of the American accession of Louisiana, a huge influx of settlers entered the Red River Valley desirous of Indian land to raise cash crops such as cotton. While the population of Natchitoches, including slaves, doubled to 2,870 people by 1810, the newly organized Rapides Parish experienced a fourfold increase to 2,200 individuals. The rapacious newcomers crowded the dwindling numbers of Indians, forcing them to continue the exodus that had begun during the final years of Spanish Louisiana. Texas remained a very inviting target for these natives since the Euroamerican population of the province had not grown significantly during the final decades of the eighteenth century. Only about 3,000 or so Tejanos lived in the colony; approximately half resided around San Antonio, while the other half lived either near Nacogdoches or La Bahía. Southeastern Texas, between the Sabine and San Antonio rivers, was almost completely devoid of Euroamericans, and open to Indian emigrants.[1]

In late 1803, Taensa chief Louis set the emigration to Spanish Texas in motion by informing Spanish officials in Rapides that his tribe, along with the Apalaches, wanted to sell their lands and relocate west of the Sabine River. The last Spanish governor of Louisiana, Juan Manuel Salcedo, approved the sale, and on January 11, 1804, the Apalaches and Taensas sold 11,230 arpents of land situated on both sides of the Red River. The Miller and Fulton firm purchased the tract for $5,200, half of which the Indians already owed the trading house. Before the Taensas and Apalaches could settle in Texas, however, they needed to obtain permission from the commandant general of the Interior Provinces, Nemesio Salcedo, brother of Juan Manuel. In order to present his case to Texas officials in person, Chief Louis traveled to Nacogdoches in March 1804, and met with the commander of the post, Juan de Ugarte. The Taensa chief impressed Captain Ugarte, who endorsed Louis's request, claiming that the tribe was "industrious, civilized, and inclined toward the Catholic religion." Shortly afterward, Texas governor Elguézabal declared that his investigation of the matter had disclosed that the Taensas and Apalaches were good Catholics, industrious farmers, and peace-loving friends of the Spaniards. Plus, their close ties to the other tribes living in Rapides Parish would prove of great value in extending Spanish influence along the Louisiana-Texas frontier. Presented with this evidence, in May 1804, Commandant General Salcedo granted the Taensa-Apalache request and instructed the governor to assign them lands near the Texas coast in the area between the Sabine and Trinity rivers.[2]

Although the Taensas and Apaches had been successful in obtaining permission to move to Texas, most tribesmen hesitated and remained in their Red River village. The other Rapides tribes, though, took advantage of the Spanish grant and small groups illegally began crossing west of the Sabine in the summer of 1804. A band of Alabamas settled on the Angelina River, just below the mouth of Attoyac Bayou. Other Alabamas, along with Coushatta and Yowani Choctaw tribesmen, moved from Louisiana and established small villages between the Trinity and the Neches. Over the next couple of years, headmen from these tribes, as well as Biloxi and Pascagoula leaders, often traveled to nearby Nacogdoches to meet with Spanish officials and receive presents. By 1806, the chiefs had persuaded Commandant General Salcedo that they could be used as a reliable buffer against the encroaching Americans, and he granted them all permission to settle in Texas.[3]

Still, many of the Indians remained in their Louisiana villages, unwilling to abandon their homes, livestock, and fields. Continued American immigration, which resulted in outbreaks of violence, soon convinced most of them to move to Texas and settle in the empty area between the Trinity and the Neches. In January 1807, an American named Samuel Watson shot and killed the brother of Coushatta headman Soulier Rouge at the salt works near Natchitoches. Although American officials tried to placate the Coushattas with presents, the tribesmen were outraged when nothing was done to punish Watson. Seeking revenge, Siache, a Coushatta man who lived in the Sabine River village, killed an American trader named O'Neal outside Natchitoches. United States troops were sent to the Coushatta village to apprehend the culprit, but Siache, like many of his fellow tribesmen, had already moved to Texas to escape retribution. Most of the remaining Alabamas and Coushattas crossed west of the Sabine in the summer of 1808 following the execution by Louisiana territorial officials of two Alabama men who had been convicted of murdering an American in Opelousas.[4]

By the end of the year nearly six hundred Alabamas and Coushattas lived in two southeastern Texas villages: the Alabamas settled on the west bank of the Neches River, nearly twenty-five miles above its confluence with the Angelina; the Coushattas, under Soulier Rouge and Pia Mingo, moved about fifty miles west to the east bank of the Trinity River. The tensions in Louisiana encouraged members of the other tribes also to seek refuge in Texas. All of the two hundred or so Yowani Choctaws crossed the Sabine and established a village about ten miles south of the Alabama town on the Neches River. Nearly one hundred Biloxis and Pascagoulas also migrated to the Neches and set up farms and houses a few miles north of the Alabamas, near the mouth of Biloxi Creek in present Angelina County. Over the next few years, Apalache and Taensa tribesmen moved to Texas and settled among the various Louisiana refugee villages. By 1810, perhaps 1,000 Indians had immigrated to the heavily forested region south of Nacogdoches—soon to be called the "Big Thicket"— between the Neches and the Trinity rivers.[5]

Other Louisiana tribesmen moved up the Red River and settled on the un-occupied Kadohadacho lands above Natchitoches that were protected from Euroamerican settlement by the Great Raft. In 1804, Apalache headman Etienne secured permission from Chief Dehahuit to establish a village within Kadohadacho territory. As a result, about one hundred Apalaches, Alabamas, and Coushattas built houses and planted corn on the east bank of the Red River, about twenty miles above the head of the huge obstacle. The Kadohadachos gladly accepted the settlement—which the confused Americans designated as being a Coushatta village—because they could be used as allies against the Osages and the Choctaws. For example, in early 1807, Osage warriors stole seventy-two horses from Kadohadacho hunters. A group of Apalaches and Alabamas came across the Osage bandits a few days later and attacked them, killing five and recovering most of the stolen horses. When the victory party returned to the Coushatta village with the five scalps, a dance was held there for all the tribes allied against the Osages. The success of the Coushatta village on the Red River encouraged further emigration, and the settlement moved upstream in 1809 to a site known today as Coushatta Bluffs, situated on the east bank of the river, about three miles northeast of the present-day town of Gilliam, Louisiana. Dehahuit did not object to the increased amount of Indians, who numbered perhaps as many as 350 individuals, for he calculated "on the benefit of their assistance against their common" enemies, the Osages and the Choctaws.[6]

Although most of the Indians that lived in Rapides Parish abandoned the area following the transfer of Louisiana, a few tribesmen remained in their villages. About two hundred Pascagoulas, Apalaches, and Taensas continued to live on the Red River in settlements located just above the newly christened town of Alexandria. Following the sale of their lands to Miller and Fulton in 1804, the remaining Apalaches had protested to the United States Board of Land Commissioners, claiming that Taensa chief Louis did not represent them and, therefore, had no right to vend their territory. As a result, the land

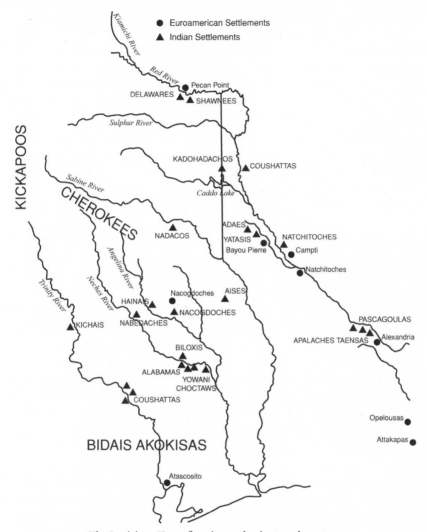

The Louisiana-Texas frontier, early nineteenth century

sale was held up until 1812, when the land commissioners voided the Apalache half of the sale and allowed the tribe to maintain title to nearly 3,000 acres of land on the Red River. Despite the continued pressure of American settlers, the Apalaches, along with members of the other two tribes, lived on this tract and nearby settlements for the next two decades. The well-established presence of the Roman Catholic Church was one reason many Apalaches remained in the area; in July 1815, the Catholic priest at Natchitoches baptized forty-two Apalache children of twenty-two sets of parents.[7]

Like the Rapides Parish tribes that moved to Kadohadacho territory, the various Indian groups that abandoned Louisiana for Texas were also welcomed by the natives of the region. Chief Negrito (Little Black), leader of the Aises who lived about thirty miles north of the Alabamas on a tributary of the Angelina River, was happy for the protection the emigrants might help provide against the marauding Choctaws. In fact, the Aises had invited the Louisiana tribes to move to Texas as early as July 1804. Also friendly to the newcomers were the Atakapan-speakers who maintained their rancherías on the Trinity River, near the Coushattas, under the leadership of Bidai chief Prieto (Dark Skin) and Caballo (Horse), head of the Akokisas. The Aises, Bidais, and Akokisas, as well as the recent emigrants, enjoyed good relations with the Spaniards in the area, often traveling to Nacogdoches to receive presents. In the first decade of the nineteenth century, the Atakapas developed especially close ties with Spanish troops stationed at the newly established fort of Atascosito, located near the mouth of the Trinity, around present-day Liberty. The tribesmen provided the soldiers with meat, acted as guides in the jungle-like forest, and alerted the Spaniards to the presence of undesirable foreigners. As a result of the alliance, the Spaniards named Nicopí as medal chief of the Bidais, while Taconá received the same distinction for the Akokisas following the deaths of Prieto and Caballo in 1808. Despite their goodwill toward the Spaniards, the lack of trade opportunities in Texas forced all of the Indians of the region to venture to Louisiana to peddle furs and horses. For example, in June 1810, a group of Coushattas traveled from Texas to Natchitoches with nineteen horses loaded with skins.[8]

The Karankawas, who lived farther south, also maintained friendly relations with the Spaniards of Texas. While most of the Karankawas hunted and fished along the coastal bays between Galveston Island and Corpus Christi Bay and only occasionally visited Mission Refugio, a few tribesmen and their families did settle down with the priests. Some Cocos and Carancaguases lived farther inland at Mission Rosario, but these neophytes joined their kinsmen at Refugio when the Spaniards closed the station on the lower San Antonio River in early 1807. By the end of 1809, a total of 103 Karankawas—most of them Cujanes—resided at Mission Refugio. These numbers increased over the next five years; on the one hand, between 1807 and 1812, Spanish priests recorded fifty-seven baptisms among the Karankawas. On the other hand, twenty-three tribesmen were buried in the mission cemetery during this period. In addition to the priests who instructed the tribesmen in the arts of Spanish civilization, the Karankawas living at Mission Refugio also came into contact with the small Hispanic settlement that grew up around the station. Between 1807 and 1821, no less than seventy individual Spanish families—usually related to one of the soldiers attached to the station—resided at one time or another at Mission Refugio.[9]

Most other Karankawas generally avoided the Spaniards, but they did not take kindly to those few Euroamericans who entered their lands near the coast. In June 1804, three Carancaguases wounded a couple of Tejanos with arrows after finding them hunting near the mouth of the Brazos. The following year a small trading vessel from Louisiana ran aground in Matagorda Bay. Karankawa warriors killed the crewmembers and ransacked the boat. On one of the few occasions that Karankawas attacked a Spaniard in the interior, two Carancaguases from Mission Rosario wounded a soldier near La Bahía in July 1806. The Spaniards captured the two culprits, tried and found them guilty, and sent them in chains to a Mexican prison. In response to this incident, the Karankawas living at the missions came together in September 1806 and elected Carancaguase leader Diego as their chief. In March 1807, the governor of Texas personally awarded Diego the Spanish medal at Mission Refugio. A Coco headman, Juan Antonio, was later named as Diego's lieutenant. Over the next few years both men successfully worked to maintain the peace between the Karankawas and the Spaniards.[10]

Relations between the Tonkawas and the Spaniards, however, proved to be not as friendly. Although the Tonkawas ranged between the Brazos and the Guadalupe, most of the time the tribesmen resided in the middle Colorado River Valley. By the beginning of the nineteenth century, Cuernitos (Little Horns) and Arocha had emerged as the main Tonkawa chieftains. Although the Tonkawas had been nominal allies of the Spaniards in Texas since the mid-1780s, both chiefs entered into a new treaty with the Spanish governor in the summer of 1805, agreeing to curtail stock thefts in return for trade. Both groups, however, found it difficult to live up to the promises made in the agreement. Angered by the lack of Spanish merchandise and cut off from access to buffalo by the Comanches and Wichitas, hungry Tonkawa men continued to prey on Spanish livestock near San Antonio and La Bahía. On occasion the Tonkawa chiefs themselves captured and punished the offenders. Other times Spanish soldiers boldly entered Tonkawa settlements and forced the men to return the horses and cattle or pay restitution. In January 1808, for example, Tonkawa men stole three cows from a Spanish rancher and killed one of his oxen. In response, Spanish soldiers traveled to a Tonkawa ranchería on the Colorado, where they forced the culprits to confess and pay a fine of seven deerskins and a horse.[11]

The aggressive stance of the Spaniards toward these thefts led to increased tensions between the two groups. Following a Tonkawa raid on a horse herd near San Antonio in early August 1808, Captain Juan José de los Santos led a Spanish force, consisting of twelve soldiers and thirty-nine militiamen, in pursuit. Traveling east, de los Santos inspected a Tonkawa ranchería on the Colorado but did not find the stolen horses. Turning north, the Spaniards encountered Cuernitos's village on the headwaters of the San Gabriel River. Captain de los Santos angered the chief by accusing him of the theft, a charge that Cuernitos hotly denied. The Tonkawa chief, however, told de los Santos that the culprits were at a ranchería located farther up the Colorado and agreed to help the Spaniards find them. Cuernitos led the soldiers to the village but discovered that the thieves had already left. When the Spanish troops began to inspect the Indians' herd anyway, the Tonkawas forcefully resisted. The frightened Spanish interpreter fired his gun at one of the Tonkawas, grazing him in the stomach. The Indian then shot arrows at the troops, wounding one of the militiamen. The skirmish ended only when the village leaders stepped in between the belligerents. After tempers cooled, Cuernitos led the troops back to his village, where he allowed the Spaniards to arrest the thieves who had returned there, though insisting that they not be put in irons. De los Santos agreed, and the following day the Spaniards set off for San Antonio. The Spanish captain, however, broke the agreement and bound the thieves after only one day's travel from Cuernitos's village.[12]

The Spaniards' disrespectful actions enraged the Tonkawas, and within a year they put out a call for war to the other Indians of Texas. Although no other tribe immediately responded to the request, Tonkawa warriors clashed with Spanish troops several times in the summer of 1809. By the following year, however, Canoso's band of Lipan Apaches had moved north from the Rio Grande to establish an alliance with the Tonkawas. Canoso had never been comfortable living near Laredo and had moved his people north to the Nueces River in 1806. Disappointed in Spanish trade and lack of protection from the Comanches, Canoso's Lipans made peace with the Tonkawas in 1810 and moved even farther northeastward, establishing several rancherías on the Guadalupe River. Over the next couple of years, both tribes stole horses in conjunction with one another from ranches near San Antonio and La Bahía. Just as events had caused the two tribes to join together in the early 1780s, the situation in the nineteenth century would tie the fates of the Tonkawas and the Lipan Apaches together for the next four decades.[13]

Whereas the United States' accession of Louisiana encouraged most of the Indians living below Natchitoches to abandon the area out of fear of the American settlers, the prospects of trade drew the Caddos, Wichitas, and to a lesser degree, the Comanches, toward the young republic. American traders desired the great amount of horses and furs the three tribes had at their disposal. Yet American officials wanted an alliance with the tribes for reasons other than trade; the manner in which the United States obtained Louisiana placed the Caddoan speakers of the Red River Valley, as well as the Comanches, in the middle of a boundary dispute between the United States and Spain. France had reacquired Louisiana from Spain in 1800, only to sell the huge expanse of territory three years later to the United States without ever taking possession or defining its borders. Thus, the boundary between Louisiana and Texas became subject to various interpretations, the most extreme being that of President Thomas Jefferson, who held that the border was the Rio Grande. Understandably, Spain scoffed at this claim, interpreting the line to be just a few miles west of the Red River, where it had been when France controlled Louisiana before 1763. In reality, the Red River became the focal point of the boundary dispute.[14]

Since the situation was so tenuous, Spanish and American officials understood that the loyalty of the native tribes along the border would be crucial in any boundary determination. The Caddos, Wichitas, and Comanches were particularly central to this dispute because the United States held that the tribes formerly allied to France were now under the jurisdiction of a new "father." Thus, both the United States and Spain claimed the allegiance of the tribes in an attempt to define the border more clearly. In addition, both nations fully expected war with each other and realized that native allies might make the difference. Therefore, the Americans of Louisiana and the Spaniards of Texas both courted the Red River Caddoans and the Comanches, and the representatives of both nations realized that trade was crucial to win the tribes' favor. Doctor John Sibley, who would become the United States Indian agent at Natchitoches, asserted that "whoever furnishes the Indians the Best and Most Satisfactory trade can always control their Politicks [sic]." Manuel Salcedo, a Spanish governor during this period, believed that Spain should establish commercial houses to supply the natives efficiently. In this way, the Spaniards "would be able to get out of [the Indians] anything [the Spanish] proposed to do because the Indians develop and behave like those who trade with them according to the degree of recognized utility, convenience, and advantages that are presented to them." Despite the Spaniards' comprehension of the situation, their lack of resources and general ineffectualness would prove no match for the wealthy and energetic Americans in winning the Indians' allegiances.[15]

Kadohadacho chief Dehahuit understood the situation and adeptly used the boundary dispute to his tribe's advantage. Officials of both the United States and Spain desired to win Dehahuit's favor because they realized that the Kadohadachos had clearly become the dominant Caddo tribe by the beginning of the nineteenth century. The Kadohadachos were by far the largest of the Caddo tribes, consisting of about 1,000 people, including one hundred warriors. Among the Indians influenced by the Kadohadachos were the one hundred or so remaining Natchitoches, Yatasis, and Adaes tribesmen, who lived upstream from Natchitoches on Bayou Pierre and the Red River. Three Hasinai tribes—the Hainais, Nabedaches, and Nacogdoches—continued to live in their traditional villages on the Angelina and Neches rivers "in great amity" with the Kadohadachos. The Hasinais, with the Nadacos who lived on the Sabine River to the northeast of Nacogdoches, had a population almost as large as the Kadohadachos. Unlike the Kadohadachos, however, all four tribes had experienced a constant turnover of chiefs due to death and disease around the turn of the century, causing them to look toward Dehahuit for direction, especially as he gained prestige from his relationship with the Americans and the Spaniards.[16]

Dehahuit quickly made the Americans realize his tribe's influential position on the Louisiana-Texas frontier and forced the representatives of the young republic to take measures designed to win his allegiance. Dehahuit made a number of trips to Natchitoches in the fall of 1803 to meet with John Sibley. The Kadohadacho chief impressed the doctor, who tried to gain his favor by promising that the Americans would give the Indians good prices for their furs and provide them with a blacksmith to repair their weapons. Daniel Clark, an Irishman who had been living in New Orleans since 1786, alerted Secretary of State James Madison of the Kadohadachos' great importance and the possibilities of an alliance, stating that "they are the friends of the whites and are esteemed the bravest and most Generous of all the Nations in the vast country." Even before the official transfer of Louisiana, the Kadohadachos and the United States were well on their way to establishing friendly relations.[17]

The officials appointed to govern the newly acquired area soon acknowledged the reports from Louisiana about the Kadohadachos' significance. On February 25, 1804, the governor of the territory of Orleans, William C. C. Claiborne, sent orders to Captain Edward Turner, the civil commandant of the District of Natchitoches, instructing him to receive visiting Kadohadachos "with friendly attention and have regard for their interest." The first step taken by Turner to gain the friendship of the Kadohadachos was to arrange, with the assistance of Doctor Sibley, a peace treaty with the Choctaws. On May 17, 1804, representatives of both tribes arrived in Natchitoches and agreed to lay down their weapons and establish peace. Both tribes also agreed that, in case one group did take up arms against the other, the victimized party would seek retribution through the mediation of United States agents rather than obtaining revenge through bloodshed. Whereas the Spaniards had been unable to assist the Kadohadachos in their battles with other tribes, the Americans quickly impressed upon the Indians their willingness to put an end to tribal warfare.[18]

More importantly, the Americans demonstrated their desire to provide ample supplies of trade goods to the Indians of the region. In August 1804, Captain Turner pleased Dehahuit by informing the Kadohadacho chief that the United States would soon establish an official trading house at Natchitoches "for the purpose of supplying their wants on moderate Terms." Two months later Dehahuit notified Turner that he was en route to Natchitoches and expected to receive presents. Turner alerted Governor Claiborne of the impending visit and stated that since the "Spaniards are exerting every means to Induce the Indians to be unfriendly. . . . [I]t would not be good policy to let him return [to his village] dissatisfied." Governor Claiborne responded by permitting Turner to award Dehahuit and his principal men $200 worth of gifts. When the Kadohadacho party arrived at Natchitoches, Turner presented them with powder, lead, and tobacco. Now assured that his tribe would receive presents from the Americans, Dehahuit asked Captain Turner for an American flag to fly over his village, for he explained it was "customary to have the Flag of the Nation who claimed his Country in which they lived." Because of the Americans' proven ability to provide the tribe with goods, the Kadohadachos informally recognized their ties with the United States in late 1804.[19]

In response to the measures taken by the United States, Spanish officials in Texas took actions designed to retain their Indian subjects. The Spanish commander at Nacogdoches, Captain Ugarte, grasped the importance of providing the natives with trade; in a letter to Governor Elguézabal he stressed the necessity of supplying the tribes with clothing and ammunition in order to avoid conflict with them and to keep their friendship. Commandant General Salcedo also realized the importance of the alliance with the native tribes of Texas. He instructed the Texas governor to "try all possible means to see that [the transfer of Louisiana] does not influence the Indian tribes to change the peaceable relations they have hitherto maintained with us." Elguézabal was ordered to "take pains to encourage their loyalty and good will."[20]

As in the late eighteenth century, the Spaniards paid particularly close attention to the Kotsoteka Comanches. Although the Comanches lived far to the west of Louisiana, the Spaniards in Texas realized that if American traders—in possession of better and cheaper trade items—could establish an intercourse with the Kotsotekas, the amicable relationship they maintained with the Comanches would seriously be damaged. Ever since allying themselves with the Spaniards in 1785, Kotsoteka leaders had successfully thwarted their young men's attempts to break the partnership by raiding Tejano horse herds to obtain wealth and glory. Although the peace had been threatened in 1803 due to the outbreak of hostilities between the Spaniards and the Panis Piques, the Spanish ability to continue to provide ample trade goods convinced the Kotsoteka chiefs to maintain the alliance. Therefore, in January 1804, Governor Elguézabal held a conference with chiefs Chihuahua and Yzazat and then sent an official trader to their rancherías. This merchant greatly pleased the Kotsotekas, and throughout the year Comanche tribesmen, including chiefs Sofais, Chihuahua, and Yzazat, visited San Antonio and Nacogdoches. Despite the good relations, young warriors, mainly from the ranchería of Pisinampe, continued to threaten the peace by stealing Tejano horses. In order to prove his commitment to the treaty, Chihuahua sent a message to Elguézabal in June, informing the governor that he had seized horses that Comanche warriors had poached from Tejano ranches. The following month, a Spanish sergeant traveled to Chihuahua's ranchería and recovered the stolen stock from the chief.[21]

While most Comanche leaders were serious about keeping the peace with Texas, the Wichitas remained divided in their feelings concerning the Spaniards. The two thousand or so Panis Piques, living in three fortified villages on the Red River, still sought vengeance from the Spaniards for the nine Taovaya warriors who had been killed near Béxar in February 1803. All three Panis Pique tribes—the Taovayas, Guichitas, and Iscanis—also eagerly welcomed a commercial and military alliance with the United States that was similar to their past relationship with the French. Likewise, American traders and officials were just as interested in friendly relations with the Panis Piques. American traders and hunters, many of whom had accompanied Philip Nolan to Texas, already knew the Panis Pique villages constituted the most important native marketplace on the southern Plains. Trade could be conducted there with the Wichitas, as well as with the numerous and powerful Comanches living to the west. American officials, through their trade informants, realized that the Panis Piques' ties with the Comanches, Tawakonis, and Kichais placed them in a strategic diplomatic position. President Jefferson even had his own private interest in the Panis Piques; mistakenly believing that the Red River was the correct highway to the Rocky Mountains (the Canadian River to the north is actually the better route), any American-sponsored scientific journey to the mountains—one of the Virginian's pet projects—would necessarily travel through their villages.[22]

While Iscani chief Awahakei and Eriascoc, leader of the Taovayas, strongly desired an alliance with the Americans, the Tawakonis and Kichais, living much closer to the Spaniards, were hesitant about abandoning their old allies. The Tawakonis, numbering about 1,500 people, lived in three proximate Brazos River villages about ninety miles above the crossing of the San Antonio

Road between San Antonio and Nacogdoches. The three hundred Kichais, led by Chief Castor (Beaver), were the closest of the Wichita tribes to the Spaniards. Their village, now situated just west of the Trinity River, was about thirty miles north of the San Antonio Road and about one hundred miles from Nacogdoches. Tawakoni chief Quiscat, who had always been one of the greatest proponents of the Spanish alliance, encouraged the Panis Piques to settle with the Spaniards, as did Comanche chief Chihuahua, who threatened to make war on the Taovayas if they did not end their hostilities. As a result, in January 1804, thirty-five Taovayas arrived at Chihuahua's village and stated that they intended to travel to San Antonio to meet with Governor Elguézabal to reestablish peace. Despite the pledge, within a week a band of Taovayas attacked four Tejanos outside of San Antonio and seized their weapons before allowing the men to escape. [23]

Soon thereafter, American traders began heading up the Red River to establish relations with the various Indian tribes. These traders prompted Spanish officials to attempt to thwart what they considered an invasion of their territory through the use of force, as well as trying to win the tribes' favor by distributing an increased amount of presents. American officials responded by sending the Indians gifts and flags, in addition to inviting them to Natchitoches in order to impress them with the great bounties the United States had to offer. In May 1804, the competition was set in motion when seven Americans led by John Davis and Alexander Dauni left Natchitoches for the Panis Pique villages. They eluded the small Spanish troop, which had recently been stationed at Bayou Pierre upstream from Natchitoches, and arrived among the Wichitas in July. The American trading party wintered there and caused the Taovayas to abandon any pretense of peace with the Spaniards. In August 1804, Taovaya warriors raided San Antonio and killed a servant boy. In April 1805, another group of Taovayas attacked a ranch near San Antonio and was pursued by Spanish troops. In the ensuing engagement the Taovayas killed two Spanish soldiers and wounded two others, while losing one warrior and suffering "many wounded." [24]

Hoping to enlist all of the Wichitas in a war against the Spaniards, the Taovayas invited the Tawakonis to join them on their raids. When Chief Quiscat died in March 1805 the Taovayas thought that his successor, Daguariscara, might be willing to alter his predecessor's pro-Spanish policy. The new Tawakoni chief, however, immediately declined the Taovaya request and tried instead to dissuade them from attaching themselves to the Americans. Daguariscara knew that the Panis Piques, following the arrival of Davis and Dauni at their villages, had sent a message of friendship through Kadohadacho chief Dehahuit to Captain Turner at Natchitoches, asking that more traders be sent up the Red River.[25]

The Americans responded to the Panis Piques' request for commerce more rapidly than the Spaniards ever had. In December 1804 President Jefferson had named Doctor Sibley to be the United States Indian agent for the region. As soon as Sibley received his appointment, Secretary of War Henry Dearborn instructed him to confer with the native tribes of Louisiana, secure their friendship, and inform them that they must break their connections with the Spanish. Sibley understood the importance of trade as a method for gaining the Indians' allegiance, and in March 1805 he answered the Panis Piques' appeal for traders by granting a passport to John House and six other Americans. Sibley supplied House with presents to distribute in his name to the Wichitas and commissioned the trader to have the Indians visit him in Natchitoches. The following month a Kichai man led House and his group past the Spanish guard at Bayou Pierre and on to the Panis Pique villages where they spent the summer exchanging guns and powder for horses and skins.[26]

The Spanish commander at Bayou Pierre, José Manuel de Castro, was helpless to stop the Americans; as a result, he asked Dehahuit to detain the traders at his village. The Kadohadacho chief, however, refused to comply with this naive request. A few months later, Castro made a bolder attempt to stop the Kadohadachos' intercourse with the United States. In the spring of 1805, Dehahuit and a few young men were on their way to Natchitoches with furs when they met Castro at Bayou Pierre. Castro warned Dehahuit that if the Kadohadacho party should return from Natchitoches with American goods, he would confiscate them. This warning angered Dehahuit, who threatened to kill the whole Spanish guard. He told Castro that the road to Natchitoches "had always been theirs, and that if the Spanish prevented them from using it as their ancestors had always done, he would soon make it a bloody road." Alarmed by Dehahuit's menacing stance, Castro meekly allowed the group to pass without incident on their return from Natchitoches.[27]

The American trade advantage over the Spaniards increased on May 23, 1805, when Agent Sibley received merchandise worth $3,000 from the government to distribute to the Indians of the region as presents and trade goods. Secretary Dearborn instructed Sibley to use all means to conciliate the tribes, especially "such natives as might, in case of rupture with Spain, be useful and mischevous [sic] to us." As soon as Sibley obtained the merchandise allocated by Congress he alerted the surrounding tribes. As a result of the House expedition and the new supply of trade goods, Taovaya, Guichita, and Tawakoni warriors traveled—despite Daguariscara's opposition—to Natchitoches in June 1805 and received presents and American flags from Sibley.

Dionisio Valle, a Spanish lieutenant at Nacogdoches, noted in the same month that an American trader passed Bayou Pierre on his way from the Wichita and Kadohadacho villages upstream. He reported that it was "openly known that the Caudacho Indians are receiving presents at Natchitoches as subjects of Louisiana," and he had no doubt that the Taovayas were being "stirred up in a similar way."[28]

The Americans were also stirring up the Hasinais in east Texas. Through the Kadohadachos, Agent Sibley had made overtures to the Hasinai tribes, and in June 1805, twenty-five Hainais appeared at the Spanish post at Nacogdoches hinting "at the offers of presents and prospects of trade" with the Americans. Although Lieutenant Valle advised them that it would be improper to accept these offers, Hainai warriors as well as Nadaco, Nacogdoches, Ais, and Adaes men visited the American post at Natchitoches in August. Valle blamed the Kadohadachos for these visits, and he feared "their instigation may lead those tribes to form a friendship with said Sibley." The American's offers even reached the Comanches; Chief Zoquiné arrived in Nacogdoches on June 27, 1805, intending to go to Natchitoches and sell buffalo skins. Only through Valle's entreaties was Zoquiné convinced to exchange his goods in Nacogdoches and refrain from traveling to Louisiana.[29]

In the meantime, Taovaya warriors, emboldened by their association with the Americans, stole a number of horses from San Antonio in October 1805. Spanish troops captured three of the Taovayas and brought them to Elguézabal's replacement as governor of Texas, Antonio Cordero, who was holding talks with Daguariscara. The Tawakoni chief immediately offered to mediate a peace between the Taovayas and the Spaniards. Daguariscara passionately told Governor Cordero that both leaders had to be the "instruments which the bloodshed by both parties on the highways may be wiped away; the ones who must smooth and strengthen a perfect and lasting peace between the said tribes and the Spaniards, and that together we may oppose the hostile acts which those whom you call the Anglo-Americans attempt against us." Impressed, Governor Cordero encouraged Daguariscara to travel to the Panis Pique villages and attempt to persuade them to withdraw from their alliance with the United States and give up their American flags.[30]

For the next six months or so, Daguariscara dedicated himself to negotiating a peace between the Taovayas and the Spaniards. In December 1805, he informed Chief Eriascoc that Agent Sibley had been deceiving the Taovayas and that they should break off relations with the Americans. The Taovaya chief, looking to see what he might obtain from the Spaniards, responded by sending two subchiefs, along with thirty other tribal members, to meet with Cordero in San Antonio. His delegates informed the governor that Eriascoc had agreed with Daguariscara's message and would appear in Béxar within a month to ratify a new peace agreement. Three months passed, however, and the Taovaya chief never arrived in San Antonio. In fact, the only Taovayas to appear in Béxar were horse thieves, who forced Daguariscara to undertake another trip to the Taovaya village in April 1806. Once again, Eriascoc appeared very receptive to the Tawakoni chief's desire for peace but refused to accompany him to San Antonio to ratify the agreement. Nonetheless, Governor Cordero was encouraged by Daguariscara's report and he ordered the commandant at Nacogdoches to urge Barr and Davenport to send traders to the Panis Pique villages.[31]

Like Daguariscara, most Comanches had yet to be tempted by American inducements and remained loyal to the Spanish. In fact, chiefs Chihuahua, Yzazat, and Sargento traveled to San Antonio in October 1805 with 350 tribesmen to welcome Cordero as the incoming governor of Texas. They greatly impressed the new official (who, as governor of Coahuila had aggressively pursued Comanche raiders) by pledging themselves to honor and respect their past agreements with the Spaniards. A series of conferences were held between the parties in which the Kotsoteka chiefs promised to fly only the Spanish flag over their rancherías and to forbid foreign traders from entering their territory. They also swore to refrain from poaching Tejano livestock and to allow the Spaniards to punish any Comanche caught in the act of stealing. To reinforce the bond between the Spaniards and the Kotsotekas, in January 1806, Governor Cordero sent envoys to the combined village of Sargento and Chihuahua, located on the San Saba River. Sargento promised to gather all the Comanche headmen and bring them to San Antonio to reconfirm the alliance. As a result, thirty-three Comanche notables met with Cordero in March and "offered their services as a proof of their loyalty" to the governor and the Spaniards of Texas. The leaders claimed to speak for the entire tribe, except for "a small group of dissatisfied Indians," led by Pisinampe, who were disposed to steal from the Spaniards. They pledged to discipline the recalcitrant Indians and reiterated that they would not resent it if the Spaniards punished any captured wrongdoer.[32]

The Comanche pledges were put to the test in April 1806, when Kotsoteka raiders from Pisinampe's ranchería stole twenty-one horses and killed a Tejano south of San Antonio. As he had done in Coahuila, Governor Cordero pressed the issue and sent Captain Francisco Amangual to the Comanche villages to reiterate to the chiefs that they were obligated to arrest the individuals who had committed the robberies. Cordero also ordered Amangual to inform the Kotsoteka leaders that, in order to improve relations with the Spaniards, they should elect one chief to act as spokesman for all the Eastern Comanche rancherías. The Comanches agreed to Cordero's request and, in Amangual's presence, chose Sargento as their principal chief.[33]

Sargento took his responsibilities seriously and immediately visited all the Kotsoteka rancherías, as well as some nearby Yamparica Comanche camps. He recovered the stolen horses from Pisinampe's band, whose members Sargento claimed had been responsible for all of the petty thefts that had been committed over the past few years. Sargento also forced Pisinampe to return with him to San Antonio and answer to the Texas governor. Pisinampe weakly explained to Cordero that illness had prevented him from welcoming the new governor to San Antonio the previous fall and from keeping order among his followers. The Comanche leader informed Cordero that he had regained control of his camp and that, although the culprits had fled westward to the Yamparicas, he had notified their chiefs and promised that they would be punished for their offenses. The Texas governor accepted Pisinampe's explanations, and both Comanche chiefs left San Antonio after reasserting their loyalty.[34]

Governor Cordero realized that the Spaniards in Texas desperately needed to maintain their alliance with the Comanches, for he knew that the Americans were about to increase their involvement with the Indians of the region. Cordero had recently learned that President Jefferson had ordered Major Thomas Freeman and Doctor Peter Custis to ascend to the source of the Red River in an attempt to define the boundary between Louisiana and Texas. In addition, Freeman and Custis were instructed to "court an intercourse with the natives as intensively as you can" and to instruct the tribes that they were no longer subjects of Spain but "henceforth [the United States would] become their fathers and friends." Although Spanish officials were unaware of this part of Jefferson's instructions, they certainly understood that the expedition would attempt to win the Indians' allegiances.[35]

For these reasons, Commandant Salcedo considered the American expedition to be an invasion of Spanish territory and was determined to thwart it. On October 8, 1805, he instructed Governor Cordero to post more troops either at Bayou Pierre or at the reinstituted fort of Los Adaes in order to "compel withdrawal of the Red River expedition." He stated that this "object must be facilitated by the Indians who live in those districts," for he recognized "the accomplishment of the expedition can be completely obstructed by the allied tribes, provided the [natives] are caused to take interest in this matter through the necessary craftiness and compensations." Obviously, Salcedo understood that the Indian tribes of the region held the key to the Red River, and only through their cooperation could the Spanish successfully arrest the American encroachment.[36]

Throughout the winter and spring of 1806, the Spaniards tried in vain to win the allegiance of the Texas tribes. Few Indians, however, responded to the Spanish entreaties. Sebastián Rodríguez, the new Spanish commander at Nacogdoches, reported in February 1806 that the "neighboring Indian tribes which have always visited this post are coming here less frequently not so much on account of lack of affection for the Spaniards," but because of the trade advantages and the greater number of presents they received from the Americans at Natchitoches. This supply of goods increased in early 1806 with the establishment of an official United States Indian trading factory in Natchitoches. The federal government had established a system of trading factories in 1795 designed to regulate commerce and to ensure that the Indians would not be swindled or given cause to take to the warpath. Like the others, the factory at Natchitoches was charged with supplying the nearby tribes with guns, ammunition, clothes, utensils, beads, and blankets at fair prices. As in previous days, the Indian trade was mainly in deerskins, buffalo robes, and bear oil.[37]

Concurrently, the tense situation on the Louisiana-Texas frontier escalated to a point that threatened to bring about the war between Spain and the United States that both sides had been expecting for two years. By the time Freeman and Custis began the expedition in mid-April 1806—when they entered the Red River at its mouth with three boats, twenty-one soldiers, and a black servant—the American presents and trade goods had swayed most of the east Texas Indians. In response to the launch of the Freeman-Custis expedition, the Spaniards mounted a troop, commanded by Francisco Viana, to stop the American party by force if necessary. As with Rodríguez, Viana tried in vain to induce the region's Indians to join with the troops he was gathering to face the encroaching Americans. Although Negrito, chief of the Aises, pledged his allegiance and claimed that he could enlist one hundred Alabama and Coushatta warriors to the Spanish cause, only seven men from the two emigrant tribes responded to his entreaties. The Spaniards also attempted to enlist the services of Hasinai warriors for battle against the Americans but were forced to admit "that not a single one of them wishes to come." Realizing that few Indians would be joining the Spanish force, Negrito and the Alabama-Coushatta warriors returned home.[38]

The Freeman-Custis expedition reached Natchitoches on May 19 and remained there until June 2. While in Natchitoches, they increased their number to forty-seven men, (including Kadohadacho interpreter, François Grappe) and seven boats to defend against the Spanish threat. The following day, Viana ordered Lieutenant Juan Ygnacio Ramón and 240 men to intercept the American party at the old Kadohadacho village near the bend of the Red River.

Because of his unfamiliarity with the area, Lieutenant Ramón hired a Yatasi man to lead him and his troops to the old Kadohadacho village, but the guide took him to the present town on Caddo Lake by mistake. Dehahuit met Ramón, who asked him accusingly if he "loved the Americans." The caddi ambiguously answered that "he loved all men; if the Spaniards had come to fight they must not spill blood on his land." Ramón accepted this vague reply and retreated to the Sabine River. Dehahuit then sent him a defiant message stating that when Freeman and Custis arrived, the chief planned to supply the Americans with guides to take the party farther upstream.[39]

Dehahuit quickly followed through on his promise to assist the approaching Americans. He sent a courier to the Coushatta village on the Red River to intercept Freeman and Custis and inform them of the presence of Ramón's troops and of their intention of stopping the Americans by force. After two weeks of struggling with the Great Raft, Freeman and Custis finally reached the Coushatta village on June 24. Upon receiving Dehahuit's message, Freeman sent the courier back to ask the Kadohadacho chief to meet the Americans at the Coushatta village. While waiting for Dehahuit's arrival, Freeman and Custis visited the Apalache, Alabama, and Coushatta settlements. On June 29, Chief Etienne accepted an American flag from Major Freeman, which he hoisted above the Coushatta village in place of the Spanish flag that had previously flown there. Two days later Dehahuit and forty Kadohadacho warriors arrived on the Red River opposite the Coushatta village and fired their guns in a salute that was returned by the Americans on the other side. As the Indians crossed the river, the members of the American expedition drew themselves up in single file to receive the Kadohadachos "with marked attention." As Dehahuit entered the camp, another salute was fired "with which he seemed well pleased; observing to the Coushatta chief that he never had been so respectfully received by any people before."[40]

Using Grappe as interpreter, the Americans clarified the objective of their mission to the Kadohadachos, telling them that France had sold Louisiana and that "henceforth the People of the United States would be their fathers and friends and would protect them and supply their wants." Dehahuit readily agreed to this, replying that he would now look to the Americans for "protection and support." He said that although he had no complaints to make against either the Spanish or the French, the Kadohadachos now had an "American father, and in the two years he had known the Americans he liked them also for they too had treated his people well." He was especially pleased by the way the members of the expedition were "treating him with respect and candor which the Spaniards did not evince in their conduct." Dehahuit added that he wanted them to proceed and meet his allies, the Panis Piques, who would also be glad to see the Americans.[41]

Major Freeman celebrated this successful meeting by distributing food and liquor to the Kadohadacho warriors. After toasting their alliance, the Americans fell into single file in order to allow each Indian to shake their hands; the new allies impressed the Kadohadachos, and the principal warrior told the American sergeant that "he was glad to see his new brothers had the faces of men, and looked like men and warriors . . . let us hold fast, and be friends forever." The next day Dehahuit informed Freeman that more Spanish soldiers were en route from Nacogdoches to intercept the Americans "and drive them back or take them prisoners." The Kadohadacho chief promised the major that he would send messengers from his village with information concerning the Spanish troops; he also ordered three other tribesmen to remain with the expedition as guides.[42]

In the meantime, Commandant Salcedo ordered about one thousand troops under the command of Lieutenant Colonel Simón de Herrera to meet Lieutenant Ramón's force at the Kadohadacho village and then proceed to their old village on the Red River to intercept the American expedition. After arriving at Nacogdoches on July 15, Herrera's force set out for the Kadohadacho village. Upon his entrance, Herrera informed Dehahuit that his town was on Spanish soil and that he would have to move eastward if he planned to continue to display the American flag. When the chief hesitated, the Spanish troops boldly cut down the flagstaff. The soldiers then taunted Dehahuit, telling him they were going after the Americans "whom they would serve in the same manner, and if resistance was made, either kill them, or carry them off prisoners, in irons." The insulting actions caused some of the Kadohadacho warriors to take up arms, but Dehahuit's cooler head quieted them. If the Kadohadacho chief had had any doubts about allying his tribe with the Americans, Herrera's visit had most certainly put them to rest.[43]

Following Herrera's departure, Dehahuit immediately dispatched three Kadohadacho messengers to find the Americans on the Red River. They met Freeman and Custis high above the Coushatta settlement on July 26, informed the party of the incident at their village, and warned them of the Spanish plan to intercept them. Three days later, the overwhelming Spanish force met the Americans, and the expedition was obliged to retreat. On August 23, Freeman and Custis reached Natchitoches and informed Governor Claiborne of their fate.[44]

The party's return initiated an exchange of letters between Claiborne and Herrera that presented both the Spanish and American claims concerning the Kadohadachos. On August 26, Governor Claiborne protested the fact that the

Spanish troops had stopped the American expedition on United States soil. By chopping down the American flag in the Kadohadacho village, in his opinion the Spanish had committed "another outrage." Claiborne further argued that while Louisiana had belonged to France, the Kadohadacho tribe had been "under the protection of the French Government . . . hence it follows Sir, that the cession of Louisiana to the United States is sufficient authority for the display of the American flag" in the village. Lieutenant Colonel Herrera, in answering Governor Claiborne two days later, agreed that the United States possessed Louisiana but asserted that the Kadohadacho village was not on American soil "and on the Contrary the place which they inhabit is very far from it and belongs to Spain." In this way, Herrera justified the removal of the American flag.[45]

Ultimately, the matter was left unresolved, and the signing of the "Neutral Ground Agreement" on November 1, 1806, by Spanish and American representatives averted war. This document remained in force until 1821 and established a neutral strip between Louisiana and Texas that, though claimed by both countries, remained ungoverned and unoccupied. Dehahuit's village fell within this neutral ground, and thus both countries continued to claim the Kadohadachos as subjects, a situation that proved most profitable for the tribe. In addition, the boundary between Louisiana and Texas was left undefined, allowing American traders the freedom to continue to travel to the Panis Pique villages.[46]

The Freeman-Custis expedition and Spain's reaction served only to propel the Kadohadachos further toward the Americans. Two weeks after the expedition was repelled, Dehahuit and a delegation of fourteen warriors met with Governor Claiborne, army officers, and leading citizens in Natchitoches. The governor asserted that the Kadohadachos were now subjects of the United States and asked that he let his "people hold the Americans by the hand with sincerity and Friendship, and the Chain of peace will be bright and strong; our children will smoke together, and the path will never be colored with blood." After smoking the ceremonial pipe, Dehahuit told the governor that the Americans were his "new friends," and he reaffirmed his agreement with Claiborne's claim of jurisdiction by stating that if "your nation has purchased what the French formerly possessed, you have purchased the country we occupy and we regard you in the same light as we did them."[47]

The United States had formally won over the Kadohadachos, but Agent Sibley did not take the alliance for granted and continued to display his gratitude to the tribe. For instance, in January 1807, when Dehahuit's house caught fire and destroyed his family's corn supply, Sibley ordered twenty-three barrels of flour to be distributed to the Kadohadachos as compensation. One month later a party of Kadohadachos arrived in Natchitoches to trade the furs they had acquired during their annual winter hunt. Sibley warmly welcomed them and presented a hat and a blue half-regimental frock coat to Cut Finger, "a particular friend and Companion" of Dehahuit, in return for his being "friendly and attentive" to Major Freeman's party. Dehahuit arrived in Natchitoches on April 14 with fifteen men and pirogues loaded with skins. Sibley presented the delighted Kadohadacho chief with a scarlet regimental coat and gave another tribesman a coat similar to Cut Finger's. All this largesse served to reassure Dehahuit and his men that the Kadohadachos had been correct in siding with the United States.[48]

Although the Spaniards had stopped Freeman and Custis before they could reach the Panis Pique villages, the Americans continued to extend their influence over the Indians living farther upstream. Following the expedition's return to Natchitoches, Agent Sibley gave licenses to a party of seven Americans, led by John S. Lewis and William C. Alexander and guided by Joseph Lucas, to trade with the Wichitas. Spanish officials resignedly allowed the traders to travel unobstructed up the Red River for they had chosen to "avoid any noisy disturbances" that might create cause for friction between Spain and the United States. Chief Awahakei welcomed the Americans at the Panis Pique villages and allowed them to winter there. A Yamparica Comanche band of 2,000 people spent the winter about forty miles upstream from the Wichitas. The American traders visited the ranchería and were greatly impressed by their herd of 5,000 horses. Quilvalparica, the Yamparica chief, promised to travel along with Awahakei to Natchitoches and meet with Sibley the following summer.[49]

The Spaniards, in the meantime, tried to compete with the American traders by having Marcel Soto, yet another grandson of St. Denis, establish a trading post at Bayou Pierre. They also hoped to entice the Indians of Texas back to their side by distributing more gifts. In early 1807, Governor Cordero invited all the Texas tribes to come to Béxar and receive presents, which had just arrived from Mexico. Some tribes were very receptive to the Spanish overtures. In March, Tawakoni chief Daguariscara came to Béxar at the same time as Sargento of the Comanches and Lipan Apache chief Canoso. Meeting independently of the governor, the three chiefs decided to put aside past feuds and agree to peace. They then took the matter to Governor Cordero who presided over a meeting attended by the three Indians. All of the chiefs spoke with "energy . . . against the evils of war," particularly the Tawakoni leader, who suggested that the tribes should follow the example of the Spaniards who had peaceably settled their recent dispute with the Americans.[50]

Iscani chief Awahakei, meanwhile, declined to attend but sent in his place a minor headman with about twenty warriors. The Texas governor gave them a "great many presents," including arms, ammunition, bridles, blankets, clothes, and three Spanish flags for the Panis Pique villages. Upon the Indians' return to their home on the Red River, Awahakei refused to fly the Spanish banners, preferring the American flag that Agent Sibley had sent him in 1805. Soon thereafter Awahakei ordered nine Panis Piques to guide the trader Lewis and one of his men back to Natchitoches and meet with Sibley. The group arrived at the post on June 25, and Lewis reported that Awahakei and the Panis Piques had treated the Americans in a "most friendly manner." Lewis informed the American agent of all that had occurred during his stay among the Wichitas and stated that Awahakei had asked for two more American flags so that each of the three villages could fly one. Sibley had none on hand but distributed presents to each Indian guide, including powder, lead, gunflints, hoes, and hatchets; other merchandise was earmarked especially for Awahakei.[51]

The Texas Indians and the United States continued to draw even closer in the latter half of 1807. In the summer Dehahuit enhanced his prestigious position on the Louisiana-Texas frontier by arranging a grand council in Natchitoches between Agent Sibley and the Caddos, Wichitas, and Comanches. By August 10, about three hundred Indians had arrived in the town, including eighty Kotsoteka Comanches, twenty-six Tawakonis and Kichais, ninety Kadohadachos, and 119 Hasinais. The following day the American agent initiated a series of meetings with various tribal leaders, paying particular attention to the Wichitas and the Comanches. Sibley welcomed four Comanche headmen, led by the anti-Spanish chief, Pisinampe, into his own home. A few days later, he presented each chief with an expressly tailored soldier's coat in front of the entire Comanche party. He then distributed even more gifts to the other tribesmen. As the gathering was breaking up Pisinampe asked for an American flag in exchange for the Spanish one that Governor Cordero had given him. Sibley eagerly responded by bringing forth a flag, which he wrapped around himself and the Comanche chief. He then presented the man with his own "Elegant Belt . . . which had a good Effect, as it was done in Presence of a Large Number of Indians of different Nations." On August 17, Sibley held a conference with the heretofore anti-American Tawakoni chief, Daguariscara, as well as Castor, chief of the Kichais. He expressed "to them the Satisfaction" he felt from the meeting and assured them that President Jefferson would also be honored.[52]

The following day Sibley addressed a gathering of headmen of the visiting tribes. He told the assembly that although Louisiana had been transferred to the United States, the boundary with Spanish Texas remained undefined.

Sibley confirmed that the Indians could be friends with both the Spaniards and the Americans, and he invited the tribes to deposit their goods at Natchitoches and accept American traders in their villages regardless of which side of the border they lived. Chief Daguariscara, the first Indian to reply, told Sibley that he approved of the speech and would deliver it to his fellow tribe members. The Tawakoni leader then demanded to know why the American traders at Nacogdoches, Barr and Davenport, sold their goods at such high prices. Sibley quickly explained that Barr and Davenport were Spanish citizens, not Americans, and promised that the Indians would never have cause for complaint against any Natchitoches-based traders. Chief Castor stated he was happy with Sibley's explanation and said that it made no difference to him that his tribe lived in Spanish territory, for he received the American's talk "like a brother," wished to live in peace, and hoped that trade would flourish with his good neighbors. Comanche chief Pisinampe said that he was glad to have traveled to Natchitoches where he had seen that the Americans "have every thing we want." He made it clear that the Comanches would "probably visit you again." Then Dehahuit rose and informed Sibley that he had told the western tribes many good things about the agent at Natchitoches, and he expressed "great Satisfaction" with the warm welcome the American had given his Indian allies. The grand council of 1807 proved mutually beneficial to the United States and the Kadohadachos, and with the aid of Dehahuit, Sibley succeeded in extending his country's influence well into Spanish Texas; likewise, Sibley's graciousness added to the esteem of the Kadohadacho chief.[53]

Despite the strong alliance with the Americans, the Kadohadachos and Hasinais did not cut their ties with the Spaniards. In November 1807, Dehahuit traveled to Nacogdoches and received food, brandy, tobacco, and a shirt from the Spanish commander during his weeklong stay. Two months later another Kadohadacho party stopped in Nacogdoches following their winter hunt and were presented with gifts as well. In the summer of 1809, Dehahuit traveled to San Antonio with the Nadaco and Nacogdoches chiefs to meet with the Spanish governor. Claiming that he was responsible for the Hasinai tribes' well-being, the Kadohadacho chief requested that the Spanish governor provide them with a much-needed trader. By the end of the first decade of the nineteenth century, it was obvious that Dehahuit had successfully used the Kadohadachos' position on the Louisiana-Texas frontier to gain status, as well as material benefits, for his tribe and himself.[54]

Following the grand council of August 1807, the Americans continued to extend their influence over groups of Wichitas and Comanches that had not attended the meeting. In October all the three Panis Pique headmen, along with about fifty tribesmen and twenty Yamparica Comanches, led by Chief

Quilvalparica, traveled to Natchitoches to meet Sibley. The American agent graciously welcomed the party to his house and showered Panis Pique chiefs Awahakei, Eriascoc, and Ecani with gifts, as well as providing Quilvalparica with a medal. He then distributed presents to the remaining Panis Piques and Comanches while informing them that the Americans were their friends and wished to cultivate a trade with them. Chief Quilvalparica answered that his tribe had brought nothing to exchange, but had come "Just to See & Satisfy themselves If it was true what they had heard of us, & he was glad to find that it was all true." He wished that Sibley would send traders to his people for "Horses and Mules were to them like grass they had them in Such plenty." Sibley told both tribes that if they returned to Natchitoches the following year with plenty of horses, mules, and buffalo robes, "they would be able to procure as Many Guns . . . as they wanted, for these things are very plenty in our Country." All the Indians responded favorably before heading home.[55]

Happy with what they received from Sibley at Natchitoches, the Panis Piques and Tawakonis—including the now-convinced Daguariscara—avoided the Spaniards all winter. The following spring, lesser-ranked Tawakoni and Taovaya officials traveled to San Antonio to meet with Governor Cordero and receive gifts. A different Taovaya group, along with some Guichitas, went to Béxar in March 1808, to steal a number of mules from the Spanish herds. As a result of the dearth of visitors, Governor Cordero ordered Marcel Soto to travel up the Red River to invite the Panis Piques to visit San Antonio and receive presents. In addition, Barr and Davenport sent a trader to the Tawakoni village to conduct business. In hope of securing the Tawakonis' loyalty, Spanish officials agreed to allow the tribe to sell surplus corn to the troops stationed at San Antonio and Nacogdoches. Eventually, this privilege was extended to the citizens of San Antonio. The following year, Barr and Davenport responded to Chief Castor's plea for a trader by sending Nicholas Pont to the Kichai village.[56]

In the meantime, the Osages resumed their attacks upon the Panis Piques. In February 1808, they raided the Red River villages and killed Chief Eriascoc. Osage attacks continued throughout the year; raiders stole about five hundred horses from the Panis Pique villages in July and followed that success with raids in August and September, netting them even more horses. Although Quicheata succeeded Eriascoc as chief of the Taovayas, the tribe still desired the Texas governor's official confirmation of the position despite their estrangement from the Spaniards. Thus, when Soto arrived in the Taovaya village in June 1808, they accepted his invitation to travel to San Antonio and meet Governor Cordero. On July 5 the governor officially named Quicheata "captain and big chief" of the Taovayas in front of a crowd of Panis Pique notables. Following the ceremony Governor Cordero promised the tribesmen that he would send a garrison to their villages to assist them in a campaign against the Osages. He also advised them that they should not have anything to do with the United States and asked them to inform him when any Americans visited their villages. The Panis Piques admitted to trading with the Americans, explaining that they were compelled to do so because of the lack of Spanish traders.[57]

Fearful of the American efforts to win the favor of the Comanches, Governor Cordero sent Captain Amangual as an emissary to the Kotsotekas in the spring of 1808. On April 12, Amangual and his party encountered Chief Sargento's ranchería, "which looked like a city, located on a beautiful plain," about thirty miles northwest of the old Spanish mission on the San Saba River. With "much jubilation," Sargento received Amangual who, in turn, delivered a walking cane and a rifle that Governor Cordero had sent the Comanche chief. Sargento then led the Spaniards up the Colorado River to the ranchería of Sofais, which contained two hundred tepees. Amangual addressed the Comanches, stressing the "loyalty and fidelity we bear them, and that they should observe the same, that they should not trade with any other nation that may come to induce them." The Spaniard also asked if they knew of any Americans entering their lands, to which both chiefs responded negatively. Sargento and Sofais then explained that that "they considered themselves Spaniards" and that they did not accept anything from other nations. Following Amangual's visit, Sargento and 225 Comanches met Governor Cordero in San Antonio and exchanged buffalo robes. When the governor asked the inevitable question about the American presence, Sargento denied having gone to Natchitoches the year before and stated that he was opposed to "any such communication and that as far as possible he has kept all his people from it."[58]

Increasingly, however, Sargento found himself helpless to stop all of the Kotsotekas from dealing with American traders, a new group of which arrived on the Texas plains in the summer of 1808. In response to a request from Iscani chief Awahakei, Agent Sibley had granted a trading license to Anthony Glass, a Natchez merchant familiar with the exploits of Nolan and his cronies. Glass gathered up merchandise worth $2,000 and, accompanied by ten men—including Alexander, Davis, and Lucas who had already visited the Panis Piques villages—headed up the Red River in July. Although Spanish officials soon learned of the Glass expedition, Commandant General Salcedo allowed it to proceed unmolested so as not to disturb the precarious peace.[59]

In early August the Panis Piques welcomed Glass and his party into their villages. A few days after the Americans' arrival, the Panis Piques staged a formal assembly in which Glass told the tribes that although the boundary between Spain and the United States had yet to be established, the president still desired their friendship. Glass announced that he had come to barter for horses and that if everything went well during his visit, other traders would surely follow. Awahakei expressed his friendship for the Americans and stated that he was very happy to have the United States flag flying over his villages. The pleased chief even housed the Americans in his own residence and furnished them with a daily supply of buffalo meat, vegetables, and fruits.[60]

A few members of the Glass party returned to Natchitoches with a herd of horses in October 1808. In the fall Awahakei led Glass and some of the other Americans southwestward to the Colorado River, trading with various Kotsoteka Comanche villages along the way, including the ranchería of Pisinampe. The Comanche leader informed Glass of his visit to Natchitoches the previous summer and stated that "he is a great friend of the Americans." Other Comanches who had accompanied Pisinampe said they "were highly pleased with the treatment they received from Doctor Sibley." In February 1809, Glass returned to the Panis Pique villages, where he carried out a profitable trade in mounts until spring. Glass and his party arrived back in Natchitoches with a horse herd in May and reported to Sibley that the Panis Piques and Comanches "appeared particularly attached" to American traders and the United States government. He also reported that the Taovayas had shown him a huge piece of metal near the Brazos River, which he thought might contain silver. This news greatly excited Sibley and others in Natchitoches, and preparations were immediately made to return to the area and retrieve the object.[61]

Meanwhile, a party of Osages made yet another attack on the Panis Pique villages in February 1809, killing two men while making off with a number of horses. In response, a Panis Pique war party traveled to the Arkansas River in June and made an ineffectual attack upon the Osages. When the Panis Piques returned to their villages in July, they found ten Americans—five of whom had been part of the Glass expedition—who wanted to purchase the piece of metal. In return for guns, ammunition, and blankets, the Panis Piques sold the metal to the Americans who, with great difficulty, dragged it back to the Red River villages. The Americans spent the winter with their Indian friends before heading to Natchitoches, which they finally reached with the metallic object—actually a meteorite—in June 1810.[62]

Spanish officials learned of the American search for the piece of metal in the summer of 1809. Although they had decided to allow American traders to deal with the Panis Piques on the Red River without interference, the Spaniards did not feel the Americans had the right to engage in "mining" activities on Spanish territory. Therefore, on October 5, 1809, a fifty-two-man cavalry force, commanded by Captain José de Goseascochea, left San Antonio to arrest the American party. Hoping to receive assistance from the Tawakonis, the Spanish force headed for their Brazos River villages but arrived after the tribe had already left for their annual winter hunt. Goseascochea headed west in search of the Americans, but without Tawakoni guides the Spanish party came up empty-handed and returned to Béxar in November.[63]

The Spaniards continued their fruitless pursuit of American traders the following year; hearing rumors that sixteen Americans were in the Panis Pique villages, the new governor of Texas, Manuel Salcedo, ordered a troop from Nacogdoches to investigate. Led by Tawakoni guides this time, Luciano García and thirty Spanish soldiers entered the Panis Pique villages on June 11, 1810, and found the Indians to be "very distrustful and suspicious." García added to the tension by demanding a portion of the herd that Taovaya warriors had recently stolen from San Antonio. Awahakei answered that the raiders refused to return the plundered horses. However, in hope of gaining García's support in fighting the Osages, whom they believed were about to attack, Awahakei promised to force the young men to return the horses to San Antonio within a few months. García agreed to stay and fight the Osages, but after waiting at the Panis Pique villages for three days without any sign of the enemy, the Spanish troops returned to Nacogdoches by way of the Tawakoni village. Once again, the Spaniards in Texas had disappointed the Wichitas living on the Red River.[64]

Soon thereafter, the alliance between the Comanches and the Spaniards began to collapse. In the spring of 1810, Chief Sargento and 108 Kotsotekas responded favorably to the New Mexico governor's request for assistance against the Mescalero Apaches and headed west. Inspired by the almost constant presence of American traders at the Panis Pique villages, hostile young Comanches took advantage of the principal Kotsoteka chief's absence and raided Spanish settlements in Texas. The Kotsoteka warriors stole horses from La Bahía and Laredo, and also attacked a small Spanish post on the San Marcos River, killing a few soldiers and stealing the entire herd. Most of the raids originated in the ranchería of Pisinampe, the Kotsoteka chieftain who had been inclined toward the Americans for several years. However, the fact that other warriors came from the village of Chihuahua, heretofore one of the leading pro-Spanish chiefs, reflected the weakening of the alliance. A lesser Kotsoteka captain named El Sordo—probably the same man the Spaniards had arrested in 1803—also engaged in the raids. Disgusted with the lack of trade goods offered by the Spaniards, El Sordo had formed his own Comanche camp near the Tawakoni village on the Brazos, from where he joined the Wichitas to plunder Spanish herds for exchange with the Americans.[65]

In response to the Comanche raids, Texas authorities contacted Chief Sargento through the New Mexico governor. The Kotsoteka chief quickly responded and in August traveled to San Antonio to meet with Governor Salcedo for the first time. With the new governor's approval, Sargento then made a tour of the various Comanche villages, investigating thefts, recovering stock, and reinforcing the alliance with the Spaniards. While making the rounds, Sargento also met with some American traders but refused their solicitations to break with his Texas allies. Sargento also had a conference with Paruaquita, one of the leading Yamparica Comanche chiefs, in which both men pledged to ensure compliance of the treaties with the Spaniards in Texas and New Mexico. Following his travels, Sargento returned to Béxar in October 1810 to inform Governor Salcedo of his accomplishments and to reaffirm the Comanches' shaky alliance with the Spaniards. Sargento was forced to admit, however, that many of the Kotsoteka young men were now beyond his limited control. The Spanish-Comanche alliance, which had been in effect for twenty-five years, was on the verge of breaking down.[66]

Although the two imperial powers had avoided war in the first decade of the eighteenth century, the tribes on the Louisiana-Texas frontier were able to take advantage of the rivalry between Spain and the United States to improve their own material situation. In fact, by the end of 1810 it had become clear that ample trade goods and skilled diplomacy had won the Red River Caddoans, as well as more than a few Comanches, over to the American side of the boundary dispute. In addition, the Tonkawas and Lipan Apaches had adopted a somewhat hostile attitude toward the Spaniards in Texas. Only the Karankawas and the tribes that had recently immigrated to southeastern Texas to escape the pressures of land-hungry settlers actually preferred, albeit luke-warmly, the Spaniards to the Americans. When warfare did break out in Texas and Louisiana in the second decade of the 1800s—surprisingly, however, not between Spain and the United States—the Indians' clear preference for the United States would greatly influence the result of the two powers' respective struggles.

4. Transformation
The Indians and the Breakdown of Spanish Texas, 1811 to 1822

Significant changes occurred in Texas and the Near Southwest during the second decade of the 1800s. Between 1811 and 1813 the Spaniards in Texas engaged in a civil conflict that all but destroyed the province by decimating the few Euromamerican settlements that had been established between the Nueces and the Sabine rivers. The Indians of Texas—natives and emigrants alike—took advantage of the resulting Spanish weakness to reinforce the dominant position they had maintained in the colony ever since its establishment a full century before. By 1821, when Mexico shook free of the Spanish empire, representatives of the newly independent nation were forced to seek peace agreements with the hostile tribes in Texas in order to reestablish a semblance of control over the shattered region. The Spanish self-destruction, combined with the United States' ability to defend itself from Great Britain in the War of 1812, allowed the Americans to fully secure their position on the Louisiana-Texas frontier. However, the tribes that had developed a close, mutually beneficial relationship with the United States prior to the war now found that the aggressive, young republic was not as interested in the Indians' well-being as before. Instead, the government allowed throngs of American settlers to enter the region, forcing the tribes to consider following the Rapides Parish Indians' example—as well as that of a new group of Indian emigrants from the United States—of taking refuge in Texas. Disease and drought also affected the Indians of the Near Southwest during this period, forcing more than a few tribes to reorganize as a means of survival. By 1822, on the eve of the full-scale American settlement of the region, the situation in Texas had altered dramatically from what it had been only a decade before.

Both Spain and the United States engaged in warfare in the early years of the second decade of the nineteenth century. In 1811, Texas was thrown into turmoil as a consequence of the Miguel Hidalgo revolt in Mexico that sparked a call for independence from Spain. A military struggle ensued in Texas between the loyal royalists' forces and the republican revolutionaries. Although the fighting concluded two years later with the royalists still in control of the colony, the few Euroamerican settlements in Texas had been shattered as a result of the fierce, internecine struggle. Meanwhile, the United States, declaring war upon Great Britain in 1812, strengthened its hand on the Louisiana-Texas frontier by defeating the British forces at New Orleans in early 1815. Although the Indians of the Near Southwest did not play an important role in either fight, the various tribes' responses to the events in Texas and Louisiana clearly demonstrated that the Americans' efforts in the first decade of the 1800s had succeeded. The region's Indians either came to the assistance of the United States forces in Louisiana, actively fought against the royalist troops in Texas, or retired from the fray and did nothing at all to help their nominal Spanish allies.

In January 1811, back-and-forth fighting began in Texas when republican forces seized San Antonio and Nacogdoches. By the summer, however, the weakened royalists had regained effective control of Texas. Taking advantage of the chaos, rebellious Kotsoteka warriors under El Sordo joined with Tawakoni and Taovaya men to steal horses and mules from Spanish ranches near San Antonio. Other Comanches, though, remained faithful to the royalist Spaniards who, pressured by the swirl of revolutionary events, took a serious misstep that ultimately led to the demise of the troubled alliance. In August 1811, Kotsoteka chiefs Sargento, Yzazat, and Chihuahua traveled to San Antonio along with Yamparica leader Paruaquita to meet with Lieutenant Colonel Herrera, acting governor in the place of the absent Salcedo. The Comanches reaffirmed their commitment to peace with the Spaniards; Paruaquita went so far as to force thieves living at El Sordo's camp to return stolen horses to Herrera. The Yamparica chief even convinced the chastised El Sordo to visit Béxar to report that the Wichitas were planning more raids. Despite El Sordo being unarmed and accompanied by only one man, two women, and a small child, Herrera could not help but be suspicious of the previously hostile visitor. Therefore, the acting governor arrested the party, placed them in irons, and sent them to jail in Coahuila.[1]

This shocking breach of diplomatic etiquette seriously damaged the already flimsy Spanish-Comanche alliance. Over the winter the angered Paruaquita gathered a Comanche party on the Colorado River to demand El Sordo's release. On April 8, 1812, the Yamparica chief appeared at San Antonio with Sargento, Pisinampe, Yzazat, and countless other Comanche warriors to ask for an explanation of the treatment of their kinsmen. Governor Salcedo, who had since returned to Texas, rode out with more than six hundred men, the largest Spanish force the Comanches had ever faced, to meet the dangerous gathering. Although the threatening group of warriors dispersed without a fight, El Sordo and his party remained in jail, causing rancor to fester among the Comanches that would eventually lead to outright war.[2]

Just as the Spanish-Comanche alliance in Texas was unraveling, the tenuous ties between the Wichitas and Spain were finally cut as well. The death of the great Panis Pique leader Awahakei while returning from a visit to Natchitoches in the autumn of 1811 was a major cause of the breakdown. Although Awahakei had followed an anti-Spanish policy ever since the American purchase of Louisiana, his leadership had provided the Panis Piques with the stability necessary to deal with representatives of both countries. Awahakei's passing, however, confused the Panis Piques because they were unable to agree on a successor and were unsure of what course to follow due to continued Osage harassment. Awahakei's death, combined with the Osage attacks, caused the Panis Piques to abandon, once and for all, the landmark villages on the Red River that had stood intact for half a century. The tribes scattered throughout the southern Plains in two directions: the Taovayas absorbed the Guichitas and headed west to establish villages on the upper Brazos and tributaries of the Red, while the Iscanis traveled south to join the Tawakonis. The newly reinforced Tawakonis, now led by Daguariscara's successor, Concha (Shell), raided Spanish settlements along with Taovayas and Kichais throughout the winter and spring of 1812.[3]

In August 1812, the Wichitas obtained Euroamerican allies in their struggle against the Spaniards when a republican force from Natchitoches invaded Texas. A Mexican, José Bernardo Gutiérrez de Lara, and a former lieutenant in the United States Army, William Magee, led this self-styled Republican Army of the North. The republican force—which included American filibusters—easily took Nacogdoches, whereupon Gutiérrez enlisted the services of the trader, Samuel Davenport, to win support from the Texas Indians. Although Davenport offered the tribes loot and trade if they would help the invaders, no Indians responded, possibly due to warnings sent out from Agent Sibley and Kadohadacho chief Dehahuit. Although the royalists also appealed to the Indians for assistance, none, not even the formerly faithful Comanches, answered the call. However, following the republicans' capture of La Bahía in February 1813, a few hundred Texas Indians, all of whom were already hostile to the Spaniards in Texas, joined the invaders. Tonkawas, Lipan Apaches, and a few Tawakonis combined with the republicans as they made their way toward San Antonio. Warriors from all three tribes assisted the republicans in their victory over the royalists at the Battle of Rosillo, fought nine miles southeast of San Antonio on March 29, 1813. In addition to weapons and other booty, the three tribes received presents worth $130 for their involvement.[4]

On April 2, the Spanish royalists surrendered Béxar to the invaders, who shockingly executed a group of officials, including Salcedo and Herrera, a few days later. The republicans then proclaimed the independence of Texas and promulgated its first constitution. Their glory was short-lived, however, for a large royalist army, commanded by Joaquín de Arredondo, marched upon San Antonio in the summer of 1813. The republicans once again called for Indian allies, and this time Taovaya warriors eager to obtain their share of the spoils of war joined the Tonkawas, Lipans, and Tawakonis. On August 13, the opposing armies met at the Medina River. Shortly after the battle began the Indians realized that the well-disciplined royalist troops, whose force was twice as large as the unorganized republican mob, would be victorious. Therefore, the Indians abandoned the field and escaped long before the battle was over. Arredondo scored a triumph at the Battle of the Medina, killing more than one thousand opponents. The victors then unleashed a wave of vengeance in Texas, using confiscation, detention, and execution to restore royal authority. The royalists did their work so thoroughly that the Euroamerican population of Nacogdoches and La Bahía was almost completely wiped out, and the settlement of Béxar was severely reduced. Following a century of existence, the Spanish colony of Texas had been returned almost exclusively to Indian hands.[5]

While the Caddo tribes had followed the advice of Kadohadacho chief Dehahuit and refused to get involved in the Texas struggle, they soon found themselves drawn into the midst of the dangerous situation that existed in the aftermath of the royalist victory. Many Americans in Natchitoches feared that the vengeful Spaniards would attempt to exact retribution in Louisiana for the filibusters' participation in the republican invasion. The United States had already gone to war with Great Britian in 1812, and it was fully expected that the war would extend to a struggle with Spain as well. Concurrently, a new threat materialized from east of the Mississippi River when the Creek Indians declared war against the United States. The Creeks sent emissaries across the river to recruit native allies, arguing that the Americans were ultimately inimical to all Indians.

Realizing the Kadohadachos' prestige on the Louisiana-Texas frontier, the Americans held a series of meetings with Dehahuit aimed at convincing him to maintain the alliance. On October 5, 1813, Agent Sibley met with the Kadohadachos, Yatasis, and Nadacos, as well as with the Alabamas, Coushattas, and Apalaches who lived above Natchitoches. Claiming that the Spaniards and Creeks were liars, Sibley implored the Indians not to join either group, assuring them that the president "continued in his friendly disposition towards his Red Children, that he wished them all clean Paths, good Crops of Corn, good hunting and happiness." Unalabahola, a young Alabama chief who had succeeded Etienne upon his death, spoke for the Coushattas and Apalaches and announced that he deferred to "his Older Brother the Caddo Chief and would always be advised by him." Dehahuit asserted that he had been allied with the Americans for a long time and promised Sibley that if the United States needed assistance all the warriors under his jurisdiction would enlist.[6]

A week later Dehahuit met with Thomas M. Linnard, the official United States trader, who assured the chief that the Creeks and Spaniards were not to be trusted. Linnard reported that Dehahuit promised "he was ready and willing to make common with [the United States] and that our enemies should be his enemies." The final council with Dehahuit occurred October 18, when he met with Governor Claiborne at Natchitoches. Claiborne recalled their meeting in 1806 and thanked the Kadohadacho chief for "the advice you have given to your own people, and to all red men with whom you have influence [which is like] that of a father to his children." He hoped "that all these people will look up to you, as an elder Brother, and hold fast your good advice" of not joining the Creek enemy. In order to express his gratitude, Claiborne gave Dehahuit a sword, since "to a Chief, a Man, and a Warrior, nothing could be more acceptable."[7]

The American conferences with Dehahuit in 1813 proved successful, and none of the tribes influenced by the Kadohadachos joined the Creeks. In fact, Dehahuit's counsel had made the tribes more than willing to join the United States in the war that continued against the British. In August 1814, Nabedache, Hainai, Kichai, and Tawakoni warriors visited Sibley in Natchitoches to offer their services. Noting that the Kadohadacho chief had "an entire influence over them," Sibley felt it would be wise to accept their offer in case of a British invasion. When the threat of a British landing in Louisiana materialized in late 1814, the Americans called upon the Indians to assist them and, under Kadohadacho leadership, the tribes proved true to their word. Governor Claiborne quickly alerted General Andrew Jackson, commander of the American forces in New Orleans, to the Kadohadachos' importance. On October 28, the governor advised Jackson to confer with Dehahuit because he was the "most influential Indian on this side of the River Grande and his friendship, sir, will give much security to the frontier of Louisiana." Although Jackson was unable to meet with Dehahuit, he nevertheless enlisted the chief's services. In December the general asked the Kadohadachos and their allies to be "mustered into the service of the United States." As promised, the Indians answered the Americans' call, sending 150 Caddo and Wichita warriors to Natchitoches to aid their allies. Since it was too late for the force to travel to New Orleans to

.intercept the British, they were held in readiness in Natchitoches in case they were needed to secure peace along the Spanish border.[8]

General Jackson's victory over the British at New Orleans on January 8, 1815, ended the War of 1812 as well as the tensions that had threatened the Louisiana-Texas frontier. Although it would be another four years before the boundary between the United States and Spain was finally determined, by the Adams-Onís Treaty of February 1819, to be the present eastern and northern border of Texas, neither country seriously challenged the other in the meantime. The Spaniards had enough trouble just holding on to the shattered colony of Texas, while the United States, now secure of its position in the Near Southwest, expanded its hold on the area by allowing land-hungry citizens to settle in the region. With the border relatively calm, Spanish and American officials paid much less attention to the well-being of the area's Indians. On their part, the weakened Spaniards in Texas could barely keep the dominant Indians at bay. The Americans' attitude toward the Indians—so courteous while the border situation was unsettled—changed once the tensions subsided, becoming increasingly hostile to the tribes that had provided such invaluable assistance in the Near Southwest. As a result of increasing Spanish weakness and rising American strength, the Indians were forced to reorient their policies vis-à-vis the two imperial powers. Some Indians, previously allies of the Spaniards, took advantage of the feeble Euromamerican presence in Texas and initiated a series of devastating attacks upon their former partners. The emigrant Indians in Texas, including a new group of tribes who settled in the northeast, more firmly established their position in the colony. Other Indians, once eager to aid the United States, now found themselves threatened by the overwhelming numbers of Americans. By 1821, when Mexico gained its independence from Spain, the Indians' situation in Texas and the Near Southwest was radically different than what it had been before the outbreak of war.

Spanish Texas lay in ruins in the aftermath of the warfare that shook the colony between 1811 and 1813. Only about two thousand Euroamericans remained in the province, three-fourths of whom lived near San Antonio, while the rest huddled around La Bahía. Nacogdoches, the third area of Spanish settlement in Texas, was almost completely abandoned; most of the townspeople had either been killed or had taken refuge in Louisiana during the armed struggle. One observer lamented that in the second decade of the nineteenth century Texas had "advanced at an amazing rate toward ruin and destruction," and that the country's resources had been drained of "everything that could sustain human life." Inept Spanish administration of the province did not help the desperate situation. In the four years following Arredondo's victory over the republicans, a succession of five interim governors ruled Texas. Finally, in 1817, Antonio Martínez began a term that proved to be the last for Spanish governors.[9]

With the colony in tatters, the few Spaniards in Texas could hardly defend themselves from the many Indian tribes that had turned hostile in the early part of the decade. When Martínez arrived at Béxar in May 1817, the new governor found the troops in a "deplorable condition . . . on foot, without a single horse, unclothed from head to foot, and meagerly supplied from day to day." Two-thirds of the weapons used by the soldiers were "unserviceable and most of them cannot be repaired." The soldiers' families, as well as the citizens of the town, were starving because, as a result of the troops' poor condition, "the Indians become so insolent that they enter the town with the greatest nerve and kill these unfortunate inhabitants with impunity." While Martínez strove to improve the situation, by 1821 he was still forced to borrow money from leading citizens to purchase corn for the few soldiers in Texas. These included the sixty-four men stationed at La Bahía and the 136 troops at Béxar. Of the latter soldiers, forty to fifty constantly patrolled the road to the Rio Grande to protect the supply trains from Mexico, which barely kept the people of the colony alive. The Spanish hold on Texas, weak during the best of times, had become virtually nonexistent after a century of occupation.[10]

The emigrant Indians took advantage of the absence of Spaniards to more firmly establish their presence in the jungle-like region of southeastern Texas. In 1815 the emigrants opened up hunting grounds on the lower reaches of the Trinity River by driving the Karankawan Cocos out of the area. Free of the Cocos, who annoyed the tribes by attacking their stock, over the next few years the emigrants set up several long-lasting villages in their new forest homeland. The Coushattas were the largest emigrant tribe, with five hundred or so tribal members living in three villages along the Trinity River. The principal Coushatta chief, Long King, resided in the Middle Coushatta village near the confluence of Tempe and Long King's creeks on the east side of the Trinity, while second chief, Calita, resided in the Lower Coushatta town, located in a horseshoe bend on the opposite bank. About four hundred Alabamas lived fifty miles east of their Coushatta kinsmen in three proximate villages—Peachtree, Fenced-In, and Cane Island—just west of the Neches River. Nearly two hundred Biloxis, Pascagoulas, Apalaches, and Taensas resided in the so-called Biloxi village, just upstream from the Alabamas on the opposite side of the river, while two hundred or so Yowani Choctaws lived in various settlements located along the Neches, Angelina, and Attoyac. Most of the emigrant families resided in well-constructed log houses, raised crops in neatly fenced fields, and kept large herds of cattle and pigs.[11]

Feeling more at home in Texas than they had in Louisiana, the emigrant tribes, along with the native Ais, Bidais, and Akokisas, were extremely jealous of outside intruders. Unfortunately, the feebleness of Spanish Texas invited invasion from Spanish and American republicans, as well as from complete foreigners altogether. Although some tribes had joined with the rebels who had invaded Texas in 1813, none of the Indians assisted the various ragtag groups that threatened the colony between 1817 and 1821. In fact, all the tribes of southeastern Texas, where most of the invasions originated, maintained their loyalty to the Spaniards. While none of the emigrant Indians or the native tribes actually provided warriors to help defend Texas, they all gave valuable service in alerting Spanish officials to the various threats. In early 1817, the Coushattas informed the Spaniards that a force of Spanish and American filibusters, led by Francisco Xavier Mina, had gathered on Galveston Island. A group of Bidais also reported the invaders' presence and noted that neither they, nor any of the other Indians of the region, wanted "to be friends with the Americans . . . [or] go to war against the Spaniards." Duly notified, Spanish forces from Mexico eventually defeated the invaders and executed Mina on November 11, 1817. The following May the Biloxi chief, along with Bidai, Akokisa, and Ais warriors, traveled to La Bahía to inform the presidial commander that a new group of one hundred or so foreigners was in the process of establishing a settlement near the mouth of the Trinity River. The invaders turned out to be French colonists who hoped to form a colony called Le Champ d'Asile (Asylum Field) as a refuge for the imprisoned Napoleon Bonaparte. Alabama, Coushatta, Biloxi, and Yowani tribesmen kept Governor Martínez informed of the developments at Le Champ d'Asile until the French abandoned the strange venture in August 1818. [12]

Despite their support of the Spaniards against the outside threats, all of the southeastern Texas tribes maintained trade ties with Americans from Opelousas and Attakapas. Lack of Spanish trade goods left the various groups with very little choice. By 1816, the Alabamas and Coushattas had established themselves as middlemen in the trade between Texas tribes and Louisiana smugglers. Realizing that Spanish Texas was suffering from a lack of manufactured goods, Biloxi, Akokisa, Bidai, and Ais tribesmen offered items obtained from Americans to the commander of La Bahía. Lacking anything of worth to trade, the Spanish officer was forced to reject the offer. These Indians, as well as the Coushattas, turned instead to the citizens of La Bahía and San Antonio, exchanging horses and mules for American goods and tobacco. By 1820, this trade had become so voluminous that Governor Martínez was forced to issue a series of orders prohibiting citizens from dealing in contraband trade with the Indians. Despite the profitable illegal trade, continuing drought during this period had a detrimental effect upon the small-scale agriculture of the remaining Atakapas of the area; as a result, the two tribes joined together around this time and the designation Akokisa was dropped in favor of Bidai.[13]

The drought in Texas, which had actually begun near the turn of the century, also impacted the Comanches through its dire effect on the buffalo population south of the Red River. Lack of rain, combined with competition with cattle and horses, limited the availability of grasses for buffalo on the plains. Wild livestock had reached such numbers in the region that the animals spread mesquite in various Texas river valleys, creating a barrier zone in which cattle and horses, but not buffalo, thrived. By the middle of the second decade of the nineteenth century all who visited the Texas plains noticed the decline in the buffalo population. Weakened by the dwindling number of buffalo, the Comanches were struck by a smallpox epidemic in the winter of 1816, which was said to have killed 4,000 people. Despite the incredible loss of life, at least ten thousand Comanches continued to roam the southern Plains, more than all the other Texas tribes combined. The smallpox epidemic and the diminishing buffalo herds affected Comanche band organization and the old designations of Kotsoteka and Yamparica soon became obsolete. The easternmost Comanche group—and the tribe that was most involved in Texan affairs—was now designated as the Penatekas, a band that ranged northwest of San Antonio between the Guadalupe and Brazos rivers. Other Comanche tribes, such as the Nokonis, Tenawas, and Kwahadas, lived farther west and north than their Penateka kinsmen.[14]

In order to make up for the population loss, the Comanches continued to kidnap Tejano women and children, as well as females and their young from other Indian tribes. Most of the nomadic Indians of Texas had always engaged in taking captives and incorporating them into the tribe, but the powerful Comanches employed this practice the most. The Comanches treated captives especially well, dedicating them for their use rather than killing them. Warriors generally took the female captives as wives and children were employed as herders and firewood gatherers, all eventually becoming full-fledged members of the tribe. By the early nineteenth century all Penateka rancherías contained Spaniards and Indians from other tribes who had been adopted as Comanches. While most of the boy and girl captives quickly became reconciled to their fate and accepted their new positions, adult females were more troublesome for the Comanches and the other tribes. If the woman proved intractable, the Indian kidnapper could either resort to killing his captive or selling her back to the Spaniards. As early as the late seventeenth century the Spaniards in New Mexico had adopted the practice of *rescate*, in which ransom was paid to free Indians that one tribe had captured from another. By the late eighteenth century, Tejanos began to pay ransom for Spanish kidnap victims, resulting in a thriving market among the various tribes, as captives were exchanged in much the same manner as horses. The Spanish weakness in Texas following the events of 1811–13 further encouraged the Indians to take Tejano captives.[15]

As with the Comanches, changes were taking place among the Wichita tribes. The Taovayas, who had established several towns on the Red and Brazos rivers following the abandonment of the Panis Pique villages in 1811, absorbed the few remaining Guichitas. Although the designation Iscani disappeared as well, a separate Tawakoni group called the Wacos emerged as an independent tribe during this period. Their village of sixty houses contained as many as nine hundred people and was situated on the west bank of the Brazos River in present-day downtown Waco. Surrounded by four hundred acres of corn, beans, pumpkins, and melons, the Waco village was reported to be "in good order." Continuing the old Wichita tradition, the Wacos surrounded the town with earthworks several feet high; within the village were five underground forts where people could take refuge in case of attack. The other Tawakonis, numbering about six hundred people, lived in various proximate towns on the Brazos, Navasota, and Trinity rivers.[16]

With Texas in ruins following its destructive wars, neither the Wichitas nor the Comanches attempted to reestablish ties with the few Spaniards who remained. Instead, both groups looked toward the United States and the numerous traders who continued to travel to Texas from Natchitoches in order to exchange manufactured goods for furs and livestock. In May 1815, a young American army officer named Reuben Ross headed an expedition into Texas and conducted trade with a huge encampment of Penatekas and Tawakonis on the Brazos River. The following year Ross joined another trading party that headed into Texas with mules loaded with arms, ammunition, and blankets. That same summer the heretofore pro-Spanish chief, Sargento, met with Sibley's replacement as the United States Indian agent, John Jamison, at Natchitoches to express his desire for friendship and trade with the Americans. Chief Chihuahua followed his fellow former supporter of the Spanish-Comanche alliance to Louisiana in 1817 and discussed rules governing trade between his tribe and the Americans. As a result of these visits, Spanish officials reported that Natchitoches traders were continually traveling to Penateka villages to exchange "powder, fusils, balls, and other merchandise in return for horses and mules."[17]

Although United States officials initially tried to regulate the commerce and manage it the way that Agent Sibley had, as time went on they significantly reduced their halfhearted attempts to prevent the eager traders from entering Texas. In March 1817, Agent Jamison reported that "hordes of hunters and licentious traders [had] entered the Indian villages and camps on Red River above Natchitoches." W. A. Trimble, commander of the western section of the 8th Military District, noted that there were five illegal traders at Pecan Point [site of the former Kadohadacho village on the Red River] and three at the mouth of the Kiamichi River who had "taken the Indian trade from Natchitoches." In order to win back the commerce, American officials moved the trading factory and Indian agency upstream from Natchitoches to the mouth of the Sulphur River in 1818. Nonetheless, John Fowler, the official trader at the Sulphur Fork Factory, reported that men left everyday from Natchitoches to barter with tribes located farther up the Red River. In May 1818, a Biloxi Indian traveling through Texas reported to the governor at San Antonio that "the traffic between the Comanches and traders from the interior continues without interruption and that arms, munitions, and other war supplies are being brought in." Some of these traders headed straight overland to the recently reconstituted town of Nacogdoches, where they supplied the Indians with "double barrel guns, good lances, and a quantity of ammunition." In 1820 alone, traders at Nacogdoches carried out a commerce with the Indians worth more than $90,000. The following year, the United States abandoned the trading factory system altogether and began issuing licenses to independent traders, thus facilitating the commerce between the Texas Indians and Louisiana traders even more.[18]

Induced by American traders to provide them with livestock, the Comanches and Wichitas turned their attention to the great horse and cattle herds that still roamed throughout south Texas, initiating the most intense Indian warfare the Spaniards in the colony had experienced in three decades. In the spring of 1814, Arredondo, the newly appointed commandant general of the Eastern Interior Provinces, attempted to make peace with the Norteños, but neither the Comanches nor the Wichitas responded to the Spaniard's entreaties. Realizing that he did not have enough men to defend San Antonio in case the Norteños attacked, Arredondo ordered the remaining Tejanos living near Béxar to abandon their ranches and fall back to protect the city. Taking advantage of the situation, within a few months the Comanches and Wichitas "had concluded to extinguish almost entirely the cattle of the province." Norteño parties also laid waste to the ranches that had recently been established between San Antonio and Laredo; they also stole from the herds around La Bahía and Mission Refugio. These raids proved to be particularly dangerous for the few inhabitants left in these areas. In addition to the three Spaniards and one Karankawa the Norteños killed near Refugio in the summer of 1814, in October they slaughtered another fourteen Spaniards on a Nueces River ranch in a single raid. By 1815, the Norteños had extended their raids south of the Rio Grande;

in November, a party of Penatekas and Tawakonis invaded the town of Gigedo and killed a judge. The following year a group of Taovayas combined with some Comanches to attack La Bahía, seizing 130 horses, most coming from the presidial herd.[19]

Competition for livestock, combined with the dwindling number of buffalo, caused the Comanches and Wichitas to wage war against the Tonkawas and Lipan Apaches as well as on the Spaniards. As a result of constant Norteño pressure, the Lipans and Tonkawas made separate peace agreements with Spanish authorities soon after Arredondo reestablished royalist control of Texas. In the summer of 1814, the new Lipan chief, El Cojo (The Lame One), went to San Antonio and agreed to hand over all stolen horses in return for a Spanish pledge not to attack his tribe. Later in the year El Cojo traveled to Monclova and agreed to the same terms with the governor of Coahuila. In October 1815, Tonkawa chief Cadena (Chain)—successor of Cuernitos and Arocha—arrived in Béxar and assured the Texas governor, Mariano Varela, that his tribe "had reconciled with the Spaniards," and had repented for past actions; he then demonstrated his desire for peace by returning a Spanish captive. Governor Varela accepted Cadena's offer and gave the Tonkawa chief a few gifts in recognition of the treaty agreement.[20]

Within two months of the establishment of peace with Chief Cadena, the Tonkawas, in conjunction with the Lipans, broke the agreement and raided Spanish ranches in Coahuila. Not only did the two tribes realize that the Spaniards could not provide them with any assistance against the Norteños, but also the Apaches and Tonkawas had developed their own trading partnership with Americans in Opelousas and other southwestern Louisiana towns. In December 1815, Lipan and Tonkawa warriors took the horses they stole in Coahuila back to their rancherías near La Bahía, where they held a trade fair with Louisiana merchants, and with Alabama and Coushatta warriors who maintained trade connections east of the Sabine River. Inspired by the prospects of further commerce, in July 1816 the Tonkawas raided La Bahía; they advanced as far as the presidial wall. Spanish troops responded by mounting a campaign against the Lipans and Tonkawas in December 1816 that resulted in the deaths of five Indians. Not intimidated by the Spanish attack, the Tonkawas killed a servant boy near La Bahía, while the Lipans attacked Mission Refugio and took a Karankawa girl prisoner. The two tribes continued aggressively to raid the Spaniards in 1817. In July the Lipans killed two soldiers who were carrying mail from San Antonio to La Bahía. Two months later a band of Tonkawas audaciously entered the presidio at La Bahía and killed three soldiers and wounded six while making off with some horses.[21]

Despite the Spaniards' inability to respond to these attacks, the Tonkawas, continuing to suffer from intensive Norteño attacks, sued for peace. In December 1817, Chief Cadena arrived at San Antonio and entered into negotiations with Governor Martínez. On February 26, 1818, after receiving permission from Commandant General Arredondo, Martínez concluded a treaty with Cadena and his brother, Joyoso, in which the Tonkawa leaders promised to refrain from stealing Spanish stock, as well as agreeing to establish their rancherías on the San Marcos River crossing of the San Antonio Road in order to guard it from invaders from the United States. In return, the Spaniards promised to provide the Tonkawas with presents, trade, and protection from their Wichita and Comanche enemies. Before the treaty could be put into effect, however, Governor Martínez demanded that Cadena return all stolen stock and Spanish captives to Béxar. Cadena responded that his tribe did not have any of the desired items due to a Penateka raid a few days earlier that had netted the attackers all of the Tonkawas' meager possessions. Unsatisfied with this explanation, the Texas governor sent Spanish troops with Chief Cadena to the Tonkawa villages to make sure he was telling the truth. Following a two-week search, Cadena and the Spaniards could not find the Tonkawa rancherías, for attacking Tawakonis had forced the tribe to move elsewhere. In April 1818, a second group of Spanish troops, guided by Joyoso, finally located the Tonkawa villages on the Colorado River crossing of the San Antonio Road and found that they contained no Spanish stock or captives. Joyoso returned to San Antonio with the force, explained the situation to Martínez, and presented the governor with the ears of a Tawakoni warrior the Tonkawas had recently killed in battle. Martínez accepted the Tonkawas' strategic position on the Colorado and announced the treaty to be in effect.[22]

The following month the Tonkawas proved their commitment to the alliance and initiated a policy the tribe would continue to follow for another half century, that of assisting Euroamericans in their battles against other Indians. On May 29, 1818, Chief Cadena arrived in San Antonio with thirty-five warriors and informed Governor Martínez that a party of Penatekas and Tawakonis had gathered just outside of town on Cíbolo Creek. The following day the Tonkawas guided Spanish soldiers and militiamen to the Norteños' camp and launched an attack that resulted in eight Comanche and Tawakoni deaths. The Spaniards and Tonkawas split between them the twenty-six horses and mules captured in the engagement, while the Texas governor gave all the recovered weapons and lances to Chief Cadena in honor of his tribe's participation in the successful battle.[23]

Within a year, however, the Spaniards had grown tired of Cadena's constant trips to San Antonio for, not only did the Tonkawa chief get drunk on his visits, but also his tribesmen killed "the few cows left on the pasture lands of this capital" as they made their way back home. Therefore, in July 1819, Martínez demonstrated his lack of respect for the tribe by gathering a group of visiting Tonkawas together and instructing them to choose a new chief. The leading men accepted the governor's command and named Joyoso as chief of the Tonkawas. Joyoso continued his brother's policy of assisting the Spaniards; in October, he alerted Spanish officials to an assembly of enemy Indians on the Colorado River that was gathering for an attack upon San Antonio. Meanwhile, the Tonkawas defied Governor Martínez in 1820 by moving their rancherías southward to the vicinity of La Bahía, where they made up for the lack of access to buffalo by feeding off Spanish cattle.[24]

In the meantime, El Cojo's band of Lipan Apaches had separated themselves from the Tonkawas and moved northwest of San Antonio to the headwaters of the Guadalupe River to continue their hostilities against the Spaniards. In May 1819, a large band of Lipan warriors attacked Spanish soldiers who were guarding Béxar's presidial horse herd. The Indians "made a long and persistent attack" but were unable to steal any horses. However, the Apaches killed five Spanish troops and two town residents in the raid. Although Governor Martínez sent a mounted force in pursuit, he admitted that the Lipans "swell with pride when they see the small number of troops in this province." The Spanish weakness encouraged further Apache aggression; in early 1820 the Lipans killed two more residents of San Antonio and attacked a small Spanish force on the Frio River, seizing all their horses and killing four soldiers. By summer the continual raids had forced the Spaniards to retaliate. In July a Spanish force of two hundred soldiers—most from Northern Mexico—and fifty militiamen left from La Bahía and discovered the Lipan ranchería on the Guadalupe River. The Spaniards launched a surprise attack early in the morning, killing eight Apaches and forcing the Lipans to abandon their village, which was filled with dried buffalo meat, ammunition, and 257 horses. They also rescued two Spanish children and took into custody three Spaniards who were working for a Louisiana Frenchman who had been trading with the Lipans.[25]

In the wake of the destruction of the Guadalupe River ranchería, a new leader, named Cuelgas de Castro, emerged among the Lipan Apaches. Born in 1762 near the ill-fated mission on the San Saba River, Castro was given his name by the priests stationed there. He was described as "enjoying a good reputation among his own people . . . a man remarkable for his urbanity and his propensity towards civilized life." Unlike El Cojo, Castro desired to make peace with the Euroamericans; however, with Spanish Texas in such disarray, for the time being his band of Lipans simply retreated farther into the Hill Country and remained aloof from the Spaniards and the rest of the tribe.[26]

El Cojo's band of Lipans, in contrast, actually made peace with the Comanches and Wichitas and joined the Norteños in their continued raids. In June 1818, Governor Martínez complained that "not a single day passes without the appearance of large bands of Comanches, Lipanes, [and] Tahuacanos . . . who harass us with the greatest tenacity." Later that summer a combined force of thirty Penatekas and Lipans attacked soldiers and residents of La Bahía who were rounding up mustangs outside of town. The following summer another Comanche-Lipan group killed four soldiers and one citizen in a skirmish near La Bahía. In October 1819, it was reported that a group of Comanches, Lipans, Taovayas, and Tawakonis had joined forces to make a concerted attack on Béxar. The raids continued into 1820 when Lipans, Tawakonis, and Penatekas killed four Bexareños in March. A month later, during Easter week, a group of Tawakonis made a midnight raid upon San Antonio only to meet a sentinel who killed two of them. The Indians responded a few weeks later by slaughtering nine Spanish soldiers in the hills north of San Antonio. Finally, in August 1820, thirty Penatekas attacked Mission Refugio and were met by a force of Karankawas, who killed two of the raiders. The victorious Karankawas took the body of the leading Comanche warrior and celebrated by cutting it into bits.[27]

The Karankawa victory over the Comanches was one of the tribe's few successes in battle with their Indian enemies during this period. In fact, continuous Comanche, Lipan, and Wichita attacks, combined with a tropical storm in September 1818 that destroyed most of the Indian dwellings at Mission Refugio, forced the few Karankawas living at the station to abandon it soon thereafter. The Indians, however, were not very sorry to leave the mission; in 1821, a band of Christianized Karankawas derisively laughed at a Spanish priest who had ventured to the coast to lure them back. By this time, the original five Karankawa tribes had melded into three overlapping groups. The largest combination consisted of about five hundred people—dominated by Carancaguases—who maintained the traditional Karankawan lifestyle, seasonally traversing through the coastal bays and lagoons between Matagorda Bay south to Aransas Bay. Although most of the Carancaguases had never submitted to mission life, they maintained friendly relations with the Spaniards. The Christianized Karankawas consisted of about two hundred Cujanes— who had absorbed the Copanes and Coapites—and a few Carancaguases. This assemblage roamed near Mission Refugio and the coast, often joining with their heathen kinsmen. The Cocos dominated the third group, a few hundred people who continued to maintain a distinct identity among the Karankawas by living farther up the coast between the mouths of the Colorado and Trinity rivers. In 1815, the emigrant tribes of southeastern Texas had forced the Cocos to move south and take refuge near La Bahía. After living off the cattle that grazed between the presidio and Mission Refugio for a few years, by 1821 the Cocos had returned to the coastal region northeast of the Colorado River.[28]

Whether heathen or Christian, all of the Karankawas continued to resist intrusions into their coastal domain, resulting in a few violent incidents between the tribe and American interlopers during the final years of Spanish Texas. The first occurred in 1817 after Louisiana buccaneer Jean Lafitte established a pirate camp on Galveston Island. When a group of Lafitte's men abducted a woman from a nearby band of Cocos, the Indians responded by killing four freebooters. While other Karankawas gathered on the island in preparation to raid the pirate settlement, Lafitte and his men—supported by two cannons—surprised the assemblage and killed thirty Indians, forcing the tribesmen to flee in their canoes to the mainland. This engagement, known as the Battle of Three Trees, resulted in the permanent removal of the Karankawas from Galveston Island. It also led the vengeful Karankawas to kill five American sailors who had shipwrecked on the northern end of Padre Island in May 1821. Later that year, another American group landed on the coast and attacked a band of Carancaguases. On the eve of the American settlement of Texas, the Karankawas had certainly learned to be wary of the numerous people who had already conquered the eastern portion of North America.[29]

A new group of emigrant Indians, already driven from their homes by land-hungry Americans, took advantage of the Spanish weakness in Texas and began to enter the northeastern part of the colony following the War of 1812. In 1817, an American official reported that Lost Prairie—the area between the Sulphur and Red rivers—abounded in game and Indians were "flocking" there and "constantly increasing by emigration from the eastward." Although the various emigrant tribes were attracted by the rich hunting grounds that continued to exist above the Great Raft, all of the Indians were sedentary agriculturalists who, living in close contact with Euroamericans for two centuries, had intermarried with them and had learned the art of husbandry. Among the eastern emigrant tribes that moved to Texas were the Kickapoos, Delawares, and Shawnees, Algonkian speakers originally from Pennsylvania and Ohio. Following the American Revolution the tribes scattered and a few splinter groups crossed the Mississippi and settled in Spanish Upper Louisiana. The Kickapoos moved into the Osage country of Arkansas, while the Delawares and Shawnees settled near the French settlement of Cape Girardeau, Missouri. The Cherokees, of Iroquoian linguistic stock, were emigrants that had originally lived in the southeastern Appalachian highlands. In 1791, the Cherokees

signed a treaty with the United States and began adopting the outward trap-
pings of Western material culture. Some tribal members, however, preferred to
move away from the Americans and, like the Delawares and Shawnees, crossed
the Mississippi and settled along the tributaries of the St. Francis, White, and
Arkansas rivers. Following the Louisiana Purchase, Americans in Missouri
and Arkansas Territories began to crowd these Indians and, after 1815, small
groups of tribal members moved southward to escape the continually growing
pressure of the settlers. By 1817, a couple of hundred Cherokees and Delawares
lived in separate villages on the east bank of the Red River, within the limits of
the United States, between forty and sixty miles upstream from the mouth of
the Sulphur River.[30]

Dehahuit welcomed both tribes; they obtained permission from the caddi
before settling in what was considered Kadohadacho territory. In return, they
showed their hosts great respect. John Fowler, the American trader at Sulphur
Fork Factory, noted that the Kadohadachos are "the oldest tribe of Indians in
this country and are looked up to with a degree of reverence by all the Indians
on Red River." Commander Trimble claimed that the Kadohadachos were
"considered the mother nation of the country and have a general superinten-
dence over all the tribes in the vicinity." A Spanish observer believed that all of
the tribes on the Louisiana-Texas frontier recognized the Kadohadacho chief
"as a superior." In addition to the respect they received, the Kadohadachos
welcomed the emigrant Indians as allies against the ever-hostile Osages. At
first, the Kadohadachos organized many of the war parties against the Osages,
but in the winter of 1819–20, political chief Duwali (or Bowl, as he was called
by Euroamericans) led another one hundred Cherokees into the Lost Prairie
Region. The Cherokees soon began to take the lead in forming war parties
against the Osages, who suffered from many destructive raids. As increasing
numbers of Cherokees and other emigrants continued to settle among both
the Kadohadachos and the Hasinais they threatened the Caddos' superior
position, and tensions between the tribes would increase in the 1820s. In
the meantime, however, Cherokee-led attacks on the Osages combined with
disease to diminish the latter tribe's threatening position in the region.[31]

A new challenge to the Indians of the Near Southwest, however, emerged
in the wake of the Osage demise as, for the very first time, American settlers
from Arkansas moved overland into the Kadohadacho territory above the Great
Raft. Some of these settlers were hunters in search of game; others were small-
scale farmers desirous of the land that had been touted as having "very rich
and productive" soil, well suited to cotton. One man went so far as to claim
that he believed the area not to be "surpassed by any part of the Union."
Although the Great Raft made it extremely difficult to get crops to market,

most observers agreed with Peter Custis, who had stated in 1806 that once the huge logjam was removed, "this country in a very short time would become the Paradise of America," a prime target for cotton planters. As early as 1811 Agent Sibley had reported that a "collection of Bad men and Some women" had settled at Pecan Point on the Red River, upstream from the Coushatta village. These intruders had built cabins and planted corn in addition to "doing great mischief Among the Indians." By 1818 there were twelve families at Pecan Point and twenty others above them at the mouth of the Kiamichi River. The Americans continued to arrive in the region, "flocking there like Doves to the Window." Within five years, 1,500 Americans had settled in the Red River Valley between the mouths of the Sulphur and the Kiamichi, competing with the Indians—emigrants and natives of the region alike—for land and game.[32]

Federal government officials on the scene did nothing to encourage the American settlement of the region, and they also did very little to stop it, particularly in the face of territorial politicians who depended upon these same settlers' votes to secure their office. In addition, since the border with Spain was no longer a pressing issue, the United States did not worry whether or not the settlers' actions alienated the area's Indians. As a result, it was not long before the Americans' aggressive behavior resulted in the outbreak of hostilities and the abandonment of the region by the newly arrived emigrant Indians. In the spring of 1819, the Delawares allowed an American named Music to help them work in the cornfields that they had recently established on the Red River. As soon as the crops were planted, Music "raised a quarrel with the Indians" and, with the assistance of other Americans, drove the Delawares from their village and took possession of the soil. Music sold the valuable river-bottom land soon thereafter. Music and an accomplice named Williams also stole cows, horses, and hogs from the nearby Cherokee village. When a literate mixed-blood Cherokee complained of the Americans' actions to a federal official, Music and Williams seized the man, severely beat him, and threatened him in such a way as to induce him to leave the country and join a different group of Cherokees on the Arkansas River. The Kadohadachos also complained to United States officials that the Americans were destroying game "in the most wanton manner," but nothing was done to dislodge them. In response to the federal government's neglect, the Kadohadachos and the emigrants stole the intruders' horses and ran off their hogs. On one occasion, the Indians seized the settlers' livestock, but an American posse recaptured them following a small skirmish that left one tribesmen dead.[33]

Illicit American traders, though, caused many more problems for the Indians on the Louisiana-Texas frontier than hunters and farmers. Unlike the Frenchmen who had dominated the Texas Indian trade in the eighteenth century, or the American merchants that Agent Sibley had closely supervised following the Louisiana Purchase, the traders who entered the region after 1815 were interested in short-term profits and therefore did not attempt to establish a longstanding relationship with the Indians that was beneficial to both parties. Instead, they sought to illegally divert the natives' commerce from the official United States trading factory and gain as much as they could through the use of alcohol. The traders were characterized as being "generally the most unprincipled men," who only practiced "the most degrading and fraudulent impositions" upon the natives by obtaining "skins with whiskey in the most fraudulent traffic." By 1817, these men had established various trading establishments on the Red River stretching from the Coushatta village upstream to Pecan Point.[34]

The traders wreaked great havoc in the Indian villages by getting the tribesmen drunk and then swindling them out of their goods. The aforementioned Williams, for instance, traded two gallons of cheap whiskey to an inebriated Cherokee for a cow, which he then immediately sold for thirty dollars. Within a short while, other Americans, by constantly supplying the Cherokees with alcohol, had "plundered these Indians" of nearly all their livestock. Cherokee leaders informed Fowler that as a result of the whiskey traders, they had "very little control over their men . . . [and] they have all become very poor and miserable." Kadohadacho chief Dehahuit complained vociferously to Jamison about the damage alcohol was causing his tribe and pressed the agent to remove the illegal traders. As a result, in April 1817, a troop of United States soldiers traveled to Pecan Point and disrupted the trade. The soldiers seized goods worth $5,000, arrested a few men, and chased other American merchants and hunters out of the area.[35]

By the following summer, however, the traders and squatters had returned, even though the official trading post and agency had been moved to the mouth of the Sulphur River in order to better manage the situation. Fowler reported that men were leaving Natchitoches every day with whiskey-filled pirogues to barter with the natives. The Kadohadachos complained to the American officials that these traders, who "almost literally drown that country with whiskey," pursued them "like wolves," cheating them out of their property and destroying game "in the most wasteful manner." Despite the Indians' constant pleas for assistance, Agent Jamison took no further action on the matter, and the illegal whiskey traders continued to ply their destructive wares. Obtaining no assistance from the federal government, in early 1819 the Cherokees warned the Americans that they would be "compelled in self defense, to come to their houses and knock the heads out of their whiskey barrels." When this threat achieved no results, the Cherokees attempted to escape from the traders by moving their village to the opposite bank of the Red River into what their leaders presumed to be Spanish territory in Texas. Unsurprisingly, the alcohol traders simply followed them across the river, seduced the Indians with liquor and "defrauded them of their property."[36]

In desperation, Chief Duwali led the Cherokees west to the Forks of the Trinity River—site of present-day Dallas—in early 1821. After harvesting their crops in the fall, however, the Cherokees returned east and settled in the un-inhabited region north of Nacogdoches. Over the next few years perhaps five hundred Cherokees established farms and ranches along the upper reaches of the Sabine, Neches, and Angelina valleys within thirty miles or so from Nacog-doches. Following the Cherokees' example, the three hundred Delawares abandoned the Lost Prairie region and moved farther up the south bank of the Red River to establish a village in Texas not far from Pecan Point. About four hundred Shawnees soon joined the Delawares in their Red River village, while eight hundred Kickapoos crossed into Texas and settled farther west on the boundary between the Sabine and Trinity watersheds. Thus, by the early 1820s, 2,000 emigrant Indians—more than a few of whom were literate English speakers—had settled in the relatively empty area of northeastern Texas, determined to carve out new lives for themselves based upon farming, stock-raising, and hunting.[37]

The Kadohadachos, threatened by the increased American presence in the region, as well as by the apathetic attitude of the new United States officials—so unlike that of their trustworthy friend, Agent Sibley—turned toward their former Spanish allies in Texas for assistance. Chief Dehahuit had already reopened relations with the Spaniards in 1816 by traveling to San Antonio, in the company of a couple of French traders at Bayou Pierre, Marcel Soto and Andres Valentin, to meet with officials and to renew their former ties. The governor, Ignacio Pérez, welcomed the "Gran Cado," for he was informed that Dehahuit "has a lot of influence with the other [Indian] nations and that he has always manifested his friendship with the Spanish government." As a result of this knowledge, Governor Pérez granted Dehahuit a Spanish colonel's commission upon his arrival. Although the meeting in Béxar went well, Dehahuit and his fellow tribesmen got so "incapacitatingly drunk" on the return trip that the Spanish soldiers accompanying them had to halt the march for a few days so that the Kadohadachos could recover from their hangovers.[38]

By the summer of 1818, Dehahuit had become so disgusted with the Amer-ican intruders and Agent Jamison's lack of response, that he returned to San Antonio to hold an official visit with Texas governor Martínez. Following this meeting, the Kadohadacho caddi returned from Texas believing that he could count on the Spaniards for support. Therefore, in April 1819, Dehahuit traveled to the Sulphur Fork Factory and angrily informed Fowler that all the lands above the Great Raft were his and threatened to drive away every American. Terribly insulted by Dehahuit, Fowler claimed that Kadohadacho chief's hatred of Americans "seems to be invisible [sic]." Put off by Dehahuit's "insolence," Fowler believed it would be wise to appoint a "more useful" chief who would be easier for the Americans to control. If this action was not taken, Fowler recommended cutting off the Kadohadachos' presents and refusing to repair their guns. He believed this would cow the tribe, for they would "soon feel the dependence of the Government, which they appear at present to have no idea of." Agent Jamison agreed with the official trader and felt that Dehahuit should be sent to Washington, for he was "vain, and with his vanity ignorant of our resources." In less than five years, the Americans' behavior following the end of the War of 1812 had turned the Kadohadachos from solid allies of the United States to enraged enemies. [39]

The American officials' outraged response, so at odds with the supportive actions of Agent Sibley, drove the Kadohadachos further into the welcoming arms of the Spaniards in Texas. By the following year the deteriorating relations with the American agents, coupled with the large number of settlers and whiskey traders on their land, caused the Kadohadachos to consider the other emigrants' example of moving to Spanish Texas. In November 1820, the Kadohadachos sent a message to Governor Martínez informing him of their desire to settle in Texas, pledging to assist the Spaniards in their ongoing battles with the Lipan Apaches, Comanches, and Wichitas. In order to prove his worth as a diplomat, in April 1821, Dehahuit arranged for a few lesser-ranked Tawakoni captains to travel to San Antonio and enter into a peace agreement, supposedly in the name of all the Wichita tribes, with the Texas governor. Realizing Dehahuit's importance, Martínez made inquiries as to how much land the Kadohadachos would need in Texas and how they planned to support themselves. Finally, in August 1821, Dehahuit and eighty-three tribal members traveled, along with a couple of French friends from Bayou Pierre, to Monterrey to discuss the move with Commandant General Arredondo. The Kadohadachos impressed the Spaniard, who offered the tribe a tract of land on the Guadalupe River above the San Antonio Road. [40]

As Dehahuit and his followers returned to their villages to consider the offer, events in Mexico radically altered the situation. On August 21, 1821, Agustín de Iturbide, leader of a movement that had been in the making for the past year, forced the Spanish viceroy to sign the Treaty of Córdoba, which recognized the end of Spain's colonial rule of Mexico. The leaders of newly independent Mexico realized that making peace with the Comanches and Apaches—nominally, the only remaining enemy tribes of Texas since the recently celebrated treaty with the Wichitas—should be the first order of business concerning the war-torn northern province. Therefore, the provisional legislative body of Mexico, the Supreme Governing Junta, adopted a report calling for the establishment of commerce and the negotiation of treaties of friendship with the Penatekas and the Lipans.[41]

Believing that the loyal and friendly Kadohadachos were still the most in-fluential Indians in Texas, the Mexican leaders turned toward Chief Dehahuit for assistance in the treaty negotiations with the Comanches and the Apaches. On September 28, 1821, Iturbide sent a letter through Commandant General Arredondo and Governor Martínez to the Kadohadacho chief asking him to gather the leaders of the Comanche and Lipan Apache tribes to visit him in Mexico City. He ordered Arredondo to provide the Kadohadachos with "every-thing they need or ask for" so that when they returned home, "they would tell the other [tribes] about all the many things they will have seen and admired, and that now we are all brothers [who] may live in peace and tranquility." Unfortunately for the Kadohadachos, the delivery of Iturbide's invitation to Dehahuit was long delayed and did not reach the chief until early the following year. Finally, on January 22, 1822, Dehahuit informed Governor Martínez that all his people were scattered on their annual winter hunt and that he could not locate any of the Lipan or Comanche leaders. Therefore, he regretted that he would be unable to travel to the capital until spring. In March Dehahuit sent Martínez yet another message promising to visit Mexico City in the future.[42]

Ultimately, Dehahuit never did make the trip to Mexico. In the mean-time, Richard Fields, the Cherokee war chief—who also handled diplomatic negotiations—took the initiative from the Kadohadachos and began corre-sponding with Mexican authorities. Fields was only one-eighth Cherokee and was married to the daughter of Kadohadacho interpreter François Grappe. Since he could read and write English and Spanish, Fields had an important advantage over Dehahuit and the Kadohadachos, who always depended on outsiders for their correspondence. Taking advantage of Dehahuit's unchar-acteristic hesitation, Fields and twenty-two Cherokees visited San Antonio in November 1822 and, after convincing the new governor of Texas, José Felix Trespalacios, that his tribe could assist in the negotiations with the Comanches and Apaches, concluded an agreement that gave the Cherokees official permis-sion to settle in Texas. Realizing that the treaty was not valid without higher approval, Trespalacios sent Fields on to Mexico City to gain an audience with Iturbide, who had recently been proclaimed emperor. Although the delegation did meet with the new commandant general of the Eastern Interior Provinces, Gaspar López, the Cherokees were unable to see Emperor Iturbide, who had been overthrown and replaced by the Mexican Congress. Despite the fact that the Trespalacios-Fields agreement had not been officially recognized, the Cherokees in Texas acted as if it were in force and took further steps to replace the Kadohadachos as the leading tribe on the Louisiana-Texas frontier. Soon thereafter, the Cherokees formed an alliance with all the emigrant tribes in northeastern Texas. Although the Cherokees never did conclude a treaty with the Lipans or Penatekas, Fields was now able to claim that he spoke for the Delawares, Shawnees, and Kickapoos, as well as for his own people.[43]

In the meantime, in light of the failure to negotiate an agreement with the warring tribes, Commandant General López commissioned a group of Texans, headed by Francisco Ruiz, to seek out the Penatekas and Lipans and offer them peace. The Ruiz commission succeeded first with the Apaches; in a preliminary council in early 1822, a group of Lipan captains agreed to break their alliance with the Comanches and make peace with the Mexican government. Accordingly, in June 1822, the two most important Lipan Apache chiefs, Cuelgas de Castro and El Cojo, traveled to Mexico City and entered into an agreement with a high-ranking official, Anastacio Bustamante, "with the noble object of securing peace and tranquility." Both parties agreed to forget all past transgressions, while the Mexicans promised to secure lands for the Apaches and deliver annual gifts of gunpowder and corn. On their part, Castro and El Cojo promised to return all Tejano captives—thirty-four people the Lipans had kidnapped, as well as another fourteen they had purchased from other tribes—in addition to providing the Mexican government with troops to act as auxiliaries against the Comanches, who had yet to agree to terms.[44]

Achieving peace with the Comanches proved more difficult than with the Apaches. Even before the Ruiz commission could meet with any Penatekas, in September 1821 the ayuntamiento of Béxar had sent a former army officer, Manuel Barrera, along with three other San Antonio residents, onto the plains to negotiate a treaty with the Comanches. At the Tawakoni village on the Brazos, Barrera met with a delegation of Penatekas, headed by the anti-Spanish chief Pisinampe, along with important new leaders, Paruakevitsi and Guonique. Barrera explained that the Spaniards no longer ruled Texas and that the Mexican government desired a settlement. Although the Penateka chiefs were interested in Barrera's offer, they threatened to kill the delegation when the Mexicans failed to deliver any presents. Following Barrera's return to San Antonio, in November 1821, Ruiz and his associates traveled northward and held a council with the three principal Penateka chiefs in front of a gathering of over five thousand Comanche tribal members. As a result of this meeting, the Penatekas agreed to send a chief to San Antonio to negotiate a truce with Mexican officials. It was not until the following summer, however, that Pisinampe led a group of Penatekas to the Texas capital to work out a preliminary settlement. Although the Comanches objected to a provision that all of the Tejano prisoners they held would be surrendered without ransom, they agreed to the terms and signed a truce on August 11, 1822.[45]

From there, Ruiz took a delegation of thirteen Penatekas, headed by Guonique, to Mexico City to sign a formal treaty. Finally, on December 13, 1822, an agreement was reached between Mexico and the Comanches that called for peace and friendship between the two nations, forgetting all that had occurred under the Spanish government. The Comanches promised to return all prisoners, defend the boundaries of Mexico from foreign invasion, and trade only with officials at Béxar. Each Penateka chief would be held responsible for any of their warriors' transgressions. In return, the Mexican government promised to deliver 2,000 pesos worth of gifts to the Comanches.[46]

By the end of 1822, following a decade of almost constant warfare, all of the Indian tribes of Texas were nominally at peace with the newly independent nation of Mexico. In addition to Mexico breaking free from Spain, great changes had occurred in Texas and the Near Southwest since 1810. Euroamerican control of Texas had become almost nonexistent, and the Indians maintained the dominant position they had enjoyed since the colony's founding a century before. Spanish weakness had encouraged new emigrant tribes to settle in northeastern Texas, and the Indians who had recently moved to southeastern Texas set down even firmer roots in the Trinity and Neches valleys. Meanwhile, the United States' success in the War of 1812 and afterward assured its superior position in the Near Southwest. As a result, American settlers flocked to the region, putting immense pressure on the Indians of the Louisiana-Texas frontier. Unfortunately for all of the tribes of the region, the example set by land-hungry Americans in Louisiana and Arkansas would be extended to Texas in the following decade, demonstrating the worthlessness of the various treaties with Mexico and threatening many of the Indians' very existence.

5. Destruction

The Indians, Mexican Texas, and
the American Intrusion, 1823 to 1835

Suddenly and dramatically the Indians' domination of Texas and the Near Southwest came to an end during the decade that followed the formation of the Mexican republic in 1823. In an attempt to develop the province of Texas, Mexican officials opened up the region to colonists from the United States. As a result, the Euroamericans in Texas came to outnumber the Indians for the first time. Most of the newcomers, like the Americans that flooded into the Red River Valley following the Louisiana Purchase, were more interested in making a profit from agriculture than from trading with the Indians or converting them to Christianity. Although the Americans in Texas would develop various strategies for dealing with the different tribes depending on the time and situation that arose, they ultimately desired the land and were determined to drive the Indians from it. This determination, combined with the Indians' tendency to help themselves to the settlers' livestock, quickly led to the outbreak of violence between the newcomers and the natives. With the assistance of Mexican troops and emigrant Indians—who were also desirous of establishing their claims to lands in Texas—the Americans would drive many of the province's Indians from the homes in which they had been so secure just a few years before. At the same time, the few remaining Indians in Louisiana would be forced by the overwhelming numbers of Americans, and the new Indian policy of the United States, to abandon the state to seek refuge in Mexican Texas. Unfortunately for them, by 1835 the newly arrived Americans would dominate the Indian and Tejano residents of Texas to such an extent that they began to contemplate breaking the province free from Mexican control altogether.

Following the overthrow of Emperor Iturbide in early 1823, the liberals who dominated Mexican politics implemented new policies that affected the Euroamerican and Indian inhabitants of Texas in various ways. Even as delegates from throughout Mexico met to promulgate a new constitution, the liberals in charge of the Mexican Congress issued decrees that reflected their beliefs. The Mexican liberals eagerly hoped to promote progress in the new independent nation by making a clean break with the colonial past, which they considered backward, unenlightened, and inefficient. Therefore, the new leaders followed liberal political theory and declared that all Mexicans were equal before the law, ending the legal distinctions between Indians, Spaniards, and mestizos that had been maintained during the colonial era. While this high-minded ideal impacted the Texas Indians only minimally, the liberal desire to reduce the powers of the Catholic Church did affect the Karankawas who occasionally visited Mission Refugio. In 1823, the federal government put forth the order to secularize the few remaining missions of Texas. The two Franciscan priests in Texas were able to stave off the final secularization of the missions at La Bahía (renamed Goliad in 1829) and Refugio until 1830, but the friar in charge of the Refugio station left it the year following the order to take up residence with his colleague at La Bahía. For all intents and purposes, the attempt to convert the Karankawas to Christianity at Mission Refugio was finally abandoned after thirty years of effort.[1]

Other liberal ideas that indirectly affected Texas tribes were included in the Mexican constitution, which was finally approved in October 1824. The Constitution of 1824 provided Mexico with a federalist form of government that permitted considerable regional autonomy and left the central government relatively weak. In the new arrangement, underpopulated Texas was joined with the more developed province to the south to form the state of Coahuila y Texas, with its capital at Saltillo. During the first years under the 1824 Constitution, all of Texas from the Nueces to the Sabine constituted a single Department of Béxar with a political chief responsible to the state's governor. Eventually, the need for more effective administration caused the state to create the District of Nacogdoches in 1831 and the Department of Brazos in 1834. These divisions increased local autonomy to some extent because each department was governed by its own political chief. As a result, local authorities were often able to deal with the Indians of Coahuila y Texas according to their own interests, free from the outside interference that had occasionally hamstrung actions in the past. More often than not, this freedom of action had detrimental consequences for the Indians of Texas.[2]

One of the most important features of the liberals' program, and the one that had the greatest impact on the region's tribes, pertained to the economy. In an attempt to promote economic development, Mexican liberals did away with the restrictive, mercantilist trading policies maintained under Spanish rule and implemented an open system of free trade, designed to foster commercial relations with the United States. Realizing that Texas would not profit from this liberal system of trade without settlers, the Mexican government and the state of Coahuila y Texas passed a series of colonization laws in the 1820s designed to promote American immigration into the relatively empty province. These laws allowed foreigners to purchase as much as 4,500 acres of land at much lower prices than could be found in the United States. Americans eager to obtain title to Mexican land generally did so under the auspices of immigration agents, known as *empresarios*, and formed part of a colony. Under Mexican law, an empresario served as an agent for the government, selecting colonists, allocating lands, and enforcing regulations in return for huge amounts of territory. Although lands contracted to empresarios quickly covered nearly all of Texas, most empresarial contracts went unfulfilled before 1830.[3]

Despite the failure of most of the empresarios, the liberal Mexican land policy caused the Euroamerican population in Texas to rise remarkably in the 1820s and 1830s. This population growth threatened the dominant position the region's Indians had enjoyed since the Spanish had established the colony over a century before. At the beginning of the 1820s, the 17,000 or so Indians who lived in Texas outnumbered the Euroamericans—most of whom were Tejanos—by eight and a half times. By 1828, however, the Euroamerican population of Texas had tripled in size from 2,000 to 6,000 people, mainly due to emigration from the United States. Over the next six years, American settlement expanded to the point that the 20,000 Euroamericans living in Texas in 1834 outnumbered the increasingly dwindling Indian population for the first time.[4]

The Euroamerican population explosion, however, was very uneven because most of the increase took place in coastal and east Texas. Therefore, the 5,000 Penateka Comanches and 1,000 Lipan Apaches maintained a numerical advantage over the Tejanos they came into contact with at San Antonio and Goliad. San Antonio's population remained steady at about 1,500 residents throughout the 1820s. In the early part of the following decade, though, Béxar increased to about 2,400 people. Goliad's population grew at a similar rate, rising from about five hundred residents to 650 by 1828, finally reaching seven hundred people in 1834. The relatively slow-growing Tejano population did not threaten the dominant position of the Penatekas and Lipans, who continued to range freely through central Texas between the Rio Grande and the Brazos River. In fact, the shift from Spanish to Mexican control did nothing to enhance the military strength of Texas as the amount of soldiers stationed in San Antonio and Goliad fell from two hundred men to fewer than sixty.[5]

As a result, relations between the Penateka Comanches, Lipan Apaches, and the Tejanos changed little from the pattern of intermittent warfare that had been established at the end of the previous century. The Comanches still maintained relations with American traders on the Red River, who were eager to exchange metal goods for stolen Tejano horses. However, for the first couple

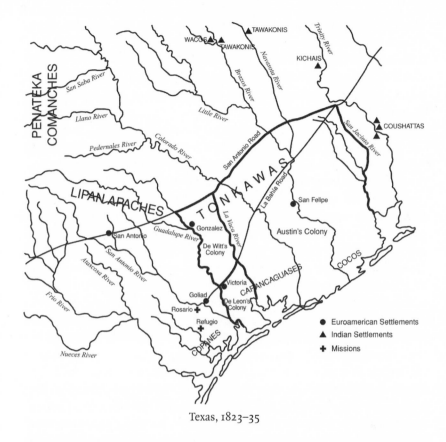

Texts, 1823–35

of years after entering into the agreement of December 1822, Penateka leaders strove to keep the peace with the Mexicans in Coahuila y Texas as they awaited the payment of the 2,000 pesos worth of goods that had been promised in the treaty. In August 1823, Chief Paruakevitsi visited Mexican officials in San Antonio to complain about the lack of gifts. Receiving no presents, young Comanche warriors made raids upon Tejano ranches between Béxar and Goliad in early 1824. Only after Coahuila y Texas governor Rafael González warned that the lack of gifts threatened a "total breakdown of peace," did the Mexican government forward the money to purchase presents for the Comanches. In response, beginning in the fall of 1824 a procession of Comanche leaders visited Mexican officials to celebrate the peace. In October, Ysachene, "one of the principal chiefs," led ten other headmen and warriors to Béxar to obtain presents; Mexican officials welcomed the Comanche dignitaries with a three-gun salute. In February 1825, a Penateka headman named Joyoso visited Monclova and received a Mexican flag as a personal gift from the president of the republic, as well other presents and a military escort to the presidio at Rio Grande. The following month Governor González awarded several visiting Comanche chiefs with officer's commissions in the militia.[6]

Despite the outward appearance of amicable relations, Comanche warriors initiated full-scale attacks in Coahuila y Texas within six months of the first distribution of the gifts. Beginning in March 1825, Penatekas stole horses and mules from herds on both sides of the Rio Grande as well as from Béxar and Goliad. In June, Ysachene and Joyoso traveled to San Antonio with a large contingent of Penatekas. Unhappy with the small amount of gifts they received and filled with bravado due to the insufficient number of Mexican soldiers, the Penatekas brazenly entered people's houses and took whatever they desired. In August, Joyoso returned to San Antonio with a small party intent on robbing horses, but a Mexican troop captured him and another warrior, as well as two women and a boy, while killing two Comanches. Ysachene traveled to Béxar and tried to negotiate for their release, but Mexican officials rebuffed the attempt. As a result, Penateka raids continued in the fall of 1825 as warriors centered their attentions on Goliad and the Rio Grande area.[7]

The Mexicans responded to these actions by planning a military expedition against the Comanches. The Mexican forces called upon their Lipan Apache allies who, for the most part, had maintained the peace since agreeing to lay down their arms in June 1822. The Lipans had, however, resumed their hostilities against the Comanches; in addition to other skirmishes, in June 1824 members of both tribes clashed outside the walls of Mission San Juan in San Antonio. Therefore, in September 1825 the Lipans eagerly answered the Mexicans' call for assistance, and fourteen Apache warriors joined with troops from Goliad to pursue Penateka horse thieves. The following month, and again in December, Lipan warriors aided Mexican troops from the Presidio del Rio Grande in operations against the Comanches. In the December campaign the Mexicans and Apaches attacked a Comanche camp in Tamaulipas, killing nine warriors and recovering 125 horses along with a kidnapped Mexican prisoner. As a result of these actions, Comanche raids in Coahuila y Texas tapered off over the next few years. In return for his assistance, the Mexican government rewarded Lipan chief Cuelgas de Castro with a lieutenant colonel's commission and a salary. Mexican officials also supplied their Apache allies with adequate amounts of arms and ammunition to continue the struggle against the Penatekas.[8]

While the new policies of independent Mexico had little effect upon the relations between the Tejanos, Comanches, and Apaches, the empresarial grants located between Galveston Bay and Corpus Christi Bay had a great impact on the Indians of the area. Stephen F. Austin, the earliest and most successful of all the empresarios, established the first American colony on the lower Brazos River in late 1821. Although most of the colonists did not arrive until 1823, by the following year Austin had fulfilled his contract by bringing three hundred families into Texas. He subsequently obtained three more contracts from the state government to import nine hundred more families, and he substantially filled each of those as well. By 1828 about three thousand people resided within Austin's colony. With its major settlement at San Felipe de Austin on the Brazos River, Austin's colony covered an immense expanse of land, bordered by the San Antonio Road on the north, the Gulf of Mexico on the south, the San Jacinto River on the east, and the Lavaca River to the west. Bordering Austin's lands on the west, between the Guadalupe and Lavaca rivers, lay Green De-Witt's colony, founded in 1825 with its principal settlement at Gonzales. Less accomplished than Austin, DeWitt procured titles for only a third of the four hundred families he had contracted to settle in Texas. By 1828, fewer than one hundred Americans lived in DeWitt's colony. Martín de León, a rancher from Tamaulipas, established a colony at the same time as DeWitt containing about one hundred Mexican citizens. Situated between DeWitt's colony and the coast, and to the southwest of Austin's grant, de León's colony centered at the town of Victoria, located on the east bank of the Guadalupe River about sixty miles downstream from Gonzales.[9]

Despite the arrival of 3,200 or so Euroamericans in the 1820s, the 4,200 Indians directly affected by the immigrants still outnumbered the new arrivals by the end of the decade. About one thousand Karankawas lived along the coast, directly within the confines of the three empresarial grants. The Cocos, living between Galveston Bay and the Colorado River, roamed through the coastal heartland of Austin's colony. The Carancaguases also moved about in all three colonies, in the lowlands around Matagorda Bay and San Antonio Bay, while the Cujanes, living south of the San Antonio River, overlapped with de León's colony. About 1,500 Tonkawas lived farther inland, along the upper reaches of the Austin and DeWitt grants between the Brazos and the Guadalupe rivers. Although the Brazos and Trinity river villages of the 1,700 Wacos, Tawakonis, and Kichais were located more than one hundred miles above the colonies of Austin and DeWitt, these three Wichita tribes were also greatly impacted by the newcomers. The Euroamerican immigrants made much less of an impression upon the other Wichita tribe, the Taovayas, whose 2,000 members lived far above their kinsmen on the Brazos and Red rivers.[10]

The tribes outnumbered the three colonies' settlers throughout the 1820s, but most of the newcomers were Americans who saw Indians in a very different light from the Spanish-era colonists of Texas. Unlike the Tejanos, a majority of the American settlers were not accustomed to Indians living in their midst.

Most of the Americans were southerners who brought with them the attitudes and beliefs of their original homeland; they were Protestants interested in expanding the same culture, based on slavery and cotton, that had rapidly spread across the South following the War of 1812. This expansion had been carried out at the expense of the region's Indians, many of whom had relinquished their lands in the South under the threat of force. Most of the newcomers were commercially minded capitalists who hoped to turn a profit by exporting Texas goods to the United States. For most of the colonists, this meant tapping into the ranching culture that already existed between San Antonio and the coast. As a result of their efforts, by the late 1820s Texas ranchers were shipping large amounts of beef, hides, and tallow to New Orleans. Used to having their way with Indians, the Americans in Texas were not about to tolerate the livestock raids that the Tejanos had often taken for granted. The Americans in Austin's colony also engaged in the highly remunerative practice of cotton production. Establishing plantations in the rich bottomlands of the lower Brazos and Colorado rivers, planters in Austin's colony soon began to export thousands of bales of cotton per year to New Orleans. In addition to developing the commercial promise of Texas, the newly arrived immigrants established the first ports along the coast to facilitate travel and trade. Austin's colony took the lead in this area since many of the settlers arrived by ship, and the export-based economy progressed faster there than anywhere else in Texas. By the early 1830s, two ports had been established in Austin's colony: Matagorda, at the mouth of the Colorado River, and Brazoria, near the mouth of the Brazos.[11]

The chaos of Mexican politics in the mid-1820s left Empresario Austin virtually in charge of dealing with the Indians in the region until 1827. Primarily concerned with the success of his own colony, Austin ably pursued a pragmatic policy in dealing with the Karankawas, Tonkawas, and Wichitas who lived in the area. He measured each tribe's strengths, weaknesses, and lifestyles, coupled that knowledge with the situation of his own settlers, and attempted to deal with the Indians in a manner that would prove most beneficial to his empresarial grant. Ultimately, Austin wisely adopted a different policy for each tribe. In the same manner, Karankawa, Tonkawa, and Wichita tribesmen formed their own strategies about how to deal with the three new colonies that appeared in their midst in the 1820s. Unfortunately for all three of the tribes, the end result was disaster.[12]

Austin developed many of his ideas concerning the three tribes during a fact-finding expedition to Texas that he undertook in the summer and fall of 1821 in preparation for the establishment of his colony. Traveling with local Texas officials, Austin learned much about the Indian situation in the region through conversations with Tejanos and by meeting representatives of the various tribes. Austin was most interested in the Karankawas, since his colony lay directly in the territory of the Cocos and the Carancaguases. While the Karankawas were certainly wary of the Americans due to the recent outbreaks of violence between the two groups, a band of Cocos warmly greeted Austin and his party as they scouted the region around the mouth of the Colorado River in September. The empresario distributed a small amount of gifts to the Cocos, but Austin quickly came to believe that coexistence with the Karankawas would be impossible. He had no intention of sharing his lands with the tribe and understood that the Karankawas had nothing valuable to trade to the Americans. He also had no desire to convert the tribesmen to Christianity or to allow them to poach from his colony's cattle herds. On their part, the nomadic Karankawas lived by exploiting their littoral environment to the fullest. Thus, they had always jealously guarded the beaches, lagoons, and river mouths from outside intruders, realizing that survival depended upon their complete control of the region. Austin understood that the huge numbers of Americans he hoped to settle in his colony would challenge the Karankawas' domination of the area and lead to hostilities. Therefore, the empresario subsequently warned his colonists that the Karankawas "may be called universal enemies to man," and stated that they killed all Euroamericans that came into their territory. He added, without any evidence, that the Karankawas were cannibals who "frequently feast on the bodies of their victims." Austin prophesized that the approach of an "American population will be the signal of their extermination for there will be no way of subduing them but extermination." This attitude, shared by most of the colonists, ultimately led to the outbreak of violence between the Americans and the Karankawas, resulting in the full realization of Austin's prediction concerning the tribe's disappearance.[13]

The first encounter between the Karankawas and the newcomers following Austin's scouting expedition occurred in June 1822, when a group of American colonists landed at the mouth of the Colorado River and encountered a Carancaguase party picking berries nearby. The Indians informed the Americans that they were intruding upon Karankawa territory and asked for provisions as a form of payment. The suspicious settlers angrily denied the request; one American told the Carancaguases that Austin would give them something later, while another aggressively shoved the gathering tribesmen out of the way. The Carancaguases responded by threatening the settlers, who drew their weapons and forced the Indians to retire. A few days later the Americans moved inland, leaving their provisions in a warehouse with a few men to protect it. Soon thereafter the Karankawas killed the guards and took the supplies.[14]

The Karankawas continued to poach from the Americans without retribution until February 1823, when some Cocos killed two colonists who had tried to prevent them from stealing a corn-filled pirogue. The Americans immediately responded by raising a company of twenty-five men, who soon located a Karankawa camp on Skull Creek. The colonists attacked the village without warning and killed nearly twenty tribal members before the Karankawas took flight. After scalping the victims, the Americans ate the food and gathered the possessions of the people they had just driven from their homes. One of the participants in the engagement justified his brutality by depicting the Karankawas as an "exceedingly fierce and warlike tribe, and also they are perfect cannibals." Another claimed that the Karankawas were "ungainly and repugnant, their cannibalism being beyond question." Although tensions continued to exist between the Karankawas and the Americans through the rest of the year, the lack of men in Austin's colony caused the settlers to hesitate before making another attack.[15]

At the same time the Americans initiated warfare against the Karankawas, the settlers laid the foundation for an alliance with the Tonkawas. The empresario had encountered a few starving Tonkawas on his 1821 trip to Texas and had dismissed them as "great beggars," who would not threaten American settlement of the region. Austin did learn, however, that the Spaniards had recently begun to manage the Tonkawas somewhat through the distribution of trade goods, and had formed a military alliance with them aimed at the Comanches and Wichitas. Although Austin did not meet any Wichitas on his scouting expedition, Texas officials informed him that the Wacos and Tawakonis living on the Brazos River constantly stole livestock from ranches at Béxar and Goliad to exchange with American traders. Realizing that his colony was closer to the Wichita villages than the Tejano establishments, Austin sought to develop a relationship with the Tonkawas similar to the one the Spaniards had established in 1818. The Tonkawas responded favorably to the entreaties of the Americans, who were wealthier and more dependable than the Spaniards had ever been. One of the Tonkawa leaders, Carita (Little Face), established an especially close friendship with Austin in early 1822. Carita began to act as a middleman in trade between the colonists and the Tonkawas, providing the newcomers with horses and deerskins in return for metal goods, firearms, and ammunition. Carita also turned to the empresario for help after the Wacos raided a Tonkawa ranchería, killing thirty women and children. In response, a few of Austin's colonists joined the Tonkawas in pursuit of the raiders. The combined force tracked the Wacos to the Trinity River, where they launched a successful attack that killed forty tribesmen.[16]

Despite the burgeoning friendship with the Americans, the hungry Tonkawas could not help but be tempted by the colonists' livestock. In the summer of 1823, Tonkawas from Sandía's and Carita's rancherías stole horses, cattle, and pigs from various settlers on the Colorado and Brazos rivers. Wishing to avoid an all-out war with the Tonkawas, Austin sent an embassy to Sandía (Watermelon) to demand the return of the livestock. Instead of complying with the order, one group of Tonkawa warriors raided settlements along the Brazos and forced the setters to give them corn. Another Tonkawa party stole horses from other colonists' ranches. Outraged, Austin surprised the Tonkawas by leading a party of Americans to Carita's ranchería on the Brazos. Instead of attacking the Tonkawas as the settlers had done with the Karankawas, Austin chose only to punish the tribe and to demonstrate his dominance over them. The empresario forced Carita to return the horses and to point out the five young men who had committed the theft. Austin then ordered the Tonkawa chief to "inflict with his own hands . . . a severe lashing on the marauders," and warned Carita that, in case of further thefts, he would have the culprits shot.[17]

Despite the threat, in April 1824 a group of Tonkawas raided Colorado River settlements below the Atascosito Road and stole about twenty hogs and a large quantity of corn. A small American party tried to arrest the thieves after tracking them to a nearby ranchería, but the Tonkawa men took up their arms and refused to give up their kinsmen. Hearing this news, Austin summoned Carita and negotiated a treaty with the chief that officially tied the Tonkawas to the Americans once and for all. In return for annual gifts of food, trade goods, and arms, the Tonkawas agreed to remain above the American settlements and act as auxiliaries against the colonists' enemies. Carita also consented to Austin's demands concerning future thefts; if a Tonkawa warrior stole from the Americans, the leaders would be forced to turn the culprit over to be whipped or have his head shaved. If not, the Americans reserved the right to find the thieves and shoot them. Following the signing of the agreement, most of the Tonkawas moved even farther up the Colorado and the Brazos to distance themselves from Austin's colony. Sandía, however, chose to abandon the area altogether and moved his ranchería west to the San Marcos River, where the Tonkawas joined with El Cojo's band of Lipan Apaches. Other tribal leaders continued to honor the treaty following Carita's death in 1825, allowing American colonists to punish Tonkawa thieves after they had poached livestock from the settlers' farms. On his part, the empresario maintained the relationship by distributing gifts to the Tonkawas; on one occasion, Austin even indemnified the tribe after he ruled that an American settler had unjustly killed a Tonkawa warrior. Austin also presented the tribesmen with seed corn and faming implements in an attempt to convince the Tonkawas to become sedentary agriculturalists. The Tonkawas, however, refused to change their nomadic ways and simply ate the seed corn.[18]

The friendship of the Tonkawas, coupled with the arrival of more colonists in 1823, allowed Austin to take an even more aggressive stance with the Karankawas. The empresario encouraged the Coushattas, Alabamas, and Yowani Choctaws living on the Trinity and the Neches rivers to attack the Cocos in return for powder and lead. The emigrant Indians were not as commercially minded as the Americans, but like the colonists they hated the Cocos for poaching from their herds. Austin instructed his colonists to "cultivate the most friendly understanding with the Coushatta and Choctaw Indians . . . and inform them that the Americans consider them as their brothers." As a result of the agreement with the empresario, in October 1823 the emigrant Indians attacked a party of Cocos, and killed the chief, his son, and three other tribal members. Austin also requested and received from Mexican officials a troop of soldiers to patrol the mouth of the Colorado River. When this unit proved insufficient to contain the Karankawas, in December 1823 Austin authorized the formation of a militia detachment. The empresario granted wide powers to the militia commander, allowing him to "make war against the Karankawas and to raise men and attack or pursue any party of said Indians that may appear on the coast or on the river . . . according to his discretion without waiting for orders" from his superiors.[19]

Now assured of their strength, in 1824 the Americans determined to remove the Karankawas from the area altogether and began attacking members of the Carancaguase and Coco tribes at every meeting. Early in the year the Americans permanently drove the Cocos from the Brazos Valley by assaulting a village just upstream from the river's mouth, destroying the camp and killing seven tribal members. In April the colonists encountered the retreating Cocos near the mouth of the Colorado River and severely wounded a warrior before the Indians fled to the safety of a cane break. The following month Austin sent an embassy to meet with a Karankawa leader near Goliad. Austin's spokesmen demanded that all of the Carancaguases and Cocos move from the colony and resettle with their Cujane kinsmen near the abandoned Mission Refugio. The embassy informed them that the Americans would consider "as enemies" any Karankawas they encountered east of the Guadalupe River.[20]

Neither the Carancaguases nor the Cocos accepted Austin's unilateral demand that they abandon their homeland. Instead, various bands remained within the colony, feeding off the Americans' cattle, which roamed between the Lavaca and the Colorado rivers. Unsurprisingly, violence broke out between the Americans and the Karankawas within a month of Austin's warning. In June 1824, a colonist surprised a group of Carancaguases on his Colorado River ranch as they were butchering a cow they had just killed. The local militia responded and shot one of the men as the Indians fled the scene. The militiamen followed the Carancaguases to a village near the river's mouth and launched an attack that killed another five men. In August the Americans discovered fifty Coco and Carancaguase warriors gathered on the Colorado preparing to make a retaliatory assault. In response, Austin himself raised about one hundred men and set out in search of the Karankawas, who fled in advance of the American force to take refuge with the Franciscan priests near Goliad. When Austin's troops were only a few miles from Goliad, the priest formerly in charge of Mission Refugio, Fray Miguel Muro, intervened on behalf of the Karankawas who had sought his protection. On September 22, as a result of Muro's mediation, Austin and Carancaguase chief Antonio signed a treaty in which the Karankawas agreed to abandon their homelands and remain west of the Guadalupe River in return for an end to attacks by the colonists. However, when the terms of the treaty were transmitted to some Carancaguases who had not been a party to the agreement, they asked that the boundary line be moved east to the Lavaca River—the southern boundary of Austin's colony—so as to regain access to their hunting and fishing grounds on Matagorda Bay. Claiming that his desire "was to guarantee a secure and permanent peace with the Indians," the empresario acquiesced and granted the Carancaguase request. [21]

Within a few months a few Cocos defied the agreement and returned to the region near the mouth of the Colorado River. By September 1825, continuing Coco stock raids had angered the Americans so much that Austin instructed the militia in that section "to pursue and kill all those Indians wherever they are found." The empresario's declaration of war initiated a series of attacks by the settlers that ultimately drove the Cocos from the colony. Following a few skirmishes between the Indians and the Americans, a large force of colonists trapped a Coco band near the mouth of the Colorado River in early 1826. In the ensuing battle, known as the Dressing Point Massacre, the Americans drove the Karankawas into the water, shooting and killing scores of men, women, and children as they attempted to swim across the river and climb the steep bank on the other side. Following this massacre the few surviving Cocos abandoned Austin's colony once and for all and joined the remaining Cujanes and Carancaguases west of the Lavaca River. [22]

The Karankawas unsuccessfully sought refuge near Goliad, as well as in the recently established colonies of de León and Dewitt. Hunger forced the

Karankawas to poach from the settlers' cattle herds, leading to the outbreak of hostilities between the Indians and the Euroamericans, who pursued the Indians just as vigorously as the settlers of Austin's colony. In desperation, Carancaguase chief Antonio asked Fray Muro to intervene on his people's behalf once more. As a result, on May 13, 1827, the Karankawas, along with the Franciscan priest, met with Mexican officials and representatives of the three empresarios in Victoria. In the ensuing treaty, the Karankawas agreed to retreat west of the Guadalupe River in return for a cession of hostilities on the part of the Americans and the Mexicans. In little more than five years, the Karankawas had been pushed off their ancestral lands between Galveston Bay and Matagorda Bay.[23]

Although Austin had chosen to go to war with the Karankawas and to develop an alliance with the Tonkawas, he followed a more cautious policy with the powerful Wichitas. Waco and Tawakoni warriors began stealing livestock from Austin's colony soon after its establishment, but did not kill any settlers until July 1823. The empresario responded prudently, stating that since the colony did not have enough men to deal with the Wichitas as well as with the Karankawas and Tonkawas, he wished "to avoid an open rupture with them for six months longer at least, by that time we shall have more strength." The following month a party of Indians "supposed to be Wacos," ventured near the settlements on the Colorado River, and Austin sent two men to collect information on the tribe. The empresario instructed the men to "treat them friendly" but also to warn the Wacos of the consequences of war. In addition, he took steps to prepare for battle by sending an emissary to the Alabama and Coushatta villages in the winter of 1823 to make arrangements for the emigrant Indians to join the colonists, if necessary, in an expedition designed to "sweep every [Tawakoni] . . . from the face of the earth.[24]

The Wacos and Tawakonis felt Austin's pressure and sent peace overtures to the Americans in the spring of 1824. In March a party of nearly two hundred Wacos and Tawakonis came to the Colorado settlements and made it clear to the colonists that they had not come to "scear [sic] the Americans from their Houses but wanted to be friendly with them." The Indians held a talk with the settlers in which they "professed every act of friendship possible towards the Americans." In response to the Waco and Tawakoni peace offer, Austin appointed Thomas Duke and William Selkirk as commissioners with the power to negotiate a treaty with the Indians. The two men traveled to the Waco village in June 1824 and met with the leaders. The commissioners, following Austin's instructions, pledged that the Americans would not attack the Indians if the Wacos agreed not to disturb the settlers of the colony. Duke and Selkirk, though, warned the Wacos that the "Americans are like the leaves on the trees—they are all good warriors—and well armed," but that, although they are always ready for war, "they prefer peace for they wish to be friends and brothers with all the Indians of this province." The Wacos responded by stating that they had not killed any Americans or stolen any livestock, despite the fact that the commissioners saw a great number of horses with familiar brands in the village. However, in accordance with Austin's peaceful intentions, the men chose not to push the matter of the stolen livestock and left the Waco village a few days later after smoking a peace pipe with the Indians. The commissioners believed they had made their point to the Wacos—that the Americans were willing and able to go to war—and Austin later reported that "the Indians are now beginning to fear us."[25]

Austin was greatly mistaken, for Wichita warriors intensified their assaults upon Texas the following year, leading to war with the colony. In the summer of 1825, Taovaya, Tawakoni, and Waco warriors combined with the Penateka Comanches to make raids upon San Antonio and Goliad. In April 1826, militiamen from Austin's colony joined Tonkawa and Lipan warriors to pursue a Tawakoni-Kichai raiding party that passed near the American settlements on the Colorado River. The Americans and their Indian allies attacked the Tawakonis and Kichais fifteen miles below the La Bahía Road and killed eight warriors. Austin followed up this victory by ordering Captain Aylett C. Buckner and 190 volunteers to assault the Wacos and Tawakonis in their Brazos River villages. Learning of the approaching force, the Indians abandoned their towns before Buckner's arrival. Soon thereafter, however, Waco and Tawakoni warriors raided Gonzales and San Antonio. In February 1827, the Wacos joined with a large band of Penatekas to overwhelm the Lipans and Tonkawas on the San Marcos River, nine miles above Gonzales. The attackers not only killed many of their enemies, they had also made off with six hundred horses.[26]

At the same time the Wichitas were engaged in hostilities, events were taking place in east Texas that would have long-lasting consequences for all of the province's Indians. As in coastal Texas, Mexican land policies promoted American immigration into the region, leading to conflicts with the Indians of the area, as well as with the resident Tejanos. Ultimately, a few newcomers staged a failed rebellion, leading Mexican authorities to question the effects their liberal policies were having on Coahuila y Texas. At the beginning of the 1820s, no more than one hundred Tejanos resided in or around Nacogdoches. In 1825, the Mexican government granted empresarial contracts to two Americans, Haden Edwards and Frost Thorn, to settle 1,200 families on lands covering most of northeastern Texas, including Nacogdoches. Within a few years, three other empresarios had received approval to establish colonies south of the Edwards and Thorn grants all the way to the coast, between the

Trinity and the Sabine. None of the empresarios came close to fulfilling their contracts and their grants were soon nullified, yet they did induce many Americans to cross the border and settle in Texas. By 1828, almost seven hundred Euroamericans lived in east Texas, mainly near Nacogdoches.[27]

Although the 4,250 Indians in east Texas easily outnumbered the newly arrived settlers, most of the tribesmen now found themselves living on lands allocated to the various empresarios. About two thousand emigrant Indians—Cherokees, Shawnees, Delawares, and Kickapoos—lived in farms and ranches northwest of Nacogdoches, within the confines of the Thorn and Edwards grants, as did the 650 native Caddos—Hainais, Nabedaches, Nacogdoches, and Nadacos—who lived in fixed villages in the Neches and Sabine valleys. Perhaps 1,300 members of emigrant tribes—Alabamas, Coushattas, Biloxis, and Yowani Choctaws—resided in southeastern Texas, along with the three hundred or so Aises and Bidais, on lands granted to empresarios between the Trinity and the Neches rivers.[28]

Therefore, the main desire of the east Texas Indians was to ensure the possession of their lands. In October 1824, even before the Mexican government had given contracts to the American empresarios, the Shawnees living near Pecan Point took advantage of the new liberal laws to petition Mexican authorities for an official grant of land. As a result, on December 24, 1824, they drew up a temporary contract with Governor González in which he authorized the legislature of Coahuila y Texas to provide each Shawnee family with one square mile of land along the south bank of the Red River. Although the Shawnee petition was tentatively approved by the state's congress, Governor González requested that the national government make a final determination. In April 1825, the federal government approved the Shawnee petition to settle in Texas while not specifically authorizing a grant of land or establishing any boundaries for the tribe. The edict only directed the Shawnees to settle along the Red River within fifty miles of the border with the United States.[29]

Although the Shawnees had received official permission to settle in Texas, the Edwards and Thorn empresarial grants of 1825 threatened the agreement the Cherokees had made with Governor Trespalacios three years before. Instead of asking the Mexican government for a land grant according to the edicts of the various colonization laws, though, Cherokee chief Fields believed that he could secure his tribe's rights to land in Coahuila y Texas by providing the Euroamericans with military assistance in the war that had recently broken out with the Comanches and Wichitas. Therefore, Fields attempted to unite all the emigrant tribes of east Texas in an alliance directed against the Norteños. While most tribes agreed to Fields's proposals, many non-Indians mistakenly feared that the Cherokees were forming a combination aimed at the two American empresarios. Hoping to avoid an outbreak of war that might spill over to his own colony, Austin wrote the political chief of Texas, José Antonio Saucedo, encouraging him to accommodate the emigrants and to provide them with secure land grants. The empresario realized that Fields was "discontented . . . he says that the government gave him the lands, but now he has understood that the land where he lives is designated to be colonized in Hayden Edwards' colony . . . I think it will not be difficult to satisfy him and the Coushattas and some of the other tribes around there by giving them some land for their people." Realizing the colonists' fears, six Cherokee headmen, including Fields and Duwali, visited Nacogdoches in December 1825, to assure the town's officials of their friendly intentions.[30]

In March 1826, Fields reiterated to Saucedo his tribe's willingness to go to war against the hostile Indians. The following month Austin accepted the Cherokee offer and plotted a campaign against the Wichitas in which his colony's militia would attack the Brazos River Waco and Tawakoni villages. He then sent an embassy to Fields, asking him to gather Cherokee, Delaware, and Shawnee warriors to make a simultaneous assault upon the Tawakoni village at the head of the Navasota River. Following the presumed successful campaign against the Wacos and Tawakonis, the American and Indian allies planned to proceed together up the Brazos to attack the Taovayas. Austin promised Fields that Cherokee involvement in the war would be "the means of securing you land in the country for as many of your Nation as wish to remove here." The Cherokees accepted Austin's offer, and the campaign was set to begin when the military commandant of Texas, Colonel Mateo Ahumada ordered it postponed until more favorable conditions prevailed.[31]

Disappointed in this missed opportunity, Cherokee leaders desperately looked for more effective means to secure their lands. Therefore, Fields and a few others cast their lot with a different group of Americans who promised to help the Cherokees in return for their assistance against the Mexicans authorities. Ironically, Haden Edwards, the empresario whose lands overlapped the Cherokees, was the leader of this American group. In early 1826, a political controversy had broken out between Edwards and the original Tejano settlers, leading the Mexican government to cancel his contract in June. Haden returned to the United States in the summer, but his brother Benjamin remained in Texas and attempted to foment support for a rebellion among the Edwards colonists. When only thirty or so Americans pledged loyalty to the Edwards' cause, Benjamin turned to the Cherokees and engaged in negotiations with Fields. Receiving a bit of encouragement from the Cherokee chief, the Edwards supporters waited until Haden returned to Texas before staging their uprising. In November 1826, the American rebels entered Nacogdoches, easily took possession of the town, and proclaimed the Edwards grant to be the independent Republic of Fredonia. On December 21, several Cherokees accompanied Fields to Nacogdoches and signed a treaty of friendship and alliance with the leaders of the Fredonian Republic. Fields pledged the Cherokees to aid the Fredonians in evicting unwelcome occupants of the grant in return for receiving title to all Texas land lying north of a line drawn from Nacogdoches westward to the headwaters of the Red River.[32]

As Mexican troops from San Antonio headed northeast to quash the rebellion, various interested parties took steps to remove the Cherokees from the alliance with the Fredonians. Colonel Peter Bean, newly appointed Indian agent of the Mexican government, wrote Fields several times, assuring the Cherokee leader that a land grant could be obtained if the application were made through proper channels. Saucedo also assured Fields that the Cherokee land claim would be protected, reiterating that the tribe needed to send another agent to Mexico. Fields rashly declined both offers, claiming they had come too late. Austin, however, met with more success; he addressed a letter to Cherokee chief Duwali, who had remained neutral during the affair. The empresario pointed out that Edwards's contract had been cancelled before the rebellion began and confirmed that the tribe's original land claim would be protected if the Indians dissolved their alliance with the rebels. In response, Duwali and the majority of the Cherokees distanced themselves from Fields who, along with Edwards's allies, fled to Louisiana in February 1827 as the Mexican army approached Nacogdoches. Soon thereafter, the Cherokees captured and executed Fields. In return for Duwali's assistance in putting down the Fredonian Rebellion, the Mexican government rewarded him with a lieutenant colonel's commission.[33]

Following the defeat of the Fredonians and their allies, the military commander of the Eastern Interior Provinces, General Anastacio Bustamante, entered Texas in the spring of 1827 to investigate the situation. Finding order restored in east Texas, Bustamante issued a proclamation warning that Mexican troops would go on the offensive if the hostile Wichitas and Comanches did not agree to peace. Intimidated by Bustamante's threat, in June the Tawakonis and Wacos entered into negotiations with Colonel Francisco Ruiz, the commander of Mexican forces at Nacogdoches. A few weeks later, Colonel Bean accompanied the headmen from the two tribes to San Antonio, where a treaty was concluded with General Bustamante. Bean also served as a peace emissary from the emigrant tribes; he gave the Tawakonis and Wacos beads and tobacco and smoked a peace pipe with them in the name of the Cherokees and the other northeastern Texas tribes.[34]

The Penateka Comanches responded to Bustamante's call for peace in July 1827, following a defeat at the hands of a joint Mexican-Lipan Apache force. Penateka headman Incoroy led a group of Comanches to San Antonio and informed the general that the principal leaders were away fighting Osages, but agreed to a truce with the Mexicans until the main chiefs returned. Although a few Penateka warriors broke the truce and raided Austin's colony in early 1828, Chief Paruakevitsi arrived at Béxar in August and held preliminary talks with Mexican officials. Over the next two months Paruakevitsi visited various Comanche rancherías and determined that all of the Penatekas desired peace. Therefore, in October he returned to San Antonio with a group of Comanche warriors and formally agreed to end hostilities against the Mexicans. As with earlier treaties, the celebration of peace with Texas officials initiated a series of visits by Comanche leaders: in July 1829, Incoroy visited San Antonio to meet the new political chief of Béxar, Ramón Músquiz; in April 1830, Paruakevitsi led a Penateka embassy to Matamoros and had an audience with Bustamante, now vice president of Mexico; the following month, Guonique, who had traveled to Mexico City in 1822, returned to the capital to reinforce the peace.[35]

The Fredonian Rebellion—and the resulting arrival of General Bustamante —proved to be a turning point in relations among the Tejanos, Americans, and Indians of Coahuila y Texas. The Edwards fiasco led directly to the sending of a high-ranking official to study the Texas situation and, ultimately, to the closing of the province to further legal American immigration. In March 1828, General Manuel de Mier y Terán entered Texas as the head of the Mexican Boundary Commission sent by the federal government to survey the border with the United States that had been established in the Adams-Onís Treaty of 1819. In addition, Terán was charged with investigating the situation of the American newcomers as well as the status of the province's Indian population. The general spent a year traveling through Texas, including a seven and a half month stopover in Nacogdoches, during which he inspected the various empresarial grants and met with members of most of the region's Indian tribes. After leaving Texas, Terán replaced Bustamante as commanding general of the Eastern Interior Provinces. Alarmed by the expansionist tendencies of the United States, as well as by the huge numbers of American settlers west of the Sabine River, in 1829 Terán made a series of recommendations designed to prevent Mexico from losing Texas to the neighboring republic. These recommendations became the basis for the law of April 6, 1830, which prohibited further emigration from the United States and rescinded all empresario contracts not yet completed. Responsibility for enforcing the law fell to a "director of colonization," and the Mexican government appointed General Terán to the position soon thereafter.[36]

In order to implement the directives of the April 6, 1830 law, Terán upgraded the Mexican military presence in Texas. He reinforced the existing garrisons in Texas—San Antonio, Goliad, and Nacogdoches—and established six new forts designed to encircle the American colonies, prevent smuggling, and keep out illegal aliens. Despite Terán's efforts, Americans flooded into Texas in the 1830s as if the law had never been enacted. Most entered Texas illegally, but a few were allowed to settle in Austin's and Dewitt's colonies as Terán allowed the two empresarios to fulfill their contracts. Within a few years the Euroamerican population in Texas had grown to such an extent that the newcomers easily outnumbered the few Tejanos and the dwindling amount of Indians. By 1834 about eight thousand people lived in Austin's colony. Within a decade of their respective foundings, DeWitt's colony contained about 1,200 Americans, while three hundred Mexicans resided within the confines of de León's empresarial grant. In the early 1830s, two teams of Irish-born empresarios founded another couple of colonies, located between the San Antonio and the Nueces rivers, which contained a total of six hundred Irish immigrants. By the mid-1830s about ten thousand newly arrived immigrants lived between the Trinity and the Nueces rivers, an area that had been almost devoid of Euroamericans just a decade before. At the same time, illegal American immigration into east Texas exploded and the population of Nacogdoches and vicinity grew to about four thousand people. Another 2,850 Americans lived farther east around St. Augustine, while 1,400 settlers lived in various settlements stretching from Liberty, near the mouth of the Trinity River, to Tenahaw, thirty-five miles northeast of Nacogdoches. By 1834, the 8,250 Euroamerican settlers in east Texas were putting immense pressure on the area's Indians, who now found that the newcomers outnumbered them by almost two to one. As a result of the crowding, the remaining Caddo tribes in east Texas consolidated into two groups, the Hainais and Nadacos, while most of the Bidais joined with the region's various emigrant tribes.[37]

Realizing the futility of preventing American immigration into the province, General Terán hoped to temper the tide of illegal settlement by providing the emigrant Indians of east Texas with title to their lands. While in Nacogdoches with the Mexican Boundary Commission Terán had been visited by embassies from the east Texas tribes, who the general opined were equal, if not superior, in character to many of the American settlers he encountered. In June 1828, Gatunwali (or Big Mush), Fields's replacement as Cherokee war chief, met with Terán and asked the general to fulfill the Mexican government's promise of providing his tribe with a land grant. The Cherokees impressed Terán, who noted that the tribe was "industrious, respects property, lives by its labor, and is obedient to the authority of its military and political chiefs. It can be hoped that . . . they will be incorporated into the Mexican nation." Shawnee and Delaware leaders also asked Terán to authorize their possession of territory in Texas. In April 1828, American settlers from Arkansas Territory had crossed south of the Red River into Mexico and threatened to attack the Shawnees and Delawares if they did not abandon their Pecan Point villages. As a result of the illegal incursion, the Shawnees moved their village south to the headwaters of the Angelina River, while the Delawares relocated to the Neches. Terán felt that the Shawnees and Delawares were "less industrious" than the Cherokees, yet he noted approvingly that they "subsist by working the land and raising cattle." The general was also favorably inclined toward the emigrant Indians living south of Nacogdoches; stopping at the Biloxi village on his trip down the Trinity River in December 1828, Terán mentioned that the house he visited "has cattle and a fair number of tools and is equal in every way to what a civilized family might possess."[38]

Therefore, in the summer of 1831, following an Alabama and Coushatta request for a land grant, Terán put in motion the process by which the east Texas emigrant tribes might gain secure possession of their territory. On July 14, Terán instructed José María Letona, the governor of Coahuila y Texas, to award a concession of land to the Alabama and Coushatta tribes. As a result, state commissioner Francisco Madero traveled to their villages to investigate the situation and to draw the boundaries of their land claims. Following Madero's inspection, Governor Letona informed Béxar political chief Músquiz that he "considered it convenient and fair that [the Alabamas and Coushattas] secure the land that they cultivate." General Terán then turned his attention to the Cherokees and their allies. On August 15 he ordered Governor Letona to send a directive to Músquiz, instructing him to put the Cherokees in possession of a fixed tract of land on the headwaters of the Trinity and along the banks of the Sabine.[39]

Just as it seemed that the emigrant tribes might finally secure legal title to their lands, events conspired to deny them once again. In July 1832, General Terán, despondent over his failure to check American immigration into Texas, committed suicide. Governor Letona died of yellow fever in the same year. Vicente Filisola, Terán's successor as the commanding general of the Eastern Interior Provinces, did not follow through on his predecessor's plan to obtain land for the east Texas Indians, for the Mexican government had awarded him the southern portion of the Thorn empresarial grant, where the Cherokees lived, in 1831. As a result, the Indians' petitions for land stalled before receiving approval from the national government.[40]

The Coushattas and Alabamas gave up their attempts to obtain legal rights to the land, but the Cherokees continued moving forward. In July 1833, Duwali traveled to San Antonio and met with Miguel Arciniega, interim political chief of the Department of Béxar. The Cherokee leader presented a petition asking the Mexicans to follow through on their promise and grant the tract of land that had been specified in 1831. Duwali defined the boundaries as lying north of the San Antonio Road, between the Trinity and the Sabine rivers. Duwali pointed out that numerous Americans had recently moved into the territory. He demanded their immediate removal, alleging that most of them had come into the region since General Terán had set aside the land for the Cherokees. The following month, Duwali and his embassy traveled to Monclova and met with the new governor of Coahuila y Texas, Juan Martín de Veramendi. After listening to Duwali's argument, Veramendi judged that, although the Chero-kees were not to be disturbed from their lands, the Indians were residing on General Filisola's grant, and that no determination pertaining to their status could be made until his empresarial contract expired. Despite the Cherokee efforts, the east Texas Indians had yet to obtain clear title to their lands as the end of the Mexican era approached.[41]

In the meantime, most of the emigrant tribes tried to secure their lands by joining with American settlers and Mexican troops in the war that erupted with other Indians soon after General Bustamante abandoned Texas in late 1827. Ironically, the Mexican army, which had been reinforced after the law of April 6, 1830, in order to contain American immigration, directed many of the campaigns against the various tribes. As a result of their efforts, the Mexican forces succeeded in reducing the Indian threat to Texas settlers, opening up the region to even greater numbers of illegal American immigrants. The numerous Americans, in turn, eventually decided to remove the Indians from Texas as well as trying to wrest control of the province from Mexico altogether. By 1835, on the eve of the American rebellion, many original Indian inhabitants of Texas had been driven from the lands that they had so securely possessed just a decade and a half before.

The Wichita tribes were the first group to feel the wrath of the Texas forces. In February 1828, Tawakoni and Waco warriors, interested in obtaining horses to exchange with illegal traders, invaded the colonies of Austin and Dewitt. In May Mexican troops pursued a group of Tawakonis and Wacos who had attacked San Antonio and killed two warriors on the Pedernales River. Two months later the emigrant tribes of east Texas pledged their assistance to the Mexican forces at a meeting held at the Cherokee village with Lieutenant José María Sánchez y Tapia, a member of the Mexican Boundary Commission. Cherokee war chief Gatunwali informed Tapia that the Wacos and Tawakonis had "begun to do harm" and warned that it was only a matter of time before their lands would "be tinged with blood." A Shawnee chief told the officer that his tribe considered the Mexicans to be friends and that tribes such as the Wacos and Tawakonis, who were "enemies of the Mexicans[,] are our enemies." Delaware, Kickapoo, Alabama, and Coushatta leaders gave similar speeches and proposed a joint campaign with the Mexicans to "exterminate" the two Wichita tribes for breaking the peace.[42]

Mexican officials did not immediately respond to the war proposals, and the Tawakoni and Waco attacks resumed in earnest. In the winter of 1828, sixteen warriors killed a Mexican resident of Austin's colony on the Colorado River. A militia force responded by attacking the retreating Tawakonis and Wacos, killing eight and mortally wounding seven. In early 1829, Tawakoni warriors made bold raids upon Béxar and Goliad and stole horses and mules, some of which had been tied to settlers' houses. Soon thereafter, counterattacks from the Mexicans, Americans, and emigrant tribes began to do irreparable damage to the Wacos and Tawakoni. In April 1829, the Cherokees invaded the Waco village at dawn and killed fifty-five tribesmen before Tawakoni warriors arrived to repel the assailants. A couple of months later the Coushattas and Alabamas joined with the Biloxis and Yowani Choctaws to attack the Wacos. Continued Wichita raids caused Austin to mount a counterattack in August 1829. Led by Lipan Apache scouts under the direction of Cuelgas de Castro's son-in-law, Flacco (Skinny), Captain Abner Kuykendall and one hundred men from Austin's colony discovered a Tawakoni hunting camp near the mouth of the San Saba River. Before Kuykendall could mount an attack, however, the Tawakonis abandoned the camp, forfeiting their entire store of winter provisions.[43]

The attacks upon the Wacos and Tawakonis increased in intensity during the following year. In June 1830, more than one hundred Cherokees, supported by a few Tonkawas, attacked the Tawakoni village on the headwaters of the Navasota River. Unable to force their way into the village, the Cherokees set fire to the Tawakoni grass houses and shot men, women, and children as they rushed from their burning homes. Before the Cherokees retreated with most of the horse herd, twenty-six Tawakonis had died and twenty-eight were wounded. Following a Tawakoni raid on San Antonio in August, the new military commandant of Texas, Colonel Antonio Elosúa, ordered Captain Nicasio Sánchez to lead 119 soldiers and thirty-three militiamen directly to the Waco and Tawakoni villages on the Brazos in order to "attack them with the greatest energy." Alerted that the Mexican force was approaching, the Wacos and Tawakonis quickly harvested their corn crop and abandoned their villages. Sánchez, finding both towns empty, destroyed the Waco and Tawakoni villages by ordering his men to burn all the houses and supporting structures. The Mexicans also took all the food that the two tribes had stored for the winter.

Sánchez and his troops pursued the fleeing Tawakonis to a hunting camp on the San Gabriel River and attacked them early in the morning on September 14. They killed eight Tawakonis, but most of the villagers escaped through the thick underbrush. The Tawakonis, however, left behind 195 horses, nine rifles, and countless buffalo hides, cooking vessels, food, and weapons for the Mexican troops to recover.[44]

Following the destructive Sánchez campaign, the Wacos permanently abandoned their village and retreated farther up the Brazos to join the Taovayas, who were in the process of moving north of the Red River and out of Texas. This retreat from the Texas settlements began in the summer of 1831 when a smallpox epidemic struck the Taovayas and Wacos. In June a Kichai warrior informed Colonel Ruiz that about forty Taovaya and Waco men had died as well as a large number of women and children. The Kichai told the colonel that the sickness continued to spread, which caused Ruiz to ask that "it be God's will that no trace shall remain of such a harmful family" of Indians. Most of the Wacos fled from the disease and settled in villages along the upper Brazos and near the mouth of the Wichita River. A few Wacos joined the Taovayas, who eventually settled in a village—near present-day Fort Sill, Oklahoma—on East Cache Creek on the southeastern edge of the Wichita Mountains, where they would remain for the following two decades.[45]

The Tawakonis, however, rebuilt their village on the headwaters of the Navasota River. While the Wacos and Taovayas preferred to remain aloof from the Texas settlements, the desperate Tawakonis resumed their raiding in order to acquire livestock for barter with illegal American traders. As the raids continued into 1831, Colonel Elosúa decided to mount the second major punitive campaign against the Tawakonis in as many years. In mid-November Captain Manuel Lafuente and two hundred Mexican troops carried out an early-morning surprise attack upon a large Tawakoni hunting camp on Cowhouse Creek, upstream from its confluence with the Leon River. The Mexicans did not follow up their initial success because they discovered a large number of friendly Penatekas within the Tawakoni camp. In fact, Chief Paruakevitsi and his son had been killed in the attack, along with six Tawakonis. The Tawakonis once again lost all their belongings, including two hundred horses, most of which Lafuente gave to the Comanches in compensation for the death of their chief. Over the course of the following week Captain Lafuente and his force pursued the fleeing Tawakonis and caught a small group of them between the Llano and Pedernales rivers. During a two-hour battle, the Mexicans killed nine Tawakonis, whose bodies they left hanging from two oak trees. Following Lafuente's brutal campaign, most of the Tawakonis retreated northwestward and established villages near the Wacos and Taovayas. By early 1832, the only

Wichitas remaining near the Euroamerican settlements in Texas were the few Tawakonis who returned to their old village on the Navasota River as well as the Kichais who still lived near the Trinity River on Keechi Creek.[46]

Soon after forcing most of the Wichitas from central Texas, the Mexican troops directed their newfound strength toward the Comanches, even though most of the Penatekas had maintained the peace in Coahuila y Texas ever since agreeing to lay down their arms in October 1828. In fact, in 1831 some Penatekas had assisted the Mexicans in their war against the Wichitas by recovering stolen horses and acting as scouts for troops pursuing Waco and Tawakoni raiders. A few young Comanche men, however, defied their leaders and began to make raids of their own upon Texas ranches. Still, the Penateka headmen tried to remain on friendly terms with Mexican officials. In August 1831, Chief Incoroy sent his son to the Goliad presidio to inform the commander that a group of Comanches were planning a raid. The warning came too late, and the Penateka war party killed a Tonkawa, an American, and two Mexican soldiers while stealing livestock. Incoroy retrieved the horses taken in the raid and returned them to San Antonio in October. The Comanche leader maintained his peaceful stance even after Mexican troops accidentally killed Paruakevitsi; informed of the chief's death while visiting San Antonio in December, Incoroy showed no sign of regret, but merely stated that the peace should be not be broken. He then traveled to Matamoros and returned even more stolen horses.[47]

Despite Incoroy's singular efforts to keep the peace, Mexican officials decided to retaliate against the Penateka horse thieves and ordered a campaign against the Comanches in early 1832. Colonel Ruiz encouraged the emigrants of east Texas to join the Mexicans in their efforts. In late January the Shawnees answered Ruiz's call and camped outside San Antonio in preparation for the campaign. At that very moment Incoroy and another Comanche headman, Isayona, were in Béxar with members of their rancherías, exchanging buffalo robes with local traders and visiting Colonel Elosúa. As the Penatekas returned home, the Shawnees ambushed Isayona's party on Leon Creek, about twenty miles north of Béxar. Following the battle, in which Isayona was killed, the Shawnees entered San Antonio and asked Elosúa to provide Mexican troops for yet another attack. Despite the friendly meeting he had enjoyed with the Comanches just a few days earlier, Elosúa ordered presidial soldiers to assist the Shawnees. The joint force caught up with the fleeing Penatekas a few days later and killed about thirty tribesmen while wounding just as many.[48]

The Mexicans immediately followed up on this successful engagement with a campaign designed to drive the Comanches from Texas altogether. In February, Captain Manuel Barragán, commander of the Presidio del Rio Grande, gathered a huge force of his own troops, militia from Béxar and Monclova, Austin's colonists, and Lipan and Tonkawa auxiliaries, and set out in search of the Penatekas. Barragán's party only found a couple of small Comanche camps on the Llano River, which they attacked, killing a dozen Penatekas and capturing fifty horses. Two months later Comanche warriors responded by kidnapping a Goliad boy and killing a party of Tejanos chopping wood near the town. Comanche raids continued throughout the summer as Penateka men stole horses and killed Mexican citizens near San Antonio and along both sides of the Rio Grande. As a result of the incursions, Captain Barragán led a troop of 115 Mexican soldiers on another campaign against the Comanches in October. The Mexican force tracked a party of Penatekas to the San Saba River, killed nine and took a large number of horses. Attacks on the Comanches continued in early 1833: in January, the Coushattas conducted an expedition to Comanche country and killed seventy Penatekas; in April, Lipan warriors assisted Captain Barragán and a troop of Mexican soldiers in a campaign against the Comanches that killed another seven warriors.[49]

Despite the yearlong assault upon Comanche rancherías, the Mexicans and their allies were unable to dislodge the mobile Penatekas, and warriors continued to raid throughout Coahuila y Texas over the next two years. In fact, Comanche young men stole the entire horse herd of Goliad in August 1834. At the same time, however, Penateka leaders began to negotiate another peace treaty with the Mexican authorities. In the summer of 1833, and again in early 1834, Comanche chiefs traveled to San Antonio to discuss a truce. In February 1835, a party of nearly four hundred Comanche men, women, and children arrived in Béxar to return 150 mules that had been stolen by young tribesmen. This peace offering impressed the Mexicans, who also received a visit from Chief Incoroy and five other headmen in May. As a result of these demonstrations, the new commanding general of the Eastern Interior Provinces, Martín Perfecto de Cos, ordered the renewal of presents for the Comanches. As events in Coahuila y Texas began to lead toward a rebellion on the part of the American settlers in the summer of 1835, General Cos became even more interested in securing peace with the Comanches. Therefore, in August 1835, Cos met with three hundred Comanches in Matamoros, and the two parties agreed to end their hostilities. On the eve of revolution, the largest and most powerful Indian tribe in Texas had once again entered into a peace treaty with the Mexican forces that controlled the province.[50]

The Mexicans failed to remove the powerful Comanches from Texas, but their soldiers succeeded in driving the beleaguered Karankawas even farther from the Euroamerican settlements. Following the agreement of May 1827, the remaining Carancaguases, Cocos, and Cujanes had been forced to rebuild their lives in the coastal plain between the Guadalupe and Nueces rivers, an area about one-third as large as their former range. Unsurprisingly, the hungry Karankawas turned toward the settlers' cattle for food. By January 1830, the citizens of Goliad petitioned the Mexican government to punish the Karankawas for repeated thefts. Mexican presidial troops responded to the request the following month and captured six tribesmen. The Karankawas continued to poach cattle from the citizens of Goliad as well as those from de León's colony. Therefore, in December 1830, a Mexican force of thirty men mounted a punitive expedition aimed at Karankawa bands on the lower Guadalupe River. Soon after departing from Victoria, the Mexicans killed two Carancaguase warriors and pursued the rest of the fleeing tribesmen downstream. Chief Antonio and fifty Carancaguase men met the Mexicans at the mouth of the river and assumed a "disposition to attack." The troops halted and then watched impotently as the Indian men, along with their families, crossed to the safety of a barrier island in a fleet of canoes. The following year not even the barrier islands provided the Karankawas a respite from the increasingly aggressive Mexican forces. In November 1831, following the deaths of two Victoria residents at the hands of Karankawa warriors, the Mexicans mounted a troop of eighty-one presidial soldiers along with seventeen residents of de León's colony to seek retribution. Crossing San Antonio Bay in boats, the Mexican force captured three Karankawa men on the coast and brought them back to the ranch of a de León colonist. The Mexicans executed two of the Indians and shot the other as he tried to escape.[51]

Persecuted and starving, some Karankawas returned north of the Guadalupe River and worked for a while as day laborers for ranchers in the colonies of Austin and DeWitt. A few Americans actually paid the Karankawas to steal horses and cattle from the Mexican settlers of de León's colony. As a result, in November 1833, a party of about one hundred de León colony residents and presidial soldiers headed northeast from Victoria in pursuit of Karankawa thieves. Before the Mexicans could locate the Karankawas, Americans from Austin's colony stood up for their Indian employees and intercepted the troops at the Navidad River. Following a short discussion, the Americans convinced the force that their pursuit of the Karankawas was futile, and the Mexicans returned home empty-handed. Soon thereafter, however, the Americans turned on the despised Karankawas living among them. Austin's colony residents enslaved thirty-five or forty of the desperate tribesmen while other colonists gunned down a small band of Karankawas on the Colorado River after the Indians had begged for corn at various farms.[52]

These hostilities drove most of the Karankawas even farther south to the area of the abandoned Mission Refugio, where they barely survived by poaching from the herds of the local Irish settlers. In the summer of 1833, Mexican troops mounted another campaign against the Karankawas but could not find any Indians because the tribesmen had taken refuge on a barrier island. Finally, in May 1834, a Mexican force located a Karankawa camp near Refugio and launched an early morning surprise attack. The soldiers fired their weapons into the village for over an hour, killing scores of Karankawas and allowing only a few to escape. The troops then pillaged and burned the camp. Following this massacre, the Mexican commander correctly proclaimed that "the country is ours." By early 1835, no more than two hundred Karankawas—twenty Cujane and Coco families, along with fifteen Carancaguase families—remained in the lowlands around Refugio. Although the Karankawas had dominated the Texas coast for a full century and a half following the arrival of Spaniards, Mexican troops and Euroamerican immigrants had driven the Indians from their homelands in fewer than fifteen years.[53]

Free from the threat of Karankawa hostilities, Americans from Austin's and Dewitt's colonies went ahead and forced their erstwhile Tonkawa allies from their midst. Denied access to the buffalo plains by the Comanches, the Tonkawas were starving and desperate for food when the Mexican Boundary Commission had visited one of their rancherías just west of the Colorado River in April 1828. Members of the commission were amazed at the tribe's poverty; one observer called the Tonkawas "one of the most wretched [tribes] in Texas." The following year, Tonkawa warriors began to steal livestock and corn from the settlers of DeWitt's colony. When the empresario confronted the Tonkawas in their Colorado River village, the headmen admitted that hunger had driven their young men to make the raids. Dewitt tried to convince the Tonkawas "to plant corn for the next year so they would not have to hunt," and even attempted to raise money in order to provide the tribesmen with agricultural tools. As they had done before, however, the Tonkawas refused the offer to become settled agriculturalists. Instead, most of the tribal members drifted westward and joined with Sandía's band, now living west of the San Antonio River with the Lipan Apaches. The few remaining Tonkawas continued to poach livestock from the Americans until 1834, when the settlers in Austin's colony attacked their ranchería and drove them from the area. By the following year, all the remaining Tonkawas lived far to the west of the American settlements in Texas.[54]

Inspired by their success with the Tonkawas, Austin's colony settlers maintained their aggressive stance the following year and forced the few remaining Kichais and Tawakonis to abandon their homes and join the general Wichita retreat northwestward. In May 1835, American settlers on the Colorado River burned the Kichai village on Keechi Creek to the ground, causing the tribesmen to forsake the east Texas location that had been their home for more than three-quarters of a century. The Kichais retreated northwestward to the headwaters of the Trinity River. The same fate befell the Tawakonis on the Navasota River soon after the destruction of the Kichai village. In July 1835, Captain Robert M. Coleman of Bastrop led a company of twenty-five American militiamen in an assault upon the Tawakoni village. The Indians, however, were ready for the attack and repulsed the invaders with heavy fire. The Tawakonis, realizing that Coleman would return with reinforcements, deserted their village and moved far up the Brazos. Coleman came back to the site a few days later with three volunteer companies and found it empty save for a few women and children, whom he captured and sold into slavery. The abandonment of the village on the Navasota unceremoniously ended the seventy-five-year period of Tawakoni occupation of central Texas. Within a decade and a half of the founding of Austin's colony, the Americans, with the assistance of Mexican troops and the emigrant tribes, had completely driven the original Karankawa, Tonkawa, and Wichita inhabitants from the region. Future American settlers in Texas would follow the example set by their predecessors and remove most of the remaining Indians from the state over the course of the next twenty-five years.[55]

At the same time that a large number of Indians were being driven from the Euroamerican settlements in Texas, Americans in Louisiana forced the various tribes living in the state to abandon their homes and seek refuge west of the Sabine River. As in Texas, the main problem for the Indians was the constantly increasing American population; between 1810 and 1830, the number of Americans and their slaves living in the Red River Valley between Alexandria and Natchitoches tripled to 15,480 people. At the same time, only about two hundred Indians resided in the area. Nearly 150 Pascagoulas and Biloxis lived in the so-called Pascagoula village downstream from Natchitoches, while about fifty Apalaches and Taensas lived in the nearby Apalache village, just above Alexandria. Another eight hundred or so Indians lived upstream from Natchitoches and the Great Raft: five hundred Kadohadachos, two hundred Coushattas, and one hundred Yatasis, Natchitoches, and Adaes. Therefore, the Americans and their slaves outnumbered the few remaining Indians in the Red River Valley by fifteen to one.[56]

As in the previous decade American settlers continued to encroach upon the Indian lands. In 1824, George Gray, the new Indian agent for the Louisiana Indians, ordered fifteen American families out of Kadohadacho territory. The following year, in order to clarify disputes with Americans living near their lands, Chief Dehahuit and Agent Gray officially delineated the boundary of

the Kadohadacho territory for the first time. In the east, the boundary was set
at the Red River, while the yet-to-be-fixed Mexican line—the present border
of Louisiana and Texas—formed the western boundary. The Sulphur River
became the northern boundary and Cypress Bayou the southern. The newly
defined Kadohadacho territory encompassed just less than 600,000 acres of
land—nearly 6,000 acres per each Indian family—much of it containing soil
eminently suitable for cotton. It would not be long before American settlers
would demand access to this land as well.[57]

During the same period two settlers tried to force the Rapides Parish tribes
off their lands. In the early 1820s, Isaac Baldwin established his Village Plantation near the Apalache town, just downstream from the Pascagoulas. Baldwin
initially tried to get the War Department to remove the Indians, but this ploy
proved futile. With the assistance of a United States senator, he also tried
unsuccessfully to have the Apalaches removed by an act of Congress. At about
the same time, a man named Joseph Gillard established a plantation near the
Pascagoula village. A few years later, Gillard expanded his operations onto land
claimed by the Pascagoulas. In 1825, the Pascagoulas complained to Agent
Gray about Gillard's encroachment and, as a result, the federal government
arranged for the Indians to congregate on the newly defined Kadohadacho
territory. Agent Gray informed Dehahuit of the government's desire; since the
tribes had always depended upon the Kadohadachos, the caddi replied that he
had no objections but stated that he should receive a small annuity from the
United States for assenting to the plan. Gray agreed to the chief's request and
was authorized to give Dehahuit $50 a year "as a token of good will . . . and for
the offer he has made the bands now in Louisiana to come and join them."[58]

In spite of the arrangement, the Rapides Parish tribes were violently driven
off their lands before they could relocate to the Kadohadacho territory. In 1826,
Baldwin launched a campaign of terror against the Indians, using his slaves
and neighbors to burn their cabins and to destroy their crops. Rather than
stay within the United States, most of the Pascagoulas and Apalaches fled to
Texas and joined their kinsmen in the Alabama, Coushatta, and Biloxi villages.
Only about thirty Pascagoulas and Apalaches remained near Alexandria. These
remnants complained to federal government officials about their treatment in
1830, but a dreadful cholera epidemic spread throughout the area in 1832,
virtually wiping them out. After seventy years of occupation, all of the Rapides
area tribes had abandoned their homes to seek refuge in Texas, following the
example set by fellow tribes three decades before.[59]

Although the Kadohadachos and the Coushattas remained in the United
States, increasing pressure in the late 1820s greatly demoralized the tribes,
causing them to turn to alcohol for solace. In 1828, a licensed trader noted that

Choctaws, in the employ of illegal American merchants, were selling liquor to the Indians within a fourth of a mile from the Indian agency, which had been moved downstream from the mouth of the Sulphur River to be closer to the Kadohadacho and Coushatta villages. On one occasion, the Kadohadachos, who had come to see Gray to receive presents, were too inebriated to conduct any business with the agent "in consequence of the whole nation arriving by some unknown person furnishing them with whiskey." When the agent's interpreter attempted to relieve the Indians of their liquor, he "was molested and compelled to retreat for Safety."[60]

Alcohol not only caused the Kadohadachos to become unruly, but it also threatened the agricultural base of the tribe. By the mid-1820s, the federal Indian agent was forced to supply the Kadohadachos with food, since their drunkenness and depression made them neglect their fields. Game near the Kadohadacho village was scarce, and the influx of American and Indian settlers forced the tribe to travel even farther west for their winter hunts. The situation reached crisis proportions following the death of Agent Gray in November 1828. His appointed successor died before assuming the position, and the Kadohadachos were without an agent until the summer of 1830. In the interim the Kadohadachos did not receive either the presents or the rations upon which they had come to depend. In desperation, they joined with their Hainai and Nadaco kinsmen in Texas to raid the livestock of the Nacogdoches-area Cherokees. As a result, in August 1830 the Cherokees prepared a retaliatory raid upon the Caddo tribes. The weaker Caddos retreated to the Kadohadacho village and begged the newly arrived agent, Jehiel Brooks, for protection. Brooks distributed powder and lead to the tribesmen and asked Texas Indian agent Bean to press the Cherokees to abandon their campaign. The Cherokees agreed to Bean's demands and soon thereafter made peace with the Caddos.[61]

After thwarting the Cherokee threat, Brooks took steps to keep the tribe from starving, since the Caddos' corn crop was destroyed by drought and general neglect. The hungry Hainais and Nadacos joined the Kadohadachos in the fall of 1830 and preyed upon the livestock of the Euroamericans living in the Bayou Pierre district. Since Brooks did not have enough food on hand to feed the combined tribes, he tried unsuccessfully to convince the two tribes to return to Texas. That winter, while the men were on their buffalo hunt, the remaining tribal members—mainly elderly men, women, and children— were reduced to begging and stealing from the local settlers because Brooks had already exhausted his allowance for provisions "in barely preserving these miserable beings from starvation." During an uncommonly severe winter, Brooks was forced to ask the secretary of war for an extra food allowance.[62]

Brooks supported the Kadohadachos in these instances, but his appointment by President Andrew Jackson represented a change in the official Indian policy of the United States. Whereas the federal government had previously attempted to provide the tribes at least nominal protection from incursion upon their lands, the Jackson administration felt that the removal of the natives would be the most beneficial policy for both the Americans—who would receive the land—and the Indians. With the passage of the Indian Removal Act in 1830, Jackson was able to implement his program of buying the natives' land and resettling them west of the Mississippi River where, free from intruders, the tribes would ideally adopt the techniques of "civilization" that would allow them to survive. As Jackson's appointee as Kadohadacho agent, Brooks shared the president's views on Indian matters. Unlike his predecessors, Brooks was more concerned with removing the Kadohadachos from their ancestral lands than with providing the tribe either protection or guidance. Also unlike his predecessors, Brooks was concerned with individual profit, as his later actions would demonstrate.

The agent showed his true intentions during a trip to Washington in the winter of 1831–32, when he visited the White House and discussed extinguishing the Kadohadacho title to the land with President Jackson. Both Brooks and Jackson knew that plans were being made for engineer Henry Shreve to remove the Great Raft, and both men realized that once the Red River was clear for navigation, the pressure on the Kadohadachos to cede their land would be great. In accordance with the new federal policy toward Indians, Jackson and Brooks felt it would be best for all parties if the tribe would relinquish their land and move west. In the spring of 1833, Captain Shreve arrived in Natchitoches to begin the process of removing the Great Raft, a prospect that greatly excited the populace. There ensued an immediate scramble for the Kadohadachos' rich lands, and citizens filed suits in court that stated the tribe had no right to the area they occupied.[63]

Due to the Americans' pressure, the Coushattas in Louisiana asked the Mexican government for permission to join their kinsmen in southeastern Texas. After investigating the situation, General Filisola denied the Coushatta request, probably fearing that their relocation would adversely affect his empresarial contract. Denied legal authorization to move to Texas, over the next few years many of the Coushattas surreptitiously crossed the border and entered the Trinity River villages. Other tribal members joined with their fellow Creeks in the lands that had recently been set aside for the tribe in Indian Territory—present-day Oklahoma—north of the Red River.[64]

At this crucial moment, when the Kadohadachos needed strong leadership the most, their esteemed caddi Dehahuit died. Bereft of guidance, the

Kadohadachos were uncertain what to do in the face of increased American hostility. One tribal faction wanted to name a war chief to lead the tribe in driving the settlers away from their lands. Agent Brooks, who caught wind of this idea, arranged a meeting with the tribe and asked the commander at nearby Fort Jesup to provide him with troops to intimidate the Kadohadachos. In June 1833, Brooks met with the tribe and conferred the title of chief upon the Kadohadachos' choice, Tarshar. With the support of the troops, the Indian agent convinced Tarshar—a much less decisive man than Dehahuit—and the rest of the tribe to promise "continued good faith to the government and friendship with the white settlers on the frontier." Brooks also informed the Kadohadachos of the various claims to their lands, to "which the Indians entirely and unconditionally" objected and asked the agent to state their protests to the government. [65]

Brooks, however, was much more attuned to his own interests than those of the Kadohadachos and immediately began to manipulate the tribe into selling their lands. In March 1834, Brooks asked Commissioner of Indian Affairs Judge Elbert Herring whether "it would not be best to negotiate for the [Kadohadacho] lands at once before the further progress of the work shall open the eyes of the tribe, as to their importance to the whites." Soon thereafter, Brooks relinquished all responsibility to the Kadohadachos, informing that he was no longer their agent and that he did "not know what [would] be done" by the United States. Whether Brooks was ordered to do this or did so on his own is unclear; whatever the case, the results were what he desired. The Kadohadachos, denied any protection by the federal government, reluctantly decided that it would be in their best interests to sell their lands for whatever price they could obtain. They hoped that by joining the Hainais and Nadacos in Texas, they would receive better treatment from the Mexican government than they had from the United States. Therefore, in early 1835 the Kadohadacho chiefs and headmen addressed a memorial to President Jackson in which they made "the sorrowful resolution of offering all our lands to you which lie within the boundary of the United States, for sale, at such price as we can agree to in council." On January 28, 1835, Jackson sent the memorial to the secretary of war for his consideration without much comment except to ask, "will it not be well to ask an appropriation to cover this expense?" [66]

In response to the Kadohadachos' memorial, Brooks, appointed as treaty commissioner, sent word to the tribe that he was ready to negotiate for the purchase of their lands. On June 25, 1835, the entire Kadohadacho tribe—as well as the few remaining Yatasis, Adaes, and Natchitoches—gathered at the Indian agency. At noon the following day Tarshar, underchief Tsauninot, and twenty-three "chosen councillors" gathered to listen to Brooks's offer. He told the Kadohadachos that he was prepared to alleviate their wants and to place them in a state of independence when compared to their "present destitution." Brooks proclaimed himself a friend sent to obtain the Kadohadacho lands, which he described as "of no more use" to the tribe. He warned them that, "right or wrong," the Americans would soon deprive the tribe of their land anyway. Therefore, Brooks offered to buy the land for goods the tribe could not "otherwise obtain, or long exist without, in this or any other country." In other words, Brooks gave the Kadohadachos the choice to sell their land for what he had to offer or lose it to rapacious Americans for nothing. [67]

Faced with this proposal, the Kadohadacho chiefs had to convince their fellow tribesmen to accept Brooks's offer. Tsauninot insisted that the tribe was "in great want" and expected Brooks to bring them "relief" by supplying them "with things of much more value . . . than these lands, which yield no game." Pointing out that the Kadohadachos were starving because of the lack of game, Tarshar claimed his tribe would not mourn the loss of the land, "which yields . . . nothing but misery." Therefore, he proposed to sell the land "and get all we can for it and not wait till the white man steals it away . . . then gives us nothing." As a result, on July 1, 1835, the Kadohadachos and the United States entered into an agreement in which the tribe agreed to sell all their land and move at their own expense to Texas within one year. In return, the federal government would pay $80,000 to the Kadohadachos; the tribe would receive horses and goods worth $30,000 immediately, while the remaining $50,000 would be paid in goods or money, in equal annual installments over the next five years. For just sixteen cents an acre, the Kadohadachos had agreed to abandon their ancient homeland. [68]

Obviously, the treaty was a bargain for the United States, but Brooks also realized a handsome profit from the treaty. Unknown to the Kadohadachos and the various witnesses to the proceedings, Brooks had introduced a secret reservation into the treaty that granted four leagues—or about twenty-three thousand acres—of land considered to be outside the Kadohadacho territory to the deceased François Grappe and his son. According to the Grappes, they knew nothing of the land grant until the United States Senate ratified the treaty and the president signed it on February 2, 1836. Brooks appeared at the Grappe's residence in Campti about two weeks later and informed them of their acquisition. The startled Grappes accepted Brooks's offer of $6,000 and a slave in return for the land, a fraction of its real worth. Brooks then went on to sell the land at a great profit. Although the tribe was not directly affected by the swindle, it was obvious that Brooks had arranged the treaty for personal profit rather than out of concern for the Kadohadachos. Unfortunately for the tribe, their dealings with Brooks had not yet ended, as he continued to be responsible for the distribution of the remaining $50,000 worth of goods as called for in the Caddo Treaty.[69]

The decade and a half following Mexico's independence from Spain had proven disastrous for many of the tribes of Texas and the Near Southwest. Nearly a third of the Indians had either been forced off their lands or had agreed to abandon their territory in the near future. Another third of the Indians lived far to the west of the Euroamerican settlements, while the remaining third still clung to their lands located in the midst of the Americans and Tejanos in Texas. The Americans' success over the Indians, however, did not yet satisfy the newcomers. Instead, it would only encourage them to continue to act aggressively in the future; first, the Americans would achieve independence from Mexico, and then they would drive nearly all of the Indians out of Texas. The Indians, who had completely dominated Texas as late as 1820, would soon find themselves being hunted and forced to flee from the only homes that many had ever known.

6. Defeat
The Indians and the Republic of Texas, 1836 to 1845

During the decade in which Texas was as an independent republic, the Indians of the province were militarily defeated by its citizens and either driven completely from the borders or beyond the extremes of the Texan settlements. Although none of the Indians were involved in the short war against Mexico for independence, the tribes of east Texas, led by the emigrant Cherokees, attempted to diplomatically play the two sides against each other in an effort to obtain the official grant of land they had desired since 1823. While the republic's first president, Sam Houston, desired peace with the Texas tribes and wanted to recognize the Cherokee claim to territory, his successor, Mirabeau Buonaparte Lamar (as well as most of the republic's citizens), refused to admit that the Indians had any rights to the soil. As a result, in 1839 President Lamar initiated full-scale warfare against tribes considered hostile. With the help of Tonkawa and Lipan Apache auxiliaries, within two years the Texans successfully forced almost all of the Indians—natives and emigrants alike—to abandon the province and take refuge in either the United States or Mexico. Although Houston, in his second term, resumed his peace policy and invited the Penateka Comanches, Wichitas, and Caddos to return to Texas, the defeated tribes then posed little threat to the settlers of the republic. All three groups, as well as the Tonkawa and Lipan Apache allies, were forced to reside far to the west of the settlers' ranches and farms. Only a few straggling remnants of the emigrant tribes of southeastern Texas remained among the Texan settlers in the Big Thicket region. By the end of 1845 when the United States annexed Texas, the province's Indians maintained an increasingly precarious existence on the borders of a region now wholly dominated by Americans.

The Texans initiated their revolt in the summer of 1835 as a result of Mexican conservatives' attempts to curb the states' powers that liberals had defined in the federalist Constitution of 1824. In reaction to a series of aggressive acts by the new, conservative president of Mexico, Antonio López de Santa Anna, a group of rebels in Texas marched on Anahuac, a Mexican fort recently established near the mouth of the Trinity River, and forced the tiny military garrison to surrender. The rebels' hope that the attack would galvanize public opinion in Texas against the centralists bore fruit in September 1835 as Mexican troops, led by General Cos, set out from Matamoros for San Antonio. Before the force could arrive, Texas volunteers defeated government troops at Gonzalez on October 2 and took possession of the presidio at Goliad a week later. Rebel forces then besieged Cos and his troops at San Antonio, forcing the Mexicans to surrender and withdraw from the town in December. In the meantime, delegates from a dozen Texas communities assembled in a "Consultation" at San Felipe de Austin and issued what amounted to a conditional declaration of independence on November 7. Accordingly, the delegates created a provisional government, formed a general council, and appointed Sam Houston commander of all troops, realizing that Santa Anna would soon send Mexican forces northward in response to the uprising.[1]

The Indians of coastal and central Texas had little to do with the events that unfolded in late 1835 as most of the tribesmen preferred to stay out of the way of the opposing forces. The Tonkawas and Lipan Apaches remained in the safety of their Hill Country rancherías west of San Antonio, while the Penateka Comanches continued to honor the peace agreement they had made with General Cos in August 1835. However, in October a few Karankawas took advantage of the unrest between the rebels and the Mexican troops and crossed east of the Guadalupe River to prey upon the settlers' cattle. In response, Thomas G. Western, future superintendent of Indian affairs for the Republic of Texas, led a rebel commission appointed to ensure the neutrality of the Karankawas and to convince them to retreat to the San Antonio River. Following initial talks, on October 29 most of the Cocos, Carancaguases, and Cujanes gathered about twenty miles downstream from Goliad and entered "into a firm and lasting peace" with the Texans. Following the signing of the treaty, the Karankawas retreated farther down the coast where they remained, out of harm's way, for the remainder of the struggle. Soon thereafter, almost all of the few surviving Karankawas abandoned Texas to take refuge near the mouth of the Rio Grande.[2]

The emigrant Indians of east Texas, as well as the native Caddo tribes, however, found themselves in the midst of a situation that was dangerous on one hand, while offering the possibility of obtaining the land grants they had desired for more than a decade on the other. Both the Mexicans and the Texans hoped to entice the Indians to join their cause. Although none of the warriors actually wanted to get involved in the fight between the opposing Euroamerican forces, Cherokee chief Duwali, self-appointed spokesman for the tribes, understood that he might manipulate the situation to the Indians' advantage by offering his men's services—as well as those of the other east

Texas tribes—to whichever side chose to recognize their claims to land in Texas. However, this was an extremely complicated endeavor. The Indians realized that the Mexican government would probably be more favorable to their claims than the Texans, but the tribes could not be sure that Santa Anna would be victorious. Duwali, therefore, was forced to play a duplicitous game, pledging the Indians' allegiance to both Mexican and Texan representatives, depending upon which side seemed to be closest to victory. Unfortunately for the tribes of the region—including the Kadohadachos still residing in the United States—the Texans ultimately defeated the Mexicans without the Indians' assistance. The Indians did not join Santa Anna's army, yet many citizens of the newly independent nation suspected the tribes of favoring the Mexicans and did not trust the many tribesmen who continued to live in their midst after the fighting was over. It would be only a matter of time before the Texans drove nearly all of the Indians out of east Texas.

In September 1835, Duwali initiated his diplomatic endeavors by traveling to San Antonio to meet with Colonel Domingo Ugartachea, military commandant at Béxar. At the conference, Ugartachea attempted to enlist the Indians of East Texas in the fight against the rebellious Texans. The colonel did not offer the Indians a guarantee to their lands, though, and Duwali returned to his Cherokee village, where he held a general council of the emigrant tribes of Texas and the Hainais and Nadacos. The Indians discussed the situation, taking note of the fact that Texans had recently killed a few Cherokees and Coushattas, in addition to surveying the natives' lands. Nonetheless, the Indians concluded that it would be in their best interests to cultivate a friendship with the revolutionaries, believing that the Mexicans in the province would have difficulty defeating the more numerous Texans. In mid-October Duwali and Gatunwali met with Texan agents and assured them that the Cherokees and their allies would remain peaceful if the rebels granted them territory.[3]

Upon the advice of the agents, the newly formed Consultation agreed to give land to the Indians, albeit a smaller tract than the tribes desired. On November 13, every member of the Consultation signed a declaration stating that the Texans recognized the Cherokee claim to lands from the San Antonio Road northward to the Sabine River, between the Neches on the west and the Angelina on the east. In late December a commission headed by Sam Houston initiated treaty negotiations with the Cherokees. Two months later, on February 23, 1836, Duwali, Gatunwali, and a few other tribal leaders entered into an agreement with the commissioners in the name of the "Cherokees and their associate bands," even though no members of the other east Texas tribes were present at the signing of the treaty. The Cherokee spokesmen compromised and accepted the Texan offer of the tract of land they had been assigned three months earlier, despite their protests that the Mexican government had acknowledged in 1833 that the claim stretched west of the Neches all the way to the Trinity. In return for the grant, the Indians were required to maintain the peace with the Texans, give up all outside land claims, and move within the boundaries of the reservation by November 1836. Although the various tribes—Kickapoos, Shawnees, Delawares, Hainais, and Nadacos—living near the land grant might have agreed to the terms of the treaty, it is doubtful whether the Alabamas, Coushattas, Yowani Choctaws, and Biloxis, whose villages lay fifty miles to the south, would have done so.[4]

At the same time Duwali and the Cherokees were negotiating with the rebels, representatives of the Mexican government increased their efforts to convince the east Texas Indians to join forces with them. In February 1836, as he crossed the Rio Grande at the head of several thousand Mexican troops, Santa Anna noted that the Cherokees "held a solemn promise from [his] government to give them lands." He suggested that if they were placated, they could be "used to good advantage." Soon thereafter, General Cos commissioned Eusebio Cortinez as Indian agent and instructed him to raise a troop of east Texas Indians to fight the rebels. Cortinez met with Duwali at his village and informed the Cherokee chief of the approaching Mexican army. Realizing that the Mexicans might be holding the upper hand in Texas, Duwali agreed to Cortinez's request that the Cherokees attack Nacogdoches and set fire to the town if called upon to do so. Having pledged his tribes' support to both sides of the struggle in Texas, Duwali and the Cherokees now sat back and waited to see who would win.[5]

The Mexican government also commissioned Manuel Flores to enlist Kadohadacho warriors to fight against the Texan revolutionaries. Throughout the fall and winter the main body of the Kadohadachos had remained quietly in their villages near the Louisiana-Texas border awaiting their first annuity payment before moving to Texas as called for in the treaty they had signed in July 1835. Flores, who was a resident of the area and longtime friend of the tribe, met with the Kadohadachos in February 1836 and promised them money and "free plunder" if they would attack the Texans, whom he shrewdly characterized as being Americans. In addition to these promises, Flores frightened the tribesmen by claiming that the United States government "intended to exterminate them." Flores's cajoling influenced the uncertain Kadohadacho chief Tarshar to lead most of the tribe's warriors into Texas along with the Mexican agent. The Kadohadachos passed Flores's offer on to the Hainais, Nadacos, and the various Wichita tribes, all of whom then gathered at the forks of the Trinity River to judge the progress of Santa Anna's army.[6]

As events in Texas unfolded quickly over the next month and a half, most of the province's Indians observed the dangerous situation from positions of safety. On March 2, only a week after the signing of the Cherokee Treaty, a convention of Texas delegates met at Washington-on-the-Brazos and formally declared independence from Mexico. They then formulated a constitution and provided a provisional government for Texas until the document could be ratified. The convention chose David G. Burnet—an empresario whose lapsed grant had conflicted with the Cherokee lands—as president, and the provisional government took no action to ratify the treaty with the Indians. Instead, the delegates, along with most of the recent settlers in east Texas, took flight toward Louisiana in the so-called Runaway Scrape after hearing the news that the Mexican army had defeated the rebel forces at San Antonio and Goliad. As the remaining Texas troops under Houston retreated eastward, the general sent a delegation to ask the nearby Alabamas and Coushattas for assistance. Like the other Texas tribes, however, both groups preferred to stay out of the fray and neither the Alabamas nor the Coushattas committed warriors to the fight.[7]

As Santa Anna's large army hotly pursued Houston's retreating forces, rumors of an imminent attack by the Cherokees and the Kadohadachos were rife among the fleeing settlers. When Duwali advised a few Nacogdoches settlers that they were in danger due to the approaching Mexican army, some Texans mistook his warning as a threat. A report soon spread that the Cherokees were in their villages "with very hostile feelings [against the Texans], and in a state of preparation for war." Others believed that the Kadohadachos, in the wake of the fall of the Alamo, were leading a force of Indians, estimated at seventeen hundred warriors, from the forks of the Trinity to pillage the emptied settlements of east Texas. As a result of these unfounded rumors, the Texans appealed to the United States for help in containing the Indians, citing an 1831 treaty with Mexico in which each country pledged to keep the tribes within its territory from crossing the border. On March 20, John T. Mason of Nacogdoches addressed an urgent dispatch to the commander of American troops at Fort Jesup near Natchitoches, begging him to send a messenger to the Indians in Texas from the United States, "particularly to the Caddoes, to make them keep quiet." Continued pleas caused General Edmund P. Gaines, the officer in charge of American troops along the Louisiana-Texas frontier, to order fourteen companies to move to the border and encamp on the east bank of the Sabine. General Gaines sent messengers to notify the Cherokees and Kadohadachos that their active involvement in the war in Texas would not be tolerated. He also dispatched soldiers to the Kadohadacho villages to investigate Manuel Flores's activities among the tribe.[8]

Even though none of the Kadohadachos, or any of the tribes of east Texas, joined the Mexican forces or attacked the Texans on their own, American and Texas officials continued to be suspicious of the Indians even after General Houston defeated Santa Anna's army at San Jacinto on April 21, a victory that gained independence for the Republic of Texas. General Gaines notified American Secretary of War Lewis Cass in early June that he believed the Kado-hadachos and Cherokees were "disposed to keep up appearances of a pacific disposition . . . until a more favorable change occurs in the affairs of those pretended friends." A few Kadohadacho warriors reinforced these suspicions in June 1836 by joining with the Kichais, Tawakonis, and Wacos to attack the residents of Robertson's colony, located on the Brazos River upstream from Austin's colony. Although most of the Caddo tribesmen had peacefully returned to their villages in East Texas and along the border with Louisiana, this raid, coupled with a rumor that another large Mexican force was headed toward Texas, caused General Gaines to order his troops across the border to occupy Nacogdoches in July.[9]

In the meantime, a few militant Cherokees, disappointed by the Texans' refusal to ratify their treaty and acknowledge the grant of land to the Indians, began to consider taking up arms against the settlers. In July a group of Cherokees visited General José Urrea, commander of Mexican troops in Mata-moros. Urrea assured the contingent that the Mexicans supported Cherokee claims to lands in Texas and informed them that troops were planning an invasion to take back the province. Inspired by Urrea's words, the Cherokee militants agreed to attack the Texans when the invading Mexican army reached the Guadalupe River. Texan officials learned about the Cherokee embassy to Mexico in August when Chief Duwali bragged to a spy, posing as a Mexican army officer, that the time would soon be right for the natives "to make a diversion" on behalf of their allies south of the Rio Grande. Hoping to win the favor of the man he thought was a Mexican soldier, Duwali stated that he "had sworn an eternal war against" the Texans and was eager to assist the Mexicans in their campaign to recover their lost territory. The Cherokee chief claimed that all of the other east Texas tribes, except the Shawnees, Delawares, and Kickapoos, were also ready to fight against the Texans. Later in the month Texas officials believed that they had corroborated Duwali's statements when they learned that Eusebio Cortinez had met with several tribes at the Cherokee village on August 29.[10]

Reports of a Mexican-Indian attack panicked the citizens of east Texas, many of whom had just recently returned to their homes following the Run-away Scrape. Sam Houston, campaigning for the presidency of the Republic of Texas, informed General Gaines of the Cherokees' activities and suggested that he reinforce the American troops occupying Nacogdoches. Houston also issued a proclamation calling for several east Texas communities to form militias in defense of an Indian uprising. These actions, combined with the inability of the Mexicans to mount an invasion of Texas, caused the Cherokee militants and their allies to abort whatever attack they might have been planning. Although most of the east Texas Indians returned peacefully to their villages, the Hainais and Nadacos, feeling threatened by the edgy Texan settlers, decided to abandon their establishments, and both tribes moved west to the Trinity River.[11]

Events taking place in Louisiana soon induced many Kadohadacho warriors to leave the United States and join their Caddo kinsmen near the forks of the Trinity. At the end of the summer of 1836, however, Chief Tarshar and most of the Kadohadachos were back in their villages on the Louisiana-Texas frontier. An American army officer, Major B. Riley, sent to investigate their situation in August, found the Kadohadachos to be "very peaceably disposed." Riley also discovered a "great abundance" of whiskey in the villages, causing him to conclude that the Kadohadachos were "a poor, miserable people, incapable of the smallest exertion, either as it regards living, or any thing else, except liquor." Indeed, Tarshar was drunk when Riley arrived at his village, and the major had to wait until the following morning to address him. The hung-over Kadohadacho chief sadly admitted that alcohol was a problem, but he insisted that his tribe had "never fought against the whites, nor ever had any disposition do so." He soothed Riley by claiming that "all of our children have been raised in this country with the Americans, and we consider ourselves their brothers and best friends, and we like them very much."[12]

Tarshar behaved obsequiously in the presence of the American officer, because the Kadohadachos were desperately awaiting their first annuity payment of $10,000 and did not want to jeopardize the transaction. Unfortunately, the tribe had given power of attorney to the devious Jehiel Brooks at the close of the treaty council in 1835, and they depended on him to deliver their money. On September 10, 1836, nine days after the payment was due, Brooks received the Kadohadacho annuity from the Treasury Department in Washington. In October Brooks met with the Kadohadacho headmen in Shreveport in order to pay the tribe. Brooks showed them ten boxes—each marked as being worth $1,000—which he claimed had been sent directly from President Jackson. Upon opening the boxes, the Kadohadacho leaders "were very much disappointed and complained that they had not received one-half of what was due to them." One witness to the transaction believed that the contents were worth only between $1,500 and $2,000. In response to Brooks's swindle, in which the American agent realized at least an $8,000 profit, a few angered Kadohadacho tribesmen entered Texas and established a small village near the Hainais and Nadacos on the Trinity River. Although a few Caddo warriors raided settlements along the Brazos River, by the end of 1836 the tense situation in east Texas had settled down, with the Indians and Texans maintaining a tenuous coexistence with each other.[13]

The large numbers of Euroamericans who moved to Texas following the revolution, however, threatened continued peaceful relations between the various tribes and the newly independent republic. Between 1834 and 1847, the population of Texas—including slaves—grew sevenfold from about twenty thousand people to just over 140,000. More than one-third of the Texans lived in northeastern counties near the 2,500 or so emigrant tribes and native Kadohadachos. Twenty-five thousand settlers resided in southeastern Texas, putting enormous pressure on the 1,500 emigrant Indians living between the Sabine and the Trinity. Incredibly, another 25,000 Texans pushed west and settled in central Texas counties stretching all the way from San Antonio northward to Dallas. The expansion of the frontier westward began to crowd the seven thousand or so Lipan Apaches, Tonkawas, and Penateka Comanches, most of whom had never lived so close to Euroamericans.[14]

The majority of the land-hungry newcomers came from the American South, and shared the earlier immigrants' hostile attitude toward Indians. They came to Texas to establish cash-crop plantations, farms, and ranches and had no desire to trade with the Indians or deal with them in any way. One of the few Texans who desired to coexist peacefully with the tribes, though, was Sam Houston, the new republic's first elected president. Houston understood the problems of the tribes and was well disposed to them, especially since he had married a Cherokee woman and lived with part of the tribe from 1829 to 1832. The president also realized the dangers and the high cost of continuing the hostilities with the tribes of Texas and, therefore, he attempted to carry out a policy of peace. In his inaugural address of October 1836, Houston stated that "treaties of peace and amity and the maintenance of good faith with the Indians, present themselves to my mind as the most rational ground on which to obtain their friendship. Let us abstain on our part from aggression, establish commerce with the different tribes, supply their useful and necessary wants, maintain even handed justice with them, and natural reason will teach them the utility of our friendship." Few other Texans, however, shared the president's idealistic vision of friendship with the Indians, and Houston's so-called peace policy ultimately ended in failure.[15]

In December 1836, the Texas Congress enacted a law "to protect the frontier" that incorporated parts of Houston's peace policy while at the same time taking measures to prepare the republic for hostile actions. This bill provided that the president should erect blockhouses, forts, and trading posts as he deemed necessary to deal with the Indians. The president was authorized to make treaties with the Indians and to appoint agents to reside among them. The bill also appropriated $20,000 to be expended in articles, presents, and gifts for the use of the Indians. In addition to these provisions devoted to maintaining the Indians' friendship, this act, as well as subsequent bills passed early in 1837, also organized a three-division corps of Texas Rangers in order to fight hostile tribes. Each division was to have attached to it a company of friendly Indians to serve as spies, guides, and auxiliaries. These Indians were to be supplied with provisions and given such pay as might be agreed upon between them and the president. [16]

Even before the passage of the bill, President Houston, anxious to implement his peace policy, appointed a two-man commission to hold a council and conclude a treaty with the Wichitas and Comanches, as well as with the Caddo tribes living near the forks of the Trinity River. Through the commissioners, the president sent the Indians a message that promised them happiness and material aid if they would agree to peace. It also informed them of Santa Anna's defeat and warned that they could not depend upon assistance from Mexico. Unfortunately for Houston, the commissioners were unable to establish contact with the various tribes. Following the commission's failure, the president turned to his old friend Duwali for assistance. In order to win the tribe's favor, Houston had resubmitted the Cherokee Treaty to the Texas Senate for approval in December 1836. Duwali, believing that his tribe now stood to profit from friendship with the Texans, agreed to act as the president's emissary. Therefore, in the spring of 1837 the Cherokee chief toured the prairies and informed the Comanches, Wichitas, and Caddos of Houston's offer of peace. [17]

The Caddos were the first tribe to respond to Duwali's entreaties. Desirous of peace so they could settle down on the Trinity and plant their crops in security, Hainai and Nadaco leaders traveled to Nacogdoches in August 1837 and signed a treaty with Texas officials. The Hainai and Nadaco agreement was the first in a series of treaties between the Republic of Texas and various Indian tribes, all of which contained virtually the same provisions. Both parties pledged perpetual peace and amity, and the Texans promised to supply the tribes with presents and an authorized trader. The Texans, however, jealously guarded their rights to the soil, and the treaty did not reserve any land for the Hainais and Nadacos, or for any of the other tribes that agreed to peace. Despite the lack of land grants, over the next several months Tonkawa chief Placido and Lipan Apache chief Cuelgas de Castro entered into peace treaties with the Republic of Texas in the name of their respective tribes. Both the Tonkawas and the Lipans hoped to maintain the Texans' favor by acting as guides and

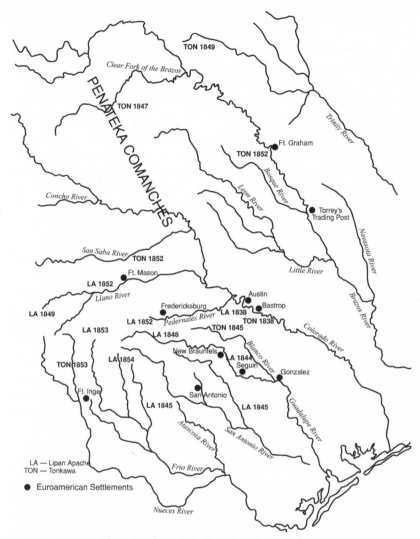

Lipan Apache and Tonkawa locations, 1838–54

auxiliaries against Indians who remained hostile to the young republic. In order to better assist the Texans, Tonkawa and Lipan tribal members moved eastward and established various rancherías in the Colorado River Valley near the settlement of Bastrop.[18]

The Wichita tribes, though, maintained their distance from the Texans. The Taovayas, Kichais, Tawakonis, and Wacos remained in their villages on both sides of the Red River, quietly tending to their fields while conducting a limited commerce at trading posts established by Auguste Chouteau on the Canadian River and Holland Coffee on the Red, across from the mouth of the Washita. The Wichitas mainly dealt in buffalo robes and refrained, for the most part, from stealing horses in Texas. Unfortunately, in the summer of 1837 an epidemic disease swept through the Wichita villages and killed a great number of the tribe. So many Wichitas died that "in many instances the dead could not be removed from the lodges for the want of proper persons to do it." In the fall, crop failure compounded the Wichitas' misery.[19]

The Kadohadachos, another tribe that lived on the extremes of the Republic of Texas, also suffered in 1837. Although a few tribal members had joined the Hainais and Nadacos near the forks of the Trinity River, the main body of the Kadohadachos remained near the Louisiana-Texas frontier, under the direction of Chief Tarshar, awaiting their second annuity payment. The Kadohadachos hoped that John Green, the man they had granted power of attorney in place of the crooked Agent Brooks, would deliver the full $10,000 due to them. Instead, Green met with the tribe in September and handed over only a few kegs of powder and one hundred pounds of lead, "not exceeding fifteen hundred dollars" in worth. Having their annuity stolen from them two years in a row caused another group of Kadohadachos to abandon the United States to unite with their kinsmen in Texas. Soon after moving to the Trinity River, the Kadohadachos, along with members of the Wichita tribes, engaged in hostilities with Texas representatives. In November 1837, eighteen Texas Rangers killed a Kichai warrior near the mouth of the Clear Fork of the Brazos. A few days later, near the headwaters of the Trinity River, a group of Wichitas and Kadohadachos intercepted the Rangers and killed half the party.[20]

President Houston's peace policy also failed to curb hostilities between the Texans and the Penateka Comanches. While the Tonkawas, Lipans, and Caddos accepted treaties that did not grant them land, the more powerful Penatekas demanded that the Texans recognize a permanent boundary between the Indians and the settlers, who were expanding dangerously close to their hunting grounds. In February 1838, more than one hundred Penateka Comanches entered San Antonio and invited Texas officials to travel to the Hill Country to discuss a peace treaty. In response, Moseley Baker, a member of the Texas Congress, accompanied the Penateka embassy to a ranchería on the Colorado River and held an informal meeting with fifteen headmen. Although the Comanche leaders expressed a desire to establish peace, they told Baker that they "would listen to no terms unless the government secured to them the full and undisturbed possession" of the country north of the divide between the Colorado and the Guadalupe rivers and west of Bastrop. Baker responded that he did not have the authority to discuss the boundary situation, but offered the Comanches a council in San Antonio with Texas officials. The Penatekas agreed, and Chiefs Eswacany and Essomanny led an embassy to Béxar that met with Texas officials in May. While the Texans tried to discuss the advantages of peace and the benefits of trade, the Penateka leaders persisted in demanding the establishment of a boundary line. When it became obvious that the negotiations were not advancing, the Penateka leaders accepted a few gifts and politely departed.[21]

At about the same time, a different group of Penatekas, led by Chief Muguara, also entered into negotiations with the Texans. A few warriors appeared at Coleman's Fort on Walnut Creek in Bastrop County and asked that a commissioner be sent to their camp to discuss a treaty. Noah Smithwick, a Ranger officer, traveled with the embassy to Muguara's village, located about thirty miles up the Colorado River. Smithwick discussed the situation with Muguara, who complained that the Texans were invading their territory, "building houses and fences, and the buffalos get frightened and leave and never come back, and the Indians are left to starve . . . if the white men would draw a line defining their claims and keep on their side of it the red men would not molest them." Smithwick responded that he had no powers to negotiate a treaty and convinced Muguara and a few others to hold talks with the Texan president. In May 1838, the Comanche delegation met with Houston and entered into a peace treaty in which the Texans agreed to appoint an agent to deal with the Penatekas and to supervise trade. Despite Muguara's insistence, the treaty made no mention of Comanche rights to the land, nor of a boundary line between the signatories. President Houston explained to the Penateka chief that even if he "could build a wall from the Red River to the Rio Grande, so high that no Indian could scale it, the white people would go crazy trying to devise means to get beyond it."[22]

The treaty between the Penatekas and the Republic of Texas proved ineffectual. The Texans' refusal to recognize a boundary line angered the Penatekas, and the Comanches killed a few traders who ventured to their villages soon after the signing of the treaty. A series of skirmishes between the Texans and Comanches ensued. In August 1838, Texas Rangers fought a group of Penatekas near the Medina River. Two months later a Comanche party killed thirteen Texans who were surveying land west of San Antonio. Penateka warriors from Muguara's band also ventured east of Béxar to raid settlements on the Guadalupe River, where they abducted a thirteen-year-old girl named Matilda Lockhart. Other Comanche war parties kidnapped women and children, along with stealing horses, from various settlements in Texas and Mexico. By the end of 1838, the treaty that had been signed in May had been all but forgotten by the Penateka Comanches and the Texans.[23]

The biggest failure of Houston's peace plan came in east Texas. In October 1837, the Texas Senate's Standing Committee on Indian Affairs issued its opinion on the Cherokee Treaty. The report stated that the Mexican government had not granted any tribe rights to the soil in Texas, and that Burnet's empresarial grant, which overlapped the Cherokee lands, was evidence that Mexico had not intended the land for Indians. Claiming the Cherokees "have been the most savage and ruthless of our frontier enemies," the report stated that the treaty concluded in February 1836 was based on Duwali's "false promises" and, as a result, "of no effect and void." Therefore, the committee advised the Senate to "disapprove of and utterly refuse to ratify" the Cherokee Treaty. Two months later, the Senate—despite the wishes of President Houston—followed the committee's advice and voted to reject the treaty.[24]

The treaty's dismissal caused Duwali and the Cherokees to be very receptive to plans being hatched south of the Rio Grande. Mexico had never given up hope of reacquiring Texas, and officials along the border had formulated a scheme that would employ the tribes of east Texas, along with a group of discontented Tejanos located near Nacogdoches, to harass the Texans until a larger Mexican force could enter the province and reclaim it. In May 1838, Mexican military commanders set the plan in motion as Vicente Córdova, a former East Texas alcalde and judge, was commissioned to organize the Tejanos of Nacogdoches. At the same time, Juan Pedro Miracle, a Mexican agent at Matamoros, was ordered to enter Texas and, with the assistance of Córdova and Manuel Flores, hold a council of all of the "captains of friendly Indians" to ask them to "take up arms in defense of the integrity of the Mexican territory in Texas." The Indians were to be given powder, lead, and tobacco, and they were to take the field immediately. Once the Indians and the Tejanos had succeeded in defeating the Texans near Nacogdoches, Mexican troops would invade across the Rio Grande and reconquer the entire province. Miracle was ordered to promise the tribes that "as soon as the campaign is over . . . a commissioner [will] give to each possession of the land they are entitled to."[25]

Learning of the plan through messengers, the Cherokees and Kadohadachos sent twenty warriors to Matamoros to escort Miracle and his force of one hundred troops across the Rio Grande on May 29. As the Miracle party made its way northeastward, Duwali arranged for a meeting of the east Texas tribes to determine a plan of action. On June 14, Cherokee, Shawnee, Delaware, Kickapoo, and Coushatta headmen charged that the Texans were "making fools of them," and they agreed that "war was inevitable" if they did not receive the land granted to them in the Cherokee Treaty. A week later a group of Kickapoos "kindly" received the Mexicans east of the Brazos River and accompanied them to the Trinity, where they met Córdova on July 5. Three days later Chief Duwali arrived to conduct Miracle and his men to the Cherokee village. On July 20, Miracle and Córdova held a conference with leading Tejanos from Nacogdoches, as well as with the headmen of the Cherokees, Delawares, Shawnees, and Kickapoos. A Shawnee warrior protested that no action should be taken until the arrival of the regular Mexican army, yet the group decided to go to war "as soon as circumstances would permit, and as speedily as possible."[26]

As Córdova assembled his troops for an assault on Nacogdoches over the next few weeks, Miracle tried to enlist more Indians to the cause. Crossing east of the Neches River, Miracle met with Chief Tarshar and a group of Kadohadachos on July 29. After Miracle informed the gathering of the planned campaign against the Texans, one Kadohadacho warrior responded that he "preferred to remain with [the Mexicans] and fight" rather than return to the United States. Complaining that the Americans had not paid them in full for their territory, Tarshar decided to throw in his lot with Miracle in hope of receiving land in Texas from the Mexicans. Soon after the meeting, Tarshar returned to the Kadohadacho villages to enlist more warriors.[27]

By the first week of August, Córdova had gathered a force of four hundred or so troops—including Cherokee, Shawnee, Delaware, Kickapoo, Kadohadacho, Coushatta, and Biloxi warriors—at a camp on the Angelina River near Nacogdoches. On August 7, however, Texan forces discovered this contingent before the planned attack could be launched. President Houston responded by asking the United States to send troops across the border because the Kadohadachos and other American Indians had joined the rebel Mexicans and were ready to attack and plunder Nacogdoches. The president also ordered General Thomas Jefferson Rusk, commander of the Texas militia, to raise a force to defend the town. Hoping to avoid unnecessary bloodshed, Houston ordered Rusk to keep his troops on the east side of the Angelina River, outside the Cherokee land claim. Houston then sent a series of letters to Duwali and Gatunwali, warning them that they must have nothing to do with Córdova's force. The president also promised to have the Cherokee boundary line surveyed in the near future despite the treaty's rejection by the Texas Senate the previous year.[28]

Fearing Córdova's force, General Rusk defied President Houston's orders a few days later by crossing the Angelina and advancing toward Duwali's village. Rather than fight the superior Texas forces, Córdova's army retreated westward and took refuge in the Kickapoo village on the Trinity River, located just downstream from the Hainai and Nadaco town. Duwali and Gatunwali, however, remained with most of the Cherokees outside of Nacogdoches. Hoping to avoid the destruction of their village, on August 15 both men met with Rusk's agents and declared their peaceful intentions. The Texans remained suspicious of the Cherokees, though, especially after Miracle was killed a few days later and his diary, which detailed his attempts to foment rebellion among the tribes of east Texas, was recovered from his body.[29]

The Córdova Rebellion, though unsuccessful, convinced many Texans that President Houston's peace policy was not working, and that the Republic of Texas should take a more aggressive stance toward Indians. During the concurrent presidential election campaign, Houston's political enemies charged that he had been ineffectual in the face of Córdova and the Indians. On September 3, 1838, less than a month after the discovery of Córdova's forces, Mirabeau Buonaparte Lamar, a proven foe of the Indians, was elected president of Texas. In his first message to the Texas Congress, Lamar boldly stated that he considered Houston's policy of pacification a complete failure and announced that the time had come for "the prosecution of an exterminating war on [Texas Indian] warriors; which will admit no compromise and have no termination except in their total extinction or total expulsion." Lamar was not inaugurated until December, but his election had immediate repercussions. The belligerence of Texas troops toward the Indians in the fall of 1838, coupled with the fact that the commanders often reported their actions to the president-elect, rather than President Houston, demonstrates that Lamar's election had unleashed the republic's hostile energies.[30]

With tensions high, and Córdova's force still at large, Texan troops responded aggressively to Indian depredations in the fall of 1838. On October 5, a large group of Indians killed eighteen Texans at the Killough settlement, located within the Cherokee land grant a few miles east of the Neches River. Three days later warriors from various tribes killed another eighteen Texans who were surveying bounty and headright grants west of the Trinity River for soldiers who had served in the Texas Revolution. Learning that Córdova and his troops were camped at the Kickapoo village, General Rusk led a force of two hundred men west to the Trinity River and assaulted the town on October 16. Following a fierce battle in which more than thirty tribesmen died, Córdova's army disintegrated as the Indians, Tejanos, and Mexicans fled to the west and south. Most of the Kickapoos retreated into the Indian Territory and established various settlements in the valleys of the Washita and the Canadian. However, one band of eighty tribesmen moved south of the Rio Grande and settled near Matamoros with the approval of the Mexican government. Future migrations would augment the numbers of the so-called Mexican Kickapoos over the course of the next few decades.[31]

After securing their western flank, the Texans turned their attentions to a perceived threat from the Kadohadachos on the eastern frontier with the United States. While most of the tribe had joined Tarshar and moved to the

Trinity River after linking with Córdova, less than two hundred Kadohadachos, under the direction of heretofore second chief Tsauninot, remained near the Louisiana-Texas boundary awaiting the payment of their annuity for 1838. On October 11, these Kadohadachos formally gave power of attorney to Charles A. Sewall, a Shreveport merchant who proved more honest than the tribes' previous agents. Sewall immediately began distributing goods from his own store to the needy Kadohadachos; in addition to blankets and other supplies, on October 25 he gave the tribe a "scant supply for hunting" that consisted of seventeen rifles, eighteen pistols, eight kegs of powder, and two kegs of lead. A few days later, just as the Kadohadachos had begun to travel west for their annual winter hunt, news spread along the frontier that a group of Indians had killed two families on the Texas side of the border. Attributing the deaths to the newly armed Kadohadachos, Texas officials ordered a company of forty militia to "destroy" the Kadohadachos in Texas or "follow them across the [boundary] line and exterminate them." Alarmed that "people on both sides of the border suspected them of hostile intentions," the Kadohadachos returned to Shreveport, and Sewall directed Tsauninot and his band to an island in the Red River where they could find game.[32]

Despite the Kadohadachos' retreat to the American side of the border, Texas officials insisted upon disarming the tribe. General Rusk, realizing the seriousness of a body of Texas troops crossing the international boundary, assumed command of the militia and added another one hundred soldiers to his force. On November 23, the Texans advanced into Louisiana and surrounded the Kadohadacho warriors and their families the following day. Realizing the futility of fighting, Tsauninot met with General Rusk, who demanded that the Kadohadachos give up their arms and ammunition to their agent in Shreveport. When Tsauninot protested that his people would starve if they surrendered their weapons, Rusk replied that the Republic of Texas would provide sustenance for the Kadohadachos as long as their arms were detained. Having little choice but to submit, Tsauninot met with General Rusk and Agent Sewall in Shreveport a few days later and finalized the agreement. Sufficiently chastised, the Kadohadachos retreated to a small peninsula between Cross Lake and Caddo Lake, where they remained for the rest of the winter.[33]

His mission successfully accomplished, General Rusk and his troops crossed west of the border to join a group of Texas soldiers who were advancing toward the three Caddo villages at the forks of the Trinity River. Upon learning of the approaching hostile force, Tarshar's band of Kadohadachos, along with the Hainais and Nadacos, hastily abandoned their encampments, leaving behind buffalo robes, blankets, and guns, and traveled west to the upper Brazos River. The Texans destroyed the remnants of the villages but broke off pursuit because it was the dead of winter and their provisions had run out. From the Brazos, the Caddo tribes eventually retreated across the Red River into the Indian Territory, abandoning Texas altogether. Thus, Texan hostility had forced all the Caddos to return to the United States despite the provisions of the treaty of 1835, which had called for the Kadohadachos to abandon American territory by the following July.[34]

Over the next few years a series of events took place that caused Tsauninot's band of Kadohadachos to join the rest of the tribe in the Indian Territory. Inquiries into General Rusk's "invasion" of Louisiana induced United States officials to order an investigation of the Kadohadachos' situation in the spring of 1839. An American army officer met with Tsauninot and found his homeless band of 162 people "destitute in every respect." Therefore, the federal government entrusted William Armstrong, agent for the Choctaw Indians (who had recently been removed to the Indian Territory), with the Kadohadacho annuity payment for 1839, which he distributed to the members of Tsauninot's band. In August 1840, Chief Tarshar sent his son, Bintah, to meet with Agent Armstrong at Fort Towson, at the mouth of the Kiamichi River, to inquire about the final annuity due the tribe in 1840. Bintah informed Armstrong that Tarshar's Kadohadacho band deserved the payment since they had yet to receive any of the previous annuities. Bintah also indicated an interest in permanently settling in the Indian Territory, as the Texans would not let them return south of the Red River. Catching wind of Tarshar's desire to obtain the final annuity payment, Tsauninot moved his band out of Louisiana and into the Indian Territory to be nearer Fort Towson.[35]

By September 1841, both Kadohadacho bands were on the Choctaw Reservation waiting to receive their annuity. That fall Tarshar and Tsauninot died, helping clear the way for the Kadohadachos' reunification. A leading man, Red Bear, assumed the position of Kadohadacho leader rather than the young and inexperienced Bintah. On November 8, 1841, Armstrong received the $10,000 from the Treasury Department and delivered the cash individually to members of both bands later that winter. Happy with the payment, the entire Caddo tribe—Kadohadachos, Nadacos, and Hainais—moved westward and planted crops in the spring of 1842 on the right bank of the Washita River. Although the village was located on lands recently granted to the Chickasaw Indians, the Caddos petitioned the United States government for permission to remain north of the Red River, free from the wrath of the hostile Texans.[36]

In the meantime, President Lamar, following his inauguration on December 10, 1838, immediately took steps to complete the goal of driving the remaining Indians from Texas. In order to enhance the republic's military capabilities, Lamar convinced the Texan Congress to pass four bills within a month concerning offensive and defensive measures against the Indians. On December 21, Congress approved an act calling for the establishment of a regiment, containing over eight hundred men, for the protection of the northern and western frontier. One week later President Lamar signed a law for the "further protection of the frontier against the Comanches and other Indians." This act provided for eight companies of mounted volunteers, or Rangers, to be stationed on the frontier. In January 1839, Congress gave President Lamar the power to accept the services of three companies of Rangers for immediate active service on the frontiers of Bastrop and Milam counties, and appropriated $1 million to support the ranger companies and the regular military. The Texans were now ready to mount campaigns against Indians on all fronts. [37]

President Lamar quickly found justification for driving the emigrant Indians from northeastern Texas. In late February 1839, General Valentin Canalizo, commander of Mexican forces stationed at Matamoros, ordered Agents Córdova and Flores to travel throughout east Texas in hope of assembling yet another Indian army to assist the effort to take back the province from the revolutionaries. The two Mexican agents were to encourage the Indians to harass the Texans in order to keep them from having the "opportunity to strengthen their establishments, and increase their population and resources," which would allow them to gather such force, "that it will be afterwards difficult to expel them." Canalizo sent letters with Flores to the Kadohadacho and Kickapoo chiefs, as well as to Gatunwali and Duwali of the Cherokees, assuring them that these operations would "ensure the quiet possession of your lands and prevent any adventurer from again disturbing the peaceful repose of your families, or from trampling under foot the soil in which are deposited the remains of your ancestors." [38]

In May 1839, before Flores could deliver Canalizo's message to the various Indian chiefs, Texas Rangers intercepted him and a company of Mexican troops on the San Gabriel River. In the ensuing battle, the Texans defeated the party and captured a packet of letters containing Canalizo's correspondence with Córdova and Flores, as well as the letters to the Indians. The packet was turned over to President Lamar who, with the assistance of his secretary of war, Albert Sidney Johnston, immediately took advantage of the evidence to demand the Cherokee removal from Texas. On May 26, Lamar sent a message to Duwali outlining his position on the Cherokees, in particular, and the Indians of Texas, in general. The president charged Duwali with conspiring with Córdova, and asserted that his village was "the chief point where our enemies have met to concert their plans and we believe that it has been partly through your tribe, that other Indians with whom we are at war, have received their ammunition and supplies." Lamar stated that the Cherokees had been erroneously acting as if the treaty of February 1836 was valid. He pointedly informed Duwali that the "people of Texas have acquired their sovereignty by many rightful and glorious achievements, and they will exercise it without division or community with another People. They can recognize no alien political power within their borders; and you and your tribe, having no legitimate rights of soil or sovereignty in this country, can never be permitted to exercise a conflicting authority. The Treaty alluded to, was a nullity when made—is inoperative now;—has never been sanctioned by this Government, and never will be." Therefore, Lamar demanded the removal of the Cherokees from the boundaries of Texas. [39]

Unsure how to respond, Duwali asked that the Cherokees be given enough time to raise and harvest the year's crops before leaving. Duwali's request was denied, and on June 27 President Lamar appointed a commission, headed by Vice President Burnet, Secretary of War Johnston, and General Rusk to "effect the immediate removal of the Cherokee Indians, and the ultimate removal of all other emigrant tribes now residing in Texas, beyond Her Territorial Limits." Supported by nearly five hundred Texan troops and forty Tonkawa auxiliaries, the commissioners held a series of meetings with Duwali, along with Shawnee and Delaware headmen, at the Cherokee village in mid-July. Realizing that it would be suicidal to fight, the three emigrant tribes agreed to sign a treaty of removal that guaranteed to them the profit from their crops and the cost of removal. Duwali, however, protested a clause that called for the Indians to be escorted to the United States under guard of Texas troops. After a few days of haggling over this issue, on July 15 the exasperated commissioners informed the Cherokees that a Texan force would march on their village immediately. [40]

Rather than fight or surrender, the Cherokees decided to abandon their village and head north on their own. The Texan troops, however, aggressively pursued the fleeing Indians and skirmished with the Cherokee rearguard a few miles north of Duwali's town. The next day the Texan force caught up with the Cherokees at the Delaware village, located on the headwaters of the Neches River. Hoping to protect their women and children, the retreating Cherokee and Delaware warriors turned and took up a defensive position in the Indians' cornfields. The Texans set fire to the Delaware huts and then attacked the Indians. In a battle that lasted nearly two hours, the Texans drove the warriors into the river bottom where they killed more than one hundred tribesmen before the Indians finally withdrew. Duwali was the last Indian standing on the field of battle; dismounting from his disabled horse he was shot twice by Texan soldiers. He walked forward a little and fell, and then rose to a sitting position. A Texas Ranger then dispatched the aged Cherokee chief by shooting him in the head at point blank range. Over the next few days the

Texans destroyed all the other Cherokee and Delaware farms in the area as the survivors retreated north across the Red River into the Indian Territory.[41]

The Texans' brutality induced Chief Linney of the Shawnees to sign a treaty of removal a few weeks after the destruction of his Indian allies' villages. On August 2, the Shawnees agreed to leave Texas peaceably in return for payment for the improvements on their land, crops, and for all property left behind. Over the next few weeks Texan agents distributed nearly $8,000 to sixty-three Shawnee headmen. In late September Texan officials escorted the Shawnees to the Red and paid for them to be ferried across the river to the Indian Territory. The tribe settled on the Canadian River and became the nucleus of the present-day Absentee band of Shawnees. Within a year of Lamar's election, the emigrant tribes of northeastern Texas had been forced to abandon their homes, in which many had resided for more than two decades, and retreat to the relative safety of the United States.[42]

Encouraged by the events in northeastern Texas, citizens of the southeastern part of the republic acted on their own to try and force the region's few remaining Indians from their midst. As their numbers dwindled in the 1830s, most of the Biloxis, Yowani Choctaws, Aises, and Bidais—as well as a small group of Pakana Muskogees who had recently arrived from the United States—had taken refuge in the Alabama and Coushatta villages. Sharing a similar culture and living in the same area for more than three decades, many of the tribal members had intermarried and all were generally recognized as being either Alabamas or Coushattas. Pressured by increased American immigration following the success of the Texas Revolution, conflicts inevitably arose between the Indians and the Texans. In June 1839, Texas settlers accused the Indians of poaching horses and responded by killing five Coushattas in the act of stealing tribal cattle. Informed of these depredations by messengers from Coushatta chief Colita, President Lamar addressed a letter to the people living near the Indians' lands. Lamar characterized the Coushattas as being a "weak and defenseless tribe, and as such not to be dreaded." Surprisingly, the Texas president implored the settlers to leave the Indians in peace, and appointed an agent to supervise their actions. In November Lamar announced in his second message to Congress that the Texan republic should officially concede land to the Alabamas and Coushattas. As a result of Lamar's support, the Texas Congress passed an act in January 1840 granting the Alabamas two leagues of land at the Fenced-in-village, and two leagues for the Coushattas, taking in Baptiste's and Colita's villages.[43]

Surveyors began marking off the Indians' lands in the spring of 1840, but heavy rains and flooding forced them to suspend their activities before the mapping could be completed. Soon thereafter the Indians clashed with settlers encroaching upon their concessions, resulting in deaths on both sides. Enraged local citizens wrote Lamar, suggesting that the president "order all of those Indians out of Texas, and if they refuse to go, authorize their removal by force . . . the whole country would turn out to effect this object." Others warned the Alabama and Coushatta agent to restrict the Indians to the "smallest limits . . . otherwise, thoughtless men will kill them." With tensions extremely high, the Alabamas abandoned their village—as well as many horses, cattle, and two hundred acres of fenced land suitable for cultivation—later in the summer. Texan settlers squatted on the Coushatta land grants, forcing the tribe to move elsewhere. Despite his previous defense of the tribes, President Lamar did nothing to recover the Indians' lands. Therefore, many of the Alabamas and Coushattas abandoned Texas and joined the Creek Indians north of the Red River, while others settled on Chickasaw territory near the mouth of the Washita River. By 1844 only a little more than two hundred Alabamas and Coushattas remained in southeastern Texas, barely scraping out a living on unclaimed lands in the Trinity and Neches valleys.[44]

At the same time that Lamar's troops were driving most of the Indians from the eastern part of the republic, Texan forces, in conjunction with Indian auxiliaries, initiated brutal warfare against the Penateka Comanches on the western frontier. In February 1839, Chief Cuelgas de Castro and sixteen Lipans guided Colonel John H. Moore and a force of sixty Texan troops to Muguara's Penateka encampment near the mouth of the San Saba River. Ignoring Castro's advice to run off the Comanche horses and then attack on horseback, Moore dismounted his men and charged Muguara's sleeping camp on foot. The militiamen fired blindly into the village, killing and wounding nearly one hundred Penatekas, many of them sleeping women and children, before being forced to withdraw. The Comanches responded by attacking frontier settlements later in the spring, but Texan troops, supported by allied Tonkawa warriors, aggressively pursued the raiders and forced all the Penateka bands to retreat far up the Colorado River in the summer of 1839. Later that fall, smallpox, which had appeared among the Mandan Indians on the Missouri River two years earlier, struck the Penatekas. The Comanches suffered terribly, and large numbers of tribal members died.[45]

Weakened by disease and warfare, some Penateka bands decided to pursue a peace settlement with the Republic of Texas. In January 1840, three Penateka emissaries entered San Antonio and informed officials that they wanted to negotiate a treaty. The Texans agreed to meet with the tribal leaders but demanded that the chiefs bring in all of their Euroamerican captives before an agreement could be worked out. The three messengers consented to the requirement and left San Antonio, stating that they would return in about a month with their principal men as well as with the prisoners. Responding to the news of this meeting, the Lamar government decided to confront the Penatekas and force them to submit to the Texans' terms once and for all. As a result, the president sent three infantry companies to San Antonio and appointed a three-man commission with orders to detain the Comanches if they did not deliver the captives. Only after the prisoners were free could the commissioners deliver the Texans' harsh peace terms. They were to inform the Penatekas that the "government assumes the right, with regard to all Indian tribes . . . to dictate the conditions of such residence . . . our citizens have a right to occupy any vacant lands . . . and they must not be interfered with by the Comanche." Therefore, the Texans reserved the right to determine where the Penatekas could settle while forbidding the tribesmen to enter Texan settlements or harm any hunters or squatters they encountered.[46]

Unaware of the Texans' determination to recover the captives or of dictating an unacceptable peace, on March 19, Chief Muguara and about sixty-five men, women, and children calmly entered San Antonio. Twelve Penateka leaders met with Texan officials in a one-story stone building known as the Council House, while the rest of the party remained outside on the plaza. The Indians delivered the only captive they had brought with them, Matilda Lockhart, whose appearance shocked the Texans. Her body was covered in bruises "and her nose [was] actually burnt off to the bone—all the fleshy end gone, and a great scab formed on the end of the bone. Both nostrils were wide open and denuded of flesh." The Comanches typically treated captives in this brutal manner as a means of instilling fear and respect. The teenage girl told the commissioners that the Comanches had many more prisoners in their village and that they planned to bring them in one at a time so as to secure a higher ransom for each. The Texan officials demanded the other captives, but Muguara stated that they were with other bands beyond his jurisdiction. Dissatisfied with this response, the commissioners ordered a detachment of soldiers into the building and then informed the Penatekas that they were now "prisoners and would be kept as hostages" until they returned the rest of the captives. The Indians chose to fight rather than submit; one man drew a knife and a general melee ensued. When the so-called Council House Fight came to an end, the Texans had killed thirty-five Comanches and imprisoned twenty-nine others.[47]

Considering the Texans' actions as duplicitous, the outraged Penatekas broke off all treaty negotiations and decided to launch an attack upon their enemy. By July 1840, a force of five hundred Comanche warriors, along with an equal number of women and children, had gathered under the leadership of a young chief named Potsanaquahip (Buffalo Hump). Following an initial series of small attacks between Bastrop and San Antonio designed to sow confusion,

Potsanaquahip guided his force down the Guadalupe River on the greatest of all Comanche raids in Texas. On August 6, the Penatekas surrounded the town of Victoria and killed about twenty people and seized more than 1,500 horses before continuing their advance toward the coast. Two days later Potsanaquahip's party reached the port of Linnville, on Lavaca Bay in present-day Calhoun County. After killing three inhabitants, the warriors forced the surprised citizens to take refuge in boats while they pillaged the settlement before burning it to the ground. Despite the destructive raid, Texan forces, along with Tonkawa auxiliaries led by Placido, regrouped and intercepted the retreating Comanches on August 12 at Plum Creek, a tributary of the San Marcos River. Fighting valiantly to protect the women and children who had accompanied them, the Penatekas lost most of their plunder and more than one hundred people before successfully making their escape. Although the Penatekas had caused a great amount of destruction in the so-called Great Comanche Raid of 1840, they ultimately suffered more losses than they could afford in the campaign against the Texans.[48]

Despite the Penatekas' withdrawal beyond the western settlements, Texan troops and their Indian allies incessantly continued to pressure the Comanches. In October 1840, Lipan chiefs Cuelgas de Castro and Flacco led Colonel Moore and a force of ninety Texans to a Penateka ranchería on the Colorado River, situated more than three hundred miles upstream from Bastrop. Attacking the unguarded Indian camp in the middle of the night, the allied troops inflicted the severest defeat the Comanches in Texas had yet to suffer. Moore and his men killed 130 Penatekas and captured thirty-four women and children while making off with the entire tribal horse herd. The Texans continued their offensive the following year; in June 1841, Captain John C. Hays and a company of Rangers killed eight Penateka warriors on the upper Frio River. Returning to San Antonio, Hays increased his force to fifty men and enlisted Flacco and about fifteen Lipan and Tonkawa warriors to assist him. The Indian allies guided the Texans to the headwaters of the Llano where they broke up a Penateka encampment, killing ten tribesmen in the process. Seeking refuge from the unceasing Texan attacks, by the end of 1841 the entire Penateka tribe had move far to the northwest to establish rancherías on the upper Colorado, Brazos, and Red rivers.[49]

In the meantime, the Texans also made war on the Wichitas living south of the Red River. In the summer of 1840 a Ranger force commanded by Jonathan Bird attacked a Waco settlement at Village Creek (south of present Arlington). The Wacos withstood the attack and drove Bird's forces away, but General Edward H. Tarrant mounted another punitive expedition against the Wichitas the following May. Leaving from Coffee's Station on the Red River, Tarrant and his force headed south toward a Tawakoni village on the West Fork of the Trinity. The Tawakonis, however, had already moved to the Indian Territory in an attempt to stay out of the fray. Finding the Tawakoni settlement abandoned, Tarrant headed for the Waco town on Village Creek. Learning of his approach, the Wacos fled from their village, which the Rangers burned upon their arrival. They also rounded up eighty horses and confiscated a large number of copper kettles and buffalo robes. Some of these Wacos settled with their kinsmen in a village located near the mouth of the Wichita River; others joined the Tawakonis north of the Red River.[50]

Thus, by the end of Lamar's two-year presidential term, the Texans had driven nearly all the Indians they considered as hostile from the boundaries of the republic. However, Lamar's war of extermination, while successful in many ways, had proven very costly to the young, financially insecure nation. Between 1839 and 1841 the Texas republic spent more than $2.5 million in its vigorous prosecution of the Indian wars. In comparison, President Houston's prior policy of peace with the Indians had cost less than $200,000 to implement. Therefore, following his inauguration to the Texan presidency for the second time in December 1841, Houston announced the resumption of his pacification program. In his first message to the Texas Congress, Houston stated that the Indians, "finding a disposition on our part to treat them fairly and justly, and dreading the loss of trade . . . would be powerfully affected, both by feelings of confidence and motives of interest, to preserve peace and maintain good faith. The hope of obtaining peace by means of war has hitherto proved utterly fallacious." President Houston implemented his policy in July 1842 when he appointed three commissioners to "treat with any and all Indians on the frontier of Texas" in an attempt to end the warfare between the tribes and the settlers. Houston's policy of peace and friendship with the Indians was not only consistently carried out by him but also by Anson Jones, his successor, who was inaugurated in December 1844 and served as president until the United States annexed Texas at the end of the following year. Since most of the beleaguered Indians also desired peace, following a period of extended negotiations members of the Caddo, Wichita, and Penateka Comanche tribes moved south of the Red River once again and, for the most part, maintained reasonably amicable relations with the Texans until the end of the republic.[51]

Hoping to return to their native lands in Texas, the Wichitas and Caddos solicited peace with the republic at about the same time President Houston put forth his own initiative. In May 1842, at a grand council of eighteen Indian Territory tribes, Chief Narshatowey (Lame Arm) of the Wacos and Tawakoni chief Kechikaroqua (Stubborn), informed the Creek Indian agent, James Logan, that they were "anxiously desirous of peace, and wish to establish terms of friendly intercourse and trade" with the Republic of Texas. They told the agent that they would have made the peace offer earlier but had hesitated out of fear of Texas hostility. The two chiefs also informed Logan that all of the tribes that President Lamar had driven from Texas, except the Cherokees, desired peace. The Wichitas asked Agent Logan to forward their request to President Houston in hope that he would respond in a positive manner. A few months later the Caddos, after learning that the Chickasaws refused to grant them permission to settle west of the Washita River, also made peace overtures to the Texans. In July Kadohadacho headman Red Bear asked Robert M. Jones, an influential Choctaw, to act as an intermediary between the Caddos and the Texans, for his tribe was "determined to lay down the hatchet" and establish peace.[52]

As a result of Jones' intercession, Caddo tribal leaders met with Houston's peace commissioners in late August and entered into an accord that began a three-year period of close relations between the tribe and the Republic of Texas. The Caddos agreed to be emissaries of peace and visit with the Wichitas and Penateka Comanches in order to invite them to negotiate an agreement with the Texans. Throughout the fall and winter Caddo representatives, along with a few Delaware Indians, met with Penateka and Wichita bands located on both sides of the Red River. Still angry because of the Council House Fight and the ensuing war, the Comanches refused to meet with the Texan officials. Despite the previous Waco and Tawakoni entreaties for peace, the Wichita chiefs also declined to attend the meeting. The Wichitas informed the Caddos that they had a "great mistrust" of the Texans and "were afraid to come by themselves" without the protection of the Indian Territory tribes. Ultimately, the Wacos agreed to send a headman named Acaquash (Short Tail) to witness the treaty council but withheld authorization for him to conclude an agreement with the Texans.[53]

After various delays the treaty council began on March 28, 1843, at newly established Torrey's Trading Post on Tehuacana Creek, about six miles southeast of the present-day city of Waco. Representatives of the Kadohadacho, Hainai, Nadaco, Delaware, and Shawnee tribes were present as well as three commissioners and one secretary from the Republic of Texas. Since the Texans had solicited the assistance of the United States in making peace with the tribes, the Cherokee agent, Pierce M. Butler, appeared on behalf of President John Tyler. A group of mixed-blood Delawares, led by John Conner and Jim Shaw, acted as interpreters, a duty they would perform for the next two decades. After the "usual preliminary of smoking" was finished, a letter from President Houston was read and interpreted for the tribes. Texas commissioner G. W. Terrell made the opening address, followed by Butler, who urged the tribes to make peace. The headmen of the individual tribes responded the following day, and each agreed to end hostilities. Wichita spokesman Acaquash informed the gathering that the site on which they were meeting had once been that of his tribe. Despite the fact that the "Whiteman now owns it," Acaquash pledged to spread the message of peace to all Wichita tribes whose homes were "now in the far west." Two days later, on March 31, 1843, all parties, except for Acaquash, signed a treaty in which it was "solemnly agreed that the war . . . should cease." The Republic of Texas gave the tribes the right to trade at Torrey's Trading Post and to establish villages any place west of it. All agreed to meet for another conference at Bird's Fort on the Trinity River in the autumn to establish a more permanent peace between the Texans and the Indians.[54]

Following the signing of the treaty, most Caddos and a few Delawares abandoned the Indian Territory and reestablished villages once again in Texas. The Shawnees, however, declined to move south of the Red River. The Kadohadachos, Nadacos, Hainais, along with a small group of Delawares, established one large contiguous village on the Brazos River, about fifty miles above Torrey's Trading Post. Most observers agreed that the Caddos and Delawares, numbering seven hundred people or so, had made a fine choice for their village site; one commented that the tribes could not have selected a "more suitable and pleasant place." The village lay "in the center of a plain two miles long," bordered by hills "covered with horses, they being fine for grazing, present[ing] a lively green as far as the eyes could reach." Flowing diagonally through the plain was a "beautiful, clear creek," on the banks of which stood "in picturesque disorder" the Caddos' traditional grass houses. Adjoining each abode were the Caddo fields; one Texas Indian agent felt that the Caddos had "about 150 acres of the finest corn" he had ever seen, in addition to "innumerable" peas, beans, and pumpkins. A group of about one hundred Caddos, known as the White Beads, stayed behind in the Indian Territory and established a settlement on Caddo Creek, a tributary of the Washita River.[55]

Successful and content in their new homes, the three Caddo tribes, as well as the Delawares, tirelessly strove to maintain the peace. Following the resettlement in Texas, Chief Iesh (or José María) of the Nadacos became the Caddos' unofficial leader, due to the death of a number of Kadohadacho and Hainai chiefs during the hard times of the late 1830s. By the time Toweash took over as chief of the Hainais in the early 1840s, he was considered to be Iesh's "second chief." Although Bintah assumed the leadership position of the Kadohadachos in 1843, the young man usually deferred to the elder Nadaco chief. Iesh's esteem and power would continue to grow over the next two decades—one Texan called him "the most influential chief on the Brazos"—

as he became one of the most important spokesman for peace between the Indians of Texas and the settlers who continued to stream into the province.[56]

Although the Wichitas had not officially entered into the agreement with the Texans, about eight hundred Kichais, Tawakonis, and Wacos settled south of the Red River without permission. The Kichais, led by Chief Sahsaroque, established a village on the Brazos River, fifteen miles below the mouth of the Clear Fork, nearly one hundred miles above the Caddos. For the next decade the Kichai village would serve as a great meeting place for all Wichita tribes and for the Penateka Comanches and the Caddos. The Tawakonis and Wacos moved to adjacent villages on the West Fork of the Trinity River, about fifty miles east of the Kichais. The Tawakonis situated their town on a hill overlooking one hundred acres of corn, beans, melons, and pumpkins. As with the Caddos, one group of Wichitas remained in the Indian Territory, as the one thousand or so Taovayas refused to abandon their village on East Cache Creek.[57]

Acaquash became the leading Wichita spokesman for peace with the Texans. In the summer of 1843 the Waco second chief accompanied J. C. Eldredge, Hamilton F. Bee, and Thomas Torrey on an expedition to invite the Wichitas and Penateka Comanches to attend the upcoming treaty council at Bird's Fort. In June, Acaquash arranged for a meeting on the Trinity River between the Texas commissioners and the Waco, Tawakoni, and Kichai chiefs. The three Texans presented Waco chief Narshatowey with two prisoners they held, for whom he thanked them profusely. Acaquash then told Chief Sahsaroque of the Kichais that "it was good to make peace" with the Texans. After "considerable discussion," Sahsaroque embraced the Texas commissioners and announced that he would attend the council at Bird's Fort "and make a firm treaty of peace." Tawakoni chief Kechikaroqua told the Texans that his tribe would also agree to make peace at Bird's Fort and that he would do all he could to convince the Comanches and Taovayas to attend as well. Accompanied by Acaquash and a few Delaware interpreters, the Texas commissioners made their way to the Taovaya village on East Cache Creek, where they also persuaded the tribal leaders to attend the meeting at Bird's Fort.[58]

Having convinced all Wichita tribes to enter into treaty negotiations with the Republic of Texas, Acaquash and the peace commission now sought out the reluctant Penateka Comanches. By the summer of 1843 most of the four thousand or so Penatekas remained in rancherías north of the Red River. In the aftermath of the smallpox epidemic and the war with Texas, four chiefs—Potsanaquahip, Pahayuko (Amorous Man), Mopechucope (Old Owl), and Santa Anna—had emerged as the main tribal leaders. Wishing to avoid further hostilities with the Texans, Penateka warriors had turned their attentions south of the Rio Grande, making a number of raids in the northern

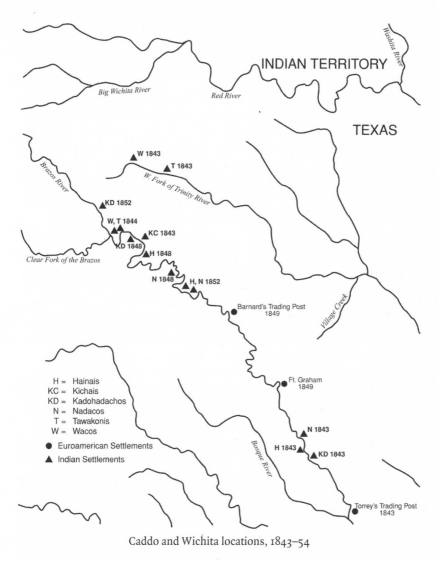

Caddo and Wichita locations, 1843–54

Mexican states of Coahuila and Nuevo León in which they stole horses and kidnapped women and children. Despite the lack of contact with the Texans, many Penatekas still wanted vengeance and had no desire to make peace with the republic. Therefore, the Comanches in Pahayuko's village, located west of the Wichita Mountains in the Indian Territory, greeted Acaquash and the Texan commissioners with mixed feelings upon their arrival in early August. Although the Penateka chief stated his desire to make peace, a number of the Comanche warriors made it known that they wanted to kill the three Texans in revenge for the Council House Fight. Acaquash was forced to save them by defending the commissioners "in a long and animated speech." The Waco headman informed the Penatekas that President Houston, "a friend of the red man," had replaced Lamar, the man who had ruled Texas at the time of the massacre. Acaquash ultimately convinced the Comanches to spare the Texans' lives and let them go in peace, but none of the Comanches agreed to attend the upcoming treaty council.[59]

The Penatekas' refusal to make peace with the Texans also caused the Taovayas, Wacos, and Kichais to skip the meeting at Bird's Fort, despite their previous promise to negotiate a treaty. Along with Caddo and Delaware headmen, Tawakoni chief Kechikaroqua was the only important Wichita leader to attend the council, held in September 1843 on the Trinity River. After a few days of negotiations the Indians and the Texans signed the Treaty of Bird's Fort, which once again called for the end of all warfare between the parties. Texan officials promised to establish a line of trading houses for the tribes on the frontier. Once the tribes had "shown that they will keep this treaty, and no more make war upon the whites, nor steal horses from them," the president would authorize the traders to provide them with guns, powder, and lead.[60]

Despite the fact that two treaties had been signed, peace between the Indians and the Texans remained incomplete as neither the Penateka Comanches nor most of the Wichitas had agreed to cease hostilities. Therefore, for much of the next year Texan officials, with assistance from the Caddos and Delawares, strove to establish a firm and lasting agreement with the two tribes. In December 1843, President Houston ordered Indian agent Daniel G. Watson and Delaware interpreter John Conner to find the Penatekas and invite them to attend a treaty council scheduled for the following spring. The entire tribe had spent the winter together on the Clear Fork of the Brazos, but the various Penateka bands had split up before the Texan representatives finally encountered Mopechucope's ranchería on the headwaters of the Colorado River in March 1844. Pahayuko's band had moved north to the Salt Fork of the Arkansas River, while Santa Anna and Potsanaquahip had led warriors on raids in Mexico. As a result, Mopechucope informed Watson and Conner that, while most of the Penatekas now wanted to negotiate a settlement with President Houston and the Republic of Texas, he regretted that the tribe was too scattered to be able to travel to Torrey's Trading Post for the upcoming conference. The Penateka chief, however, said that the entire tribe planned to gather on the Clear Fork of the Brazos in September and would, therefore, gladly attend a peace conference in the fall. In the meantime, Mopechucope promised to send messengers to the other Penatekas to instruct them not to molest the Texan settlements. Heeding Mopechucope's instructions, Penateka warriors avoided

Texas throughout the rest of the summer and instead continued to raid only south of the Rio Grande.[61]

The Wichitas were not as mobile as the Comanches and did not have the resources to travel as far south as Mexico to steal the horses they needed to maintain commerce with American traders. Therefore, Wichita warriors often attacked settlements in Texas over the following year. In December 1843, Chief Narshatowey and forty Wacos killed a slave and seized horses from ranches on the Little River in Milam County. Two months later, while searching for the Comanches, Agent Watson, accompanied by Kadohadacho headman Red Bear, arrived at the Clear Fork of the Brazos and found the Wacos and Kichais driving stolen horses. Red Bear forced them to give up the mounts and threatened to report their actions to President Houston. A few days later at the Nadaco village, Chief Iesh pressured Narshatowey to admit to Watson that he had stolen horses from the Texan settlements near Gonzales. Angered at the Waco and Kichai thefts, Watson left certificates with Iesh and Red Bear stating that even if the Texans traced stolen horses to the Caddos, blame should be placed on the Wichitas instead, since their villages were on the road that passed through the Caddo towns. The certificate also stated that the Caddos "were doing their best to stop the [Wichitas] from coming down" to the Texas frontier.[62]

Caddo pressure, combined with the continued efforts of Acaquash, persuaded Narshatowey and Kichai chief Sahsaroque to join with Chief Kechikaroqua of the Tawakonis and attend the treaty council held at Tehuacana Creek in May 1844. Acaquash had met with Houston in March and then spent the following month delivering the president's message of peace to the Wichita villages south of the Red River. Leading Texan officials, including Superintendent of Indian Affairs Thomas G. Western, accompanied by Caddo and Delaware headmen, greeted the Wichita chiefs at Torrey's Trading Post on May 11. The council opened the following day with "purtty Severe" talks from the Delaware and Kadohadacho chiefs, who chastised the Wichitas for continuing to commit depredations upon the Texan settlers. Both men implored the three Wichita leaders to make peace with the republic.[63]

For the most part, the Wichitas responded positively to the demands of their fellow Indians. Acaquash spoke first and stated that "I want to eat out of the same dish, drink of the same water, smoke the same pipe with Houston and my white brothers in peace. . . . I do not like my young men to steal the white man's horses." Kechikaroqua answered by saying that he was "strong for making a firm peace. War is like an arrow sticking in the side; I have plucked it out and now I am for peace." He offered to travel to the Taovaya village and retrieve horses stolen from Texas. Although Narshatowey and Sahsaroque gave similar responses, both hinted that all was not settled. Narshatowey stated that his Wacos would "walk in the white path" only after the Texans gave them presents. A disappointed Sahsaroque, though, found it difficult to believe that President Houston had not attended the meeting. Ultimately, the council ended in failure; the meeting that took place on the final day of the council broke down as each tribal headman accused the other of stealing Texan horses. The next day, the Wacos, Tawakonis, and Kichais angrily left the council grounds after the Texan commissioners refused to give them powder and lead. The officials informed the Wichitas that they would not receive presents until they returned stolen mounts to a Texan Indian agent at Torrey's Trading Post.[64]

Instead of delivering horses to the agent at Tehuacana Creek, the angered Wacos plotted to attack Torrey's Trading Post and the Texan settlements farther downstream. In late July 1844, Waco women harvested their crops and headed west as the men began their descent toward the trading establishment. The Caddos and Delawares, however, discovered the Wacos' hostile actions and sent word of the impending attack to the Texans. Kadohadacho headmen Red Bear and Bintah began mobilizing their forces to fight the Wacos and invited Texan settlers to join them. Upon hearing this news, Nadaco chief Iesh hurried to the Kadohadacho village to prevent them from battling the Wacos. Iesh's counsel proved decisive, and the Kadohadachos called off their attack, as did the Wacos once they learned the Caddos had betrayed them. In return for his good offices, Superintendent Western instructed a Texas Indian agent to embrace the Nadaco chief "for me as my brother, and say that Gen Houston will approve of his conduct that he was right in preventing bloodshed . . . [Iesh] is a great man and a good friend." Fearing retribution from the Texans, the Tawakonis and Wacos abandoned their settlements on the West Fork of the Trinity and sought refuge near the Kichais. The two tribes formed a contiguous village on the north bank of the Brazos, six miles above the Kichais and nine miles below the mouth of the Clear Fork.[65]

Despite the Wichitas' fear of the Texans, in September Agent Watson, supported by Delaware interpreters John Conner and Jim Shaw, ventured up the Brazos and convinced the Waco, Tawakoni, and Kichai chiefs to attend another treaty council at Torrey's Trading Post. The Texan representatives then traveled another two hundred miles up the river and met with the gathered Penatekas. Although Pahayuko's and Santa Anna's bands were absent, Watson and the Delawares persuaded Penateka chiefs Potsanaquahip and Mopechucope to accompany them to the council grounds on Tehuacana Creek. President Houston, realizing the magnitude of convincing the Comanches to negotiate an agreement, personally appeared at Torrey's Trading Post on October 7 to open the largest and most important of all the republic's Indian treaty councils.[66]

The Caddo and Delaware headmen were also in attendance, yet Houston addressed most of his comments to the Penatekas and the Wichitas. The president reminded the Indians that Lamar, the "bad chief" who had succeeded him, had broken the peace he had made with Comanche chief Muguara in 1838. Houston stated that President Lamar "made war on the Comanche and murdered them at San Antonio" in the Council House Fight. He admitted that this wrong had "to be mended [since] war can do us no good." The president then called on the Indians, particularly the Wichitas, to refrain from stealing Texan horses and promised to supply trade goods and deliver presents once all parties agreed to peace. Potsanaquahip responded favorably to Houston's address the following day. The Penateka chief stated that "what I came here for was to hear the words of peace. I have heard them and all is right; peace is peace." After receiving the Comanches' blessing, President Houston felt free to berate the Wacos for continuing to poach Texan horses. The president told Chief Narshatowey that if he returned the horses "he will find my heart straight towards him" but warned that if he continued to let his men steal, hundreds of mounted troops would come "and they will sweep the Wacos away." When Narshatowey meekly replied that some of the stolen horses might be dead, Houston bluntly stated that "for every horse that's dead or missing a Waco shall be hung."[67]

Despite such harsh words to the Wacos, the president presented a treaty that he had drawn up to all the gathered tribes the following day. In addition to agreeing to peaceful relations and promising the tribes the right to trade at designated posts, Houston gave in to the longstanding Comanche demand and included a boundary line setting off the Indian lands from those of the Texans. Houston's line ran from the Red River through the upper Cross Timbers to Comanche Peak (a promontory near the west bank of the Brazos River), then southwest on a line through the abandoned Spanish mission on the San Saba to the Rio Grande. However, after reviewing Houston's terms, Potsanaquahip emphatically rejected the proposed line. Claiming the buffalo frequently roamed much farther east than this line, the Penateka chief proposed that the border be drawn just west of Austin and San Antonio, and then along the road to the Presidio del Rio Grande (south of present-day Eagle Pass). President Houston refused to accept Potsanaquahip's line for fear that it would bring the Indians too close to the Texan settlers. Instead, Houston convinced the Indians, including the Penateka and Wichita chiefs, to sign the peace accord without mention of a boundary line. Houston then distributed presents to all tribes, except for the Wacos, for once again their presents were withheld until they delivered the stolen horses.[68]

Despite the lack of an agreement concerning the boundary line, the Penateka Comanches respected the peace treaty through the end of the republic. In fact, the Penatekas joined with the Caddos and Delawares in their effort to force the recalcitrant Wichitas to cease hostilities. Within a month of leaving the council grounds, the infuriated Wacos broke the peace by continuing to steal Texan horses. Waco warriors also invaded Austin and kidnapped the son and daughter of a Texan settler. Superintendent Western immediately sent word of the theft to the Caddos in the hope that they would be able to recover the children. Upon receiving the information, the Caddos informed the Penatekas, who forced the Wacos to turn the kidnapped boy—the girl had died in the interim—over to Chief Pahayuko. Of the four leading Penateka headmen, Pahayuko and Santa Anna were the only ones who had yet to agree to peace with the Republic of Texas. Therefore, in January 1845, Pahayuko used the occasion of returning the child to Texan officials at Torrey's Trading Post to announce his intention to abide by the treaty signed the previous October. Accompanied by Mopechucope, Pahayuko informed Agent Benjamin Sloat that he was "anxious . . . to make peace, and what I say now I will stick to as long as I live."[69]

Pahayuko remained true to his word and, along with the other Penateka leaders, successfully strove to enforce the peace between the Indians and the Texans. Soon after the meeting at Torrey's a small hunting party of Delawares from the Indian Territory killed three Comanche men on the headwaters of the San Marcos River. In response, some Penateka warriors swore that they would wreak vengeance on any Indians allied to the Texans. Wishing to avoid cause for bloodshed, Pahayuko sent word of the dangerous situation to Texas officials, informing them that no Texan or Delaware Indian "would be safe in their Country at present." Potsanaquahip and Mopechucope intervened to peacefully settle the dispute between the Delawares and the Comanches a few months later. Pahayuko also took actions to curb continued Wichita hostilities. In June, following a raid on Austin in which Waco warriors killed and scalped two Texan settlers, Pahayuko traveled to the Clear Fork of the Brazos and severely reprimanded the Wichitas for the murders, stating that he had made peace with the Texans and that they "must do the same." The Penateka chief informed Acaquash that he would do all in his power to assist the Waco second chief's efforts to establish a lasting peace between the Wichitas and the Texans. Continued Comanche pressure caused the Wichitas to refrain from raiding Texas ranches for the rest of the year. Finally, in November Pahayuko and Acaquash convinced representatives of all the Wichita tribes, including the Taovayas, to meet with Texas officials at Torrey's Trading Post. Following a round of talks in which each headman—including Kechikaroqua and Sahsaroque—admitted that the continuing struggle with the Texans had impoverished their people, the Wichita leaders signed a treaty and pledged to cease their attacks. Officially, at least, the Republic of Texas and all of the Wichita tribes were at peace for the first time.[70]

Peaceful relations between the Penatekas and the Texans caused both groups to also work together against another common enemy, Mexico. In May 1845, a large group of Penatekas encamped on the Little River, within fifty miles of Torrey's Trading Post, as the warriors made preparations to cross the Rio Grande into Mexico. The Penatekas sent word of their planned raid to Texas officials and asked the government for permission to approach near Austin and San Antonio on their way to the border. The Comanches promised not to bother any Texan settlers and asked for the same treatment in return. In response to the Penateka request, Superintendent Western ordered Agent Sloat to deliver passports to the Comanches and to accompany them on their way south, making sure that the war party stayed at least twenty-five miles west of the settlements. Sloat was also ordered to furnish the Penatekas with corn and beef on the trip so that the Texans' livestock would not tempt them. Ultimately, through the cooperation of the Comanches and the Texans, the Penateka raid met with great success because the warriors returned with a large drove of horses from Mexican ranches located on the other side of the Rio Grande from Laredo. Encouraged by the results of working with the Texans, in August Potsanaquahip and 150 warriors left Mopechucope's village on the San Saba River and traveled to San Antonio to invite a troop of Rangers to accompany them on yet another raid into Mexico. Although the Texans declined the offer, they gave beef and other provisions to the Comanches, who left town "well satisfied" with the treatment they received. Joined by Santa Anna's war party, Potsanaquahip and his followers stole horses and took captives in Nuevo León. Following the productive raid, in November Santa Anna completed the Penateka peace agreement with the Republic of Texas by informing officials at Torrey's that "he wished to have peace with the whites as long as the sun continued to give light." Finally, four years after President Houston had announced the reimplementation of his peace policy with the Indian tribes, all the Caddos, Wichitas, and Comanches on the northwestern frontier had agreed to cease hostilities against the Texans.[71]

Ironically, Houston's peace policy had dire effects upon the Tonkawas and Lipan Apaches who had assisted President Lamar's previous attempt to expel the tribes considered hostile from the boundaries of Texas. During the wars most of the Tonkawas and Lipans had settled in various rancherías located along tributaries of the Colorado River near Bastrop to be able to join Texas troops on their expeditions. By the summer of 1842, when President Houston began negotiations with the tribes that Lamar had forced to take refuge in the Indian Territory, six hundred or so Lipans resided in Texas, led by chiefs Flacco, Chiquito, and Ramón Castro (following the recent death of his father, Cuelgas). About seven hundred Tonkawas lived near their Apache allies under the direction of Placido, Campos, and Ocquin. Although warriors from both tribes had fought alongside the Texans in many battles, newly arriving immigrants who established farms and ranches in the region between Bastrop, Austin, and San Antonio were uncomfortable having so many Indians nearby and began threatening the Tonkawas and Lipans. Realizing that there were "some persons on the frontier who have a disposition to molest" the two tribes, President Houston appointed Thomas J. Smith as their agent with orders to "take active measures to protect them" from the hostile citizenry. Unfortunately, the efforts of Smith and other agents would be ineffectual, and by the end of the republic most Tonkawas and Lipans would be forced to move westward away from the Texan settlements.[72]

One violent incident, however, caused some tribal members to abandon Texas altogether to take refuge south of the Rio Grande in Mexico. In retaliation for three separate Mexican invasions of Texas in 1842, in November President Houston ordered Alexander Somervell to lead a force of about seven hundred men on an expedition to the Rio Grande. Flacco the younger, son of the Lipan chief, and another warrior served as guides for the expedition, a portion of which retreated from Mexico in late December. The two Apaches, who had stolen about fifty Mexican horses during the invasion, were passing south of San Antonio on their way home when Texan bandits killed them for their herd. Fearing that the Lipans would seek to avenge young Flacco's murder, Texas authorities blamed Mexican thieves for the deed. President Houston even wrote a poem in honor of the slain young man in an attempt to console his heartbroken father. Chief Flacco, however, investigated the incident and concluded that Texans had committed the crime. As a result, Flacco led his band into Mexico, leaving only about four hundred Lipans in Texas. Fearing the Texan settlers near Bastrop, two hundred Tonkawas joined the Lipans south of the Rio Grande in early 1843. As with the Caddos and Wichitas still living in the Indian Territory, the Lipan and Tonkawa bands in Mexico would provide a refuge for the tribesmen remaining in Texas over the next decade and a half. Throughout the period Indians would be forced to flee from Texas when the settlers' hostility inevitably erupted and became too much for the tribesmen to bear.[73]

Epidemic disease, which broke out among the Lipans and Tonkawas in the late summer of 1843, caused the rest of the Apaches to leave the Bastrop area and begin their westward movement. The epidemic raged through the fall, killing thirteen Indians in a single two-day period in October. The sickness affected men more than women, and nearly one-fifth of the Lipan and Tonkawa warriors died. Fleeing from the disease, by February 1844 most of the Lipans had settled on the Guadalupe River west of the Texan settlements of Seguin and Gonzales. They remained there for the rest of the year, but the Apaches were forced to move again early in 1845, soon after colonists of the Adelsverein, or Society of German Noblemen, established the town of New Braunfels at the confluence of the Comal River and the Guadalupe. Ramón Castro's band eventually settled on Cíbolo Creek southeast of San Antonio, while Chiquito and his Lipans moved southwest of Béxar to establish a ranchería on Hondo Creek. Both bands planted extensive gardens at their settlements—Chiquito's band enclosed forty acres of corn on the Hondo—because they hoped to remain in the vicinity for a long while.[74]

The beleaguered Tonkawas continued to reside in their villages on Cedar and Buckner creeks in the vicinity of Bastrop. In addition to the problems caused by the outbreak of disease, Waco warriors had stolen most of the Tonkawas' horses by the end of 1843. Unable to travel westward to hunt buffalo, over the next year Tonkawa men enraged local settlers by poaching cattle from nearby ranches. They also got drunk in Bastrop and Gonzales on money their women made from picking cotton on Colorado River plantations. To avoid a confrontation with the settlers, in February 1845 Superintendent Western appointed Robert S. Neighbors as the Lipan and Tonkawa agent and ordered him to gather the Tonkawa tribe and "move them out of the settlements, as fast as practicable." By the end of the summer Agent Neighbors, who would be the most important liaison between the Texas Indians and the settlers during the next decade and a half, had convinced the Tonkawas to relocate to vacant lands southwest of Austin, where they established rancherías on the Blanco River. In September, Agent Neighbors brought the Tonkawa and Lipan Apache leaders to the annual conference at Torrey's Trading Post where Campos and Ramón Castro both agreed to maintain peaceful relations with the Texans and the other Indians of the nation.[75]

Thus, by the end of 1845, when the citizens of Texas gave up their independence and joined the United States, all of the province's Indian tribes had signed treaties of peace with the Lone Star Republic. However, unlike the agreements the Indians had made with Mexico two decades before, this time the tribes had been forced to acknowledge the dominant position the Americans now held in the region. The Texans had militarily defeated the Indians, and it was only through the whim of the government that the tribes were allowed to reside in the province at all. Although the Indians continued to be self-sufficient, over the following decade their situation would decline dramatically as settlers encroached further upon their territory and the amount of game in the region dwindled. Increasingly, the Indians' survival would become dependent upon the power of the federal government, which, in the face of the state's unique entrance into the Union, proved to be very limited in Texas.

7. Desperation
The Indians and the United States, 1846 to 1853

By late 1845, when the Republic of Texas gave up its autonomy to join the United States, the province's Indian tribes had been thoroughly defeated and had come to accept their dependent position vis-à-vis the dominant Euroamericans. The Indians were grossly outnumbered, constantly threatened by the settlers' infringement upon their lands, and faced increasing difficulty in raising crops or finding game. Therefore, all the tribes transferred their allegiance to the United States with the full expectation that the federal government would secure their territory and at least provide them with the moderate amount of protection the Texans had during the final years of the republic. Unfortunately, the United States was unable to fulfill its acknowledged responsibilities to the Texas Indians, and the tribes suffered inordinately during the decade following annexation.

The federal government actually attempted to tend to the Indians' needs, but the unique circumstances of Texas' entrance into the Union hampered the United States' efforts. Unlike the other states, Texas retained complete control of its public lands upon joining the Union. This presented a complex legal problem, for the land occupied by the Texas tribes was not the domain of the United States, a fact that rendered the federal government's Indian laws inapplicable. For this reason, the United States Senate was forced to remove provisions from various treaties that extended the federal trade and intercourse laws over Texas Indians and protected them from trespassers. To make matters more difficult, the laws of Texas did not acknowledge that the Indians had any rights to the land.[1] Commissioner of Indian Affairs William Medill spelled out the problem in March 1847, upon Major Neighbors's appointment as special agent to manage Indian affairs in Texas. Medill informed Neighbors that "it is difficult if not impossible to determine at present how far the department has the power and jurisdiction with respect to the Indian country in Texas." Since the trade and intercourse laws, as well as other laws regulating Indian affairs, could not be applied to Texas, the federal government was almost powerless to deal effectively with the Indians, illegal traders, or encroaching Texans.[2]

To add to the problem, the state of Texas, upon turning over responsibility for the Indians to the federal government, became hostile to the tribes' interests once again. In the latter years of the Texas republic, the government had been forced to adopt an Indian peace policy and had pledged paternal protection over the tribes. Now, however, the Texans washed their hands of the Indian problem and gave almost no assistance to the helpless agents of the federal government. As time wore on, the Texas government's Indian policy harkened back to that of President Lamar. Matters were made worse by the fact that the United States was at war with Mexico between 1846 and 1848, and all federal troops were sent there. Thus, the only soldiers the federal Indian agents could turn to for assistance were the Texas Rangers, who were controlled by the state governor. Although United States troops established forts on the state's western frontier following the conclusion of the U.S.-Mexican War, their presence only emboldened the Texas settlers' desire to occupy Indian lands. The federal government's inability to protect the tribes from encroachment left the Indians at the mercy of the Texas government, which continually opposed any attempts to establish reservations. By the time the Texans finally did agree to donate land to the federal government for the use of the tribes, the state's Indian population had been seriously reduced through hunger, disease, and outmigration to either Mexico or to the Indian Territory.

Following Texas' entrance into the Union on December 29, 1845, the federal government quickly took steps to assume its constitutional duty of supervising relations with the states' Indian tribes. In fact, even prior to annexation, the War Department had commissioned Cherokee agent Butler and M. G. Lewis to negotiate a treaty with the Indians of Texas. On January 8, 1846, the commissioners, along with a party of about fifty people—including representatives from the Cherokee, Seminole, Choctaw, and Chickasaw tribes—left the Indian Territory and crossed the Red River into Texas. Through Delaware interpreter Jim Shaw, Butler and Lewis hired a group of Kickapoos to notify the various tribes to meet them at Comanche Peak on the Brazos River, about seventy miles above Torrey's Trading Post. In a comic turn of events, it took the commissioners a full month to finally locate the assigned meeting place. Once there the American emissaries spent nearly two months holding talks with representatives of the various tribes. The most important meeting took place on March 7 when Comanche chiefs Potsanaquahip and Mopechucope informed Butler and Lewis that they could not speak for the entire Penateka tribe, thus making it necessary to meet later in the spring to conclude the treaty.[3]

Finally, on May 12 the largest of all Indian treaty councils in Texas commenced when the leading chiefs of every tribe met with the American agents at Torrey's Trading Post. Three days later an agreement, called the Treaty of Council Springs, was reached between the United States and the Penateka Comanche, Hainai, Nadaco, Kadohadacho, Lipan Apache, Tonkawa, Kichai, Tawakoni, Waco, and Taovaya tribes. The Indians "acknowledged themselves to be under the protection of the United States," and perpetual peace was pledged between the two parties. The Indians agreed to surrender stolen property and prisoners and to trade only with licensed officials. In turn, the federal government pledged to provide the tribes with blacksmiths, teachers, and "preachers of the gospel." The United States also agreed to set up official trading posts for the Indians and to present them with an undetermined amount of gifts in the fall of 1846. Article Three of the treaty implied that there would be a line dividing Indian territory from the rest of Texas. Thus the tribes believed the federal government had agreed to the longstanding Comanche demand for a boundary. The definite adjustment of the line was not established in the Treaty of Council Springs, so the commissioner of Indian affairs asked that Texas citizens refrain from trespassing on lands in question until the boundary could be determined once and for all. Ultimately, however, the federal government's lack of jurisdiction over the public lands in Texas would preclude the running of the line beyond which Americans were forbidden, and the encroachment of settlers on Indian lands would continue.[4]

Following the signing of the treaty, Butler and Lewis prevailed upon a number of chiefs to visit Washington in an attempt to overawe them with the strength and resources of the United States. On their part, the Indians hoped to establish the definitive boundary line between themselves and the Americans. Nearly fifty Indian headmen made the trip, including Nadaco chief Iesh, Wichita leaders Tosaquash (the Taovaya chief), Acaquash, and Kechikaroqua, as well as Penateka headman Santa Anna. On July 25, the party traveled to the White House to meet with President Polk, who presented Iesh with a testimonial of friendship. Although the chiefs were quartered in the outskirts to give them more room and freedom from the crowds, a few became ill, and the entire party returned to Texas soon after the interview with Polk. Despite the brevity of their stay in Washington, most of the chiefs were impressed. Acaquash told the president that he would return home and advise his people not to wage war. Iesh later remarked that he had observed the ways of the Americans and knew it was "folly to fight them." Santa Anna stated that before he traveled east, he thought that the Penatekas "could whip any nation in the world," but now he realized that the Americans were "more numerous than the stars, and that he could not count them." For the rest of their lives all three men would maintain a policy of peace and cooperation with the United States, for they understood that their tribes had no viable alternative.[5]

Despite the relative success of the trip to Washington, the Indians were disappointed that the federal government's representatives had not discussed the definite adjustment of a boundary line. They were also unhappy that they had not yet received the gifts promised by Butler and Lewis. Due to the United States Senate's failure to promptly ratify the Treaty of Council Springs, no appropriation had been made for the purchase of gifts. Therefore, by the fall of 1846 some of the tribesmen began to lose faith in the federal government's good will. Comanche spokesmen complained to Thomas Torrey that President Polk "has a forked tongue . . . [he] sends word that he had no money to buy presents, and we must wait until the big captains agree to our treaty." In order to appease the doubting tribesmen, Torrey advanced Major Neighbors—the appointed but not yet confirmed United States Indian agent—nearly $8,000 worth of goods on credit, which he distributed to members of the various Texas tribes in a council held at Tehuacana Creek in December. Neighbors explained to the Indians that the federal government would fulfill its obligation to them as soon as the treaty was ratified. The Indians accepted Neighbors' words, and the agent claimed that the council was successful for it "resulted in establishing that good understanding which had heretofore existed with these tribes, and remov[ed] anything like dissaffection."[6]

Most of the Indians reinforced Neighbors's optimism by continuing to maintain peaceful relations with the settlers in Texas. The tribes' actions concerning the German colonists, in particular, demonstrated their strong desire to abide by the Treaty of Council Springs. Following the establishment of New Braunfels in 1845, German settlers of the Adelsverein founded the settlement of Fredericksburg, about seventy miles west of Austin, the following May. Despite the Germans' intrusion into country that had heretofore been dominated by the Indians, during the settlers' first six months at Fredericksburg, members of various tribes—Caddos, Delawares, Lipan Apaches, and Penatekas—helped keep the struggling colonists alive by selling them fresh deer and bear meat, as well as horses, mules, and hides. Inspired by the situation at Fredericksburg, in early 1847, John O. Meusebach, commissioner-general of the Adelsverein, decided to survey the recently purchased Fisher-Miller grant, which included lands between the Llano River on the south and the Colorado River on the north, in preparation for further settlement. Realizing that much of the grant lay directly in the country claimed by the Penatekas, Meusebach decided to work out an agreement with the Comanches before proceeding.[7]

Assisted by Major Neighbors and Delaware interpreter Jim Shaw, Meusebach and a party of ten men met with Penateka chiefs Potsanaquahip,

Mopechucope, and Santa Anna on March 1 in a village near the mouth of the San Saba River. Meusebach proposed that in return for $3,000 worth of presents and goods as well as the right to trade at all the German settlements, the Penatekas would allow the colonists to travel to the Fisher-Miller grant without fear of attack. The following day Mopechucope spoke for the Comanches and agreed to the German proposal, stating that he had consulted with his fellow tribesmen, who had decided to "abandon the war path and travel on the white path of peace, as [Meusebach] proposed yesterday, and I will do my utmost that we remain forever on this path." The treaty made between Meusebach and the Penatekas was ratified at Fredericksburg on May 9, 1847, and both parties lived up to their obligations for several years thereafter. In fact, Santa Anna's band accompanied German surveyors on the upper San Saba River in the summer of 1847, while various Penateka groups peacefully traded at newly established settlements on the north bank of the Llano in the fall and winter. Santa Anna, Mopechucope, and a lesser-ranked headman named Sanaco, conducted trade in Fredericksburg and New Braunfels several times following the signing of the treaty.[8]

The Penateka Comanches agreed to allow the German colonists to settle on their lands south of the Colorado River, but they still strongly desired the establishment of a boundary line between themselves and the Americans. Therefore, the Penateka headmen were very unhappy when Major Neighbors informed them in May 1847 that the United States Senate had struck Article Three, calling for the establishment of a clearly defined Indian country in Texas, from the Treaty of Council Springs, which President Polk had signed into law two months before. Potsanaquahip was the most outspoken Penateka chief, angrily informing the federal agent that "for a long time a great many people have been passing through my country; they kill all the game. . . . I believe our white brothers do not wish to run a line between us, because they wish to settle in this country. I object to any more settlements, I want this country to hunt in." Pahayuko and Mopechucope supported Potsanaquahip's protestation, claiming that they were "violently opposed to any extension of [the] settlements, and much annoyed by, and very suspicious of, any persons that visit their country." After lengthy discussions, Major Neighbors ultimately convinced the Penatekas to accept the treaty and to do all in their power to compel their men to observe it. However, he warned that unless something was done to prevent the intrusion of surveying parties, hostilities would likely soon develop.[9]

The intentions of most of the Texas Indians were friendly, but continuing Wichita raids south of the Red River threatened the tenuous peace. In the summer of 1846, even while their comrades were being overawed in Washington,

Taovaya and Tawakoni warriors stole horses from a Texas Ranger encampment near Austin. Another band of Taovayas later raided through Fannin County. In retaliation, a Texas Ranger company, accompanied by Delaware guides, traveled to the Indian Territory and attacked the Taovaya village near the Wichita Mountains. Although several Taovayas were killed in the fight, Wichita warriors continued to make raids in Texas throughout the rest of the year and beyond. The following spring Caddo tribesmen pursued and killed two Wacos who had stolen horses from them as well as from various Texas settlements. In an attempt to force the Wichitas to stop their raids, Major Neighbors, accompanied by Hainai chief Toweash and six Delawares led by John Conner, traveled to the Kichai village on the Brazos River in June 1847. Having won the confidence of the Caddos and Delawares, the federal Indian agent adopted a bold stance with the gathered Wichitas, believing "that the friendly Indians would sustain me in any measure I might adopt towards them." In the face of Neighbors' assertiveness, the Wichitas agreed to cease their hostilities and returned several stolen horses to the major.[10]

Nonetheless, in the summer of 1847 a few renegade Wichita warriors resumed their attacks, which seriously threatened to disrupt the peaceful relations that had been maintained between most of the Indians and the Texans for several years. In July, Waco tribesmen killed four Germans who were surveying land on the San Saba River. Panicked Texan settlers, however, initially assumed that the Penatekas had committed the murders. As a result, they formed a militia to attack a huge Comanche ranchería—which included the bands of Pahayuko, Mopechucope, and Potsanaquahip—located on the Colorado River about one hundred miles above Austin. By the time Major Neighbors quieted the settlers and convinced them that the distant Wacos had committed the murders, much damage had already been done. Learning of the planned expedition, the Penatekas hurriedly broke camp and retreated northwestward to the upper reaches of the Brazos River. The Tonkawas also fled from the American settlements and took up residence on the Brazos between the Wichitas and the Comanches. At the same time, Texas Rangers mistook a Lipan Apache hunting party as being hostile and attacked them. Frightened, the Lipans abandoned their rancherías on Hondo and Cíbolo creeks and moved to the Pecos River, far to the west of the Americans.[11]

Hoping to diffuse the volatile situation by informing the tribes that an additional shipment of presents had recently arrived at Torrey's Trading Post, Major Neighbors toured the Indian country in the late summer. On August 28, he met with the Caddo headmen in their Brazos River villages and "found them all perfectly peaceable and friendly." Neighbors then traveled up the river to the Kichai village and met with representatives of all four Wichita tribes. The

Wacos, now led by Acaquash following Narshatowey's recent death, extended a warm welcome to Neighbors and explained that the tribesmen who had killed the German surveyors had moved north of the Red River. A group of Penateka Comanches, led by Mopechucope, arrived at the Kichai village, and on September 6 Neighbors assembled all the tribes in council and invited them to meet at Torrey's later in the month to receive their presents. Unable to locate the Lipan Apaches, Major Neighbors returned to Tehuacana Creek in late September to prepare for the grand council.[12]

Over two thousand Indians, mainly Caddos, Wichitas, Penateka Comanches, and Tonkawas, had arrived at Torrey's Trading Post when the council began on September 27, 1847. Although the Indians were happy to receive the presents that had been promised for signing the Treaty of Council Springs, they voiced a few complaints to the federal Indian agent. The Caddos announced that the excessive heat of the summer had recently destroyed their corn crop, and Nadaco chief Iesh complained that his people found it difficult to find game since the increasing American population had caused the buffalo and deer to "almost entirely disappear" from the central prairies of Texas. The Wichitas and Comanches informed Neighbors that they were also having trouble obtaining enough food to survive. Therefore, the Penatekas reiterated their demand for the establishment of a boundary line between the Americans and the Indians. In view of the federal government's helplessness concerning the disposition of the public lands of Texas, Neighbors asked Governor J. Pinckney Henderson for assistance. Hoping to avoid an outbreak of hostilities, Governor Henderson agreed to establish a temporary boundary line twenty miles below Torrey's Trading Post. The temporary line satisfied the tribes, and each principal chief pledged to assist Major Neighbors in "carrying into full effect the several stipulations" of the Treaty of Council Springs. The "friendly dispositions" of the Indians convinced Neighbors that they were "sincere in their many professions of friendship for the government and citizens of the United States." The agent informed Commissioner Medill that he felt "fully assured that, unless the Indians are improperly interfered with, we have nothing to fear for the future."[13]

Unfortunately, American settlers lost no time in interfering with the Indians as they began passing beyond the temporary line within a few months of its establishment. In November 1847, a man named Spencer settled on the council grounds near Torrey's Trading Post and "threatened to shoot the first Indian that came on the land claimed by him." Major Neighbors, with the assistance of Governor Henderson and a troop of Texas Rangers, removed Spencer below the line soon thereafter. Following Spencer's ejection, Neighbors was absent from the area for about a month. When the Indian agent returned in January 1848, he found that the situation had radically changed for the worse. The newly inaugurated Texas governor, George T. Wood, in conjunction with Colonel Peter H. Bell, commander of the Texas Rangers, had decided to abandon the temporary line agreement. They ordered the Ranger company quartered on the Brazos River to move their station fifteen miles west of Torrey's Trading Post and instructed them not to "interfere or prevent any settlers" from moving to the area. As a result, American settlement had pushed ten miles west of Torrey's by February 1848. Seven other Ranger companies, stationed at intervals from the Rio Grande to the Red River, also moved farther west at the same time, inviting settlers to accompany them upstream into Indian country.[14]

The Americans' westward advance reinforced the decision—suggested by Major Neighbors the previous fall—made by most of the Caddo tribesmen in Texas to move nearly one hundred miles up the Brazos River to settle near the Wichitas. The Kadohadachos, now led by Haddabah after Bintah's death over the winter, settled on the south bank of the river, directly across from the Kichai village. Toweash's Hainais assembled thirteen miles below the Kadohadachos on the north bank of the Brazos. Among the Caddo tribes, only the Nadacos under Iesh refused to move their village, which was now located only about forty miles from the nearest American settlements. Following the Nadacos' return from their winter hunt in late February, Major Neighbors met with Iesh and found him "perplexed." The Nadaco chief confessed that he was hesitant to settle and plant corn since the Americans might drive his tribe off before harvest time. Neighbors, in an attempt to restore Iesh's confidence in the United States, advised him to remain where he was, for the federal government "would do him justice" even if the settlers moved beyond his village. Major Neighbors, however, was not as confident in his March 2, 1848 report to Commissioner Medill. He stated that "a crisis has now arrived" and that the Americans' insistence upon settling on Indian lands "regardless of the consequences . . . must necessarily and inevitably lead to serious difficulty."[15]

Major Neighbors' forecast of trouble soon proved correct as violence broke out on the frontier, and the animosity between the Texans and the Indians came boiling to the surface. In late March 1848, following the murder of a German settler near Fredericksburg, a company of Texas Rangers attacked a Taovaya and Waco party on the Llano River and killed twenty-five men. Two weeks later the Taovayas retaliated by killing and scalping three surveyors of the Texas Emigration and Land Company near the headwaters of Aquilla Creek, about sixty miles northwest of Waco. The day after the surveyors' murder, a group of Texas Rangers traveling to the Aquilla to supervise the surveyors' burial killed a teenaged Kadohadacho boy they encountered. Enraged, the Kadohadachos immediately flew to arms, resolving to obtain vengeance for the murder of the boy, who had been hunting with his father. However, Nadaco chief Iesh, recognized leader of all the Caddos, stepped in and pacified the warriors "with great difficulty." In late April Iesh met with local trader Charles Barnard and "promised to keep his people quiet" and to abide by the stipulations of the Treaty of Council Springs, which stated that any American citizen charged with the murder of an Indian would be tried and punished by the laws of Texas.[16]

The Nadaco chief attempted to maintain the peace, but Texas Ranger commander Bell refused to arrest the soldiers responsible for the death of the Kadohadacho boy. In response to the Wichita and Caddo actions, between two and three hundred Texas settlers organized a militia to "drive the [Indians] out of the country." The Texas Rangers prevailed upon the citizens to desist in their planned attack, but in the face of such hostility Colonel Bell chose not to bring the soldiers to justice. Only after Iesh and the Caddos protested vehemently to Major Neighbors did Commissioner Medill use his influence to force Colonel Bell to resolve the matter. In September 1848, five months after the incident, Texas Ranger representatives met with the Kadohadachos at Torrey's and agreed to provide goods worth $500 as compensation for the boy's death. Mistrustful of the Rangers and crowded by encroaching settlers, the Nadacos decided to move far up the Brazos to join with the Kadohadachos and Hainais following their annual winter hunt. In early 1849, the Nadacos settled into their new home—situated directly across the river from the Hainais—by constructing traditional grass houses and, with the other Caddo tribes, made "very creditable efforts" at raising corn, beans, pumpkins, and melons.[17]

In the meantime, the Penateka Comanches also conflicted with the Texans over the temporary line agreement, which they came to realize would only be enforced against Indians and not the American settlers. In early 1848, a Texas Ranger captain told Mopechucope that, "under [no] circumstances" would he permit the Penateka chief and his small hunting party to follow the buffalo below the regiment's Colorado River post. Mopechucope quarreled with the Ranger officer, claiming that the Penatekas had hunted in the region long before the man was born. The Comanche chief questioned why the Texans kept "so many soldiers on the line if [they] wish to keep the peace." Informing Major Neighbors of the incident, Mopechucope charged that "you told me that the troops were placed there for [the Indians'] protection as well as the [Texans']; that I know is not so." A few months later, when Chief Santa Anna visited Austin to have a "friendly talk" with the governor, a few citizens "became alarmed," and the Penateka party was ordered to return west of the Ranger stations. Exasperated, the Comanches complained that "when we made a treaty, we believed the [Texans] wished to be friendly. If they are not friendly, and the Comanches cannot go to their houses, there is no use in making treaties."[18]

Despite their anger over the lack of a boundary, the Penatekas still tried to abide by the treaty. In January 1848, warriors from Northern Comanche tribes—mainly Tenawas, Nokonis, and Kotsotekas—stole horses and killed a couple of American settlers near San Antonio. Not wanting to be blamed for the crimes, Penateka chief Mopechucope sent word for Major Neighbors to visit his ranchería, located far above the Wichita villages on the Salt Fork of the Brazos. Upon the federal agent's arrival, Mopechucope explained the situation and told Neighbors that his tribe had "used every exertion to prevent further difficulty, and to return the stolen property" to Texas authorities. He even arranged a conference between Neighbors and a few visiting Northern Comanches, who told the federal agent that they would follow the Penatekas' lead and abide by the Treaty of Council Springs.[19]

Nonetheless, the Penatekas reserved the right to continue to make raids in Mexico. Throughout the summer and fall of 1848 Comanche war parties continually pillaged south of the Rio Grande, returning to their rancherías with large numbers of horses, mules, and prisoners. Despite the Penatekas' desire to maintain peaceful relations with the Americans, Texas Rangers—now stationed in the path of the raiders' routes to Mexico—harassed the men as they made their way to and from the Rio Grande. In a few instances, blood was spilled on both sides. Fearful that these incidents might lead to full-scale war, in September 1848 Major Neighbors traveled to Santa Anna's village high upon the Clear Fork of the Brazos. The Penateka headman explained the dangerous situation to Neighbors, who impotently suggested that the raiders should move their routes to Mexico farther west or attempt to obtain passes from the Rangers before heading south. The Indian agent, however, was forced to admit that his advice would not "put an end to serious difficulties, growing out of the collisions between our troops and the Indians."[20]

Ironically, the Texas Rangers' clashes with the Penatekas had already resulted in the outbreak of hostilities with the Lipan Apaches, who had been allies of the Americans in Texas for more than two decades. After spending the winter near the mouth of the Pecos River, the Lipans had established rancherías on the headwaters of the Guadalupe River in the spring of 1848. In April, Major Neighbors traveled to the Guadalupe and met with Chief Chiquito, who stated that since the Ranger attack the previous summer, the Lipans had been afraid to approach the Texan settlements. Hoping to reestablish peaceful relations, Neighbors escorted Chiquito and a few other Apaches back to Austin and distributed the presents that were due them for signing the Treaty of Council Springs. The friendly relationship, however, was soon disrupted by the continuing dispute between the Penateka Comanches and the Texas Rangers. On two occasions during the summer of 1848, Penateka war parties returning from Mexico stole horses from Ranger stations and then passed by the Lipan rancherías on their way northward. Both times the Rangers traced the stolen mounts to the Lipans and attacked them without warning, killing a total of thirty Apaches and making off with two hundred horses. Chiquito protested to Major Neighbors, whose investigation proved that the Penatekas were actually guilty of stealing the horses. The federal agent then informed Ranger commander Bell of the unfortunate misunderstanding. As with the murder of the Kadohadacho boy, though, Colonel Bell was hesitant to take any actions against his troops or to provide restitution to the aggrieved Indians. As a result, vengeance-seeking Lipan warriors broke the peace by killing twenty settlers while stealing horses from ranches between the Guadalupe and San Antonio rivers. By the fall of 1848, Major Neighbors was forced to admit that "a feeling of strong resentment exists in the minds of some [Texas] citizens towards Indians in general, and the Lipans in particular; and I have heard threats made by some to shoot the first Indians they meet."[21]

There were no outbreaks of violence in the winter of 1848–49, but Major Neighbors realized that the quiet situation was temporary, and that the tribes' position would continue to deteriorate unless bold steps were taken to resolve the Indian matter in Texas. On March 7, 1849, Neighbors put forth his solution to Major General William J. Worth, commander of the United States' military forces that were being deployed at a string of forts established on the Texas frontier following the end of the U.S.-Mexican War. Neighbors called for a reservation system to be implemented in Texas in which the Indians would be placed under federal jurisdiction and separated from the settlers. He proposed that the federal government acquire land from the state of Texas for the "permanent location and settlement of the Indians; said land to be divided among the several bands and tribes according to their numbers." The federal trade and intercourse laws would be extended over the Texas Indians, and agents would be provided for them. To protect the tribes on the reservation, Neighbors called for the federal government to establish military posts in the Indian country whose commanders would be in "full cooperation with the Indian agent in carrying into effect all laws or treaty stipulations." Although the newly installed Whig administration of President Zachary Taylor removed Neighbors from his position as Indian agent in the summer of 1849, the establishment of a reservation in Texas soon became the federal government's goal.[22]

Unfortunately for the Texas tribes, the actual implementation of the policy did not come immediately, and the Indians suffered miserably over the next few years. The new Indian agent, Judge John Rollins, was an elderly man in poor health who did not arrive in Texas until late November 1849 and did not bother to meet with any tribal members until the following spring. This left the Indians of Texas virtually without a representative of the federal government, which, in view of the state's hostile attitude, was their only ally. As a result, most of the tribes kept their distance from the American settlements in Texas. The four hundred or so Lipan Apaches, made up of a "disproportionate amount of old people," retreated far to the west and established rancherías on the upper reaches of the Llano River as well as on the Concho and the Pecos. While the Lipans at least engaged in small-scale agriculture, some of the six hundred "wretched and destitute" Tonkawas were reduced to begging for food and clothing near various Texas Ranger stations. Others chose to hunt deer on the range between the headwaters of the Trinity and the upper Brazos. A few tribal members from both the Lipans and the Tonkawas abandoned Texas and joined their kinsmen in Mexico.[23]

Many Wichitas and Caddos, feeling pressured by American settlers, also left Texas to take refuge with their comrades in the Indian Territory. In March 1849, the United States Army established Fort Graham on the Brazos River about one hundred miles below the Wichita and Caddo villages. Within six months, eager surveyors arrived at the Nadaco town to mark off the land for future settlement. As a result, over the next couple of years more than one hundred Caddos crossed north of the Red River and joined the Whitebead band near the newly established Fort Arbuckle on the Washita River. By 1851, fewer than five hundred Caddos (161 Kadohadachos, 202 Nadacos, and 113 Hainais) remained on the Brazos River. An even greater number of Wichitas fled from Texas; nearly all of the three hundred or so Kichais moved to the Indian Territory and established a settlement on Choteau Creek, near its confluence with the Canadian River. Another couple of hundred Wacos and Tawakonis left the Brazos to join the Taovayas, who had recently moved their village eastward, from the foot of the Wichita Mountains to the headwaters of Rush Creek, a tributary of the Washita. Less than three hundred Wichitas (thirty-eight Kichais, 114 Wacos, and 141 Tawakonis) stayed behind in their Brazos River settlements. More than one hundred Delawares lived about fifty miles downriver from the Wichitas and Caddos, near a trading post recently established by Charles Barnard.[24]

In the spring and summer of 1849, an outbreak of cholera seriously reduced the number of Penateka Comanches in Texas. In addition to killing hundreds of tribesmen, the epidemic also took the lives of chiefs Santa Anna and Mopechucope. Through their absence, Potsanaquahip and Pahayuko were spared the wrath of the disease; Potsanaquahip helped Major Neighbors (along with Delaware guides) establish a road, called the California Trail, from Torrey's Trading Post to El Paso, and Pahayuko spent the early part of the year on the Arkansas River. In the aftermath of the disease, however, Pahayuko chose to live with the Kotsotekas, the Northern Comanche tribe of his wife, leaving Potsanaquahip the most authoritative Penateka chief in Texas. Three younger men—Saviah (Yellow Wolf), Sanaco, and Ketumse—assumed leadership positions of the other Penateka bands. In September the twelve hundred remaining Penatekas gathered on the Clear Fork of the Brazos to discuss their future. Potsanaquahip, who had led the greatest of all Comanche raids against the Texans in 1840, now warned his fellow tribesmen that it "would be foolish to" fight the Americans, for the Penatekas had previously been unable to defeat them when the tribe had been strong. Therefore, the weakened tribesmen chose to maintain the policy of peaceful relations with the Americans while continuing to conduct raids in Mexico. Following the council, Potsanaquahip and Ketumse traveled to Fredericksburg to inform United States military officers at Fort Martin Scott of their decision. They also implored the American soldiers to have patience and not kill Penateka warriors for committing minor infractions on their way to and from the Rio Grande.[25]

Understanding the dire situation of the Texas tribes, in 1850 the federal government seriously began to push for the establishment of an Indian reservation in the state. The Texans, however, refused to accede to the wishes of the United States. The February 1850 session of the state legislature rejected a specific proposal authorizing the federal government to extend the trade and intercourse laws to the Indians of Texas. The situation became so desperate that President Millard Fillmore personally tried to persuade Texas to "assign a small portion of her vast domain for the provisional occupancy of the small remnants of tribes within her borders." Commissioner of Indian Affairs Luke Lea suggested the appointment of a commission to confer with Texas authorities "for the purpose of effecting the conventional arrangements indispensable to a satisfactory adjustment" of the state's Indian affairs. William M. Williams, chairman of the Texas House Committee on Indian Affairs, responded favorably to these entreaties. In August 1850, he called upon his state to adopt the proposals of the federal government, yet once again the Texas legislature refused to comply.[26]

In the face of the Texas legislature's inaction, Judge Rollins decided to forge a treaty with the Indians that included a boundary line agreement. In September 1850, Rollins traveled throughout the state, meeting with representatives of the Lipans, Caddos, Wichitas, and Penateka Comanches—he failed to locate any Tonkawas—to invite them to attend a treaty council on Spring Creek, near the mouth of the San Saba River. Headmen of each tribe—including Chiquito of the Lipans, Acaquash of the Wacos, and Potsanaquahip, Saviah, and Ketumse of the Penatekas—met with Rollins there in December and concluded an agreement that was basically a restatement of the Treaty of Council Springs, except for Articles Fifteen and Eighteen. Article Fifteen established a temporary line at the Llano River, south of which the Indians agreed not to travel without the special permission of an army officer; Article Eighteen stated that within the next year a definite line would be established between the Indians and the Americans, "so that the Indian country may be known and respected." Despite Rollins's best intentions, the Treaty of Spring Creek proved worthless, as the United States Senate refused to ratify it because of the federal government's lack of control of the public lands in Texas.[27]

Soon thereafter, however, Congress agreed to assist Judge Rollins in his duties by passing legislation providing for two Indian subagents in Texas. Eventually, Jesse Stem was appointed special agent to the Wichitas, Caddos, and Tonkawas, while John Rogers was placed in charge of the Penateka Comanches and the Lipan Apaches. The new subagents, though, proved unable to improve the situation of the Texas Indians. Both men clashed personally with the infirm Judge Rollins, who died in September 1851. Over Agent Stem's objections, George T. Howard was appointed as Rollins's successor the following January. In May 1852, Agent Rogers resigned and was replaced by Horace Capron. The constant turnover of agents, combined with their inability to get along with one another, only further added to the federal government's impotence concerning Indian affairs in Texas at a time when the tribes needed the United States' assistance the most.[28]

The continued increase in the number of American settlers in Texas and their constant encroachment upon tribal lands and hunting grounds caused the few remaining Indians in Texas to suffer inordinately over the next half decade. In the three years since 1847 the settler and slave population of Texas had grown from about 140,000 to more than 210,000 in 1850. While most of the citizens lived in the eastern portion of the state, more than 25,000 settlers had established over fifteen hundred farms and ranches in the fourteen westernmost counties stretching from the San Antonio River north to the Red. The Texans not only forced the Indians to abandon their villages and crops and move even farther westward, they also caused a dramatic decline in the number of deer and buffalo in the region. Whereas immense herds of buffalo had ranged as far south as the San Gabriel River in the final years of the Republic of Texas, by 1850 few buffalo crossed south of the Red River. In 1852 the appearance of just a few small herds west of Fort Worth was regarded as a

highly unusual occurrence. Unfortunately for the tribes of Texas, including the
Penatekas, the Northern Comanches fiercely guarded the ranges on which the
buffalo still roamed between the Red and the Canadian rivers in the western
portion of the Indian Territory. As a result, many of the Indians in Texas were
starving, causing all the tribes—even the hunting and gathering Comanches
and Tonkawas—to beg the federal government to secure lands on which they
could safely settle and raise crops.[29]

Chief Ketumse was the first Penateka leader to discuss the possibility of
settling down on a reservation. As early as May 1850, Ketumse had complained
to Judge Rollins that the Penatekas were starving due to the lack of game.
He hinted to the Indian agent that his band of three hundred people might
be willing to abandon the chase and learn to farm, but he feared that the
Americans would soon come along and drive them away from the place they
had chosen to make their home. A year and a half later, in October 1851,
Ketumse met with Agent Rogers and reiterated his band's desire to settle
down and become sedentary agriculturalists. The Penateka headman stated
that his people had been "driven from their homes where their parents were
buried . . . by the white men and have no home or resting place. We want land
and homes, of our own." Ketumse promised that if the president of the United
States would give his tribe a section of the country "to settle on and cultivate
that we can call our own," his band of Penatekas would gladly move there
and live under the protection of the federal government. Agent Rogers was
helpless to act, though, since the Texas legislature continued to refuse to grant
any land to the Indians.[30]

All of the Penateka bands suffered during the following winter as the encroaching American settlements forced them to move even farther west than
their usual range. In April 1852 an American official encountered Ketumse and
his group, "very much in want," on the headwaters of the San Saba River. The
Penateka headman, along with thirty tribesmen, traveled to Fort Martin Scott
and met with Agent Howard, who provided them with much needed food.
Ketumse reiterated his band's desire to settle on a reservation and raise crops,
but he demanded that the Indian agent show them the "lands that we are to live
on." Receiving no satisfactory response, Ketumse's band spent the summer
with Sanaco's people fruitlessly searching for game in the Concho River Valley.
By September both bands, numbering seven hundred people, were "suffering
extreme hunger, bordering upon starvation." Meeting with Agent Capron at
Camp Johnston on the North Concho River, the two Penateka headmen asked
how they could "attempt the cultivation of the soil, or raising of cattle, so
long as we have no permanent home? . . . Over this vast country, where for
centuries our ancestors roamed in undisputed possession, free and happy,

what have we left? The game, our main dependence, is killed and driven off, and we are forced into the most sterile and barren portions of it to starve. . . . Give us a country we can call our own, where we may bury our people in quiet." Once again, the federal Indian agent could not do anything for the suffering tribesmen, and Ketumse and Sanaco led their bands northward to the Clear Fork of the Brazos where they spent the winter with the Penatekas under Potsanaquahip and Saviah. In the spring of 1853, all four bands moved to the Colorado River, upstream from the mouth of the Concho, and hunted in vain for adequate amounts of game. In November the starving tribal members gathered near Fort Chadbourne, where American officials distributed 8,000 pounds of beef and 125 bushels of corn to the Penatekas so they could survive the winter.[31]

In the meantime, the hunting and gathering Tonkawas suffered so much that they actually attempted to raise crops for the first time in their history. Competing for scarce game with the agricultural tribes of the Brazos River, in 1851 Tonkawa hunters clashed several times with Wichita warriors, who usually got the better of them; on one occasion a group of Wacos killed thirteen of the fourteen Tonkawa men they encountered. As a result, about half of the Tonkawas migrated from the prairies of Texas to take refuge with their kinsmen in Mexico. In early 1852, Chief Placido led the remaining three hundred Tonkawas to Fort Graham to ask Agent Stem for food and clothing. The desperate Indians "presented a sad picture of suffering and destitution" to the Indian agent, who helped the Tonkawas establish a ranchería a few miles west of the fort on the Bosque River. Stem provided the tribe with seed, and the starving Tonkawas, with the assistance of the Indian agent, planted corn. Unfortunately, in August drought and grasshoppers destroyed their crop, forcing the Tonkawas to move farther south to hunt between the Colorado and the Llano for the remainder of the year. The following spring the desperate Tonkawas begged for food from the soldiers at Fort Mason, located near the Llano River. One officer characterized them as being "squalid [and] half-starved looking," while another stated that the Tonkawas were the "most ragged, filthy, and destitute Indians" he had ever seen. The soldiers at Fort Mason took pity on the suffering Indians and provided them with small quantities of corn and damaged pork and bacon. Wearing out their welcome at Fort Mason, in late 1853 the Tonkawas moved southward to the headwaters of the Nueces River and began scrounging for food at nearby Fort Inge.[32]

By 1853, after much hardship and suffering, the remaining Lipan Apaches in Texas also had taken refuge in the Nueces Valley. In early 1852, however, most of the Lipans had established a ranchería on the Pedernales River, about fifteen miles southwest of Fredericksburg. Although the Apaches maintained the peace, tending to their gardens and hunting in the area, the German colonists were uneasy with the Indian camp being so close to the town. Hoping to avoid an outbreak of violence, in July Agent Capron met with Chiquito and Ramón Castro and informed them that they should move farther from the German settlements and establish their villages on the Llano River. Resignedly, the Lipan headmen agreed to relocate and, with the exception of a few men left behind to harvest their crops, in August the tribe established a new ranchería a few miles from Fort Mason. Since game was scarce in the region, the Lipans were "in a most destitute condition," forcing Agent Capron to provide them with meager portions of beef and corn, in addition to a much needed supply of blankets, throughout the fall. As winter set in the Lipans moved northwestward to the headwaters of the San Saba River in search of game. [33]

In late December 1852, while the Apaches were hunting on the San Saba, a Texas citizen reported to General William P. Harney, recently appointed commander of the military department of Texas, that a party of Lipans had stolen horses and wounded several people at a ranch forty miles south of San Antonio. Agents Capron and Howard, as well as Delaware interpreter John Conner, were certain that the bandits had been Mexicans disguised as Indians, but they were unable to convince the newly arrived general of the Lipans' innocence. Therefore, Harney ordered troops from San Antonio to attack the Lipans in the dead of winter, authorizing them to "kill all the men and make all the women and children prisoners." As a result, an American force surprised the unsuspecting Lipans in their camp on the San Saba, killing perhaps twenty-five tribal members and making off with most of the Apache horse herd before burning the village to the ground. Whereas most of the Lipan survivors, "turned loose upon the borders at an inclement season of year," decided to take refuge with their kinsmen in Mexico, in March 1853 Chiquito and Juan Castro led the remaining one hundred or so tribal members to the headwaters of the Nueces River. Hoping to make amends, General Harney returned a few horses to the Lipans and provided them with blankets and clothing. Several citizens gave the Apaches seed so they could resume planting corn. Nonetheless, the Lipans in Texas remained wary of the American settlers and were ready to move to Mexico at the first sign of hostility. [34]

Continued American encroachment also forced many members of the agricultural tribes of the Brazos River villages to abandon their homes and seek refuge outside of Texas. In June 1851, two representatives of the federal government made separate visits to the Caddo and Wichita towns on the Brazos. Colonel Samuel Cooper, with Major Henry H. Sibley and a company of the Second Cavalry, left Fort Graham on June 5 and spent a week among the various tribes. Almost as soon as Cooper left the villages, Agent Stem and

Colonel William J. Hardee arrived at the Nadaco and Hainai towns. Colonel Cooper and Agent Stem held talks with the Caddo and Wichita headmen, and their reports were very similar. Both claimed that the tribes were "perfectly peaceable" and "professed the most cordial feelings toward our government and people." However, the tribes' leaders strongly desired that "a permanent boundary should be fixed, so that they might have a country where they could be secure from encroachments of the white settlements." Only then could they build up their villages and raise crops without fear of being "forced to abandon their homes, the fruits of their labors, and the graves of their kindred." Nadaco chief Iesh—whom Stem felt was the "most influential chief on the Brazos"— complained to the agent that the boundary line was constantly being crossed by settlers "who marked trees, surveyed lands in [the Indians'] hunting grounds, and near their villages . . . and this is not just." The Caddos and Wichitas also complained that the sparseness of game made it difficult to obtain enough to eat, and at times they were "in a starving condition." They "expressed a desire" to be provided with better farming implements, which had been promised in the Treaty of Council Springs, so that they might cultivate their crops "to better advantage and to greater extent." The headmen asked to be furnished with a few cows and hogs to compensate for the depletion of game. Colonel Cooper recommended that the government should supply the tribes with the these items, which "would greatly contribute to their comfort, and might through their influence, effect a salutary change in the temper and feelings" of some of the other tribes.[35]

Stem's and Cooper's reports concerning the tenuous situation of the agricultural tribes of the Brazos did not persuade the federal government to protect them. In fact, the establishment of Fort Belknap on the Brazos River in the summer of 1851 worsened the tribes' situation. The post, located west of the Wichita and Caddo villages, served as an invitation for American settlers to stream into and beyond the Indian towns. Following their annual winter hunt, the Nadacos and Hainais returned to their homes in early 1852 only to find the area surveyed and surrounded by Americans. As a result, the frightened tribal members moved down the Brazos to an unoccupied tract of land near Comanche Peak. This land was of a lesser quality, and their corn crop was "unusually small." Combined with their inability to construct adequate shelters, the Nadacos and Hainais "experienced an unusual amount of sickness and mortality" throughout the year. Agent Stem reported that their precarious situation had caused them to "have no courage for vigorous and hopeful effort." The Kadohadachos, meanwhile, moved their village upstream to Fort Belknap. Realizing the desperate situation of the tribe, Major Sibley purchased the land on which the Kadohadachos resided and gave them written permission to live on his property for five years. However, since the land was "previously uncultivated," the Kadohadachos were only able to "make but little" corn for the year.[36]

The American settlers' encroachment forced almost all of the Wichitas to move to the Indian Territory, where they joined their kinsmen at the Taovaya village on Rush Creek. Only Acaquash and a small band of Wacos remained in Texas where, for protection, they eventually relocated near the post Agent Stem established on the Clear Fork of the Brazos at the crossing of the road between Fort Belknap and Fort Phantom Hill. The hardship and hostility caused by these forced removals led the Wichitas north of the Red River to resume their raids upon the Texans. In June 1852, a group of Taovayas invaded Texas and robbed a wagon train of eight horses and mules. Agent Stem sent a member of Acaquash's band of Wacos to Rush Creek, where he was able to retrieve the stolen animals. Two months later a troop from Fort Belknap visited the Wichita encampment on Rush Creek and convinced them to give up six more stolen horses and mules. The soldiers' visit quieted the Wichitas for the rest of the year. In January 1853, however, the Wichitas began to make raids into Texas in earnest. By late February five separate parties had committed depredations in Texas, often using Acaquash's camp as a rendezvous point.[37]

The uneasiness between the Wichitas and the Americans soon led to bloodshed, which ultimately forced the entire tribe to take refuge in the Indian Territory. On February 22, Agent Stem intercepted twenty-two Taovaya warriors, led by Koweaka, accused them of committing "many depredations over the past year," and ordered them back across the Red River to obtain the stolen property. Koweaka did not deny the charges, and he and his party returned to Rush Creek. Koweaka reentered Texas on March 23 with eight warriors and several women and children and returned fourteen horses to the Indian agent. Despite this demonstration of good faith, Stem and Major Sibley decided to hold Koweaka's party hostage in an attempt to recover the large number of horses that had been stolen in the past few months. Two of the Taovayas were sent to the Indian Territory to retrieve the horses, and Koweaka and his party were disarmed and put under guard in their own camp. That night Koweaka sacrificed himself and his family so that the rest of the Taovaya hostages could escape. He stabbed his wife and child in the heart and then rushed one of the guards with the knife and was killed. In the confusion the others slipped away. This shocking incident raised the level of tension between the Wichitas and the Americans. A few days later Acaquash and his band of Wacos killed five head of Agent Stem's cattle with "no explanation or apology." Stem, accompanied by a troop of soldiers commanded by Major Sibley, visited the Waco camp and demanded three horses as payment. While Acaquash feigned compliance, the

Waco men began driving their horses away to safety. When Major Sibley tried to stop them, shots were traded between the parties, and the Waco warriors were forced to retreat. The Waco women immediately decamped, burned the lodges, and the entire Acaquash band headed north to join their kinsmen. The last of the Wichitas had finally abandoned Texas.[38]

Although most of the Caddos remained south of the Red River, their situation was not much better than that of the Wichitas. The untimely death of Chief Haddabah in the summer of 1853 exacerbated the Kadohadachos' problems. George W. Hill, Stem's replacement as Indian agent, met with the tribe in August and reported that there was no clear successor to Haddabah's position, and that the tribe was "much scattered and divided in sentiment." In their misery the Kadohadachos had again taken up drinking whiskey, which they had obtained from the soldiers at Fort Belknap. Hill told the old men of the tribe to gather the people and select a chief, and he promised to "remove as far as possible [the] evils" of liquor. In September the Indian agent returned to the Kadohadacho village and met with the headmen who, "after much effort" had still been unable to choose a new leader. They requested that Hill "give them one," whom they promised to "hold up and make strong." Expecting this, Hill had gathered information about the various headmen and chose Tinah, a "sensible and good man," to be the new Kadohadacho chief. Tinah promised to help his tribe refrain from drinking whiskey and requested that Hill give them a permanent home. Although the agent was unable to fulfill this request, he did travel with a group of Kadohadachos to Barnard's Trading Post and purchased "articles of necessity to enable them to make" their fall hunt. Hill also held a council with Hainai and Nadaco tribesmen in which Chief Iesh "urged with force the necessity" of the government procuring a home for him and his people, around which "his white brother could pass" to the west. He told the agent that "the buffalo was gone and but a few deer were left," and thus again asked to be provided with cattle and hogs. As before, Hill was forced to reply that he could not do anything for the Indians until he received permission from the federal government.[39]

In late 1853, just in time to save the desperate Indian tribes from further despair, the Texas government at last realized that something had to be done. Following his dismissal as Indian agent in 1849, Major Neighbors had been elected to the Texas House of Representatives two years later. Appointed as chairman of the Committee on Indian Affairs, Neighbors, along with Senator John S. "Rip" Ford, sponsored a bill that the legislature passed in February 1852 authorizing the governor to negotiate an agreement with the United States that would set aside public lands in Texas for the settlement of the state's tribes. Although Governor Bell—the former commander of the Texas

Rangers—took no immediate action on the bill, in May 1853 the Democratic administration of President Franklin Pierce reappointed Neighbors to the position of Texas Indian agent. Neighbors, along with Secretary of War Jefferson Davis, put pressure on Governor Bell to provide for the establishment of federally supervised Indian reservations in Texas. As a result, in his message to the Texas legislature on November 9, the governor finally recommended that the United States be given the authority to settle the Indians on reservations to be located within the boundaries of the state. The Texas legislature followed the governor's advice and passed an act on February 6, 1854, giving the federal government jurisdiction over twelve leagues of the state's vacant land "for the use and benefit of the several tribes of Indians residing within the limits of Texas." The reservation proposal of Major Neighbors was at last being put into effect, a full five years after it had first been suggested. With the federal government finally receiving the full authority to protect them, most of the Indians of Texas hoped that they could settle down on a reservation and end the suffering they had been forced to endure for the past decade.[40]

8. Disappearance
The Indians and the Texas Reserves, 1854 to 1859

By the 1850s the Indian policy of the United States had evolved from simply removing the tribes from the path of encroaching settlers to the development of the reservation system. Small parcels of land were to be "reserved" out of the tribes' original holdings as an alternative to extinction. On the reserves the federal government's trade and intercourse laws would be implemented, the Indians would be protected, and their country preserved from land-hungry settlers. In return for agreeing to settle on the reservation, the Indians would be provided with weekly food rations as well as periodic distributions of presents such and clothing and blankets. The ultimate goal of the reservation system, however, was not just to protect the Indians but also to transform them. The notions of Major Neighbors, who was placed in charge of the two Texas reservations in 1854, neatly summarized the general policy of the federal government concerning the reservation system. Neighbors saw himself as a "civilizing agent" who would help the Indians convert to the ways of the American settlers. The Indians would be taught advanced agricultural techniques and the art of stock raising and would be provided with the tools necessary to implement these practices. English education would be provided for the children, and attempts would be made to convert the tribes to Christianity. Neighbors claimed that his efforts, as well as those of his subagents, "would be directed particularly to give individuality to the Indians, and to teach them the value of property . . . to encourage each head of a family to settle and cultivate his own farm."[1]

The optimistic goals and practices of the reservation plan, however, were not actually appropriate for all the different tribes that resided in Texas. On one hand, the Caddos and Wichitas seemed particularly well suited to proving that the reservation experiment could work in Texas. They were traditionally sedentary and agricultural, had given up any hope of living independently of Euroamericans, and were very eager to obtain a parcel of land they could permanently call their own. The Caddos and Wichitas had painfully learned the lesson that the Texans were not to be deterred in their westward march, and the tribes realized they would need to adapt to the Americans' ways if they wished to survive. Although not ready to give up their traditional way of life, the tribes saw nothing wrong with adopting new measures—such as raising cattle or having their children attend school—that would profit them. The Caddos and Wichitas' optimistic attitude went far in the success they experienced in the four years they spent on their Texas reservation. On the other hand, the nomadic hunting tribes, the Penateka Comanches and Tonkawas, had a more difficult time adopting to reservation life. Before the Indians could even settle down, Texan hostility caused many Penatekas and Tonkawas—as well as the entire Lipan Apache tribe—to refuse to move to the reserves. The tribesmen that did settle on the reservations then had to be coaxed into performing the laborous agricultural tasks required of them. Although a core group of Penatekas and Tonkawas eventually came to accept their new lives and had begun to make progress on the reservations by the time they were closed in 1859, neither tribe was able to match the accomplishments of the agricultural Caddos and Wichitas.

With more time, however, even the Penateka Comanches and the Tonkawas might have proven the feasiblity of the reservation system in Texas. Unfortunately, the experiment was not undertaken in a vacuum, and there were two mutually antagonistic groups who violently opposed its success: Northern Comanches and Texan settlers. From the moment they were opened in 1855, the two reservations in Texas were susceptible to attacks from both groups. Ultimately, the reservations were left in an untenable position, and the tribes were forced to give up their lands and move into the Indian Territory, this time abandoning Texas for good. By the end of 1859 the only Indians remaining in Texas were the few hundred Alabama and Coushatta Indians who lived in the Big Thicket on a small plot of land purchased for them by the state.

Although legislation had been passed in February 1854 for the establishment of reservations for the Indians of Texas, it took a full year before the various tribes were actually able to settle on them. In the meantime, most of the Indians continued to suffer. The three Caddo tribes of Texas had a particularly difficult year; grasshoppers destroyed their first corn crop in early spring, and torrential rains—combined with an extremely dry summer—injured their second crop. Their harvest was so small that it had been consumed by September. Caddo tribesmen tried to supplement their food supply through the chase but met with little success, as their hunting grounds had been severely reduced by the encroaching Texan settlements to the southeast and by the Northern Comanches who controlled the land to the northwest. As a result, Agent Hill distributed food throughout the year to prevent the Caddos from starving. Unhappy with their dependence on rations, about one-third of the five hundred Caddos in Texas chose to move to the Indian Territory, where they joined the two hundred or so Whitebeads at their well-established village near Fort Arbuckle.[2]

The seven hundred Wacos and Tawakonis also spent the entire year in dire straits north of the Red River, either at the Kichai village on Choteau Creek or at the Taovaya settlement on Rush Creek. Along with the Caddos, the two Wichita tribes were eager to settle down permanently in Texas. Therefore, in July 1854, Waco chief Acaquash and Chief Ocherash of the Tawakonis traveled to Texas and met with Captain Randolph B. Marcy and Major Neighbors to discuss the proposed reservation. Iesh—representing both the Nadacos and the Hainais—and Kadohadacho chief Tinah were also present, along with six Delawares, led by John Conner, who acted as guides and interpreters. Captain Marcy explained to the Indian leaders that he had been chosen to survey the country and to select a site for their reservation. Iesh informed Marcy that although he realized the Americans had the "abundant power" to send his people wherever they chose, the Caddos wished to live on the Brazos at a point downstream from Fort Belknap in order to receive protection from the Northern Comanches. The Nadaco chief stated that although the Americans had driven his tribe from their home many times, Iesh said he preferred to live near them since "they generally allowed him to eat a portion of what he raised, but that the Comanches took everything." The other headmen concurred with this opinion. There was only one parcel of land below Fort Belknap on the Brazos that had yet to be claimed by onrushing settlers, so Marcy and Neighbors traveled there with the various chiefs. Situated about fifteen miles below Fort Belknap near the old Caddo and Wichita villages, the tract consisted of eight leagues, or 37,152 acres. Within the tract was a "large body of valley land of the most preeminent fertility upon either side" of the Brazos. The uplands were "covered with luxuriant grama grasses," which provided the tribes with good pastureland. There were several streams of fresh spring water, which afforded "an abundance of water at all seasons." The tribes gladly accepted this rich land as their reservation, which came to be known as the Brazos or Lower Reserve.[3]

Soon after Marcy and Neighbors selected the site on the Brazos for the Caddos and Wichitas, the two men sent a message to the twelve hundred Penatekas requesting a meeting with their headmen in order to assign a location for the Comanche reservation. In early August, Chief Ketumse met with Marcy and Neighbors in their camp on the Clear Fork of the Brazos and informed them that the Penatekas wanted to "avail themselves of the present opportunity to change their wandering life" and that, although his people were "perfectly ignorant of every thing relating to agriculture," they wanted to settle down on a reservation and learn how to farm. Ketumse explained that most of the Penatekas were suffering, since few buffalo ventured south of the Red River, and the Northern Comanches jealously guarded their hunting grounds in the western portion of the Indian Territory. Therefore, the Penatekas maintained a precarious existence based upon a dwindling amount of deer and antelope. Increasingly, the tribal members were forced to subsist on their own horses and mules and, as a result, their herds had greatly declined over the past five years. The desperate situation caused many Penateka men to succumb to the attraction of alcohol for the very first time. Ketumse hoped to end the Penatekas' cycle of decline by living under the protection of the federal government on land designated as their own.[4]

Not all of the Penatekas, though, were as eager as Ketumse to become sedentary agriculturalists. A few days later Chief Sanaco arrived at the camp and insisted that the entire Penateka tribe had authorized him, not Ketumse, to deal with the American representatives. Although Sanaco stated that many in his tribe shared Ketumse's willingness to settle down and farm, the Penateka leader said that he and others had misgivings about the prospect. He resignedly explained, however, that even though everyone knew that his tribe controlled all the land between the Red and the Colorado rivers, since the Americans wanted the Penatekas to live on the narrow limits of a reservation, "we shall be forced to do so whether we desire it or not." Despite this sour note, Sanaco reluctantly agreed to bring the Penatekas to the Comanche or Upper Reserve, a parcel of land containing four leagues, or 18,576 acres, which Marcy and Neighbors ultimately located on the Clear Fork of the Brazos, about fifty miles above its mouth. Nonetheless, Sanaco's doubts concerning the reservation, coupled with the leadership conflict with Ketumse, would ultimately prove detrimental to the Penatekas' attempt to alter their nomadic ways.[5]

Continued American hostility caused the few remaining Lipan Apaches and Tonkawas in Texas to have similar concerns about Neighbors' proposal of settling them on the Brazos Reserve, far north of their traditional range. By early 1854 the three hundred desperate Tonkawas under Chief Placido had established a ranchería on the Frio River, a few miles from Fort Inge, in hope of obtaining rations from the soldiers. Chief Chiquito's one hundred or so Lipans, meanwhile, settled in the nearby Sabinal Valley and begin planting "considerable fields" of corn and melons, around which they also constructed fences. In March, despite the Apaches' efforts, area settlers complained about the Indians' presence to Agent Howard in San Antonio, who sent a message to the Lipans ordering them to abandon their crops and move to the uninhabited Nueces Valley. They refused, and Juan Castro traveled to San Antonio with three family members to plead the Lipans' case to Howard.[6]

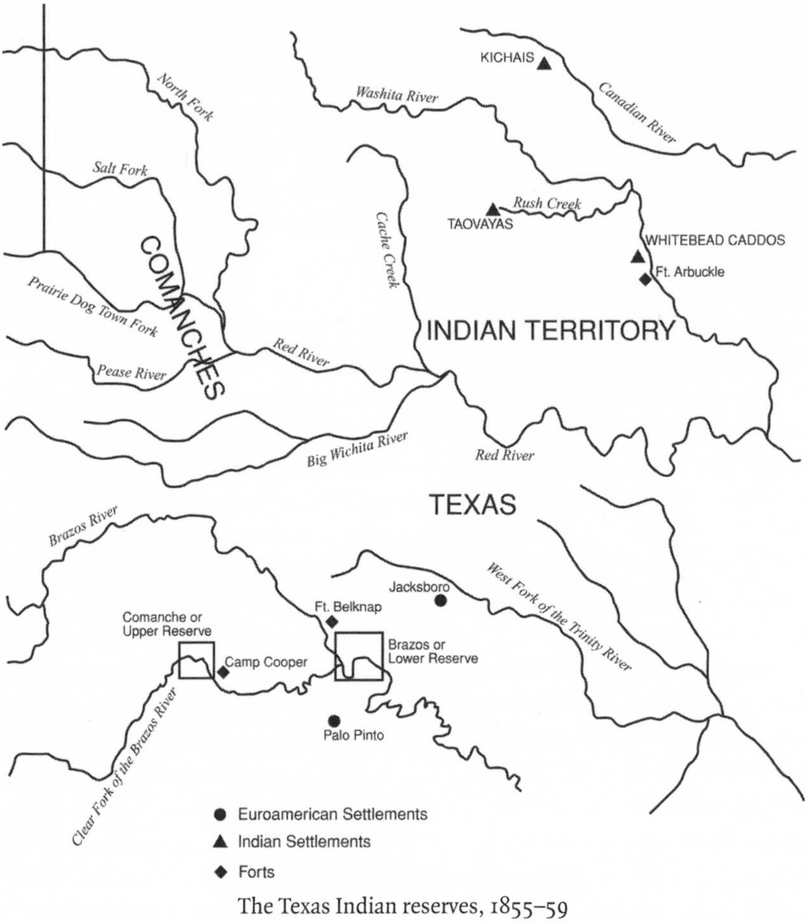
KICHAIS
North Fork
Washita River
Canadian River
Salt Fork
Rush Creek
TAOVAYAS
WHITEBEAD CADDOS
Ft. Arbuckle
Cache Creek
COMANCHES
Prairie Dog Town Fork
INDIAN TERRITORY
Red River
Pease River
Big Wichita River
Red River
TEXAS
Brazos River
West Fork of the Trinity River
Jacksboro
Ft. Belknap
Comanche or Upper Reserve
Camp Cooper
Brazos or Lower Reserve
Clear Fork of the Brazos River
Palo Pinto
Euroamerican Settlements
Indian Settlements
Forts
The Texas Indian reserves, 1855–59

While Howard and Castro discussed the situation, news arrived that unidentified Indians had killed a group of settlers on the Medina River, twenty miles northwest of San Antonio. Although Castro volunteered to guide American soldiers in pursuit of the murderers, Agent Howard remained suspicious of the Indian and held Castro's family in the Béxar County jail as hostages until the Lipans could be wholly absolved of the crime. Castro, however, abandoned the troops on the trail and, as a result, Howard arrested Chiquito and a few other Apaches and confined them to the guardhouse at Fort Inge. Ultimately, it turned out that a rogue group of Tonkawas had killed the settlers, and that Castro fled because a soldier had threatened his life. By May all of the hostages had been released, but soon thereafter the Tonkawas and Lipans were moved near Fort Clark in the Nueces Valley to keep them away from the

Texan settlements. A few Tonkawas moved to Mexico, leaving only about 250 tribal members in Texas to await their removal to the Brazos. Disgusted by the Americans' treatment and unwilling to relocate northward out of fear of the Comanches and the Texans, in the fall of 1854 Chief Chiquito led the remaining Lipans across the Rio Grande to join their kinsmen and the Mescalero Apaches in Mexico. Except for a few brief forays across the river during the next few years, following more than two centuries of habitation the Lipan Apaches had abandoned Texas for good.[7]

The remaining Indians in Texas began to settle on the reservations in the fall of 1854. By October the three Caddo tribes had eagerly arrived at the Brazos Reserve "without assistance or encouragement." They set up temporary shelters, and small hunting parties ranged between Fort Belknap and Comanche Peak in search of game. Over the winter Agent Hill distributed rations of flour and beef to the tribesmen. In November Waco and Tawakoni warriors returned stolen horses to Hill and evinced "anxious desire" to settle on the Brazos Reserve since they were starving in the Indian Territory. Hill furnished them with the remaining rations but convinced them to wait until spring to move south of the Red since he had no more food at his disposal. Finally, on March 1, 1855, Agent Hill gathered the Caddos and the two Wichita tribes together and, after consulting with the headmen, distributed the land. The Kadohadachos, along with the small group of Delawares they were associated with, chose land near the east line of the reserve near Caddo Spring, on the north bank of the Brazos. The Nadacos and the Hainais settled on the same side of the river, about one and a half miles west of the Kadohadacho village, at the mouth of Anadarko Creek. As a result of Iesh's leadership over the two tribes, the term Nadaco began to be used for both tribes, and the designation of Hainai was dropped for the time being. The Waco and Tawakoni village was located five miles west of the Nadacos, one mile north of the Brazos, near Salt Creek. Agent Hill decided to construct the agency buildings of the Brazos Reserve about one and a half miles north of the Waco and Tawakoni village, six hundred yards south of the northern boundary of the reserve. Upon completion, the agency complex consisted of separate houses for the agent, laborer, and interpreter, as well as an office, a storehouse, a schoolhouse, and a blacksmith's shop. Laborers' houses were also built at the various Indian villages. Two Delawares, Jim Shaw and George Williams, acted as agency interpreters.[8]

Unlike that of the Wichitas and Caddos, the Tonkawas' trip to the Brazos Reserve did not go smoothly. Notifying the tribe of their imminent departure, in March 1855, Agent Howard gathered 239 Tonkawas near Fort Inge. Howard purchased wagons, arranged a contract for beef and other supplies for the trip, but fell ill before he was able to lead the tribe northward. As Major Neighbors made his way to the Frio to conduct the Tonkawas to the Brazos in place of Howard, a party of twenty Texas settlers approached the tribe's camp intent on stealing their horses. Learning of the planned raid, Chief Placido sent the women and children to the hills while the Tonkawa men forced the Texas horse thieves to withdraw. Neither Howard, nor the troops stationed at nearby Fort Inge, did anything to protect the Tonkawas. By the time Neighbors arrived on April 5 all the Tonkawas had fled to the surrounding mountains. Soon thereafter Howard resigned his position and Neighbors returned to the Brazos Agency without the Tonkawas. In the meantime Placido assembled about two-thirds of the Tonkawas near Fort Clark on the Nueces River. Fearing further attacks by Texan citizens, the other tribesmen joined the Tonkawas and Lipans who had already crossed the Rio Grande for the safety of Mexico. Finally, in June 1855, Placido led his band of Tonkawas, numbering 171 individuals, north to the Brazos Reserve. Upon their arrival, Agent Hill assigned the Tonkawas land near the western boundary of the agency, about five miles west of the Waco and Tawakoni village.[9]

As with the Tonkawas, the Penateka Comanches' attempt to settle on their reservation was disrupted by fears of Texan hostility. Following the death of Saviah earlier in the year, the remaining Penatekas had divided into three bands under Ketumse, Sanaco, and Potsanaquahip. By late 1854, most of the Penatekas had gathered on the Clear Fork of the Brazos to await the final preparations for the Comanche Reserve. A short time later, however, a trader at Fort Chadbourne on the Concho River informed a visiting party of Sanaco's band that the Americans were planning to kill all the Penatekas once they settled on the reservation. The rumor quickly spread among the wary Comanches, and the people in Sanaco's and Potsanaquahip's bands— many of whom were already reluctant to settle down—panicked and fled to the northwest. Ketumse and his group of 177 Penatekas were the only tribal members to remain in the camp. In order to more easily provide the starving Comanches with rations, in early 1855 Agent Hill moved Ketumse's people temporarily to the Brazos Reserve where the Caddos and Wichitas were already making preparations for their new homes. In March Ketumse sent runners to the other Penateka bands inviting them to return to the reserve; a few heeded the call, and in late May the 226 Penatekas on the Brazos were finally moved to the Comanche Reserve. Members of Sanaco's band continued to drift to the Clear Fork of the Brazos over the next few months, and by October, when the ill-chosen John R. Baylor assumed the position of agent, 419 Penatekas resided on the Comanche Reserve in a village located near the river. Baylor established the agency complex—ultimately consisting of a few houses, a main building, an office and a commissary—about one mile from the Penateka camp. The agency employees consisted of a farmer and a laborer, as well as Delaware interpreter John Conner.[10]

Thus, after more than a year of great hardship, the Texas Indian tribes had finally settled on the two reserves and were now ready to establish permanent homes. Through hard work and great desire, the Caddos and Wichitas, residing on the Brazos Reserve along with the Tonkawas, proved the feasibility of the reservation experiment in Texas. Both tribes—including, for the very first time, the Waco and Tawakoni men—went to work in the fields immediately upon their arrival in the spring of 1855. The federal government provided each tribe with a farmer and a laborer, and the Caddos and Wichitas plowed and planted corn on 295 acres of land. However, the late period of planting, coupled with dry weather, caused the yield to be fairly small, a little over one thousand bushels. In addition to the corn, the Indians raised a "good supply" of melons, pumpkins, and beans. Following the harvest of 1855 the three tribes were provided with a five-yoke team of oxen as well as plows, a wagon, and "all the necessary farming utensils." Three hundred head of cattle, along with a few chickens and hogs, were also distributed among the tribes in an effort to wean them away from hunting. With the new equipment, the tribes—including the heretofore hunting and gathering Tonkawas, who shared the Wichitas' farmer and laborer—made great progress in preparing their fields for planting in 1856. The Kadohadachos cultivated 150 acres of land, the Nadacos only ten fewer. The Wacos and Tawakonis together planted 150 acres, the Tonkawas one hundred. All of the tribes built fences around the crops to protect them from the cattle and pigs. Despite their efforts, the tribes' yield again was not high. Grasshoppers destroyed the first crop in the spring, and summer dryness caused the second crop to produce only half of what was expected. The new Indian agent on the Brazos Reserve, Shapley P. Ross, realized that raising corn was difficult, if not impossible, this far west and began making preparations to raise wheat the following year.[11]

Finally, in 1857 the Brazos Reserve Indians had a successful agricultural year. The Kadohadachos and the Nadacos were very industrious, keeping their wagons and oxen "constantly at work, hauling in their crops and fencing their farms." The Caddos' labor was rewarded, for together they raised 4,000 bushels of corn as well as six hundred bushels of wheat. In addition, there was "a very large crop of peas and beans, an abundance of pumpkins and squashes [and] . . . a large crop of melons." Working "admirably," the Wacos and Tawakonis raised eighteen hundred bushels of corn apiece, while the Tonkawas harvested four hundred bushels of corn; however, the tribes' wheat crop was destroyed by a spring frost. The Brazos tribes also had success in raising stock, and some of the Caddo women learned to milk the cows and make their own butter. According to Agent Ross, the crops of the Brazos Reserve Indians were better than those of the average Texan settler in the area. The agent gave the Kadohadachos and Nadacos permission to make small hunting parties in the winter as a reward for their diligence, which had proved them "perfectly reliable." This was done, "more [as] a matter of recreation than profit," for the Caddos had raised enough food in 1857 to make a winter hunt unnecessary.[12]

The year 1857 proved to be the agricultural high point for the Indians of the Brazos Reserve. Their efforts were greatly hampered the following two years by troubles with both the Northern Comanches and the Texan settlers. Comanches stole much of their stock, and settler hostility forced the tribes to remain on the reservation, unable to collect the cattle that had roamed out on the open range. In addition, the increased tensions caused the tribes to pay far less attention to their crops. The Brazos Indians were still able to keep a good stock of domestic animals though. By 1859 the tribes of the reserve had collected 597 hogs. Even after the Comanches and the Texans ran off with much of their stock, the Caddos still owned two hundred head of cattle, eight yoke of oxen, and 605 horses. The Wichita tribes were less successful than the Caddos at raising stock; the Wacos and Tawakonis had only 225 horses, forty-eight mules, and fifty-five head of cattle. The Tonkawas held no cattle, but owned 159 horses and two yoke of oxen. Except for the oxen, the animals were held individually rather than communally. The tribal members had always owned their own horses, and this form of ownership was extended to the rest of the stock they acquired. Following tradition, the leading members of the tribe owned more animals than the rest. For example, Chief Iesh owned nearly a fifth of all the hogs on the reservation.[13]

The three tribes had also begun setting up permanent villages soon after they arrived at their new home. By 1856 the Caddos and Wichitas were described as having "neat cottages," made of both grass and logs. During the following year the Kadohadachos built seven log houses and the Nadacos ten, while the Wacos and Tawakonis raised sixteen between them. The leading members of each tribe were housed in these nontraditional abodes, some of which were quite impressive. By 1859 the Kadohadachos and the Nadacos had raised seventy-three traditional grass houses, the Wacos and Tawakonis another forty-nine. As with most matters, the Tonkawas' progress lagged behind the agricultural tribes; they resided in government-supplied tents until late 1857, when they finally began to build log houses. By 1859 the Tonkawas lived in sixty-one rudely constructed "shanties." Nonetheless, the Indian agents attributed the general good health of the Brazos Reserve tribes "to the cleanliness of themselves and their lodges."[14]

The Indians' success on the Brazos Reserve is best demonstrated by their ability to stabilize their population after years of decline. The Caddo census of March 31, 1855—taken soon after the opening of the reserve—numbered 364 (204 Nadacos and 160 Kadohadachos), a loss of 110 people since the previous enumeration in 1851. The Wichita population had decreased from 255 to 202 (eighty-seven Wacos and 115 Tawakonis) in the same period. Much of this loss can be attributed to the defection of tribal members north of the Red River, but Agent Hill also claimed that many Indian children had died during that period for "want of proper food, and increase of exposure." Both tribes' population grew steadily, however, once they settled on the Brazos Reserve. The number of Caddos rose to 445 in 1857 and to 479 two years later. The Nadaco totals peaked in May 1859 at 235, an increase of forty people, while the Kadohadachos gained eighty-four members to reach 244. Both Wichita tribes' populations peaked in late 1857; the Waco total had doubled since 1855 to 172 members, while the Tawakonis gained ninety-eight members to reach a total of 213. Most of the increase can be attributed to the return of the refugees from the Indian Territory; the agents noted a continual stream of these new arrivals from the north. Overall, 181 Wichitas and 105 refugee Caddos joined the Brazos Reserve during its four-year existence. However, conditions on the reserve in and of themselves were sufficient for a natural increase in population. Major Neighbors felt that, "by being well clothed, having houses to live in, and relieved from the continued anxieties of attending a roving life, their health has greatly improved, and [they] now, for the first time in several years, begin to raise healthy children." In fact, there were twenty-two Caddo children born between 1855 and 1859, but there were only seven deaths. The Waco and Tawakoni numbers were less dramatic; six births and three deaths. The amount of Tonkawas on the reserve actually dropped from 171 in June 1855 to 168 in June 1857. The following spring, though, eighty "starving" Tonkawas abandoned their camps in Mexico and arrived at the Brazos Reserve. In May 1859 the Tonkawa totals peaked at 258 individuals, mainly due to the return of the refugees and the stabilizing effect of the agency.[15]

Although the Penatekas improved their situation a bit on the Comanche Reserve, ultimately they were not able to match the accomplishments of the three tribes on the Brazos. The main problem for the Penatekas was that most of the tribesmen found it extremely difficult to abandon their nomadism and permanently settle down. Despite receiving government rations, many Penatekas did not want to engage in the laborious duties of planting, harvesting, and building fences that were expected of them on the reservation. In addition, these agricultural efforts often went unrewarded in the dry climate of the Upper Brazos Valley, causing many disappointed Penatekas to succumb to temptation and join with their brethren—as well as with the Northern Comanches—who ranged nearby, hunting and making raids in Texas and Mexico. Major Neighbors complained that the Penatekas' "progress . . . [does] not compare favorably with" the Brazos Reserve tribes due to the "influence exercised by that portion of the [Comanches] who still roam at large and continue to depredate . . . it has been found impossible to . . . prevent the young men from quitting the reserve to join in the continued forays made by them upon our frontier and that of Mexico." The constant raiding, combined with the comings and goings of the Indians on the Comanche Reserve, raised the ire of the nearby settlers, leading to citizens' calls for its destruction almost as soon as it had opened.[16]

The power struggle between Sanaco and Ketumse also exacerbated the difficult situation on the reservation, leading to a further exodus of tribesmen. In late 1855, Sanaco arrived at the Clear Fork of the Brazos with his band, but failed in his attempt to supplant Ketumse as chief of the reservation Penatekas and angrily left soon thereafter. Fear of the Americans also kept many tribesmen from settling on the Comanche Reserve. In January 1856, the United States Second Cavalry established Camp Cooper only one mile from the Penateka village and stationed two infantry companies and two cavalry companies at the post. The coming of the soldiers frightened some of the reserve Penatekas and many took flight once more, some joining the Comanches north of the Red River. A cold winter, however, induced a number of starving tribesmen—including Potsanaquahip and his party of ninety-three people—to return to the reserve in the spring. By June over five hundred Penatekas were on the Comanche Reserve; three months later the Comanche population had increased to 557, the most that would ever reside on the reservation during its four-year existence.[17]

The Penatekas at the reserve, however, were soon disappointed by the returns of their first effort to raise crops, leading many to have doubts about the transition to agriculture. With the assistance of a government farmer and laborer, the Penateka women—the men refused to work in the fields—had planted corn, melons, beans, peas, and pumpkins on 160 acres of enclosed land in the spring of 1856. Agent Baylor also distributed cattle to the Indians. All looked well until July, when the lack of rain caused the corn crop to fail. Baylor reported that the Comanches were bewildered, and that it "was difficult to make them understand how it is they can't make a crop." Frustrated, a few Penateka men left the reserve and joined Nokoni and Tenawa raiding parties heading south. About five hundred or so tribal members stayed on the Clear Fork of the Brazos throughout the winter, living in tepees and eating government rations.[18]

Almost one-third of the remaining Penatekas, however, abandoned the reserve the following spring and never returned. In March 1857, just as spring planting was due to begin, a soldier at Camp Cooper got drunk and accidentally shot himself. Believing that the Comanches were responsible for the man's death, United States troops went to the Penateka villages to investigate, causing the women and children to "stampede" out of fear. Chief Ketumse was away looking for stray cattle and, therefore, was not able to prevent a large number of tribesmen—including Potsanaquahip's entire band—from leaving the reserve. Although order was soon restored after the commanding officer at Camp Cooper, Colonel Robert E. Lee, assured the remaining Penatekas that they would not be punished for the soldier's inadvertent demise, the Comanche men refused to allow their women work in the fields until Baylor distributed presents. The agent refused, but he was able to coax the Penateka women to begin planting by promising them gifts after the crops were sown. Soon, Neighbors relieved Agent Baylor of his duties after he misappropriated funds, and the reserve Penatekas were left on their own. By the time Matthew Leeper assumed the position of Comanche agent in mid-May, the women had planted corn, wheat, beans, and melons on twenty acres of land, but only 387 Penatekas—a decline of 190 since the previous September—remained on the reserve. Once again dry weather ruined most of the Comanches' crop; they harvested only fifty bushels of wheat and five hundred bushels of corn in the fall. Almost all of the tribe's cattle had wandered off as well.[19]

Nonetheless, most of the Penatekas that remained on the Clear Fork under the leadership of Chief Ketumse had decided to make the Comanche Reserve their permanent home, and the population stabilized at just under four hundred—about one-third of the entire tribe—for the rest of the reservation's existence. Leeper believed that the Comanches who stayed on the reservation were "determined to pursue a quiet, civil life, and to follow, as far as possible, the good examples of" the American agents. In the fall of 1857 a few Penatekas followed the lead of Ketumse and began to construct log cabins. Most of the tribe, however, resided in tepees until the following spring when they occupied the buildings at Camp Cooper after most of the Second Cavalry relocated to Fort Belknap at the end of March 1858. A few troops came back six months later, though, forcing the Penatekas to return to their tepees for the remainder of the year. The reserve Comanches had their first successful agricultural year in 1858. For the very first time, some Comanche men joined with their women to plant crops—mainly wheat and corn—in the spring. Due to a new system in which each family was allowed to cultivate small parcels apart from a common field, the Penatekas "worked with a great deal more energy and spirit" than in previous years and planted crops on 150 acres of enclosed land. Although the wheat crop yielded only fifty bushels in the fall, the Comanches' corn crop, "which is one of the best of the country," produced an average of twenty bushels per acre. The tribe also made progress raising stock; in addition to the 1,000 horses they owned, by 1859 the Penatekas had recovered nearly 150 head of cattle as well.[20]

Although the reserve Penatekas' success did not match the achievements of the Brazos Reserve tribes, the Indians on both reservations shared an inclination toward educating their young. As the various tribes had gathered in the Upper Brazos Valley in 1855, Major Neighbors noted that there were 344 children younger than twelve years of age among the population. The agent informed Commissioner of Indian Affairs Charles E. Mix that the tribes of both reserves were "anxious to have a school for their children." Government officials, however, took no action on the proposal in 1856, although Agent Ross alerted them that a number of children were "growing up in ignorance and superstition, which might be averted by a suitable appropriation for educational purposes." Ross claimed that the majority of the Indians on the Brazos Reserve understood "that schools would prepare the rising generation for the more useful walks and occupations of life." Comanche agent Leeper added that a "school is also deemed necessary, and it is desired by the Indians themselves." He felt that a school on the Comanche Reserve "would produce a more beneficial effect than the same amount of expenditure in any other way."[21]

In light of such endorsements, in 1857 Congress appropriated funds for the establishment of a school on both reserves. Following the construction of a small schoolhouse near the Comanche agency buildings, Daniel Simpson opened the Penateka school on January 1, 1858. Ten eager Penateka boys attended the opening classes and appeared "delighted by it." Throughout the first session, which lasted until June 30, between five and fifteen boys went to school, primarily learning how to read. Although Simpson "acquitted himself well as a teacher," Leeper dismissed him for conduct that rendered him "an unsuitable person to remain on the reserve." In August Simpson's replacement, Richard Sloan, opened the second school session on the Comanche Reserve. Housed in a larger building located closer to the Penatekas' village, the school drew thirty-seven full-time students, including twelve girls. The students, who evinced "a great deal of sprightliness," were characterized as being "very attentive," spending six to eight hours a day studying the few elementary reading and spelling books held in the school's "library."[22]

The Brazos Reserve school, which opened on June 1, 1858, was even more successful than its counterpart on the Comanche Reserve. Sixty students, most of them boys, enrolled in the school, which was directed by Zachariah Ellis

Coombes, an optimistic young teacher. Coombes reported that average attendance, however, was only about thirty students a day. Although the children
knew no English and were hard to control, "being accustomed to no restraint
or coercion," a good many of the students had learned the alphabet by September. Most of the children were Kadohadachos and Tawakonis, for those two
tribes "manifest[ed] considerable interest in getting their children to school."
Coombes prepared a "report card" on October 19, which listed fifteen "scholars." Among the comments that Coombes made was that Sam Houston, a
twelve-year-old Kadohadacho boy, had "learned his letters [and was] very
kind." Fourteen-year-old Kadohadacho Jim Shot Gun had "progressed well at
first, but is very headstrong." Shantano, a Nadaco boy of thirteen, "progressed
slowly at first [but] advances now rapidly." A twelve-year-old Tawakoni named
Naquah was progressing slowly because he was "fond of talk and trade." Following six months of school, Coombes felt that the students needed a rest, and
the children were given a month's vacation. Coombes reported that by the end
of the first session in November 1858, one student was studying arithmetic,
sixteen were learning how to read and write, seventeen were studying spelling,
and twenty others were learning the alphabet.[23]

Unfortunately, the educational progress made at the Brazos and Comanche
Reserves in 1858 was not increased during the following year. Intense Texan
hostility to the Indians threw both reserves into an uproar in early 1859, and
it was difficult for the teachers to get the children to attend. On February 28,
Coombes reported that the number of scholars at the Brazos Reserve school
had dropped from sixty to forty-six, because of the parents' fear for their
children's safety. Coombes remained optimistic though and believed that it
"would be very difficult in any school of red or white people to find as much
good will and as great harmony." Cause for optimism about either school,
quickly dwindled. By the end of March the Comanche Reserve school had
closed for good, while Coombes felt that neither the pupils nor the parents
had a desire to continue the school on the Brazos Reserve. Average attendance
during April dropped to only twelve students per day; two months later, the
Brazos Reserve school closed its doors forever. It would be many years before
the children of the various tribes would again receive educational instruction.[24]

Thus, the Indians who had agreed to settle down on the two Texas reservations had done their part in proving the feasibility of the reservation system.
The tribesmen had established farms and houses, accepted whatever innova-
tions the agents proposed, and had even sent their children to school. They
were able to support themselves and seemed well on the way to adapting to
the changes that had ocurred around them. In order to fully complete the
transformation to the reservation way of life, however, the tribes would need

more time. Unfortunately, patience with any Indians, friendly or hostile, was not something that many Texans had to spare. Although the tribes made great strides within the reservation system, uncontrollable external forces hampered the overall success of the Texas reserves. The Northern Comanches emerged as the primary enemy, attacking both the Indians on the Brazos Reserve and the frontier Texan settlements. Despite the Brazos Reserve tribes' many demonstrations of friendship, the Northern Comanches' unceasing attacks upon the hapless Texans caused the settlers to become increasingly suspicious of all the reservation Indians and eventually to oppose their existence. Although the Reserve Indians might have been able to withstand the attacks of the Northern Comanches, the additional hostility of the Texans placed them in an untenable situation.

Northern Comanche hostilities actually grew out of a treaty they, as well as the Kiowas and Kiowa-Apaches, signed with the United States in 1853. In the Treaty of Fort Atkinson the federal government agreed to present the tribes with trade goods worth $18,000 annually in return for free right of travel on the Santa Fe Trail and the right to establish military posts in Indian Country. Assured of receiving goods from the United States at Fort Atkinson in Kansas, the Northern Comanches began to raid into Texas with impunity. Penateka warriors from Potsanaquahip and Sanaco's bands who had refused to settle down with Ketumse's group on the Comanche Reserve occasionally joined in on these raids. Their actions caused the Texans to suspect all Comanches, including those on the reserve. [25]

Northern Comanche raiding began almost as soon as the Indians on the two reserves had settled down. In September 1855, Agent Ross received word that Tenawa Comanches had killed an American settler about ten miles northwest of Fort Belknap. Ross sent runners to the various tribes on the Brazos Reserve asking for their assistance, and the next morning sixty-six warriors were mounted and ready to pursue the raiders. The party stayed on the Comanches' trail for two days before concluding that it would be impossible to overtake them. The following week, however, a Comanche raiding party stole forty head of horses from the Brazos Reserve Indians and an undetermined number from the Texas settlements. A combined Kadohadacho-Delaware force pursued the Comanches across the Red River, skirmished with them, and recovered the horses. They also learned that the Northern Comanches had "declared war upon all people south of Red River, white and red." [26]

In the spring of 1856, Comanche assaults upon the Brazos Reserve and the surrounding Texan settlements increased dramatically. In addition to Tenawa and Nokoni attacks, warriors from Sanaco's band of Penateka Comanches also joined in the raids. In response, Colonel Lee, commander of the Second

Cavalry at Camp Cooper, mounted a punitive expedition in June. Fifteen Brazos Reserve Indians, mainly Caddos and Delawares led by Jim Shaw, accompanied Colonel Lee's soldiers as scouts. After following Indian trails for a few days on the upper reaches of the Colorado and Brazos rivers, the force surprised a party of four Comanches, killing two and capturing a woman. Upon questioning, the woman reported that she had accompanied twelve men on a raiding expedition through Mexico and Texas. Although she was a Northern Comanche unattached to the Upper Reserve, the Indian scouts took here there because she claimed to have relatives among the Penatekas.[27]

The return of the woman, and the news that the Caddos and Delawares had joined Colonel Lee's expedition, caused about seventy-five Penatekas from the Comanche Reserve to march on the Nadaco village on July 23. Led by Ketumse and Potsanaquahip, the Penateka Comanches advanced to within one hundred yards of the Nadaco camp before being met by Iesh, who told them that his men were ready for battle if they wanted to fight. Faced with this bold stance, the Penatekas replied that they only wanted to talk. Agent Ross was summoned, and a council was held between the headmen of both tribes. Ketumse protested the Caddo scouts' assistance to the Second Cavalry and inquired if Iesh intended to continue allowing his tribe to fight the Comanches. Agent Ross answered for the chief, insisting that the Caddo tribe had every right to take measures to detain and kill any thieving Indians. Ross then persuaded the Penatekas to return peacefully to their own reservation. However, both the agent and the angry Penatekas were certain the Caddos had not been "dissuaded from stopping [the Comanche's] stealing."[28]

Comanche depredations upon the Brazos Reserve and the Texan settlements continued throughout the fall and winter of 1856. As the raids increased in intensity the following year, so did the settlers' hostility to the Indians of both reserves, although the Brazos tribes were "always rendering assistance to citizens in pursuing thieves." The country around the reservations was rapidly filling up with settlers, many from the "older states who are not accustomed to Indians." In early 1857, Young County (in which the Brazos Reserve lay) was organized. Agent Ross claimed that when the reservations were opened in 1855 only twelve families lived in the area embraced by the county. Three years later he estimated that about 150 families resided in Young County. By 1860 the county's population stood at 592. The surrounding area was also experiencing a similar growth; by the end of the decade 2,922 people lived in the other five counties—Jack, Palo Pinto, Shackleford, Stephens, and Throckmorton—that bordered on the two Indian reserves. The Indian raids also affected the 9,798 Texans living in nearby Erath, Parker, and Wise counties. The new settlers, exasperated by the constant attacks, were inclined to lay the blame for hostilities at the feet of the 1,500 or so Reserve Indians, particularly the Penateka Comanches, who lived in their midst.[29]

"Reckless and designing men" helped encourage the prejudices of the Texas citizens against the Reserve Indians. Chief among these unprincipled few was John Baylor, who Neighbors had dismissed as Comanche agent in 1857. The vengeful Baylor began to do all that he could to secure the removal of the major; he stated that he was collecting "all the evidence I can against the Indians and Neighbors," for he wanted his friend, Allison Nelson, to assume the position of principal Texas Indian agent, and promised to do "all in my power to aid him." Over the next two years Baylor, Nelson, and others spread many libelous and dangerous rumors among the Texan settlers designed to raise their ire toward the two reserves and the Indian agents who presided over them. Continuous Indian attacks and raids also encouraged the Texans to suspect the Reserve Indians. During the last two months of 1857, hostile Indians killed seven citizens, stole six hundred horses, and damaged property worth an estimated $60,000. Investigations by Nadaco warriors, led by second chief Jim Pock Mark, discovered the guilty parties to be primarily from the Nokoni and Tenawa Comanches, living north of the Red River. Many local settlers, however, blamed the Penatekas on the Comanche Reserve. In December 1857, the citizens of two Texas counties presented separate petitions to the Secretary of the Interior calling for the removal of Major Neighbors as Indian agent. The citizens charged the Penatekas of the Comanche Reserve Indians with stealing their horses, while Neighbors "persists in the face of proof" to do nothing to stop them. The settlers protested that "the very Indians we are taxed to feed and clothe are the ones who inflict the greatest injuries upon us."[30]

Captain W. G. Evans of the Second Cavalry was ordered to investigate the charges against the Penatekas. In January 1858, Evans reported that he was "fully convinced that robberies in the neighborhood were committed by the Northern Comanches" but did not rule out the possibility that they may "have many facilities afforded them by their relations" on the Comanche Reserve. Regardless of the truth, Captain Evans stated that every citizen in the area believed the Penatekas were involved in the depredations. Major Neighbors, in contrast, vehemently denied any involvement on the part of the Reserve Indians in the attacks on local settlers. Fearing for the safety of the Indians on both reservations, Neighbors implored Commissioner Mix to provide increased military protection in order to prevent further Northern Comanche raids. Unless the attacks were stopped, he correctly predicted that it would be "impossible to prevent the people of Texas from making an indiscriminate war on the Indians" in which the reservations would also be destroyed.[31]

In response to the increased settler hostility, the tribes of the Brazos Reserve took matters into their own hands in an attempt to prove their friendliness. In January 1858, a party of Waco warriors took up the trail of Comanche raiders and returned a month later with two captured men, sixty-seven stolen horses, and seven stolen mules, all of which they turned over to Agent Ross. The Brazos Reserve headmen, along with the agent, then held a council in which the two prisoners were questioned. The Comanches assured their inquisitors that Tenawa and Nokoni Comanches had carried out most of the raids in Texas. They did admit, however, that Sanaco's son had led Penateka warriors on several thieving campaigns south of the Red River. Following the interrogation, a firing squad of Indians chosen from the several tribes executed the two captured Comanches. The Brazos Indians then assured Agent Ross that "they would use every means in their power to maintain the friendship of the whites, [and that they] were willing and ready whenever called upon to cooperate with the government forces in putting a stop to all stealing and marauding on this frontier."[32]

The Brazos Reserve tribes were soon given the opportunity to fulfill their pledge to Agent Ross. The citizens of Texas had recently elected a new governor, Hardin R. Runnels, on a platform that included a promise to provide the frontier settlements with adequate protection from attacking Indians. Governor Runnels implemented that policy on January 28, 1858, when he appointed Rip Ford as senior captain of the Texas Rangers and authorized him to enlist another one hundred men to take action against the hostile Indian forces. By late February Ford had established Camp Runnels on the Clear Fork of the Brazos near the two Indian reserves in preparation for a campaign against the Northern Comanches. Captain Ford enlisted the help of Agent Neighbors and Ross in the recruitment of the Brazos Reserve Indians to be used as scouts and auxiliaries. Ross encouraged as many Indians as could be spared from farming to join Ford "in order to satisfy the minds of the citizens" that they were on the side of the Texans. The recruitment was successful and on April 22 when the 102 Rangers finally broke camp, 109 auxiliaries from the Brazos Reserve joined them. The Caddo contingent, led by Jim Pock Mark, was the most numerous, providing twenty-nine Nadaco and twenty Kadohadacho warriors. In addition, thirty-five Tonkawas, sixteen Tawakonis, and nine Wacos accompanied the Caddos. On April 29, the expedition crossed the Red River, and eleven days later the Indian scouts began reporting signs that showed a large Comanche encampment nearby. The Brazos Indians soon located the Comanche village on the north side of the Canadian River near the Antelope Hills, and Ford launched an attack at dawn on May 12. After a few hours of slaughter and destruction, Ford's troops counted seventy-six dead Comanches, eighteen women and children captured, and three hundred horses taken, most of which were turned over to the Reserve Indians. Only one Waco and two Texas Rangers had been killed. Learning from the prisoners that Potsanaquahip and a large band of Penatekas were camped only a few miles away, Ford ordered his force to return quickly to Texas.[33]

Thanks to the role played by the Indians of the Brazos Reserve, the fight with the Comanches on the Canadian River was an overwhelming success. Ford acknowledged the effort of the Indian troops in his report to the governor, claiming that "in justice to our Indian allies I beg leave to say they behaved most excellently on the field of battle. They deserve well of Texas and are entitled to the gratitude of our frontier people." Upon hearing news of Ford's success, Governor Runnels addressed a message to the men of the expedition, which stated that the "deeds of gallantry and valor, performed by each and all of you who were engaged in the fight, gallant Rangers and brave Indian allies . . . will be held in grateful remembrance by the people of Texas." A celebration was held at the Brazos Reserve upon the return of the victorious warriors, for the situation at the reservation had been tense since the Indian troops had left. Two settler families had been murdered eighteen miles north of the reserve only a few days after the Indians had joined Ford's command. This incident increased the suspicions of the surrounding Texans concerning the reserve, and in an attempt to prevent a confrontation the agent had not permitted the remaining Indians to leave the boundaries of the reserve to collect their stock. However, the news of the returning warriors' participation in Ford's successful campaign quieted (temporarily, at least) the fears of the citizenry. Agent Ross optimistically noted that a "great change of feeling has taken place in the minds of our frontier citizens in favor of the [Reserve] Indians . . . and . . . they have obtained both credit and position that will allay any prejudice existing against the Reserve."[34]

Soon after the Indian troops returned to the Brazos Reserve, Major Neighbors traveled to Washington to inform the government of the tense atmosphere that surrounded the reserves in Texas. As a result, Thomas T. Hawkins, a special agent, was sent there to investigate Neighbors's administration of Indian affairs. He stayed at both reserves for five weeks and in that time invited complainants to appear before him and testify, but very few did so. In fact, no one came to present evidence against Neighbors. In his report, Hawkins commended the agents very highly and stated that the Reserve Indians had made "great moral and physical advancement." Hawkins was not alone in these conclusions. Many settlers living near the reservations did not believe the Indians were guilty and readily endorsed Neighbors's efforts. Captains Ford and E. N. Burleson of the Texas Rangers, both of whom had been directed by the governor to watch the reserve Comanches closely, had found no evidence of guilt. Captain Ford particularly praised Agent Ross, calling him an "able efficient, and energetic agent, whose successful manner of conducting the affairs of the Agency can be seen by anyone who will examine the houses, the fields, and the Indians." [35]

In the fall of 1858 the Indians of the Brazos Reserve were once again given the opportunity to demonstrate their worth to the settlers of Texas. Captain Ford's successful campaign against the Northern Comanches had quieted them during the spring and early summer, but by August they had resumed their raiding. The Comanches aimed many of their forays at the stock of the Brazos Reserve Indians, for they expressed "a determination to revenge themselves . . . for damage done them by the expedition of Captain Ford." This time the army of the United States responded, and Major Earl Van Dorn, new commander of the Second Cavalry, was ordered to cross north of the Red River and search for Comanche bands. Van Dorn, like Ford, sought the assistance of the Indians of the Brazos Reserve. Once again they responded to the call, and while preparations for the campaign were still under way, Agent Ross's son (and future governor of Texas), Lawrence Sullivan (Sul) Ross, led a force of 125 Reserve Indians to Otter Creek, north of the Red River. Here they established a base named Camp Radziminski and were joined by Van Dorn's troops in late September 1858. [36]

Waco and Tawakoni spies soon learned that an encampment of six hundred Comanches, mainly Potsanaquahip's Penatekas, was located near the Taovaya village on Rush Creek, about ninety miles northeast of Camp Radziminski. As his force made its way to the Comanche village, Major Van Dorn was unaware that Potsanaquahip was in the process of making peace with the American authorities in the Indian Territory. Following Ford's attack on the Comanche village in May, the Penatekas under Potsanaquahip had begun stealing horses from the Taovayas in the mistaken belief that they had assisted the Texas Rangers. The Taovayas finally convinced the Penatekas that they had not been with Captain Ford and invited Potsanaquahip to come to their village for a council on August 22 with Lieutenant J. E. Powell from Fort Arbuckle. New Taovaya chief Isadowa related the misunderstanding to Powell, who then gave the Penatekas permission to settle on Rush Creek, provided Potsanaquahip would travel to Fort Arbuckle in the near future to finalize a peace agreement. [37]

Tragically, Potsanaquahip was making preparations for his peace mission to Fort Arbuckle on the morning of October 1 when Van Dorn and his Indian allies reached the Penateka village. Van Dorn ordered an attack, and in the resulting ninety-minute fight, the Comanches were once again routed. Their losses were particularly heavy as the Reserve Indians inhibited the Comanches' retreat by stampeding their horses. Van Dorn labeled the so-called Battle of the Wichita Village a "complete and decisive" victory. The bodies of fifty-six Penateka Comanches were counted in the vicinity, and many more were presumed to have been killed. More than three hundred horses were captured, and the entire camp of 120 lodges burned. Only five members of Van Dorn's command were killed and twelve were wounded, including the major. The Indians of the Brazos Reserve lost no men, and only a few were wounded. Coombes reported that the Reserve Indians returned from the expedition on October 11, "all safe and bringing in new ponies as the fruit of their victory." The teacher looked forward to seeing the tribesmen perform an "exulting victory dance."[38]

The Taovayas, however, were not so lucky. Fearing the surviving Comanches would accuse them of a double cross, they abandoned their village on Rush Creek (and its one hundred acres of corn) and took refuge with the White-bead Caddos near Fort Arbuckle on the Washita. The Kichais and the newly appointed Wichita agent, Samuel Blain, soon joined them. Agent Blain had arranged for the refugee Wichitas to be cared for over the winter, but 754 blankets purchased for their warmth failed to arrive after the steamboat that was carrying them sank. In the spring of 1859 the Taovayas and Kichais were uncertain if they should plant crops, for the Indian agents could not decide whether the Wichitas should be allowed to remain with the Whitebead Caddos.[39]

Ultimately, a crisis concerning the Brazos Reserve Indians and the surrounding settlers forced the federal government to end the reservation in Texas and settle all the tribes in the Indian Territory. The crisis was precipitated in the latter portion of November 1858 when Tom, a Choctaw Indian who had married into the Nadaco tribe, received permission from Agent Ross to take a group—consisting of twenty-seven Nadaco and Kadohadacho men, women, and children—below the agency boundary. The young men in the party had just returned from Major Van Dorn's campaign and they wanted to graze their horses on the luxuriant grass that grew on the banks of the Brazos River downstream from the reserve. The men were eager to get their horses ready for another expedition against the Comanches, which Van Dorn had scheduled for the spring of 1859. Choctaw Tom's party camped above Golconda, the Palo Pinto county seat, and spent much of early December "conducting themselves in a peaceful and quiet manner," visited occasionally by friendly settlers who lived nearby. A few citizens, however, did not approve of the Indians' presence and went to the Caddos' camp and "firmly but kindly" told them to return to the reservation, warning the Indians that the settlers "would raise men and kill them" if they remained. Although the Caddos agreed to head back to the reserve, a few tribesmen moved down the Brazos River to hunt bear at the mouth of Keechi Creek. Enraged by the Indians' movements, a party of settlers attacked the Caddos while they slept in the early morning hours of December 27, killing four and wounding eight, including women and children.[40]

A few of the survivors raced back to the reserve and informed chiefs Iesh and Tinah of the massacre. The Caddo young men immediately took to arms in order to "go back and execute summary vengeance on the murderers." As he had done before, Iesh stepped in and persuaded them to wait and attempt to seek justice through official channels. Since Agent Ross was absent at the time, the following morning the two headmen went to the agency farmer, J. J. Sturm, with the grim news. Sturm, with four men and thirty Kadohadacho and Nadaco warriors, started immediately for Choctaw Tom's camp and arrived there shortly before sundown on December 28. Sturm characterized what he viewed as being "a more horrible sight I never expect to see." Lying on their beds were the riddled bodies of "the best and most inoffensive Indians on the reserve . . . their eyes closed and their bodies stretched at full length, their countenances indicating that they passed from calm sleep to the sleep that knows no waking." The relief party covered the bodies with brush and stones and attended to the wounded. Sturm and the Indians found a place near the camp where the murderers had evidently awaited their chance to surprise the sleeping Caddos.[41]

The relief party camped that night about five miles from Golconda and was met the next morning by a Palo Pinto County citizens' committee that had been sent to explain the circumstances. They informed Sturm that on the evening of December 26 a party of twenty men from Erath County, led by Peter Garland, had encamped near Golconda. They stated that Garland's party had left in the middle of the night only to return to Golconda in the morning with the news that they had attacked Choctaw Tom's camp. Garland and his men happily claimed that through this attack "they had opened the ball and the people there should dance to the music." Believing that Garland's men had precipitated an Indian war, the settlers in Palo Pinto County began to abandon their homes. The citizens' committee explained to Sturm and the Caddo headmen that they did not approve of the attack on the Indian camp and that they wished to "live in peace and amity." The Caddo chiefs immediately assured Sturm that they would not "retaliate on the innocent" and asked that a messenger be sent to inform the people to return to their homes.[42]

Despite the assurances of both parties, tensions on the frontier remained high. Upon the return of the Caddo party to the agency with the details of the slaughter, a few members of the reserve tribes decided to cross the Red River to take refuge in the Indian Territory. Fearing further attacks, the Indians who remained on the reserve left their villages and assembled around the agency

buildings "for their better protection." Captain T. N. Palmer of the Second
Cavalry was ordered to take a detachment of troops from Fort Belknap to
the Brazos Agency to prevent a collision between the settlers and the Reserve
Indians. Captain Palmer arrived on January 5, 1859, and found the Indians
"much alarmed" because they had heard a rumor that the citizens of Palo
Pinto and Erath counties were assembling to attack and break up the reserve.[43]

The rumor proved to be partly true. On January 4, Garland and his band had
published a signed letter, addressed to the "people of Texas," in which they
took full responsibility for the attack on Choctaw Tom's camp. They claimed
they had had the "wool pulled over" their eyes long enough by the Brazos
Reserve Indians and thus offered no apology for what they had done. They
further asserted that they were "sustained by hundreds" of their fellow citizens.
Two days later two hundred citizens of Coryell, Bosque, Comanche, Erath, and
Palo Pinto counties began assembling at Stephenville. The settlers chose an
executive committee of twenty-four men, five of whom had been involved in the
attack on the Caddo camp. They also formed a military organization called the
"frontier guards" and organized companies headed by those who had attacked
Choctaw Tom. Captain Allison Nelson, the man Baylor had been pushing to
replace Agent Neighbors, was unanimously chosen commander-in-chief. The
executive committee then selected three commissioners to travel to the Brazos
Reserve to evaluate the situation and attempt to reach a peaceful agreement.
The commission arrived on January 8 and met with Captain Palmer and Farmer
Sturm, who was acting in place of the still-absent Agent Ross. Three days later
the headmen of the various tribes met with the commissioners, who quickly
became "satisfied that there was no danger to be apprehended" from the
Indians of the Brazos Reserve. On January 12 they returned to Stephenville and
made their report to the assemblage, after which it was agreed that everyone
should return home. Further violence had been temporarily averted.[44]

The authorities in Texas responded to the attack on the Caddos in a manner
that seemed to indicate that Garland's vigilantes would be prosecuted. On
January 10 Governor Runnels issued a proclamation that denounced the attack
upon the Caddo camp and "warned all persons against joining any hostile
expeditions" aimed at the Reserve Indians. The governor directed that the
offenders should be arrested and brought to trial; he additionally requested
that "all good and law abiding citizens give all necessary and lawful aid" to
the authorities. On January 14, District Judge N. W. Battle of Waco ordered
the arrest of the men in Garland's party, but the local civil officers refused
to carry out the injunction out of fear for their lives. Three days later Judge
Battle ordered Captain Ford of the Texas Rangers to arrest Garland. Major
Neighbors, anticipating a trial, hired Waco lawyer E. J. Gurley to act as counsel

for the Caddos in order to ensure they would be "properly represented before the legal tribunals" of Texas. Neighbors finally arrived at the Brazos Agency on January 22, eight days after the return of Ross. The Indians were still gathered around the agency buildings, and Neighbors held a council with the headmen there. He read them the governor's proclamation and explained the measures taken by state authorities to have the murderers apprehended and brought to trial. The chiefs of the tribes agreed to remain peaceful and to "abide by the decision of the civil authorities" of Texas. Following Neighbors's reassurances, the Indians agreed to return to their villages and farms, which had suffered from neglect after being left unattended for nearly a month.[45]

The Texas authorities soon demonstrated, however, that they were not serious about apprehending Garland and his men. Captain Ford, despite being a friend of the Caddos, informed Gurley that he could not legally arrest the murderers since he could only act as an assistant to a civil officer. He stated that he would need an order from the governor to implement Judge Battle's command. Neighbors then protested the lack of action to Governor Runnels. The governor advised Judge Battle to issue new writs of arrest to a civil officer and promised that Captain Ford would assist in their execution. Despite these promises, by mid-February Garland and his men remained free. The Indians of the Brazos Reserve received another blow to their cause in February when the United States Army decided that nearby Fort Belknap would be abandoned in the near future. Major Neighbors, realizing it would be "impossible to maintain the reserve without a military force," suggested to the commissioner of Indian affairs on February 22 that the Indians be removed north of the Red River and that they "abandon the reserves to the lawless bands of white barbarians" that abounded nearby.[46]

In the meantime, the Brazos Reserve tribes returned to their farms and began planting crops and repairing fences. Unfortunately, in their absence much of the Indians' livestock had run off the limits of the reserve. This stock was in danger of being permanently lost because the Indians refused to leave the reserve for fear of being killed by the citizens of the surrounding counties. In addition, raiding Northern Comanches and unscrupulous settlers had stolen many reserve horses while the tribes had taken refuge around the agency buildings. On February 23, Northern Comanches stole another eighty horses from the Caddos and also attacked some settlers' ranches. Agent Ross sent a message to Captain Ford, who was encamped nearby with group of Rangers. He had earlier refused to arrest the Garland party, but now Ford agreed to assist the Caddos in a retaliatory expedition against the Comanches. On the morning of February 24, forty Kadohadachos and Nadaco warriors joined Ford's Rangers for this ill-timed campaign.[47]

Learning that the Caddo warriors had left the agency with Captain Ford, citizens of Erath, Jack, and Palo Pinto counties began raising a force to attack the unprotected Brazos Reserve and to prevent any attempt to arrest Garland's party. Agent Ross received the news from various sources and immediately requested a company of troops from Major George Thomas, new commander of the Second Cavalry. On March 5, Ross held a council with the headmen of the Brazos Reserve tribes and informed them that the citizens were planning to attack the agency. Although twenty Caddo warriors had returned from their fruitless pursuit of the Comanches, the Indians of the reserve nevertheless left their villages and took up a defensive position around the agency buildings. By March 20, about one hundred Texans, under the command of Neighbors's enemy, John Baylor, had gathered at Rock Creek, about twelve miles from the Brazos Agency, where they awaited Captain Nelson's reinforcements, who were gathering at nearby Jameson's Peak. On March 23, however, Second Cavalry Captain John King arrived at the agency with troops and an artillery piece. This strong show of force caused the citizens to lose their nerve, and only thirty-five men—not enough to assist Baylor—showed up at Jameson's Peak. On March 26, Baylor and Nelson resolved to "suspend operations" for six weeks to allow the government to remove the Indians from the state. Even though the danger of an attack had passed for the moment, both the Kadohadachos and Nadacos refused to return to their villages long after the Tonkawas and Wichitas had abandoned the agency buildings.[48]

It was becoming obvious to all parties that the situation in Texas had become untenable for the Indians of either reserve. Finally, on March 30, 1859, Commissioner Mix informed Major Neighbors that the two reserves in Texas "must be discontinued . . . the Indians removed where they can be protected from lawless violence, and effective measures adopted for their domestication and improvement." Mix believed that the Reserve Indians should be moved, along with the Wichitas and Whitebead Caddos living near Fort Arbuckle, to the western part of the Indian Territory known as the Leased District. In June 1855, a treaty had been concluded in which the Choctaw and Chickasaw tribes agreed to lease to the United States their territory located between the Canadian and Red rivers and the 98th and 100th meridian for the settlement of the Wichitas and whatever tribes the federal government might desire. Accordingly, Mix ordered Elias Rector, Indian Territory superintendent, to proceed with Wichita Agent Blain to the Leased District and choose sites for an agency, a military post, and a suitable location for the tribes to settle. Since all this would necessarily take time, Mix did not believe that the Indians could be removed until the fall or winter, and he hoped they would be "permitted to remain in peace and quiet, where they are, till then."[49]

Unfortunately, this was not to be. Neighbors notified Governor Runnels immediately after receiving the commissioner's notification for removal and then had the news published in all the leading newspapers on the frontier. This action, however, led Baylor and his group to undertake even "more energetic endeavors to bring about hostilities" between the settlers and the Indians. Rather than indict Garland and his men for murder, the Palo Pinto County grand jury charged Nadaco chief Iesh with stealing a mule. The grand jury also characterized the Brazos Reserve as an "intolerable nuisance" and concluded their report by claiming that "it is now the prevailing sentiment that we must abandon our homes and take up arms against the Reserve Indians." On April 25, Captain Baylor and his cronies held a meeting at Golconda and made speeches using "very threatening language against the agents and Indians." One hundred twenty-eight men signed a petition that demanded the immediate resignation of Neighbors and his assistants. Baylor and about fifty armed men subsequently left Golconda with the "avowed intention of taking scalps of reserve Indians." Upon being informed of Baylor's activities, Agent Ross notified the Indians and sent for reinforcements from the Second Cavalry. The frightened tribesmen once more assembled around the agency buildings.[50]

It was at this inopportune moment that about sixty or seventy warriors from the Brazos Reserve once again decided to join Major Van Dorn in an expedition against the Northern Comanches. As usual, the opportunity to exact revenge on their foes, to recover stolen horses, and to gain other booty proved too much for the Brazos Reserve Indians to resist. In addition, the Indians continued to hope that their friendly actions might cause the surrounding citizens to cease their hostilities. The expedition—the third and final one the Brazos Reserve Indians would participate in against the Comanches—rode out from Camp Radziminski on April 30 and traveled north in search of their enemies. On May 10 they entered Kansas Territory, and two days later Van Dorn's command attacked a Penateka Comanche village on Crooked Creek, a tributary of the Cimarron River. The village contained about one hundred people, led by the ill-fated Potsanaquahip. Major Van Dorn's force successfully routed the Comanches—killing forty-nine warriors and capturing thirty-six. One hundred horses were recovered from the Penatekas, and all of their camp supplies were either taken or destroyed. Four of the Reserve Indians were killed, and several were wounded. Major Van Dorn's casualties were two dead and fifteen wounded.[51]

Although the Reserve Indians had aided Van Dorn, their absence served to embolden their Texan enemies. On May 7 a Kadohadacho man named Fox, along with six other warriors, was returning from Fort Arbuckle in the Indian Territory with messages to Major Neighbors from Agent Blain. Just as they reached the boundary of the Brazos Reserve fifteen Texans fired on them. The shots killed three of their horses, but all of the Kadohadacho party except for Fox made it safely back to the agency to report the attack. Lieutenant William E. Burnet had arrived from Camp Cooper, and he led one hundred Indian warriors, two soldiers, and Farmer Sturm in search of Fox. They went to the site of the ambush, found the dead horses, and concluded that Fox had been taken prisoner. They followed the trail for a mile and a half until they came upon a postal station. The employee there told Lieutenant Burnet that fifteen men, calling themselves the Jacksboro Rangers, had arrived at the station about three hours before with Fox and a pair of saddlebags containing the mail from Fort Arbuckle. They "cursed and abused" Fox and told him he had no business with the papers and no right to be there. They then read the letters and continued on the road to Jacksboro with the captured Kadohadacho man. Lieutenant Burnet and the party followed the trail for twelve miles until they found Fox's body lying about twenty steps from the road; he had been shot through the chest and scalped. The Indians, including Fox's brother and cousin, gathered around the body "and each looked at him, but no one spoke a word." They wrapped Fox's dead body in a blanket and covered it with branches in a nearby ravine. The party followed the trail into Jacksboro and camped for the evening. It rained heavily that night, and the next morning the trail was impossible to follow. Lieutenant Burnet decided to abandon the chase, and the group returned to the agency. Burnet characterized the Indians as being "very much exasperated" and vowing to "have revenge for these things some time or other."[52]

For the time being, however, the Brazos Reserve Indians were forced to remain gathered around the agency buildings awaiting the next move of the hostile settlers. Baylor—eager to bring his two-year vendetta to a successful climax—quickly began gathering more men at Jacksboro; by May 20 he had led five hundred armed men to a position about eight miles below the Brazos Reserve. They stole cattle from the Indians and those settlers in the area who had refused to join the band. In an attempt to starve out the inhabitants, Baylor's men intercepted a wagon train loaded with flour headed for the reserve. In response, Captain Joseph B. Plummer arrived from Camp Cooper with the First Infantry to begin directing the defense of the agency. The troops erected a picket work, arranged with flanking bastions and traverses, large enough to protect the gathering of Indians and soldiers. A six-pound cannon was brought over from Camp Cooper and placed within the works. By May 22 the agency was ready for Baylor's attack.[53]

The following morning Indian scouts reported that a party of 250 to three hundred men were a mile and a half from the agency and were moving forward.

The soldiers of Captain Plummer's command took up their position and at the same time the Indians mounted their horses for a cavalry attack. Baylor and his men halted half a mile from the troops and waited. Captain Plummer sent Captain Charles C. Gilbert with fifty men to ask Baylor why he had "come upon the reservation with an armed body of men." Baylor answered that he had "come to assail certain Indians of the reserve, but he did not wish to fight the troops. Nevertheless, Baylor warned Gilbert that if the troops did fire at his men, he would attack them as well. Captain Gilbert returned to the agency and informed his commander of Baylor's message. Captain Plummer in turn sent Lieutenant Burnet to direct Baylor to leave the reserve, as he intended to carry out his orders to protect the Indians from "the attacks of armed bands of citizens." Baylor defiantly answered that this message did not alter his determination and that he was intent on destroying the Indians on both reserves even "if it costs the life of every man in his command." Lieutenant Burnet returned to the agency buildings, and the troops and the Indians prepared for Baylor's attack.[54]

It never came. Instead, Baylor's party apprehended an old Indian couple in their nineties and retreated. While still in sight of the Reserve Indians, they killed and scalped the man and the woman; this brutality infuriated the warriors, and about sixty or seventy mounted Indians attacked the retreating Texans. A running fight ensued for six or seven miles before the Texans finally took shelter at a nearby ranch. Baylor's party occupied the house, outhouses, and livestock pens in anticipation of the fast-approaching warriors. Throughout the rest of the day, the Indians "annoyed" Baylor and his men but were unable to draw them out to fight. Jim Pock Mark rode up to the house and called for Baylor to "come out and give him single combat," an invitation the once-boastful Baylor "respectfully declined." The Indians returned to the agency at nightfall. During the battle, five Indians were wounded, and one was killed. Two of Baylor's men were killed, and six were wounded.[55]

The troops and Indians at the agency remained on their guard, as they fully expected another attack from Baylor and his men who had returned to their encampment eight miles away. Baylor did send numerous scouting parties throughout the area to intimidate the Indians, keeping them at the agency for several days. The agency's close quarters and unclean conditions caused the outbreak of a disease, "something like the Cholera." In five or six days about forty Indians died, and many more were very sick; the disease then spread to the soldiers but did not cause any deaths. Although it was quickly becoming necessary to break up the camp and send the tribes back to their villages, Baylor's army remained in the way. Luckily, Major Van Dorn had just returned to Camp Cooper from his campaign against the Comanches, and Lieutenant

Burnet wrote him and requested that he send back the Indian auxiliaries and any other troops he could spare. Immediately, Van Dorn sent these Indians and three companies of soldiers to the Brazos Agency while sending two companies to protect the Comanche Reserve. Upon hearing the news of Van Dorn's advance, Baylor's men broke camp and fled back to their homes. This retreat allowed the Brazos Reserve Indians finally to return to their villages, and the spread of sickness abated.[56]

Although the Brazos Reserve Indians had survived Baylor's "attack," they did suffer serious losses during his "campaign." The tribes lost a large portion of their stock in addition to the crops they had planted in the spring, and forty Indians had succumbed to disease. With danger ever present, the Indians refused to take up cultivation again. Major Neighbors considered the reserve "virtually broken up." He held a council with the headmen of the various tribes and reported that "although they think themselves badly treated," they "expressed full confidence that the general government will do them justice" and hoped they would be allowed to move immediately north of the Red River. The newly appointed commissioner of Indian affairs, A. B. Greenwood, recognized the gravity of the situation and authorized Major Neighbors on June 11, "to take measures forthwith for the removal" of the Reserve Indians to the Leased District. He instructed Neighbors to "proceed at once" in order to gather both reservations' Indians and their movables and "make everything ready to start them up as soon as" the United States troops arrived to provide a military escort. In less than half a decade, the reservation experience in Texas had come to an abrupt end.[57]

Despite the announcement that the various tribes would soon be moving to the Indian Territory, tensions remained high near the Brazos Reserve following the retreat of Baylor's force. In response, on June 6 Governor Runnels appointed a five-man peace commission to travel to the reserve to "prevent all future violence" between the settlers and the Indians. The governor empowered the commission to call, if necessary, for a force of one hundred men "for the purpose of preserving the peace." Upon reaching the area, the commissioners found that the settlers of the surrounding counties had undertaken "extensive and formidable preparations" for another attack on the Brazos Reserve. Therefore, the commissioners raised a troop, commanded by John Henry Brown, to prevent a clash between the Indians and the settlers. Unsurprisingly, the formation of Captain Brown's force enraged the local Texans. On June 24, Baylor chaired a Parker County citizens council meeting that branded Brown's troop a "gross insult" to the settlers of the frontier. The citizens' council also recommended that the county organize a militia for the "purpose of the immediate removal of the Indians and the utter destruction of all reservations on our frontier." The citizens appointed a committee to correspond with other counties to request that they raise a militia as well. The Texans' continued hostile stance forced the Brazos Reserve tribes to remain confined within its boundaries, unable to collect their stock, which had wandered off during Baylor's previous campaign.[58]

In the meantime, the Indians of both Texas reserves, as well as the Wichitas and the Caddos in the Indian Territory, began to make preparations for their removal to the Leased District. On June 18, Taovaya chief Isadowa, White-bead Caddo headman George Washington, and a few Kichais and Delawares traveled from Fort Arbuckle to the Leased District with a party headed by Superintendent Rector and Wichita Agent Blain and picked out village sites in the Washita and Canadian River valleys. On their return to Fort Arbuckle, Rector's party met with Major Neighbors and the headmen from each of the six tribes from the two Texas reserves and informed them that sites had been selected for their new homes. The two agents also explained that the tribes controlled all the territory between the Red and the Canadian rivers and the 98th and 100th meridian, and would remain there "as long as the waters should run, protected from all harm by the United States." Rector and Neighbors apologized to the assembled chiefs for having to relocate them but promised that the federal government would pay for all losses incurred by the removal. The headmen of the reserves responded favorably by declaring "themselves entirely satisfied" with the region—which they all knew very well—and proclaimed that they were ready to relocate immediately.[59]

Neighbors and the headmen returned to the Texas reserves and began preparations in earnest for the Indians' departure to their new homes. The tribes of both reservations gathered the possessions that could be easily transported to the Leased District, while Neighbors appraised all of the Indians' immovable property—such as their houses—so the government could repay them for their losses. Because they could not survive the long trip, nearly six hundred hogs belonging to the Brazos Reserve Indians were sold to the surrounding settlers. The preparations carried out entirely within the boundaries of the agency went smoothly, but the matter of collecting the tribes' lost stock caused further conflict with the neighboring settlers. At least seven hundred head of cattle and horses had been lost from the two reserves since March 1859. The majority of the stock had strayed from the reservations, but a considerable number had been stolen by the Texans and were being sold openly in public auction at Jacksboro. Gathering the strayed horses and cattle, however, proved to be very dangerous. On July 22, a rancher named Patrick Murphy killed a Tawakoni warrior fifteen miles from the Brazos Reserve boundary line. Two days later a more serious engagement took place near the Comanche Reserve between a detachment of Captain Brown's troops and a party of Reserve Penatekas in which two soldiers and one Indian were wounded. To avoid future incidents of this nature, the Reserve Indians abandoned any further attempts to collect their stock, and Major Neighbors arranged for friendly settlers to gather whatever strays were left after the Indians' departure.[60]

Neighbors also continued to make final preparations for the trip to the Leased District. He purchased provisions for the march north and made arrangements for cattle to be slaughtered en route. The major also hired eighty ox-drawn wagons to carry the Indians' goods. Despite the obvious intent of the reserve tribes to move north of the Red River peacefully, Baylor and the other hostile Texan settlers threatened to attack the Indians on their march. Since Captain Brown's regiment had shown that it could not be trusted to protect the Indians, federal troops from Camp Cooper were ordered to accompany the tribes on the journey to the Indian Territory. Arrangements were made for Major Thomas and two companies of the Second Cavalry and one company of the First Infantry to travel north with Neighbors, Agent Ross, and the Brazos Reserve Indians. Another First Infantry company was instructed to protect Agent Leeper and the Penatekas as they made their way from the Comanche Reserve to the Red River, where they planned to meet Neighbors' party.[61]

During the rain-swept day of July 31, the tribes of both reserves gathered to begin their own "trail of tears," leaving, once and for all, their traditional homelands south of the Red River in Texas. Agents Ross and Leeper distributed firewood, coffee, sugar, tobacco, and flour to the Indians for the trek. Both assemblies were huge; in addition to the 1,049 Brazos Reserve Indians—462 Caddos, 344 Wichitas, and 243 Tonkawas—there were at least one thousand horses and five hundred head of cattle to be driven. While there were only 370 Penatekas remaining at the Comanche Reserve, the tribal members owned over nine thousand horses. The following morning, both groups of Indians, accompanied by the federal troops and the Indian agents, began the slow march northward. After a week of travel, on August 7 the Comanche Reserve party met the Brazos Reserve caravan at the Red River, two miles below the mouth of the Big Wichita. The Indians of the two reserves spent the entire following day safely crossing the Red River. Major Neighbors felt that by fording the stream he had "crossed all the Indians out of the heathen land of Texas and [was] now out of the land of the philistines." The reserve tribes spent their first night in the refuge of the Indian Territory at a camp located on Whiskey Creek, three miles north of the Red River.[62]

Nonetheless, the philistines, in the form of messengers from Captain Brown, arrived at the camp that night. Due to the Texans' threats to attack the Indians en route, their departure date had been kept a secret from the local settlers. Captain Brown had not learned of the Reserve Indians' withdrawal until August 2, whereupon his command immediately took up the trail in order to monitor their progress. The next day Patrick Murphy, who charged that the Brazos Reserve Indians had stolen five horses from him as they were leaving, met Brown's troops. In an attempt to investigate Murphy's charges, Brown hurriedly continued his quest to overtake the slow-moving caravan before it crossed into the Indian Territory. Unsuccessful in his attempt, Captain Brown sent troops across the Red River to inform Major Thomas of the theft of Murphy's horses and to protest the fact that the Texans had not been allowed to examine the Indians' livestock for stolen property before the tribes left the agencies. The federal officer answered that the citizens had been given every opportunity to search the Indians' herd for stolen cattle, and that since then none of the tribal members had left the line of march or caused any mischief. This bold stance induced Brown's messengers to cross back into Texas without causing any further difficulties.[63]

After resting for a day, the caravan traveled twelve miles to Beaver Creek on August 10. Before leaving that morning, Neighbors sent four Kadohadacho warriors to locate Agent Blain—who had left Fort Arbuckle for the Leased District on July 26 with the Taovayas, Kichais, and Whitebead Caddos—and inform him of the Reserve Indians' approach. Five days later the party finally arrived at waters flowing north to the Washita River. On August 16, Major Thomas and the cavalry departed for Texas, leaving the Indians in the hands of Captain Plummer and the infantry for the final day of travel. After seventeen grueling miles, the party arrived safely at its Washita River destination and made camp opposite the mouth of Sugar Creek. On the following day the camp was moved four miles upstream where there was spring-fed water and good grazing land. The Indians received all the remaining rations and then settled down to await the arrival of Agent Blain and his party.[64]

The Texas Indians and Major Neighbors were very happy with the success of the trip and with their new home. While waiting for Agent Blain, the headmen of the various tribes accompanied Neighbors on a tour of the countryside. They inspected the village sites that had been chosen and found them "to their entire satisfaction." Agent Blain, the Taovayas, Kichais, and Whitebead Caddos arrived at Neighbors's camp on August 19. The next day Captain Plummer returned to Camp Cooper with his infantry troop. On September 1, Neighbors officially transferred jurisdiction over the Indians to Agent Blain and headed for home. The Texas Indians were greatly saddened by the departure of their old friend, and every warrior shook hands with the major before he left. Some of the older men clung to Neighbors, refusing to let him go; Tonkawa chief Placido "cried like a child." When Neighbors—accompanied by Agents Ross

and Leeper—finally did ride away, the Indians "threw themselves upon the
ground, yelling, in the wildest grief." Neighbors stated that he was so moved
that it required all his "fortitude to leave them."[65]

Driving the Reserve Indians out of Texas, though, had not yet quenched the
vengeful settlers' thirst for blood. The Texans' aimed their fury at Major Neighbors and the two Indian agents for the close ties they had developed with the
state's tribes. On the morning of September 14, Major Neighbors was walking
through the streets of the small town of Belknap, waiting for the high waters
of the Brazos River to recede so he and the other two agents could complete
their return trip. The vengeful Patrick Murphy angrily confronted Neighbors,
but before the major could answer he was shot in the back and killed by
Edward Cornett, Murphy's brother-in-law. Soon after Neighbors' murder, the
citizens of Belknap convened to discuss the fates of Leeper and Ross, but
ultimately decided to let the two men go unpunished. Informed of the murder,
Commissioner Greenwood stated that Neighbors had incurred the "vengeful
animosity" of many Texans by "his zealous and uncompromising efforts to
protect the Indians and their property from wrong." Neither Neighbors nor
the Reserve Indians had been able to overcome the Texas settlers' intense
prejudice and, as a result, the tribes were forced to abandon the state and seek
the federal government's protection in the Indian Territory.[66]

Therefore, after centuries of dominating the region, the only Indians that
remained in Texas were the few hundred Alabamas and Coushattas who lived
in the jungle-like forests of the Big Thicket. Since 1840, when settlers had
driven both tribes from lands set aside for them by the Republic of Texas,
the remaining Alabamas and Coushattas had eked out a marginal existence
on unoccupied lands in the southeastern part of the state. Eventually, the
Coushattas returned to their old settlement at Colita's Village, where the new
owner, a recent Polk County settler, allowed them to establish homes and plant
crops. Likewise, another Texas citizen permitted the Alabamas to remain on
his lands, located at the junction of Big and Little Cypress creeks, in Tyler
County. Realizing the insecure nature of this settlement, in October 1853
Alabama chief Antone, with the assistance of leading Polk County residents,
petitioned the Texas state legislature for a grant of land in compensation for
the wrongs and losses they had suffered. As a result of the request, in 1854
the state purchased 1,110 acres of land for the Alabamas on the headwaters of
Big Sandy Creek in Polk County. The following year, with the support of Sam
Houston, the Coushattas presented a memorial to the Texas Congress asking
for their own land grant. In "consideration of their services to the country, and
their devotion to the early settlers of Texas," the legislature appropriated funds
to purchase 640 acres of land in Polk County for the Coushattas.[67]

The Alabamas quickly prospered on their new reservation. Within a year of its establishment, more than one hundred tribal members had settled in farms and homesteads along the banks of Big Sandy Creek. Most of the Alabamas resided in log cabins with floors, chimneys, and porches. Working together, the Indians cleared the forest and planted corn, potatoes, and fruit trees. The Alabamas also owned a sufficient number of cattle and horses and had several thousand hogs to supply meat for the whole tribe. In addition to working in their own fields, the Alabamas supplemented their income by toiling for wages on the nearby farms of Texas citizens. Following the fall harvest, the tribe broke up into hunting parties that entered the deep forest of the Big Thicket, returning in spring with bear oil, deer meat, and deerskins for their own use and for market. The Alabamas' success on their reservation caused one observer to note that the tribal members were "happy people, kind, warm-hearted and gay, docile and confiding, happy in their domestic relations, and with unlimited hospitality."[68]

The eighty or so remaining Coushattas did not fare as well as the Alabamas. Despite the legislature's appropriation, the tribe did not obtain a reservation since there was no available land remaining in Polk County. Although one Texan citizen allowed the chief, Chickasaw Abbey, to live on his property with about ten other tribesmen, the rest of the Coushattas were forced to scatter throughout the region. In an attempt to improve the Coushattas' condition and separate the Indians from the surrounding Texan settlements, state officials encouraged both tribes to move from their forest homeland to the Brazos Reserve in the summer of 1858. The Coushattas' situation was desperate, but neither they nor the Alabamas agreed to relocate after tribal headmen made an inspection tour of the dry, treeless reservation in the fall. Therefore, early the following year the Alabamas gave the Coushattas permission to settle on their own reservation. Secure on their lands for the first time in a generation, the Coushattas built upon the success of their Alabama kinsmen. On the eve of the Civil War, the 213 tribal members living on the state-administered Alabama-Coushatta Reservation were the only Indians that remained in Texas. Together, the two tribes raised corn and cotton on four hundred acres of land while owning three hundred cows, 350 horses, and about two thousand hogs. Meanwhile, more than six hundred thousand settlers and slaves lived in the state of Texas in 1860. Most Texan citizens resided on farms, raising food crops and cotton on more than 2.5 million acres of improved land. In addition, Texan farmers and ranchers owned more than 2.5 million head of cattle along with a little over 1 million hogs.[69]

Much of the Texans' achievements, most of which had been accomplished in little more than four decades, had come at the expense of the province's

Indian tribes. As late as the early 1820s, the Indians who had dominated the area for over fifteen millennia had remained in control of Texas and the Near Southwest. However, the huge number of Americans who entered the province over the next forty years ultimately had no use for the Indians, whose population dwindled dramatically due to disease and warfare. Within a quarter century of gaining of independence from Mexico, the citizens of Texas had caused almost all of the Indians to disappear from the region entirely. Although Indians had been at the center of most events in Texas prior to 1860, they would have less than a minimal impact upon the state following the outbreak of the Civil War.

Epilogue

Unfortunately, trouble and hardship followed the Caddos, Wichitas, Tonkawas, and Penateka Comanches north of the Red River after their forced removal from Texas. The tribes had just settled into their homes at the newly established Wichita Agency when the Civil War broke out in April 1861. Union troops quickly abandoned the Indian Territory, and Confederates from Texas occupied Fort Cobb, which had served to protect the Agency Indians from enemy Northern Comanches and Kiowas. Although the four tribes signed a treaty with Confederate agents in August 1861, most of the Indians were uneasy with the new situation. Matters came to a head when Union-allied Shawnees and Delawares from Kansas attacked and destroyed Fort Cobb and the Wichita Agency in October 1862. During the melee, the Caddos, Wichitas, and Penatekas settled old scores with the Tonkawas for the assistance the tribe had given to Texan troops during Lamar's presidency. Nearly half of the three hundred Tonkawas were killed in the massacre, including Chief Placido, and the survivors fled south of the Red River to take refuge near Fort Belknap. Reassuming their ties to the Texans, the Tonkawas helped protect the undermanned frontier during the remainder of the Civil War. Following the war, the Tonkawas settled near United States troops at Fort Griffin, established on the Clear Fork of the Brazos in 1867. Over the course of the next eight years, Tonkawa scouts and auxiliaries provided assistance to the American forces, who finally defeated and subdued the Northern Comanches and Kiowas in 1875. The Tonkawas, whose numbers were rapidly declining due to hunger and disease, continued to squat on private property in the vicinity of Fort Griffin even after its abandonment in 1881. Finally, in 1885 the Bureau of Indian Affairs secured a reservation of 91,000 acres in the northern part of the Indian Territory, near the Salt Fork of the Arkansas River, for the ninety-two remaining Tonkawas.[1]

The Caddos, Wichitas, and Penateka Comanches fled to Union controlled Kansas following the destruction of the Wichita Agency. It was not until 1867, following five years of grave suffering during which more than one-fourth of their people died, that the three tribes were able to return to the Indian Territory. Upon their arrival, the Indians were surprised to find that the federal government had set aside all the land south of the Washita River in the Leased District—territory promised to the Caddos, Wichitas, and Penatekas in the Fort Arbuckle Agreement of July 1, 1859—to the previously hostile Kiowas and Comanches, along with a few Apaches. Eventually, the three hundred remaining Penatekas joined the 2,500 or so tribal members on the Kiowa, Comanche, and Apache Reservation, 3 million acres of land located between the Washita and Red Rivers. Nearly one hundred Delawares settled down with the six hundred Caddos and seven hundred Wichitas, who were forced to accept their reduced reservation of 720,000 acres, unilaterally defined by the federal government in 1872 as being bounded by the Washita and Canadian rivers. The two reservations were administered separately until the federal government consolidated the Kiowa, Comanche, and Wichita Agency head-quarters at Anadarko, located on the south bank of the Washita River, in 1878.[2]

Finally settled on lands they felt they could securely call their own, the Caddos, Wichitas, and Delawares successfully adapted to the federal government's attempt to "civilize" the Indians through agriculture, education, and religion. Over the following two decades, individuals from each tribe joined with their families to establish private farms and ranches, on which they raised grain, horses, and cattle. Along with the Kiowas and Comanches, the three agricultural tribes also sent their sons and daughters to local government boarding schools and also to off-reservation schools such as the Carlisle Indian Industrial School in Pennsylvania and the Chilocco Indian Agricultural School in north-central Oklahoma. By the end of the century, the tribes of both reservations had accepted Christianity and worshipped at various Catholic and Protestant churches established near Anadarko. Despite the "progress" the Caddos, Wichitas, and Delawares made on the reservation, their population declined by nearly one-third between 1870 and 1900.[3]

Although the Kiowas and Comanches agreed to educate their children and to attend Christian churches, individuals from neither tribe settled down on farms to raise crops, preferring instead to herd cattle and horses communally, or to lease their lands to Texas cattlemen for cash payments. Their refusal to become farmers (shared by most tribes who were previously nomadic), along with the universal insistence of American Indians to retain their tribal identities, and the desires of whites to gain access to Indian lands, caused government officials and philanthropists to support the passage of the Dawes Severalty Act in 1887. Designed to break up the reservations and give each Indian family its own plot of land on which to raise crops, the Dawes Act allotted 160 acres of land to each family head and lesser amounts to unmarried or orphaned Indians. The government auctioned off all excess land to land-hungry whites, with the money from sales going into Indian accounts. Supporters of the Dawes Act hoped that allotment would force the Indians to end their ties to the tribe, realizing instead the virtues of individual ownership of private property.[4]

Despite unanimous protests by Indians throughout the country, as well as separate lawsuits put forth by the tribes of the Kiowa, Comanche, and Wichita Agency, the disastrous allotment process went forth nonetheless. Although the humanitarian part of the Dawes Act failed miserably in achieving its goals— ultimately the Indians did not assimilate and actually became more dependent upon the federal government—the disposal of reservation lands was a complete success as whites gained 86 million of 138 million acres of Indian land between 1887 and 1934. In 1895 the Tonkawas were the first tribe from Texas subjected to allotment. The results were predictable, as the Tonkawas lost more than four-fifths of their lands to homesteaders. Surrounded by covetous whites and receiving minimal federal supervision, the Tonkawas declined in numbers and lost their language during the first half of the twentieth century. By 1937 only fifty-one Tonkawas remained; within fourteen years these few tribesmen had intermarried with other Indians or whites to the extent that they were no longer distinguishable as a separate tribe. In 1901 the Indians belonging to the Kiowa, Comanche, and Wichita Agency were forced to accept allotment. When the allotment process was completed, fewer than one thousand Wichitas, Caddos, and Delawares maintained title to just over one-fifth of their lands as they were allotted 152,714 acres, while 586,468 acres was opened to white settlement. The three thousand Kiowas and Comanches fared even worse as they lost more than five-sixths of their huge reservation.[5]

The tribes of the Kiowa, Comanche, and Wichita Agency continued to resist assimilation, and have retained their identities to the present. For the first three decades of the twentieth century, tribal members struggled as best they could to survive on their parcels of land. The acreage was generally too small for successful cattle raising, and the weather was too dry for productive agriculture. Most of their children continued to attend federal boarding schools, and returned to their homes in southwestern Oklahoma following graduation. Almost all learned English, and most attended one of the many Christian churches in the area. Despite constant federal pressure to suppress their traditional cultures, the Indians resisted. Tribal members continued to perform their traditional dances—sometimes in secret—while many Indians became involved in nativist movements such as the peyote ritual and participated in the formation of the Native American Church. Elders kept other tribal customs and rituals alive and handed them down orally to the next generation.[6]

Finally, in the 1930s, Franklin Delano Roosevelt and his New Dealers radically changed federal Indian policy for the first time since the founding of the United States. The Indian New Deal, as embodied in the Indian Reorganization Act of 1934 and the Oklahoma Indian Welfare Act of 1936, sought to promote Native American self-determination, the preservation of tribal cultures, and the retention of Indian-owned land. These acts included provisions that allowed each tribe to write a constitution and bylaws in order to organize as a whole for the benefit of tribal members. A federal charter provided that the tribe could administer credit, operate production market efforts, and provide consumer protection as well as land management.[7]

The Caddos, Wichitas, Delawares, and Comanches took advantage of the shift in federal Indian policy to reassert control over their own lives, albeit · using different methods. In 1938 the federal government issued a corporate charter to the Kadohadachos, Hasinais, and Nadacos, as the Caddo Indian tribe of Oklahoma, and the tribe adopted a constitution and bylaws. By the 1970s the Caddos recognized that this document had become obsolete, and in 1976 a new constitution was written and ratified. Today the three thousand Caddos maintain a complex located on thirty-seven acres of tribal-controlled land about seven miles north of Gracemont in Caddo County, Oklahoma. In addition to promoting self-government, the Caddos created the Whitebead Hasinai Cultural Center in 1975 in an effort to retain their cultural identity through the preservation of "tribal values and traditions."[8]

Unlike the Caddos, the Wichitas did not organize under the Oklahoma Indian Welfare Act and chose instead to govern themselves through traditional means on an unwritten constitutional basis. In 1961 its governing rules were approved by resolution and adopted by the tribe, and the fifteen hundred Wichitas—most of whom also live in Caddo County—continue to be governed by these means. Like the Caddos, the Wichitas have taken active measures to preserve their culture; the tribe has created a complex on ten acres of land once controlled by the Riverside Indian School on which dances are held and tribal songs are recorded. The Delaware Tribe of Western Oklahoma did not organize until 1958 when they approved the establishment of home-rule government by resolution. Fifteen years later the tribe approved and ratified a constitution and bylaws. During the 1980s, the one thousand Delawares joined with the Wichitas and Caddos to form the WCD Enterprise Corporation to promote economic development. The Comanches, like the Wichitas and Delawares, also chose not to organize during the New Deal, preferring instead to be governed by a joint resolution and bylaws shared with the Kiowa and Plains Apache tribes. In 1966, however, the Comanches adopted a constitution and established their own government, which has operated ever since in a bustling complex near Lawton, Oklahoma. Today the Comanches have an enrollment of nearly ten thousand people scattered throughout the United States.[9]

The two hundred or so Alabamas and the Coushattas, despite being the only Indians who remained in Texas following the dissolution of the Brazos and Comanche Agencies in 1859, did not fare much better than the tribes that were forced to move north of the Red River. Following the Civil War, Texas officials tried to get the federal government to take over administration of the two tribes but nothing came of it, and for the next several decades the state virtually ignored the Alabamas and Coushattas. Not only were the tribes overwhelmed by the influx of white settlers into the Big Thicket, but their land base also declined when more than one-third of the 640-acre reservation was accidentally granted to a railroad company in 1876.[10]

However, with the help of Presbyterian missionaries and sympathetic Polk County citizens, the Alabamas and Coushattas gradually improved their situation as the federal government took note of their plight. In 1918 Congress appropriated $8,000 for education and to investigate whether to purchase land for the tribes. Ten years later Alabama and Coushatta leaders testified in Washington about their people's condition. As a result, Congress appropriated $40,000 to the newly constituted Alabama-Coushatta tribe for the purchase of 3,000 acres of land adjoining the original reservation as well as for livestock and feed. The following year the state of Texas provided $47,000 for the construction of a hospital, gymnasium, and reservation housing. Following the passage of the Indian Reorganization Act in 1934, the Alabamas and Coushattas drew up a constitution that officially united the two tribes. Despite the official federal recognition, the Alabama-Coushattas had limited contact with federal and state governments during the next decade or so.[11]

In 1953 officials from the Department of the Interior convinced the tribe to accept termination of the federal government's trust responsibility. This trust, along with their lands, was eventually transferred to the Texas Commission for Indian Affairs. Under the purview of Texas, the Alabama-Coushattas experienced mixed results. Although their land base declined once more, the state assisted the tribe in its effort to promote tourism by providing money for a museum, restaurant, and an arts and crafts shop. Nevertheless, by 1985 the Alabama-Coushattas were not happy with the Texas Indian Commission's administration of their resources and successfully appealed to the federal government for trust protection. With the restoration of federal recognition, the

Bureau of Indian Affairs began providing the Alabama-Coushattas with social services and economic programs, helping the tribe to build a cultural center as a tourist attraction in the 1990s. Today about half of the one thousand or so enrolled Alabama-Coushattas reside on 2,800 acres of tribal controlled land, located on Big Sandy Creek in Polk County.[12]

Notes

Abbreviations

ADM   Bolton, Herbert Eugene, ed. *Athanase de Mézières and the Louisiana-Texas Frontier, 1768–1780.* 2 vols. Cleveland: Arthur H. Clark, 1914.

AP   Barker, Eugene C., ed. *The Austin Papers.* 3 vols. Washington DC: Government Printing Office, 1924–27.

ASP   *American State Papers.* Washington DC: Gales and Seaton, 1832.

BA   Béxar Archives. Microfilm Copy. University of North Texas Library. Denton, Texas.

BAT I   Béxar Archives Translations. Series One. Microfilm Copy. University of North Texas Library. Denton, Texas.

BAT II   Béxar Archives Translations. Series Two. Microfilm Copy. University of North Texas Library. Denton, Texas.

CAL   Bureau of Indian Affairs. Letters Received by the Office of Indian Affairs. Caddo Indian Agency, 1824–42. Microfilm Copy. National Archives. Fort Worth, Texas.

FC   Secretaria de Fomento-Colonizacíon. Transcript Copy. Center for American History. University of Texas at Austin.

HED   United States Congress. House of Representatives. *Executive Documents.*

HR   United States Congress. House of Representatives. *Reports.*

LAMG   Taylor, Virginia H., ed. *The Letters of Antonio Martínez, Last Spanish Governor of Texas, 1817–1822.* Austin: Texas State Library, 1957.

LAMV   Taylor, Virginia H., ed. *Letters from Governor Antonio Martínez to the Viceroy Juan Ruiz de Apodaca.* San Antonio: Research Center for the Arts and Humanities. University of Texas at San Antonio, 1983.

LBC   Rowland, Dunbar, ed. *Official Letter Books of W. C. C. Claiborne.* 6 vols. Jackson: Printed for the Mississippi State Department of Archives and History, 1917.

NA   Nacogdoches Archives. Transcript Copy. Center for American History. University of Texas, Austin.

NSFFL   Bureau of Indian Affairs. Letterbook of the Natchitoches-Sulphur Fork Factory, 1809–1821. Microfilm Copy. National Archives. Fort Worth, Texas.

NPCR   Natchitoches Parish Conveyance Records. Microfilm Copy. Genealogy Library. The Church of Jesus Christ of Latter Day Saints. Dallas, Texas.

PC   Papeles Procedentes de Cuba. Archivo General de Indias. Seville, Spain.

PI   Provincias Internas. Transcript Copy. Center for American History. University of Texas at Austin.

RDLF   Records of the Diocese of Louisiana and Florida. Microfilm Copy. Williams Research Center. New Orleans, Louisiana.

SA   Saltillo Archives. Transcript Copy. Center for American History. University of Texas at Austin.

SED   United States Congress. Senate. *Executive Documents.*

SMV   Kinnaird, Lawrence, ed. *Spain in the Mississippi Valley, 1765–1794.* 3 vols. Washington DC: Government Printing Office, 1946–49.

SR   United States Congress. Senate. *Reports.*

SWHQ   *Southwestern History Quarterly* (from July 1897 to April 1912, this appeared as the *Texas State Historical Association Quarterly*).

TAL   Bureau of Indian Affairs. Letters Received by the Office of Indian Affairs. Texas Agency, 1846–59. Microfilm Copy. National Archives, Fort Worth, Texas.

TIP   Winfrey, Dorman, ed. *The Indian Papers of Texas and the Southwest, 1825–1916.* 5 vols. Austin: Texas State Library, 1959–61.

TP   Carter, Clarence E. *The Territorial Papers of the United States.* 28 vols. Washington DC: Government Printing Office, published continuous since 1933.

TRP   Jenkins, John, ed. *The Papers of the Texas Revolution, 1835–1836.* 8 vols. Austin: Texas State Library, 1959–1961.

WAL   Bureau of Indian Affairs. Letters Received by the Office of Indian Affairs. Wichita Agency, 1857–78. Microfilm Copy. National Archives, Fort Worth, Texas.

WSL   Bureau of Indian Affairs. Letters Received by the Office of Indian Affairs. Western Superintendency, 1832–51. Microfilm Copy. National Archives. Fort Worth, Texas.

Preface

1. Other works of this genre include Brown, *Indian Wars and Pioneers of Texas*; Wilbarger, *Indian Depredations in Texas*; DeShields, *Border Wars of Texas*; and Webb, *Texas Rangers*. The most notable exception to this trend is Newcomb, *Indians of Texas*.

2. For example, Weddle, *French Thorn*; Gutierrez, *When Jesus Came, the Corn Mothers Went Away*; Chipman, *Spanish Texas, 1519–1821*; Weber, *Spanish Frontier in North America*; Usner, *Indians, Settlers, and Slaves in a Frontier Exchange Economy*; De la Teja, *San Antonio de Béxar*; Alonzo, *Tejano Legacy*; Frank, *From Settler to Citizen*; Brooks, *Captives and Cousins*.

3. Among the many works are Noyes, *Los Comanches*; Kavanagh, *Comanche Political History*; Schilz and Schilz, *Buffalo Hump*.

4. Schilz, *Lipan Apaches in Texas*; Carlisle, "Spanish Relations with the Apache Nations East of the Rio Grande"; Schilz, "People of the Cross Timbers"; Himmel, *Conquest of the Karankawas and the Tonkawas*.

5. Perttula, *Caddo Nation*; Cecil Elkins Carter, *Caddo Indians*; Smith, *Caddo Indians*; Smith, *The Caddos, the Wichitas, and the United States*; Smith, *Wichita Indians*; La Vere, *Caddo Chiefdoms*.
6. Ricklis, *Karankawa Indians of Texas*; Himmel, *Conquest of the Karankawas and the Tonkawas*.
7. Everett, *Texas Cherokees*; H. Anderson, "Delaware and Shawnee Indians and the Republic of Texas," 231–60; Flores, "Red River Branch of the Alabama-Coushatta Indians," 55–72; Martin, "Polk County Indians," 3–23; Hunter, "Their Final Years," 3–45; Hook, *Alabama-Coushatta Indians*.
8. Aten, *Indians of the Upper Texas Coast*, touches upon the Atakapas a bit.
9. Gannett, "American Invasion of Texas."
10. Meredith, *Dancing on Common Ground*.
11. La Vere, *Life among the Texas Indians*, 3–48.
12. G. Anderson, *Indian Southwest*.
13. La Vere, *Texas Indians*.

1. Dominance

1. La Vere, *Life among the Texas Indians*, 5–10.
2. The best overviews of Indian-Euroamerican relations in Texas during the sixteenth and seventeenth centuries are John, *Storms Brewed*, 3–195; Chipman, *Spanish Texas*, 1–62; G. Anderson, *Indian Southwest*, 9–66.
3. These epidemic "events" discerned by scholars through historic references occurred in 1592–93, 1617–19, 1635–38, 1647–48, 1671, 1687–91, and 1708–10. See Vehik, "Problems and Potential in Plains Indian Demography," in *Plains Indian Historical Demography and Health*, 115–18; Perttula, "European Contact and Its Effect on Aboriginal Caddoan Populations between AD 1520 and AD 1680," 3: 504–6; Ewers, "Influence of Epidemics on the Indian Populations and Cultures of Texas," 104–15.
4. The process of ethnogenesis is best described in G. Anderson, *Indian Southwest*, 3–5.
5. To avoid confusion, I have chosen to use one of the many Spanish spellings of Karankawa, Carancaguase, to differentiate the individual tribe from the whole group. I have done the same thing in similar cases with other tribes.
6. Ricklis, *Karankawa Indians of Texas*, 4–8, 127–31.
7. Secondary studies of the Karankawan culture include Gatschet, *Karankawa Indians*; Newcomb, *Indians of Texas*, 59–81; Lipscomb, "Karankawa Indians," 1031–33.
8. Ricklis, *Karankawa Indians of Texas*, 101–10, 137–42; Gatschet, *Karankawa Indians*, 63; Newcomb, *Indians of Texas*, 67–71; Lipscomb, "Karankawa Indians," 1031.
9. Newcomb, *Indians of Texas*, 29–57; Newcomb, "Coahuiltecan Indians," 171–74.
10. Aten, *Indians of the Upper Texas Coast*, 27–66; Newcomb, *Indians of Texas*, 315–25; Campbell, "Deadose Indians," 546; Burch, "Indigenous Indians of the Lower Trinity Area of Texas," 36–52; Andree F. Sjoberg, "Bidai Indians of Southeastern Texas," 5–22, 54–78; G. Anderson, *Indian Southwest*, 39.
11. Newcomb, *Indians of Texas*, 325–28; Couser, "Atakapa Indians," 272.
12. La Vere, *Caddo Chiefdoms*, 10–15; Smith, *Caddo Indians*, 5–14.

13. Smith, *Caddo Indians*, 11–13; La Vere, *Caddo Chiefdoms*, 21–25.

14. La Vere, *Caddo Chiefdoms*, 29–34; Smith, *The Caddo Indians*, 8–9.

15. Smith, *Wichita Indians*, 3–5.

16. Smith, *Wichita Indians*, 5; Smith, *The Caddos, the Wichitas, and the United States*, 6–7.

17. Smith, *Wichita Indians*, 15–17.

18. La Vere, *Life among the Texas Indians*, 11–12.

19. Brooks, *Captives and Cousins*, 48–51; Schilz, *Lipan Apaches in Texas*, 1–4; G. Anderson, *Indian Southwest*, 105–10; Carlisle, "Apache Indians," 210–11.

20. John, *Storms Brewed*, 59–63; La Vere, *Life among the Texas Indians*, 11–12.

21. G. Anderson, *Indian Southwest*, 112–16; Smith, *Caddo Indians*, 15–16; Smith, *Wichita Indians*, 17–18.

22. Studies of the Comanches include Wallace and Hoebel, *Comanches*; Noyes, *Los Comanches*; Kavanagh, *Comanche Political History*.

23. Wallace and Hoebel, *Comanches*, 22–24; Kavanagh, *Comanche Political History*, 26–62; John, *Storms Brewed*, 307–8.

24. Noyes, *Los Comanches*, 32–37; Wallace and Hoebel, *Comanche Indians*, 33–66; 245–84.

25. Schilz, "People of the Cross Timbers," 32–35; Campbell, "Ervipiame Indians," 886; Carlisle, "Tonkawa Indians," 525–26; Himmel, *Conquest of the Karankawas and the Tonkawas*, 22–33.

26. Newcomb, *Indians of Texas*, 136–41; Carlisle, "Tonkawa Indians," 525–26; Schilz, "People of the Cross Timbers," 36–37; Himmel, *Conquest of the Karankawas and the Tonkawas*, 32–33.

27. Chipman, *Spanish Texas*, 101–4; Burton, "Family and Economy in Frontier Louisiana," 18–21.

28. La Vere, *Life among the Texas Indians*, 16–17.

29. Usner, *Indians, Settlers, and Slaves*, 13–76; Hall, *Africans in Colonial Louisiana*, 2–27; Burton, "Family and Economy in Frontier Louisiana," 31–32.

30. Smith, *Caddo Indians*, 36–55; Chipman, *Spanish Texas*, 105–26; Weddle, *French Thorn*, 190–212.

31. Smith, *Wichita Indians*, 25–34.

32. For the best definition of the "middle ground," see White, *Middle Ground*. La Vere, "Between Kinship and Capitalism," 198–206; Mills, ed., *Natchitoches, 1729–1803*, 4, 97, 101; D. Lee, "Indian Slavery in Lower Louisiana during the Colonial Period," 68–70; Burton, "Family and Economy in Frontier Louisiana," 229–35.

33. A. Lee, "Fusils, Paint, and Pelts," 50–56. Although this study examines the later Spanish period, it reflects the system that had been developed during the French era. Bridges and De Ville, "Natchitoches in 1766," 145–58.

34. Weber, *Spanish Frontier in North America*, 92–121; Smith, *The Caddo Indians*, 20–35.

35. Chipman, *Spanish Texas*, 105–26; De la Teja, *San Antonio de Béxar*, 3–18.

36. Smith, *Caddo Indians*, 55–56; Ricklis, *Karankawa Indians of Texas*, 143, 165.

37. G. Anderson, *Indian Southwest*, 70–72.

38. G. Anderson, *Indian Southwest*, 72–84.

39. G. Anderson, *Indian Southwest*, 59–61; Jackson, *Los Mesteños*, 11–37.

40. Himmel, *Conquest of the Karankawas and the Tonkawas*, 24–25; Chipman, *Spanish Texas*, 147–56; Schilz, "People of the Cross Timbers," 73–88.

41. Gilmore, "Indians of Mission Rosario," 233–34; Ricklis, *Karankawa Indians of Texas*, 144; Wolff, "Karankawa Indians," 8–10; Chipman, *Spanish Texas*, 163–66.

42. Chipman, *Spanish Texas*, 156–60.

43. Weddle, *San Sabá Mission*, 61–89.

44. Smith, *Wichita Indians*, 30–33; Chipman, *Spanish Texas*, 170–79.

45. Rollings, *Osage*, 134–36; Din and Nasatir, *Imperial Osages*, 61–70; Smith, *Wichita Indians*, 46.

46. ADM 1: 66–75; Nasatir, *Borderland in Retreat*, 15–18; Alejandro O'Reilly, Proclamation, December 7, 1769, SMV 1: 125–26.

47. Usner, *Indians, Settlers, and Slaves*, 60–61; Kniffen, Gregory, and Stokes, *Historic Indian Tribes of Louisiana*, 83–84, 123–25.

48. Usner, *Indians, Settlers, and Slaves*, 130; Census of the Post of Rapides for the Year 1773, PC 189a; Mills, ed., *Natchitoches, 1729–1803*, 201–2, 215.

49. Flores, "Red River Branch of the Alabama-Coushatta Indians," 55–57; Martin, "Polk County Indians," 3–4; Kniffen, Gregory, and Stokes, *Historic Indian Tribes of Louisiana*, 83–84; Valentin Layssard to Bernardo de Galvéz, March 1, 1778, PC 191.

50. Smith, *Caddo Indians*, 68.

51. Chipman, *Spanish Texas*, 173–86; Weber, *Spanish Frontier in North America*, 203–20.

52. Chipman, *Spanish Texas*, 189–92.

53. Smith, *Wichita Indians*, 52–60.

54. Wolff, "Karankawa Indians," 11–12; Himmel, *Conquest of the Karankawas and Tonkawas*, 15–16.

55. Schilz, *Lipan Apaches in Texas*, 26–27; Himmel, *Conquest of the Karankawas and Tonkawas*, 17.

56. Chipman, *Spanish Texas*, 201–2; Roell, "Nuestra Señora del Espíritu Santo de Zuñiga Mission," 1062–65.

57. Wolff, "Karankawa Indians," 14–18; Himmel, *Conquest of the Karankawas and the Tonkawas*, 16.

58. Usner, *Indians, Settlers, and Slaves*, 114–15; Valentin Layssard to Gálvez, January 22, 1778, PC 191; State of livestock in Rapides, May 25, 1783, PC 196; Census of the nations of Rapides, April 15, 1789, PC 202; Esteban Miró to Layssard, May 7, 1784, PC 197; Din, *Spaniards, Planters, and Slaves*, 94–102.

59. General census of the residents and slaves at the post of Natchitoches and its dependencies, August 17, 1787, PC 201; Contracts are from NPCR, 2–15; Coutts, "Boom and Bust," 289–309; Statement of the quantity of . . . pounds of tobacco made in the post of Natchitoches in the harvest of the present year of 1791, December 15, 1791, PC 17; Mills, ed., *Natchitoches Colonials*, 68–75; General census of the residents . . . at the post of Natchitoches and its dependencies, August 17, 1787, PC 201; Burton, "Family and Economy in Frontier Louisiana," 239–54; 260–67.

60. Land sale, Tsaoua Camté to Manuel Trichel and Dame Veuve Alexis, March 26, 1778, NPCR 12; Land sale, Hyamoc to Jean Baptiste Laberry, June 13, 1780, NPCR

16; Mills, *Natchitoches Colonials*, 71; List of inhabitants and merchants of this post of Natchitoches who have presented since January 19, 1791 until the present date . . . the number of carrotes and pounds of tobaco that they have made in this last harvest, March 15, 1791, PC 203; La Vere, *Caddo Chiefdoms*, 88; General census of the residents . . . at the post of Natchitoches and its dependencies, August 17, 1787, PC 201.

61. Report of the council at San Antonio de Béxar, January 5, 1778, ADM 2: 166; Census of Indian Allies, September 1780, PC 193a; State of the nations of Texas and the numbers of individuals, March 13, 1783, PC 196; Lists of debts of Mr. Joseph Capuran, August 12, 1785, NPCR 20; Rousseau to Miró, September 9, 1785, PC 11; Miró to Rousseau, October 5, 1785, PC 3.

62. Smith, *Caddo Indians*, 63–74; Daniel Clark to James Madison, September 29, 1803, TP 9: 63; Manuel Salcedo, Report on the number and location of Indian tribes of Texas, 1808, BA 39.

63. De la Teja, *San Antonio de Béxar*, 21; Tjarks, "Comparative Demographic Analysis of Texas," 291–338; Chipman, *Spanish Texas*, 204–7.

64. G. Anderson, *Indian Southwest*, 136–39; Schilz, *Lipan Apaches in Texas*, 25–29; Himmel, *Conquest of the Karankawas and the Tonkawas*, 26–27; Domingo Cabello to Jacobo Ugarte y Loyola, June 12, 1786, BAT I, 138: 90–93; Vigness, "Nuevo Santander in 1795: A Provisional Inspection by Félix Calleja," 491; de Mézières to Croix, September 7, 1779, ADM 2: 274; Census that manifests the number of individuals that comprise the Nations of Indian Gentiles, situated in the province of Texas . . . deduced from Don Nicolas Lamathe in the year 1781, March 5, 1783, PC 70a.

65. Himmel, *Conquest of the Karankawas and the Tonkawas*, 16, 27; Ricklis, *Karankawa Indians of Texas*, 134–35; de Morfi, *History of Texas*, 2: 79–80; Census that manifests the number of individuals that comprise the Nations of Indian Gentiles, situated in the province of Texas . . . deduced from Don Nicolas Lamathe in the year 1781, March 5, 1783, PC 70a.

66. Smith, *Caddo Indians*, 74; Report of the council at San Antonio de Béxar, January 5, 1778, ADM 2: 166; de Mézières to Croix, August 26, 1779, ADM 2: 262; Census of Indian Allies, September 1780, PC 193a; State of the nations of Texas and the numbers of individuals, March 13, 1783, PC 196; Sibley, "Historical Sketches of the Several Indian Tribes in Louisiana, south of the Arkansas, and between the Mississippi and River Grande," ASP, Class II, Indian Affairs, 721; Manuel Salcedo, Report on the number and location of Indian tribes of Texas, 1808, BA 39.

67. John, *Storms Brewed*, 635–37, 652–53; Himmel, *Conquest of the Karankawas and the Tonkawas*, 27–28; Schilz, "People of the Cross Timbers," 120–27.

68. John, "Nurturing the Peace," 346–47; G. Anderson, *Indian Southwest*, 218–20; Kavanagh, *Comanche Political History*, 93–109; John, "Inside the Comanchería." 49; Francisco Xavier Ortíz to Juan Bautista de Anza, May 20, 1786, in Thomas, ed., *Forgotten Frontiers*, 321–24.

69. Smith, *Wichita Indians*, 65–66; de Mézières to Teodoro de Croix, April 18, 1778, ADM 2: 201–2; de Mézières to Croix, September 7, 1779, ADM 2: 274; Census that

manifests the number of individuals that comprise the Nations of Indian Gentiles, situated in the province of Texas . . . deduced from Don Nicolas Lamathe in the year 1781, March 5, 1783, PC 70a; Census of Indian Allies, September 1780, PC 193a; Louis de Blanc to Esteban Miró, January 10, 1784, PC 197.

70. Smith, *Wichita Indians*, 77–78; John, ed., "Inside the Comanchería," 27–56; Chipman, *Spanish Texas*, 198–99.

2. Tenuous Coexistence

1. Cabello to José Antonio Rengel, December 9, 1786, BAT I, 135: 110–14; Cabello to Rengel, December 24, 1785, BAT I, 135: 142–46; Cabello to Rengel, January 10, 1786, BAT I, 136: 36–41; Cabello to Rengel, February 20, 1786, BAT I, 136: 136–40.

2. Cabello to Rengel, March 14, 1786, BAT I, 137: 29–30; Cabello to Jacobo Ugarte y Loyola, July 31, 1786, BAT I, 139: 94–96; John, *Storms Brewed*, 694–95; Diary of events at Béxar, September 1798, BA 28; Diary of events at Béxar, October 1798, BA 28.

3. Cabello to Ugarte, July 30, 1786, BAT I, 139: 92–93; Cabello to Ugarte, August 28, 1786, BAT I, 140: 171–72; Kavanagh, *Comanche Political History*, 148–50, 177–88; John, *Storms Brewed*, 705; G. Anderson, *Indian Southwest*, 230–33; Chipman, *Spanish Texas*, 199.

4. Gil Ibarvo to Rafael Martínez Pacheco, November 12, 1787, BAT I, 148: 62; Martínez Pacheco to Juan de Ugalde, May 22, 1788, BAT I, 154: 98–99; Martínez Pacheco to Ugalde, June 7, 1788, BAT I, 155: 7–8; Martínez Pacheco to Ugalde, June 20, 1788, BAT I, 155: 19–20; de Blanc to Miró, February 28, 1790, SMV 2: 301–3; Schilz, "People of the Cross Timbers," 128–29.

5. Report on the cost of maintaining fifteen Taovayas, March 18, 1787, BAT I, 144: 109; Martínez Pacheco to Ugalde, August 27, 1787, BAT I, 146: 40–41; Report on gifts and food provided visiting Indians, September 3, 1787, BAT I, 146: 62; Martínez Pacheco to Ugalde, September 16, 1787, BAT I, 146: 91.

6. Diary of events at Béxar, November 1788, BAT I, 157: 95–100; Diary of events at Béxar, December 1788, BAT I, 157: 187–89; Martínez Pacheco to Ugalde, January 4, 1789, BAT I, 158: 33–35; Diary of events at Béxar, January 1789, BAT I, 158: 92–94; Diary of events at Béxar, March 1789, BA 19.

7. Martínez Pacheco to Juan de Ugalde, February 13, 1789, BA 19; Martínez Pacheco to Ugalde, March 16, 1789, BA 19; Martínez Pacheco to Ugalde, July 6, 1789, BA 19; Ibarvo to Martínez Pacheco, August 11, 1789, BA 19; de Blanc to Miró, January 20, 1790, SMV 2: 295–97; de Blanc to Miró, September 2, 1790, SMV 3: 9; de Blanc to Miró, March 30, 1791, SMV 3: 408–10.

8. Report of passports issued at San Antonio, July 27, 1792, BA 22; Cristóbal de Córdova to Muñoz, April 27, 1793, BA 23; Córdova to Muñoz, April 29, 1793, BA 23; Pedro de Nava to Muñoz, April 10, 1794, BA 24; Nava to Muñoz, April 27, 1794, BA 24; Nava to Muñoz, May 21, 1794, BA 24.

9. De Blanc to Muñoz, July 21, 1794, PC 29; Nava to Muñoz, July 8, 1795, BA 25; Muñoz to Bernardo Fernández, March 27, 1796, BA 26.

10. Haggard, "House of Barr and Davenport," 66–88; José Miguel del Moral to Juan

Bautista de Elguézabal, May 21, 1800, BA 29; Músquiz to Elguézabal, July 1, 1801, BA 30; Barr and Davenport to José María Guadiana, September 2, 1809, BA 42.

11. Cabello to Ugarte, November 20, 1786, BAT I, 143: 5–6; Loomis, "Philip Nolan's Entry in Texas in 1800," 120–33.

12. Nava to Muñoz, April 23, 1794, BA 24; Muñoz to Ibarvo, April 27, 1794, BA 24; Muñoz to Ibarvo, April 30, 1794, BA 24; Córdova to Muñoz, July 2, 1794, BA 24; Fernández to Muñoz, February 2, 1795, BA 25; Juan Cortés to Muñoz, April 22, 1795, BA 25; Guadiana to Muñoz, March 26, 1797, BA 27; Muñoz to Guadiana, April 25, 1797, BA 27; Nava to Elguézabal, September 18, 1799, BA 27.

13. Cabello to Ugarte, July 3, 1786, BAT I, 139: 34; Revillagigedo to Miró, March 2, 1791, SMV 2: 404–6; Cortés to Baron de Carondelet, March 22, 1792, SMV 3: 18–19; Córdova to Muñoz, November 12, 1792, BA 22; Muñoz to Córdova, November 17, 1792, BA 22; Muñoz to Carondelet, April 30, 1794, SMV 3: 274–75; Elguézabal to Nemesio Salcedo, April 11, 1804, BAT II, 293–95.

14. Cabello to Rengel, January 24, 1786, BAT I, 136: 61–64; Cabello to Ugarte, June 12, 1786, BAT I, 138: 90–93; Cabello, Strength Report for June 1786, BAT I, 138: 122–25; Cabello to Ugarte, July 3, 1786, BAT I, 139: 29–34.

15. Cabello to Ugarte, July 2, 1786, BAT I, 139: 24–28.

16. Cabello to Ugarte, July 3, 1786, BAT I, 139: 29–34; Cabello to Ugarte, July 30, 1786, BAT I, 139: 92–93; Cabello, Strength Report for July 1786, BAT I, 139: 102–5; Ugarte to Cabello, August 3, 1786, BAT I, 140: 39–41; Cabello to Ugarte, September 10, 1786, BAT I, 141: 60–61; Cabello to Ugarte, September 11, 1786, BAT I, 141: 64–65; John, Storms Brewed, 728–29; Kavanagh, Comanche Political History, 148; Smith, Wichita Indians, 82.

17. Chipman and Joseph, Notable Men and Women of Spanish Texas, 220; John, Storms Brewed, 724–25; Martínez Pacheco, Lists of Gifts, February 23, 1787, BAT I, 144: 84; Martínez Pacheco to Ugarte, March 10, 1787, BAT I, 144: 103–8.

18. Martínez Pacecho to Ugalde, Decmeber 9, 1787, BAT I, 149: 40–42; Martínez Pacheco to Ugalde, December 24, 1787, BAT I, 149: 71–72; Martínez Pacheco to Ugalde, January 7, 1788, BAT I, 151: 13–14; Martínez Pacheco to Ugalde, January 17, 1787, BAT I, 151: 32–33; Martínez Pacheco to Ugalde, September 15, 1788, BAT I, 156: 52; Pacheco to Ugalde, September 29, 1788, BAT I, 156: 77; Diary of Ugalde, April 13, 1788–June 12, 1788, PI 111.

19. Diary of events at Béxar, February 1789, BA 19; Martínez Pacheco to Ugalde, March 16, 1789, BA 19; Diary of events at Béxar, June 1789, BA 19; Martínez Pacheco to Ugalde, August 31, 1789, BA 19; Martínez Pacheco to Ugalde, September 9, 1789, BA 19.

20. Ugalde to Martínez Pacheco, December 20, 1789, BA 20; Martínez Pacheco to Ugalde, December 23, 1789, BA 20; Martínez Pacheco to Ugalde, December 24, 1789, BA 20; Diary of events at Béxar, December 1789, NA; Martínez Pacheco to Conde de Revillagigedo, March 1, 1790, NA.

21. Diary of events at Béxar, December 1789, NA; Manuel Muñoz to Revillagigedo,

September 1, 1790, PI 159; Castañeda, *Our Catholic Heritage in Texas*, 5: 19; Carlisle, "Spanish Relations with the Apache Nations East of the Rio Grande," 341–42.

22. Espadas to Martínez Pacheco, March 4, 1790, BA 20; Martínez Pacheco to Espadas, March 21, 1790, BA 20; Espadas to Muñoz, August 17, 1790, BA 20; Muñoz, Report on Indian nations in the province of Texas, November 16, 1790, BA 20; State of the number of deaths, captives, and robberies of livestock . . . executed by the Lipan Apaches in the towns of Laredo, Revilla, and Mier, September 26, 1790, PI 159; Muñoz to Revillagigedo, October 25, 1790, PI 159; Treviño to Muñoz, January 14, 1791, PI 162; Treviño to Muñoz, January 20, 1791, PI 162; Muñoz to Revillagigedo, February 4, 1791, PI 162; Revillagigedo to Miro, March 2, 1791, PI 162.

23. Espadas to Martínez Pacheco, May 21, 1790, BA 20; Martínez Pacheco, Report on measures taken to secure peace with the Lipan Indians, July 3, 1790, BA 20; Martínez Pacheco to Ugalde, July 23, 1790, BA 20; Diary of events at Béxar, August 1790, BA 20; Muñoz to Revillagigedo, September 1, 1790, PI 159; Muñoz to Revillagigedo, December 1790, PI 159.

24. Nava to Revillagigedo, February 8, 1791, PI 224; Nava to Revillagigedo, March 21, 1791, PI 224; Revillagigedo to Nava, March 2, 1791, PI 162.

25. Juan Gutierrez de la Cueva to Muñoz, May 2, 1791, BA 21; Muñoz to Revillagigedo, May 9, 1791, PI 162; Muñoz to de la Cueva, May 18, 1791, BA 21; Muñoz to Revillagigedo, May 10, 1791, NA; Muñoz to Revillagigedo, May 21, 1791, NA; Treviño, Diary . . . of what occurred on the expedition against the Lipans, June 6, 1791, PI 162; Ibarvo to Muñoz, June 13, 1791, BA 21; Muñoz to Revillagigedo, June 20, 1791, PI 162; Muñoz to Revillagigedo, July 31, 1791, PI 162; Ramon Castro to Muñoz, September 24, 1791, BA 21; Courbière to Muñoz, October 27, 1791, BA 21; Castañeda, *Our Catholic Heritage in Texas*, 5: 114.

26. Cortés to Condé de Sierra Gorda, July 9, 1792, BA 22; Cortés to Muñoz, October 3, 1792, BA 22; Muñoz to Cortés, October 9, 1792, BA 22; Cortés to Muñoz, October 19, 1792, BA 22; Cordova to Muñoz, November 12, 1792, BA 22; Muñoz to Córdova, November 17, 1792, BA 22; Revillagigedo to Muñoz, January 16, 1793, BA 23; Muñoz to Nava, January 26, 1793, BA 23; Muñoz to Nava, May 2, 1793, SA; Manuel Merino to Nava, July 5, 1793, SA; Muñoz to Revillagigedo, November 6, 1793, PI 99.

27. José Lafuente to Felix María Calleja, March 17, 1798, PI 12; Calleja to Lafuente, April 28, 1798, PI 12; Sierra Gorda to Miguel José de Azanza, January 30, 1799, PI 12; Sierra Gorda to Azanza, March 13, 1799, PI 12; Sierra Gorda to Azanza, April 14, 1799, PI 12; Nava to Azanza, July 23, 1799, PI 12; Diary of events at Béxar, May 1799, NA; Diary of events at Béxar, April 1800, BA 29; Diary of events at Béxar, July 1801, BA 30.

28. Summary of developments that occurred at the presidios of San Antonio de Béxar and La Bahía . . . during the course of the month of July, 1786, BAT I, 139: 106–10; Luis Cazorla to Cabello, December 6, 1786, BAT I, 143: 30–31.

29. Martínez Pacheco to Ugalde, September 15, 1787, BAT I, 146: 78–84.

30. Cazorla to Martínez Pacheco, August 2, 1787, BAT I, 146: 8; Cazorla to Martínez

Pacheco, August 5, 1787, BAT I, 146: 13; Martínez Pacheco to Ugalde, September 15, 1787, BAT I, 146: 78–84.

31. Manuel Espadas to Ugalde, February 12, 1789, PI 159; Diary of events of campaign, Athanase de Mézières, February 13, 1789, PI 159; Espadas to Martínez Pacheco, February 12, 1789, BA 19; Espadas to Martínez Pacheco, February 22, 1789, BA 19; Martínez Pacheco to Ugalde, March 2, 1789, BA 19.

32. Ricklis, Karankawa Indians of Texas, 155–56; Espadas to Martínez Pacheco, November 10, 1789, BA 20; Espadas to Martínez Pacheco, November 13, 1789, BA 20; Antonio Treviño, Diary of Expedition against the Carancaguases, December 12, 1789, BA 20; Espadas to Martínez Pacheco, December 12, 1789, BA 20; Espadas to Martínez Pacheco, December 29, 1789, BA 20; Espadas to Martínez Pacheco, January 29, 1790, BA 20; Martínez Pacheco to Revillagigedo, March 1, 1790, NA.

33. Espadas to Martínez Pacheco, April 9, 1790, BA 20; Father José Mariano Reyes to Revillagigedo, May 1, 1790, BA 20; List of inhabitants of Mission Rosario, May 1, 1790, BA 20; Espadas to Martínez Pacheco, May 6, 1790, BA 20; Espadas to Martínez Pacheco, May 20, 1790, BA 20; List of inhabitants of Mission Rosario, July 2, 1790, NA; Espadas to Muñoz, September 10, 1790, BA 20; Fray José Mariano Reyes to Muñoz, November 18, 1790, BA 20.

34. Silva to Muñoz, April 26, 1791, BA 21.

35. Garza to Muñoz, June 13, 1791, BA 21.

36. Oberste, History of Refugio Mission, 21–60.

37. Diary of Mariano Rodríguez, March 13–May 23, 1793, BA 23; Garza to Muñoz, July 21, 1793, BA 23; José Antonio Cadena to Muñoz, June 8. 1794, BA 23; Muñoz to Juan Cortés, June 10, 1794, BA 23; Oberste, History of Refugio Mission, 131–36.

38. Muñoz to Cortés, May 31, 1794, BA 24; Muñoz to Cortés, August 4, 1794, BA 24; Muñoz to Nava, November 7, 1794, BA 25; Muñoz to Nava, November 30, 1794, BA 25; Silva to Muñoz, January 12, 1795, BA 25; Cortés to Muñoz, January 16, 1795, BA 25; Muñoz to Nava, January 26, 1795, BA 25.

39. Oberste, History of Refugio Mission, 163–64; Census report of Indians at Mission Refugio, October 23, 1795, BA 25; Ricklis, Karankawa Indians of Texas, 159–68.

40. Castañeda, Our Catholic Heritage in Texas, 5: 190–92; Elguézabal to Muñoz, July 3, 1797, BA 27; Census of Indians at Refugio, June 30, 1797, BA 27.

41. Father Antonio de Jesús Garavito to José Miguel del Moral, October 13, 1798, BA 27; Juan Bautista de Elguézabal to Muñoz, January 17, 1798, BA 28; Garavito to Elguézabal, March 25, 1798, BA 28; Elguézabal to Muñoz, March 28, 1798, BA 28; Father Bernardino Vallejo, Report on Texas Missions, August 26, 1803, BA 31; Oberste, History of Refugio Mission, 230–53.

42. Nava to Muñoz, April 4, 1797, BA 27; Antonio Cordero to Muñoz, April 28, 1798, BA 28. Nava to Muñoz, May 24, 1798, BA 28; Castañeda, Our Catholic Heritage in Texas, 5: 118–20.

43. Diary of events at Béxar, March 1799, NA; Diary of events at Béxar, April 1799, NA; Bustamante, Diary of campaign against Comanches, April 2, 1799, PI 12; José Menchaca to Cordero, April 26, 1799, PI 12; Muñoz to Nava, June 5, 1799, PI 12;

Muñoz to Felix Calleja, June 5, 1799, PI 12; Nava to Azanza, July 23, 1799, PI 12; Diary of events at Béxar, March 1800, BA 29; Diary of events at Béxar, May 1800, BA 29.

44. Sibley, "Historical Sketches," 723; Smith, *Wichita Indians*, 94; Appointment of Atourisoc (Eriascoc) as chief, July 22, 1799, BA 29; Nava to Elguézabal, September 18, 1799, BA 29; Moral to Elguézabal, August 26, 1800, BA 29; Nava to Elguézabal, September 1, 1800, BA 29; Nava to Elguézabal, November 24, 1800, BA 29.

45. Wilson and Jackson, *Philip Nolan and Texas*, 65–75; Guadiana to Elguézabal, September 1, 1801, BA 30.

46. Nava to Elguézabal, July 7, 1801, BA 30; Nava to Elguézabal, November 12, 1801, BA 30; Músquiz to Elguézabal, November 8, 1801, BA 30; John, "Nurturing the Peace, 347–48; Kavanagh, *Comanche Political History*, 149–50.

47. John, "Nurturing the Peace," 348; Kavanagh, *Comanche Political History*, 150.

48. Juan Ignacio Arrambide to Elguézabal, February 13, 1803, BA 31; N. Salcedo to Elguézabal, February 24, 1803, BA 31; Músquiz to Elguézabal, February 27, 1803, BA 31; John, "Nurturing the Peace," 350–52.

49. Diary of events at Béxar, March 1803, BA 31; N. Salcedo to Elguézabal, April 26, 1803, BA 31; N. Salcedo to Elguézabal, August 2, 1803, BA 31; Diary of events at Béxar, July 1803, BA 31; N. Salcedo to Elguézabal, November 7, 1803, BA 31.

50. N. Salcedo to Elguézabal, September 26, 1803, BA 31; N. Salcedo to Elguézabal, October 11, 1803, BA 31; John, "Nurturing the Peace," 352; Kavanagh, *Comanche Political History*, 149–50.

51. José de la Peña to Miró, August 17, 1787, SMV 1: 232–33; de Blanc to Jean Filhiol, July 26, 1791, PC 213; de Blanc to Carondolet, May 3, 1792, PC 25a; Layssard to Miró, December 28, 1789, PC 202; Layssard to Carondolet, August 6, 1793, PC 207; proces múbetween Vincent Michel and Widow Remy Toutin, May 14, 1794, NPCR 24; de Blanc to Carondolet, June 3, 1796, PC 219; Felix Trudeau to Manuel Gayoso de Lemos, August 19, 1798, NPCR 50.

52. Rousseau to Miró, March 3, 1786, PC 198a; Miró to Francisco Cruzat, March 24, 1786, SMV 2: 171–73; Rousseau to Miró, April 18, 1786, PC 199; Miró to Bernardo de Gálvez, August 1, 1786, SMV 2: 182–84; Paul Bouet Laffitte to Rousseau, August 24, 1786, PC 199; Rousseau to Miró, August 24, 1786, PC 199; Din and Nasatir, *Imperial Osages*, 157–76.

53. Rousseau to Miró, April 18, 1786, PC 199.

54. Rousseau and de Blanc to Miró, March 20, 1787, SMV 2: 198–99; José de la Peña to Miró, September 22, 1787, SMV 2: 234.

55. De Blanc to Miró, August 5, 1788, SMV 2: 259; de Blanc to Miró, March 27, 1790, SMV 2: 316–17.

56. De Blanc to Miró, September 30, 1790, SMV 2: 281; de Blanc to Miró, March 27, 1790, SMV 2: 316–17; de Blanc to Miró, March 30, 1791, PC 17; de Blanc to Miró, August 4, 1791, PC 17; de Blanc to Carondolet, April 16, 1792, PC 25a; de Blanc to Carondolet, August 23, 1792, PC 25a.

57. Succession of Zachary Martin, September 29, 1791, NPCR 21; de Blanc to Carondo-

let, February 18, 1792, SMV 3: 9–11; Carondolet to Ignacio Delino, June 29, 1792, SMV 3: 56; de Blanc to Carondolet, July 6, 1792, PC 25a.

58. Din and Nasatir, *Imperial Osages*, 217–90; Rollings, *Osage*, 167–212; Kinnaird and Kinnaird, "Choctaws West of the Mississippi," 349–51; de Blanc to Carondolet, April 16, 1792, SMV 3: 25–27; de Blanc to Carondolet, May 3, 1792, PC 25a; de Blanc to Carondolet, December 1, 1792, SMV 3: 99–100.

59. Córdova to de Blanc, June 27, 1792, BA 22; Córdova to Muñoz, July 26, 1792, BA 22; Carondolet to de Blanc, October 18, 1792, SMV 3: 92–93; de Blanc to Carondolet, December 1, 1792, SMV 3: 99–100.

60. De Blanc to Manuel Gayoso de Lemos, May 20, 1794, PC 28; de blanc to Carondolet, May 22, 1794, PC 28; Córdova to Muñoz, June 20, 1794, BA 24; Caddo chiefs to de Blanc, April 28, 1795, PC 31; de Blanc to Jean Filhiol, September 20, 1795, PC 213; de Blanc to Carondolet, February 15, 1796, PC 33; de Blanc to Carondolet, May 14, 1796, PC 33; Kinnaird and Kinnaird, "Choctaws West of the Mississippi," 354–56.

61. François Grappe to Trudeau, July 8, 1796, PC 34; Trudeau to Carondolet, July 9, 1796, PC 34; Trudeau to Carondolet, July 24, 1796, PC 212b; Fernández to Muñoz, July 25, 1796, BA 26; Trudeau to Carondolet, September 6, 1796, PC 212a; Fernández to Muñoz, September 25, 1796, BA 26; Trudeau to Carondolet, October 3, 1796, PC 212b; Guadiana to Muñoz, October 23, 1796, BA 26; Trudeau to Carondolet, October 26, 1796, PC 34; Guadiana to Muñoz, November 25, 1796, BA 26; Guadiana to Muñoz, March 3, 1797, BA 27; Trudeau to Carondolet, September 17, 1797, PC 35.

62. Layssard to Filhiol, October 17, 1797, PC 213; Layssard to Gayoso de Lemos, October 27, 1797, PC 212b; Kinnaird and Kinnaird, "Choctaws West of the Mississippi," 367–68.

63. Trudeau to Gayoso de Lemos, August 19, 1798, PC 50; Trudeau to Layssard, August 28, 1798, PC 215b; Trudeau to Layssard, September 15, 1798, PC 215b; Layssard to Gayoso de Lemos, September 20, 1798, PC 215b; Cesaire Archinard to Gayoso de Lemos, at the requisition of a Choctaw chief named Apiache, dictated from his mouth, September 20, 1798, PC 215b; José Miguel del Moral to Elguézabal, January 28, 1800, BA 29; Trudeau to Marqués de Casa Calvo, January 28, 1800, PC 71a; Moral to Elguézabal, June 26, 1800, BA 29; Sibley, "Historical Sketches," 721.

64. Rousseau and de Blanc to Miró, March 20, 1787, SMV 2: 198; de Blanc to Miro, March 30, 1791, PC 17; de Blanc to Carondolet, May 25, 1792, PC 25a; Carondolet to de Blanc, August 9, 1792, PC 18; de Blanc to Carondolet, November 20, 1792, SMV 3: 98–99; Land sale, André Rambin to Louis de Blanc, April 10, 1794, NPCR 24; Census of the inhabitants of the parish of Natchitoches, February 24, 1803, RDLF, Roll 12; Sibley, "Historical Sketches," 721–22.

65. Layssard to Miro, July 10, 1792, PC 206; Layssard to Carondolet, January 24, 1793, PC 207; Kinnaird and Kinnaird, eds., "Red River Valley in 1796," 93; Census of savages of Rapides, January 23, 1793, PC 207; Layssard to Casa Calvo, September 6, 1800, PC 217a; List of Rapides inhabitants who made tobacco this year, December 15, 1791, PC 204; Sibley, "Historical Sketches," 724; Flores, ed., *Jefferson and Southwestern Ex-*

ploration, 112; Mills, ed., *Natchitoches, 1729–1803*, 251–53, 316, 327, 338–39; Bishop Luis Penlaver y Cárdenas, Proceedings of the visit to El Rapido, to the village of the Apalache Indians, and to Avoyelles, November 21, 1796, RDLF 5; Father Isidro Quintero to Penlaver y Cárdenas, November 21, 1796, RDLF 5; Layssard to Gayoso de Lemos, March 15, 1797, PC 215b.

66. Kinnaird and Kinnaird, eds., "Red River Valley in 1796," 93; Census of savages of Rapides, January 23, 1793, PC 207; Layssard to Carondolet, January 24, 1793, PC 207; Layssard to Carondolet, April 27, 1793, PC 207; de Blanc to Carondolet, June 3, 1796, PC 34; Father Isidro Quintero to Bishop Luis Penlaver y Cárdenas, November 21, 1796, RDLF 5; Layssard to Gayoso de Lemos, June 1, 1798, PC 215b; Hunter, "Their Final Years," 14.

67. Land sale, Pascagoula Indians to Louis de Blanc, attorney for Colin La Cour, April 9, 1795, ASP, Public Lands, 2: 781; Testimony of Layssard, January 29, 1812, ASP, Public Lands, 2: 782; Archinard to Gayoso de Lemos, May 18, 1798, PC 215b; List of Foreign Irish Americans and others introduced in the Rapides district in the previous year, November 20, 1800, PC 217a.

68. Hunter, "Their Final Years," 17–18; Layssard to Casa Calvo, October 15, 1800, PC 217a; Land sale, Choctaw Indians to Alexander Miller and William Fulton, May 14, 1802, ASP, Public Lands, 2: 789–90; Land sale, Pascagoula and Biloxi Indians to Miller and Fulton, May 14, 1802, ASP, Public Lands, 2: 790.

69. Sibley to the Commissioners of the Land Office of the Northern Division of the Territory of Orleans, Opelousas, January 26, 1806, ASP, Public Lands, 2: 801–2; Sibley, "Historical Sketches," 724–25; Flores, ed., *Jefferson and Southwestern Exploration*, 113; Sibley to Eustis, May 8, 1809, in Garrett, ed., "Doctor John Sibley and the Louisiana-Texas Frontier," SWHQ 47 (January 1944): 319; Flores, "Red River Branch of the Alabama-Coushatta Indians," 57–58; Francisco Xavier Uranga to Elguézabal, November 29, 1803, BA 31.

70. Sibley, "Historical Sketches," 721–23; Trudeau to Casa Calvo, January 29, 1801, PC 72; Trudeau to Casa Calvo, April 28, 1801, PC 72; Trudeau to N. Salcedo, August 26, 1801, PC 77b; Smith, *Caddo Indians*, 85.

3. Contested Boundaries

1. United States Census of 1810, Microfilm Copy, University of North Texas Library; Chipman, *Spanish Texas*, 205–6.

2. Ennemond Meullion to Juan Manuel Salcedo, November 11, 1803, PC 220b; J. M. Salcedo to Meuillion, November 9, 1803, PC 220b; Land Sale, Apalache and Tensaw Indians to Miller and Fulton, January 11, 1804, ASP, Public Lands, 2: 796–97; Elguézabal to N. Salcedo, February 29, 1804, BAT II, 1: 169; Diary of events at Nacogdoches, March 1804, BAT II, 2: 240; Juan de Ugarte to Elguézabal, April 3, 1804, BAT II, 2: 250; N. Salcedo to Elguézabal, May 8, 1804, BAT II, 2: 388; N. Salcedo to Elguézabal, May 21, 1804, BAT II, 2: 421.

3. Diary of events at Nacogdoches, June 1805, BAT II, 2: 20: 4; Guadiana to Viana, May

31, 1806, BAT II, 2: 21: 107; N. Salcedo to Antonio Cordero, August 16, 1806, BAT II, 2: 22: 40.

4. Sibley to Dearborn, January 10, 1807, in Garrett, ed., "Doctor John Sibley and the Louisiana-Texas Frontier," SWHQ 45 (January 1942): 294; Sibley to Dearborn, March 12, 1807, in Garrett, ed., "Doctor John Sibley and the Louisiana-Texas Frontier," SWHQ 45 (January 1942): 297; Sibley to Dearborn, July 3, 1807, in Garrett, ed., "Doctor John Sibley and the Louisiana-Texas Frontier," SWHQ 45 (April 1942): 380; Sibley to Dearborn, August 8, 1807, in Garrett, ed., "Doctor John Sibley and the Louisiana-Texas Frontier," SWHQ 46 (July 1942): 83; Sibley to Dearborn, August 7, 1807, in Garrett, ed., "Doctor John Sibley and the Louisiana-Texas Frontier," SWHQ 46 (January 1943): 272–73; Sibley to Dearborn, September 7, 1808, in Garrett, ed., "Doctor John Sibley and the Louisiana-Texas Frontier," SWHQ 46 (January 1943): 275; William C. C. Claiborne to James Madison, July 11, 1808, LBC 4: 183–84; Claiborne to Dearborn, August 8, 1808, LBC 4: 185; Claiborne to Sibley, August 9, 1808, LBC 4: 188–89; Claiborne to Dearborn, November 5, 1808, LBC 4: 237–39.

5. Manuel Salcedo, Report on the number and location of Indian tribes of Texas, 1808, BA 39; Sibley, Report from Natchitoches in 1807, 96–97; Morse, ed., Report to the Secretary of War, 373; Kniffen, Gregory, and Stokes, Historic Indian Tribes of Louisiana, 88–89.

6. Hunter, "Their Final Years," 19–20; Sibley, "Historical Sketches," 724; Sibley, Report from Natchitoches in 1807, 15–16; Sibley to Dearborn, April 3, 1807, in Garrett, ed., "Doctor John Sibley and the Louisiana-Texas Frontier," SWHQ 45 (January 1942): 297–98; Sibley to Samuel Eustis, October 20, 1809, HR 1035: 105–6; Flores, "Red River Branch of the Alabama-Coushatta Indians," 58–59, 64–68; Sibley to Dearborn, May 8, 1809, in Garrett, ed., "Doctor John Sibley and the Louisiana-Texas Frontier," SWHQ 47 (January 1944): 320; Morse, ed., Report to the Secretary of War, 373.

7. Hunter, "Their Final Years," 27–30; ASP, Public Lands, 2: 797; Statement showing the names and numbers of different tribes of Indians now remaining within several States and Territories, and the quantity of land claimed by them, respectively, January 10, 1825, ASP, Indian Affairs, 2: 545–47; Mills, ed., Natchitoches, 1800–1826, 96–97, 102–7.

8. Deposition of William Graham, September 9, 1804, TP 9: 292–93; Diary of events at Nacogdoches, August 1804, BAT II, 3: 207–8; Diary of events at Nacogdoches, September 1804, BAT II, 4: 2; Diary of events at Nacogdoches, December 1804, BAT II, 5: 5; Strength Report at Béxar, December 31, 1805, BAT II, 10: 218; Guadiana to Viana, May 31, 1806, BAT II, 15: 107; M. Salcedo, Report on the number and location of Indian tribes of Texas, 1808, BA 39; Cordero to N. Salcedo, December 10, 1808, BA 39; Juan José Calderon to Cordero, January 25, 1809, BA 40; Diary of José Antonio Cuellar, January 30, 1809, BA 40; M. Salcedo to Bernardo Bonavía, September 12, 1809, BA 42; Pedro López Prieto to M. Salcedo, April 17, 1810, BA 44; Report of Francisco Antonio de Leon, June 25, 1810, BA 45; Padilla, "Texas in 1820," 50–51.

9. M. Salcedo, Report on the number and location of Indian tribes of Texas, 1808, BA 39; Oberste, History of Refugio Mission, 256–75.

10. Diary of events at Nacogdoches, June 1804, BAT II, 3: 5–6; Elguézabal to N. Salcedo, July 18, 1804, BAT II, 3: 49–50; Francisco Amangual to Elguézabal, May 9, 1805, BAT II, 7: 191; Viana to Cordero, November 16, 1805, BAT II, 10: 12–14; N. Salcedo to Cordero, August 14,1806, BAT II, 17: 30; N. Salcedo to Cordero, October 3, 1806, BAT II, 17: 173; N. Salcedo to Cordero, November 6, 1806, BAT II, 18: 90; Cordero to N. Salcedo, March 22, 1807, BAT II, 23: 6–7; N. Salcedo to Cordero, August 25, 1807, BAT II, 28: 139; N. Salcedo to Cordero, October 6, 1807, BAT II, 30: 24; N. Salcedo to Cordero, November 2, 1807, BAT II, 30: 172.

11. Cordero to Mariano Varela, September 11, 1805, BAT II, 8: 340; Cordero to N. Salcedo, November 6, 1805, BAT II, 9: 221; Cordero to N. Salcedo, June 16, 1806, BAT II, 16: 3; Cordero to N. Salcedo, February 10, 1808, BAT II, 33: 73–74; José Manuel Granados to M. Salcedo, February 13, 1808, BAT II, 33: 148.

12. Juan José Santos, Diary of operations, August 13–29, 1808, BAT II, 38: 76–79.

13. M. Salcedo to Bernardo Bonavía, July 9, 1809, BA 42; M. Salcedo to Bonavía, July 11, 1809, BA 42; Santos to M. Salcedo, July 23, 1809, BA 42; Pedro Prieto to M. Salcedo, August 6, 1809, BA 42; M. Salcedo to Bonavía, August 16, 1809, BA 42; José Manuel Granados to Mariano Varela, September 5, 1809, BA 42; Cordero to N. Salcedo, June 16, 1806, BAT II, 16: 4; José de Goseascochea to M. Salcedo, November 20, 1810, BA 47; José Felix Pérez, Diary of an expedition against the Tonkawas and Lipan Apaches, May 16–June 2, 1812, BA 51; Schilz, *Lipan Apaches in Texas*, 36; Padilla, "Texas in 1820," 56.

14. Background on the boundary dispute can be found in Flores, ed., *Jefferson and Southwestern Exploration*, 24–31.

15. Sibley to William Eustis, November 28, 1812, in Garrett, ed., "Doctor John Sibley and the Louisiana-Texas Frontier," SWHQ 49 (January 1946): 418; Benson, ed., "A Governor's Report on Texas in 1809," 614.

16. Sibley, "Historical Sketches," 721–24; Sibley, *Report from Natchitoches in 1807*, 96; M. Salcedo, Report on the number and location of Indian tribes of Texas, 1808, BA 39; Smith, *Caddo Indians*, 83–86.

17. Sibley to Claiborne, October 10, 1803, TP 9: 75–76; Daniel Clark to James Madison, September 29, 1803, TP 9: 63.

18. Claiborne to Edward Turner, February 25, 1804, LBC 1: 386; Smith, *Caddo Indians*, 88–89.

19. Claiborne to Thomas Jefferson, August 30, 1804, LBC 2: 287; Turner to Claiborne, October 13, 1804, LBC 2: 385; Claiborne to Turner, November 3, 1804, LBC 2: 390; Turner to Claiborne, November 21, 1804, TP 9: 336.

20. Ugarte to Elguézabal, November 26, 1803, BA 31; N. Salcedo to Elguézabal, May 22, 1804, BAT II, 2: 425.

21. Elguézabal to N. Salcedo, January 4, 1804, BAT II, 1: 58; Diary of events at Béxar, May 1804, BAT II, 2: 449; Elguézabal to N. Salcedo, July 4, 1804, BAT II, 3: 27; Elguézabal to N. Salcedo, August 15, 1804, BAT II, 3: 170; Diary of events at Béxar, August 1804, BAT II, 3: 213–15.

22. Flores, ed., *Jefferson and Southwestern Exploration*, 32–38; Smith, *Wichita Indians*, 93–94.

23. Smith, *Wichita Indians*, 94; Elguézabal to N. Salcedo, February 1, 1804, BAT II, 1: 102–4.

24. Ugarte to Elguézabal, June 3, 1804, BAT II, 1: 463; Elguézabal to N. Salcedo, September 12, 1804, BAT II, 3: 247–48; N. Salcedo to Elguézabal, October 7, 1804, BAT II, 4: 22; Dionisio Valle to Cordero, October 3, 1805, BAT II, 9: 21–22; Cordero to N. Salcedo, November 24, 1805, BAT II, 10: 41–49.

25. N. Salcedo, to Elguézabal, April 22, 1805, BAT II, 7: 38; Valle to Elguézabal, May 4, 1805, BAT II, 7: 61; Turner to Claiborne, November 21, 1804, TP 9: 335–37.

26. Dearborn to Sibley, December 13, 1804, TP 9: 352–53; Diary of events at Nacogdoches, March 1805, BAT II, 7: 4–7.

27. Sibley, "Historical Sketches," 721–22.

28. Smith, *Caddo Indians*, 91–92; Valle to Elguézabal, June 11, 1805, BAT II, 7: 161–62; Valle to Elguézabal, October 3, 1805, BAT II, 9: 21–22.

29. Diary of event at Nacogdoches, June 1805, BAT II, 8: 10; Valle to Elguézabal, August 10, 1805, BAT II, 8: 239.

30. Cordero to N. Salcedo, November 24, 1805, BAT II, 10: 41–49.

31. Cordero to N. Salcedo, December 27, 1805, BAT II, 10: 187–18; Cordero to N. Salcedo, May 4, 1806, BAT II, 15: 5–7.

32. Cordero to N. Salcedo, October 5, 1805, BAT II, 9: 28–30; Cordero to N. Salcedo, December 27, 1806, BAT II, 10: 180; Mariano Rodríguez to Cordero, January 13, 1806, BAT II, 11: 115–17; Cordero to N. Salcedo, January 24, 1806, BAT II, 11: 174; Cordero to N. Salcedo, March 12, 1806, BAT II, 11: 200.

33. Although the principal chief took the governor's name, Cordero, as his own, I will continue to refer to him as Sargento so as to avoid confusion. N. Salcedo to Cordero, May 19, 1806, BAT II, 15: 70–71; N. Salcedo to Cordero, June 3, 1806, BAT II, 15: 130–31.

34. Cordero to N. Salcedo, June 16, 1806, BAT II, 16: 1–2.

35. Quoted in Flores, ed., *Jefferson and Southwestern Exploration*, 55.

36. N. Salcedo to Cordero, October 8, 1805, BAT II, 9: 47–48.

37. Sebastian Rodríguez to Cordero, February 13, 1806, BAT II, 11: 70–71; Smith, *Caddo Indians*, 93.

38. Guadiana to Viana, May 31, 1806, BAT II, 15: 107; Juan Ygnacio Ramón to Viana, June 2, 1806, BAT II, 15: 130.Viana to Cordero, June 3, 1806, BAT II, 15: 137–38; Guadiana to Viana, June 5, 1806, BAT II, 15: 162; Guadiana to Viana, June 20, 1806, BAT II, 16: 32.

39. Viana to Cordero, June 3, 1806, BAT II, 15: 137–39; Viana to Cordero, June 6, 1806, BAT II, 15: 152; Ramón to Viana, June 20, 1806, BAT II, 16: 33–34; Flores, ed., *Jefferson and Southwestern Exploration*, 145–46.

40. Flores, ed., *Jefferson and Southwestern Exploration*, 145–67.

41. Flores, ed., *Jefferson and Southwestern Exploration*, 160–67.

42. Flores, ed., *Jefferson and Southwestern Exploration*, 166–74.

43. Flores, ed., *Jefferson and Southwestern Exploration*, 173; Smith, *Caddo Indians*, 95.

44. Flores, ed., *Jefferson and Southwestern Exploration*, 193–207.

45. Claiborne to Herrera, August 26, 1806, LBC 3: 384; Herrera to Claiborne, August 28, 1806, LBC 3: 392.

46. The limits of the Neutral Ground were never officially described beyond a general statement that the Arroyo Hondo on the east and the Sabine River on the west were to serve as boundaries. Haggard, "Neutral Ground Agreement between Louisiana and Texas," 1001–28.

47. Address to the Caddo Chief, September 5, 1806, LBC 4: 3–5.

48. Sibley, *Report from Natchitoches in 1807*, 20–24; Sibley to Dearborn, July 3, 1807, in Garrett, ed., "Doctor John Sibley and the Louisiana-Texas Frontier," SWHQ 45 (January 1942): 381.

49. Sibley, *Report from Natchitoches in 1807*, 40–42; Sibley to Dearborn, July 3, 1807, in Garrett, ed., "Doctor John Sibley and the Louisiana-Texas Frontier," SWHQ 45 (April 1942): 49–51; Cordero to N. Salcedo, July 30, 1808, BAT II, 37: 139–40.

50. Cordero to N. Salcedo, February 4, 1807, BAT II, 22: 10–11; Cordero to N. Salcedo, March 31, 1807, BAT II, 23: 41–44; N. Salcedo to Cordero, August 25, 1807, BAT II, 28: 138; Cordero to Viana, November 3, 1807, BAT II, 30: 175.

51. Sibley, *Report from Natchitoches in 1807*, 40–45; Sibley to Dearborn, July 3, 1807, in Garrett, ed., "Doctor John Sibley and the Louisiana-Texas Frontier," SWHQ 45 (April 1942): 381–82.

52. Sibley, *Report from Natchitoches in 1807*, 49–50, 53–55.

53. Sibley, *Report from Natchitoches in 1807*, 56–66.

54. Record of goods supplied by Barr and Davenport, November 11, 1807, BAT II, 30: 201–5; List of Indian Presents, January 11, 1808, BAT II, 32: 142–44; M. Salcedo to Guadiana, August 19, 1809, BA 42; Barr and Davenport to Guadiana, September 2, 1809, BA 42.

55. Barr and Davenport to Guadiana, September 2, 1809, BA 69–76.

56. List of goods distributed to Indians at Nacogdoches, October 19, 1807, BAT II, 30: 80–82; Viana to Cordero, December 16, 1807, BAT II, 31: 136; Cordero to N. Salcedo, February 1, 1808, BAT II, 33: 43–44; Cordero to Marcel Soto, March 15, 1808, BAT II, 25: 148–51; Juan Ignacio de Arrambide to Cordero, March 19, 1808, BAT II, 34: 195–96; Barr to Cordero, April 28, 1808, BAT II, 35: 275; Juan José Zepeda to Cordero, May 4, 1808, BAT II, 36: 26; Cordero to N. Salcedo, July 11, 1808, BAT II, 37: 30; Cordero to N. Salcedo, July 27, 1808, BAT II, 37: 127–28; Barr and Davenport to Guadiana, September 2, 1809, BA 42.

57. Cordero to N. Salcedo, April 20, 1808, BAT II, 35: 245; Commission of Quicheata as Taovaya Captain, July 5, 1808, BAT II, 37: 16; N. Salcedo to Cordero, August 26, 1808, BAT II, 38: 66; Flores, ed., *Journal of an Indian Trader*, 50–53, 64–65.

58. Diary of Francisco Amangual from San Antonio to Santa Fe, March 30–May 19, 1808, in Loomis and Nasatir, *Pedro Vial and the Roads to Santa Fe*, 466–74; Cordero to N. Salcedo, July 30, 1808, BAT II, 37: 139–41.

59. Sibley to Dearborn, November 20, 1808, in Garrett, ed., "Doctor John Sibley and

the Louisiana-Texas Frontier," SWHQ 47 (July 1943): 49–51; Flores, ed., *Journal of an Indian Trader*, 26–30.

60. Flores, ed., *Journal of an Indian Trader*, 46–52.

61. Flores, ed., *Journal of an Indian Trader*, 52–81; Sibley to William Eustis, May 10, 1809, in Garrett, ed., "Doctor John Sibley and the Louisiana-Texas Frontier," SWHQ 47 (January 1944): 321–23.

62. It turned out that the metal did not contain any silver at all and was not discovered to be a meteorite until a few years later. It was eventually shipped east, and today it is at the Peabody Museum of Natural History at Yale University. Flores, ed., *Journal of an Indian Trader*, 80–81, 88–89; Sibley to Eustis, May 10, 1809, in Garrett, ed., "Doctor John Sibley and the Louisiana-Texas Frontier," SWHQ 47 (January 1944): 321–23.

63. Diary of Captain José de Goseascochea, October 5–November 21, 1809, BA 43.

64. Diary of Luciano García, May 20–July 2, 1810, BA 45.

65. José Ramon Diaz de Bustamante to Felix Calleja, April 1, 1810, PI 201; Vicente Lozano, Diary of expedetion against Indians, May 20, 1810, PI 201; Herrera to Calleja, May 30, 1810, PI 201; Bustamante, Diary of expedition against the Comanches, May 17–June 7, 1810, PI 201; Affadavit of José Mannrique, June 16, 1810, BA 45; Arrambide, interrogation of Comanche Indian prisoner, August 2, 1810, BA 46; Arrambide to Bonavía, October 19, 1810, BA 46; Herrera to Bonavía, October 19, 1810, BA 46; M. Salcedo, interrogation of Comanche Indian prisoner, 1810, BA 47.

66. Conference with Comanche chief Cordero, July 31, 1810, BA 46; Bonavía to Cordero, August 1, 1810, BA 46; Bonavía to N. Salcedo, August 15, 1810, BA 46; Testimony of Chief Cordero, October 25, 1810, BA 47; John, "Nurturing the Peace," 360–61; Kavanagh, *Comanche Political History*, 156–57.

4. Transformation

1. Chipman, *Spanish Texas*, 232–34; Herrera to N. Salcedo, August 7, 1811, BA 48; Herrera to Arrambide, August 16, 1811, BA 48; Herrera to N. Salcedo, August 29, 1811, BA 48; N. Salcedo to Herrera, September 17, 1811, BA 48; N. Salcedo to M. Salcedo, April 27, 1812, BA 51; John, "Nurturing the Peace," 362–63; Kavanagh, *Comanche Political History*, 156–57.

2. Cristobal Domínguez to M. Salcedo, April 29, 1812, BA 51; John, "Nurturing the Peace," 363–64; Kavanagh, *Comanche Political History*, 157–58.

3. Sibley to Eustis, December 31, 1811, in Garrett, ed., "Doctor John Sibley and the Louisiana-Texas Frontier," SWHQ 49 (January 1946): 403; W. A. Trimble to John C. Calhoun, August 7, 1818, in Morse, ed., *Report to the Secretary of War*, 258–59; Smith, *Wichita Indians*, 106; Herrera to Felipe Arciniega, January 7, 1812, BA 49; M. Salcedo to N. Salcedo, January 8, 1812, BA 50; Felipe de la Garza to M. Salcedo, March 21, 1812, BA 50; José Guadalupe Charles, Diary of an expedition against Indians, April 26–May 1, 1812, BA 51; de la Garza to M. Salcedo, May 10, 1812, BA 51.

4. Chipman, *Spanish Texas*, 234–36; Smith, *Caddo Indians*, 99–100; Schilz, *Lipan Apaches in Texas*, 36–37; Schilz, "People of the Cross Timbers," 133–35; Smith, *Wichita Indians*, 107.

5. Chipman, *Spanish Texas*, 236–37; Hatcher, ed., "Joaquín de Arredondo's Report on the Battle of the Medina," 226.

6. Sibley to General John Armstrong, October 6, 1813, in Garrett, ed., "Doctor John Sibley and the Louisiana-Texas Frontier," SWHQ 49 (April 1946): 602–3.

7. Linnard to General John Mason, September 13, 1813, NSFFL; Linnard to Mason, October 14, 1813, NSFFL; A Talk from Claiborne . . . to the Chief of the Caddo, October 18, 1813, LBC 6: 276–77.

8. Sibley to Armstrong, August 10, 1814, in Garrett, ed., "Doctor John Sibley and the Louisiana-Texas Frontier," SWHQ 49 (April 1946): 609; Claiborne to Jackson, October 28, 1814, LBC 6: 293–94; Claiborne to James Monroe, December 20, 1814, LBC 6: 238–29; Smith, *Caddo Indians*, 102.

9. Weber, *Mexican Frontier*, 10; Chipman, *Spanish Texas*, 238–40.

10. Antonio Martínez to Viceroy Juan Ruiz Apodaca, May 31, 1817, LAMV, 3; Martínez to Apodaca, June 13, 1817, LAMV, 4; Martínez to Apodaca, January 20, 1821, LAMV, 50; Martínez to Apodaca, 1821, LAMV, 50.

11. Fray Antonio Díaz de Leon to Mateo Ahumada, August 21, 1825, quoted in Oberste, *History of Refugio Mission*, 314; Martin, "Polk County Indians," 5–7; Padilla, "Texas in 1820," 49–50; Berlandier, *Indians of Texas in 1830*, 104–5, 124, 127; M. B. Benard to Edmund P. Gaines, July 21, 1836, WSL; Henry M. Morfit to John Forsyth, August 27, 1836, TRP 8: 334–38; Report of Standing Committee on Indian Affairs, October 12, 1837, TIP 1: 22; Jackson, ed., *Texas by Terán*, 128–32, 253–57.

12. Ignacio Pérez to Martínez, August 20, 1817, BA 59; Martínez to Apodaca, May 8, 1818, LAMV, 16; Martínez to Arredondo, May 31, 1818, LAMG, 136–37; Martínez to Juan Castañeda, July 30, 1818, BA 61; Juan Manuel Zambrano to Martínez, August 23, 1818, BA 61; Chipman, *Spanish Texas*, 238–39.

13. Castañeda to Mariano Varela, June 30, 1816, BA 56; Pérez to Arredondo, July 31, 1816, BA 56; Report of Antonio Aguirre, March 14, 1817, BA 58; Martínez to Arredondo, May 31, 1818, LAMG, 136–37; Arredondo to Martínez, October 28, 1820, BA 65; Arredondo to Martínez, November 18, 1820, BA 65.

14. G. Anderson, *Indian Southwest*, 229; Kavanagh, *Comanche Political History*, 172–75, 475–78; Trimble to Calhoun, August 7, 1818, in Morse, ed., *Report to the Secretary of War*, 259.

15. G. Anderson, *Indian Southwest*, 220–23; Weber, *Spanish Frontier in North America*, 126–27.

16. Smith, *Wichita Indians*, 111–12.

17. G. Anderson, *Indian Southwest*, 195–96; Kavanagh, *Comanche Political History*, 172; Pérez to Arredondo, October 14, 1816, BA 57.

18. John Jamison to Calhoun, March 31, 1817, TP 15: 257; Trimble to Calhoun, August 7, 1818, in Morse, ed., *Report to the Secretary of War*, 259; John Fowler to Thomas McKenney, August 10, 1818, NSFFL; Martínez to Arredondo, May 31, 1818, LAMG, 136–37; Letter of a Citizen of Béxar, March 15, 1821, BA 67.

19. G. Anderson, *Indian Southwest*, 253–54; Benito Armiñan to Arredondo, August 1, 1814, BA 54; Proceedings concerning the investigation of damages by the Co-

manches around Béxar, August 16, 1814, BA 54; Oberste, *History of Refugio Mission*, 275–76; Frederico Falcon to Varela, November 24, 1815, BA 55; Pérez to Arredondo, November 21, 1816, BA 57.

20. Armiñan to Arredondo, July 11, 1814, BA 54; Arredondo to Armiñan, July 21, 1814, BA 54; Varela to Arredondo, October 25, 1815, BA 55.

21. Matias Jiminez to varela, December 4, 1815, BA 56; Varela to Francisco Adam, December 19, 1815, BA 56; Varela to Adam, January 3, 1816, BA 56; Arredondo to Juan José Elguézabal, February 17, 1816, PI 239; Felix de Cevallos to Arredondo, March 6, 1816, PI 239; Leandro Ramón to Arredondo, March 7, 1816, PI 239; Juan Castañeda to varela, June 30, 1816, PI 239; Pérez to Arredondo, July 31, 1816, PI 239; Pérez to Arredondo, September 12, 1816, PI 239; Pérez to Arredondo, January 2, 1817, PI 239; Pérez to Arredondo, January 30, 1817, PI 239; Pérez to Arredondo, February 27, 1817, BA 58; Martínez to Arredondo, July 15, 1817, LAMG, 22–23; Martínez to Arredondo, September 13, 1817, BA 59.

22. Martínez to Apodaca, December 9, 1817, LAMV, 10–11; Martínez to Arredondo, February 28, 1818, LAMG, 105–6; Martínez to Apodaca, March 6, 1818, LAMV, 14; Martínez to Arredondo, March 22, LAMG, 107; Martínez to Pérez, April 12, 1818, BA 60; Martínez to Arredondo, April 25, 1818, LAMG, 121–22; Martínez to Apodaca, April 26, 1818, LAMV, 15.

23. Martínez to Apodaca, June 2, 1818, LAMV, 20; Martínez to Arredondo, June 2, 1818, LAMG, 137; Martínez to Arredondo, October 28, 1818, BA 61.

24. Martínez to Arredondo, July 20, 1819, LAMG, 246; Martínez to Arredondo, October 20, 1819, LAMG, 268; Martínez to José Ramirez, August 24, 1820, BA 65; Ramirez to Martínez, September 17, 1820, BA 65.

25. Berlandier, *Journey to Mexico*, 353; Martínez to Arredondo, May 12, 1819, LAMG, 228–29; Martínez to Apodaca, May 12, 1819, LAMV, 33; Martínez to Arredondo, May 15, 1819, BA 62; Martínez to Arredondo, March 2, 1820, LAMG, 308; José Sandoval to Martínez, June 24, 1820, BA 64; Sandoval to Martínez, August 1, 1820, BA 64.

26. Carlisle, "Lipan Apaches and the Anglo-Texans"; Berlandier, *Journey to Mexico*, 269.

27. Martínez to Apodaca, June 18, 1818, LAMV, 22; Martínez to Arredondo, September 23, 1818, LAMG, 179–80; Rafael Casillas to Martínez, June 28, 1819, BA 62; Martínez to Arredondo, March 7, 1820, LAMG, 310; Martínez to Arredondo, April 1, 1820, LAMG, 313; José Ramirez to Martínez, August 20, 1820, BA 64.

28. Oberste, *History of Refugio Mission*, 275–91; Francisco García to Martínez, March 17, 1821, BA 66; Fray de León to Ahumada, August 21, 1825, quoted in Oberste, *History of Refugio Mission*, 312–18.

29. Wolff, "Karankawa Indians," 21–22; Himmel, *Conquest of the Karankawas and Tonkawas*, 18; Martínez to Apodaca, June 13, 1817, LAMV, 4; José Guadalupe de los Santos to Martínez, May 30, 1821, BA 67; Testimony concerning the murder of Americans near the Refugio Mission by the Karankawa Indians, May 31, 1821, BA 67; García to Martínez, June 2, 1821, BA 67; Gatschet, *Karankawa Indians*, 30.

30. Fowler to McKenney, May 9, 1817, in Magnaghi, ed., "Red River Valley, North of Natchitoches," 291; Jamison to Calhoun, May 10, 1817, TP 15: 302–3; Fowler to

McKenney, July 4, 1818, NSFFL; H. Anderson, "Delaware and Shawnee Indians and the Republic of Texas," 231–60; Gibson, *Kickapoo Indians*; Everett, *Texas Cherokees*, 3–24, 51.

31. Fowler to McKenne, August 10, 1818, NSFFL; Trimble to Calhoun, August 7, 1818, Morse, ed., *Report to the Secretary of War*, 259; Padilla, "Texas in 1820," 47; Jamison to Calhoun, May 10, 1817, TP 15: 302–3; Everett, *Texas Cherokees*, 16; Miller to Calhoun, June 20, 1820, TP 19: 195; David Brewls to Calhoun, April 26, 1821, TP 19: 285; Rollings, *Osage*, 236–85.

32. Sibley to Eustis, July 17, 1811, in Garrett, ed., "Doctor John Sibley and the Louisiana-Texas Frontier," SWHQ 49 (July 1945): 119; Fowler to McKenney, May 19, 1817, in Magnaghi, ed., "Red River Valley, North of Natchitoches," 291; Flores, ed. *Jefferson and Southwestern Exploration*; Trimble to Calhoun, August 7, 1818, in Morse, ed., *Report to the Secretary of War*, 258–59; Jamison to Calhoun, June 16, 1819, TP 19: 76–77; Arkansas Territorial Assembly to Calhoun, October 18, 1823, TP 19: 602–3.

33. Fowler to McKenney, June 14, 1819, TP 19: 73–74; Fowler to Jamison, June 1, 1819, TP 19: 75–76; Grand Jury presentment in Hempstead County, April 20, 1820, TP 19: 196–98; Miller to Calhoun, June 20, 1820, TP 19: 194–96.

34. Fowler to McKenney, April 8, 1817, in Magnaghi, ed., "Red River Valley, North of Natchitoches," 289; Trimble to Calhoun, August 7, 1818, in Morse, ed., *Report to the Secretary of War*, 259; Fowler to Jamison, June 1, 1819, TP 19: 75–76.

35. Jamison to Calhoun, March 31, 1817, TP 15: 257–58; Jamison to Calhoun, May 10, 1817, TP 15: 302–3; Fowler to McKenney, July 4, 1818, NSFFL; Fowler to Jamison, June 1, 1819, TP 19: 75–76; Everett, *Texas Cherokees*, 18.

36. Fowler to McKenney, July 4, 1818, NSFFL; Fowler to McKenney, August 10, 1818, NSFFL; Fowler to McKenney, August 29, 1818, NSFFL; Fowler to McKenney, June 14, 1819, TP 19: 73–74; Fowler to Robert L. Coomb, December 29, 1819, TP 19: 134; Everett, *Texas Cherokees*, 18.

37. Everett, *Texas Cherokees*, 23; José Felix Trespalacios to Gaspar López, November 8, 1822, BA 73; Gaspar Flores to Rafael Gonzalez, October 30, 1824, FC 4; Frost Thorn to Stephen F. Austin, July 22, 1828, AP 2: 74–75; Wharton Rector to William Izard, May 8, 1828, TP 21: 677; Sánchez, "A Trip to Texas," 280, 283; Berlandier, *Indians of Texas in 1830*, 113, 125, 127, 142; Juan N. Almonte to Secretary of Interior and Exterior Relations, June 16, 1834, FC 8; Benard to Gaines, July 21, 1836, WSL; H. Anderson, "Delaware and Shawnee Indians and the Republic of Texas," 233–34.

38. Trudeau to Varela, July 12, 1816, BA 56; Passport for Andres Valentin and Chief Cado, July 20, 1816, BA 56; Soto to Varela, July 23, 1816, BA 56; Pérez to Arredondo, October 14, 1816, BA 56; José Ignacío Flores to Pérez, November 16, 1816, BA 56; Padilla, "Texas in 1820," 47–48; Grand Jury Presentment in Hempstead County, Arkansas, April 1820, TP 19: 197.

39. Fowler to Jamison, April 16, 1819, TP 19: 70–71; Jamison to Calhoun, May 26, 1819, TP 19: 69–70.

40. Francisco Maynes to Martínez, November 10, 1820, BA 65; José Vivero and Francisco del Corral to Martínez, March 28, 1821, BA 67; Martínez to Vivero, April 16, 1821,

BA 67; Accord between Martínez and the captains of the Tawakoni nation, April 23, 1821, PI 251; Martínez to Arredondo, April 30, 1821, PI 251; Arredondo to Martínez, May 9, 1821, PI 251; Deposition of Pierre Rublo, December 11, 1840, HR 1035: 33–34; Deposition of Joseph Valentin, December 15, 1840, HR 1035: 35.

41. McElhannon, "Imperial Mexico and Texas," 122–23.
42. Martínez to Béxar Ayuntamiento, November 22, 1821, BA 69; Martínez to Gaspar López, January 20, 1822, BA 70; Dia Juin to Martínez, January 22, 1822, BA 70; Gran Cado to Martínez, March 4, 1822, BA 70.
43. Richard Fields to Martínez, February 1, 1822, BA 70; José Felix Trespalacios to López, November 8, 1822, BA 73; López to Trespalacios, December 14, 1822, BA 73; Everett, *Texas Cherokees*, 25–35.
44. Francisco Ruiz to Martínez, October 15, 1821, BA 68; López to Martínez, June 7, 1822, BA 71; López to Trespalacios, July 9, 1822, NA; Manuel Herrera to Anastacio Bustamante, August 17, 1822, BA 71; Cuelgas de Castro to Trespalacios, October 29, 1822, BA 73; Schilz, *Lipan Apaches in Texas*, 40.
45. Juan Cortés to Martínez, October 16, 1821, BA 68; Cortés to Martínez, October 23, 1821, BA 68; Manuel Barrera to José Angel Navarro, December 3, 1821, BA 69; Ruiz to Béxar Ayuntamiento, April 2, 1822, BA 71; López to Trespalacios, July 9, 1822, NA; López to Martínez, August 11, 1822, BA 72; Kavanagh, *Comanche Political History*, 194–96.
46. Kavanagh, *Comanche Political History*, 196–97.

5. Destruction

1. Weber, *Mexican Frontier*, 20, 43–50, 53–56; Oberste, *History of Refugio Mission*, 303–9.
2. Weber, *Mexican Frontier*, 19–26.
3. Weber, *Mexican Frontier*, 161–63.
4. Weber, *Mexican Frontier*, 164–77.
5. Martínez to Gaspar Lopez, February 8, 1822, AP 1: 472–74; Sánchez, "A Trip to Texas," 257–58; Berlandier, *Journey to Mexico*, 293, 374; Juan N. Almonte, "Statistical Report on Texas," Castañeda, ed., SWHQ 28 (January 1925): 186; Weber, *Mexican Frontier*, 108.
6. Ruíz to Luciano García, August 10, 1823, BA 75; Rafael González to Juan de Castañeda, March 3, 1824, BA 76; Lucas Alamán to José María Zambrano, June 1, 1824, BA 77; Alamán to José Antonio Saucedo, September 3, 1824, BA 77; Flores to Castañeda, October 14, 1824, BA 78; Antonio Elosúa to Saltillo commandant, February 16, 1825, BA 78; Rafael González to Castañeda, March 1, 1825, BA 79; Elosua to La Bahía, San Fernando, and Rio Grande commandants, March 15, 1825, BA 79; Elosúa to Monclova Paymaster, April 10, 1825, BA 80; Kavanagh, *Comanche Political History*, 198.
7. Mateo Ahumada to Juan José Llanos, June 1, 1824, BA 77; Ahumada to Nicasio Sánchez, August 17, 1825, BA 83; Ahumada to José Bernardo Gutierrez de Lara,

August 17, 1825, BA 83; Ahumada to Elosúa, August 21, 1825, BA 83; Weber, *Mexican Frontier*, 89; Kavanagh, *Comanche Political History*, 199.

8. Gaspar Lopez to Trespalacios, February 7, 1823, BA 74; Castañeda to Rafael González, June 24, 1824, BA 77; Rafael González to Elosúa, December 1, 1824, BA 78; Casamiro León to Elosúa, September 10, 1825, BA 84; León to Elosúa, September 16, 1825, BA 84; Cayetano Andrade to Elosúa, October 12, 1825, BA 84; Deposition of José Ibarra, November 16, 1825, BA 85; Andrade to Elosúa, December 16, 1825, BA 85; Elosúa to Ahumada, December 16, 1825, BA 85; Francisco Rojo to Ahumada, May 24, 1826, BA 93; Elosúa to Bustamante, October 4, 1827, BA 108; Sánchez, "A Trip to Texas," 250.

9. Weber, *Mexican Frontier*, 164–65; Barker, ed., "Descriptions of Texas by Stephen F. Austin, 1828," 102; Jackson, ed., *Texas by Terán*, 213–14; Berlandier, *Journey to Mexico*, 383.

10. Fray Díaz de León to Ahumada, August 21, 1825, quoted in Obereste, *History of Refugio Mission*, 312–18; Berlandier, *Indians of Texas in 1830*, 114, 123, 146–49; Padilla, "Texas in 1820," 51, 56; Smith, *Wichita Indians*, 111–12.

11. Jackson, ed., *Texas by Terán*, 56; Himmel, *Conquest of the Karankawas and the Tonkawas*, 40–42; Almonte, "Statistical Report on Texas," 201.

12. Cantrell, *Stephen F. Austin*, 141–42.

13. Cantrell, *Stephen F. Austin*, 96–97; Barker, ed. "Journal of Stephen F. Austin on His First Trip to Texas, 1821," 304–5; Himmel, *Conquest of the Karankawas and the Tonkawas*, 46–47.

14. John Tumlinson to José Felix Trespalacios, January 7, 1823, BA 73; Statement of Mirabeau Buonaparte Lamar, undated, LP 4: 255–57; Himmel, *Conquest of the Karankawas and the Tonkawas*, 47.

15. Tumlinson to Trespalacios, February 26, 1823, BA 74; Burnam, "Reminiscences of Captain Jesse Burnam," 15–16; Himmel, *Conquest of the Karankawas and the Tonkawas*, 47–48.

16. Austin, "Journal," 297; Martínez to Lopez, February 8, 1822, AP 1: 472–74; Salvador Carrasco to Agustin Iturbide, May 25, 1822, BA 71; Kuykendall, "Recollections of Early Texans," 30–32; Himmel, *Conquest of the Karankawas and the Tonkawas*, 55; Schilz, "People of the Cross Timbers," 139–40.

17. Austin to Luciano García, August 28, 1823, AP 1: 688–89; Austin to Garcia, October 20, 1823, AP 1: 701–2; Kuykendall, "Reminiscences of Early Texas," 31–32.

18. James Cummins to Austin, May 3, 1824, AP 1: 783; Austin to Amos Rawls, June 22, 1824, AP 1: 840; Austin to Ahumada, March 27, 1826, AP 1: 1280–83; Affadavits concerning Indian hostilities, relative to an attack on the Tonkawas, April 23, 1826, AP 1: 1319–21; Austin to Saucedo, May 19, 1826, AP 1: 1341–44; Cantrell, *Stephen F. Austin*, 140.

19. J. Child to Austin, February 1, 1824, AP 1: 735–36; Austin to Alcalde, May 24, 1824, AP 1: 800; Moses Morrison to Robert Kuykendall, August 3, 1823, 676; Austin to Luciano García, October 20, 1823, AP 1: 701–2; Austin to Guerra, November 1823, AP 1: 711; Austin, Militia Organization, December 5, 1823, AP 1: 715.

20. Statement of William Pettus, undated, LP 4: 245–48; Austin to Military Commandant of Texas, April 20, 1824 AP 1: 768; Austin to Alcalde of San Felipe, May 25, 1824, AP 1: 803; Kimmel, *Conquest of the Karankawas and the Tonkawas*, 49–50; Obereste, *History of Refugio Mission*, 309.

21. Amos Rawls to Austin, June 13, 1824, AP 1: 830–31; Austin to Rawls, June 14, 1824, AP 1: 831–32; James Cummins to Austin, August 25, 1824, AP 1: 879; Austin to Baron de Bastrop, August 26, 1824, AP 1: 883; Austin, Diary of a Campaign against the Karankawas, August 30–September 7, 1824, AP 1: 885–87; José Gerónimo Huizar to José Antonio Saucedo, October 1, 1824, AP 1: 910; Flores to Austin, October 6, 1824, BA 78; Austin to Authorities of La Bahía, November 1, 1824, AP 1: 930–31.

22. De León to Ahumada, August 21, 1825, quoted in Obereste, *History of Refugio Mission*, 312–18; Austin to Ahumada, September 10, 1825, AP 1: 1198; Austin to Ahumada, March 27, 1826, AP 1: 1280–83; Statement of William Pettus, undated, LP 4: 246; Wilbarger, *Indian Depredations in Texas*, 210; Gannett, "American Invasion of Texas," 102–4; Himmel, *Conquest of the Karankawas and the Tonkawas*, 50–51.

23. Rafael Antonio Manchola to Ahumada, October 10, 1826, BA 97; Green DeWitt to Austin, April 3, 1827, AP 1: 1624–25; Treaty with Karankawa Indians, May 13, 1827, AP 1: 1639–41; Anastasio Bustamante to Austin, May 14, 1827, AP 1: 1641–42; Gannett, "American Invasion of Texas," 104–6; Himmel, *Conquest of the Karankawas and the Tonkawas*, 51.

24. Austin to J. M. Guerra, July 18, 1823, AP 1: 674–75; Austin to Josiah H. Bell, August 6, 1823, AP 1: 681–83; J. Child to Austin, February 1, 1824, AP 1: 735–36.

25. James Cummins to Austin, March 23, 1824, AP 1: 755; Austin to Waco Indians: A Talk, June, 1824, AP 1: 844–45; Thomas Duke to Austin, June, 1824, AP 1: 842–43; Austin to the Alcalde of San Felipe de Austin, May 25, 1824, AP 1: 803.

26. Austin to Ahumada, September 8, 1825, AP 1: 1196–97; Austin, Referendum on Indian Relations, September 28, 1825, AP 1: 1208–11; Austin to Ahumada, March 27, 1826, AP 1: 1280–83; Austin to Ahumada, April 6, 1826, AP 1: 1304–5; Schilz, *Lipan Apaches in Texas*, 42; Austin to James Ross and Aylett C. Buckner, May 13, 1826, AP 1: 1332–33; Austiin to Ahumada, May 18, 1826, AP 1: 1338–40; DeShields, *Border Wars of Texas*, 21–22; Austin to Saucedo, July 17, 1826, AP 1: 1374; James Kerr to Austin, July 18, 1826, AP 1: 1377–78; Alexandre Curcier to Austin, September 5, 1826, AP 1: 1449–50; Kerr to Austin, February 26, 1827, AP 1: 1607.

27. M. Henderson, "Minor Empresario Contracts for the Colonization of Texas, SWHQ 31 (April 1928): 16; Sánchez, "A Trip to Texas," 283.

28. Sánchez, "A Trip to Texas," 276, 280, 283; Berlandier, *Indians of Texas in 1830*, 104–5, 113, 124–25, 127, 142, 253–57; Almonte to Secretary of Interior and Exterior Relations, June 16, 1834, FC 8; Benard to Gaines, July 21, 1836, WSL; H. Anderson, "Delaware and Shawnee Indians and the Republic of Texas," 233–34. Smith, *Caddo Indians*, 106; Padilla, "Texas in 1820," 49–50; Benard to Gaines, July 21, 1836, WSL; Morfit to Forsyth, August 27, 1836, TRP 8: 334–38; Report of Standing Committee on Indian Affairs, October 12, 1837, TIP 1: 22.

29. J. Norten to Alcalde of San Antonio, October 25, 1824, FC; Gaspar Flores to Rafael

González, October 30, 1824, FC; Rafael González to Padilla, December 24, 1824, FC; Approval of Shawnee Petition, April 15,1 825, FC; H. Anderson, "Delaware and Shawnee Indians and the Republic of Texas," 233–34; Everett, *Texas Cherokees*, 39–40.

30. Austin to Saucedo, September 8, 1825, AP 1: 1194–95; Saucedo to Samuel Norris, February 2, 1826, NA; Everett, *Texas Cherokees*, 32–37.

31. Fields to Saucedo, March 20, 1826, NA; Austin to Cherokees, April 24, 1826, AP 1: 1307–8; Austin to Ahumada, April 30, 1826, AP 1: 1317–18; Austin to Ahumada, May 18, 1826, AP 1: 1338–40; Everett, *Texas Cherokees*, 40–42.

32. McDonald, "Fredonian Rebellion," 1163–64; Everett, *Texas Cherokees*, 42–45; Patricio de Torres to Ahumada, December 29, 1826, BA 99; Fredonian Declaration, December 21, 1826, NA.

33. Peter Bean to Austin, December 31, 1826, AP 1: 1553; Saucedo to Fields, January 4, 1827, AP 1: 1563–64; Austin to Cherokee Chiefs, January 24, 1827, AP 1: 1592–94; Austin to Sam M. Williams, March 4, 1827, AP 1: 1610–11; Everett, *Texas Cherokees*, 45–47; Cantrell, *Stephen F. Austin*, 183–88.

34. Ruiz to Austin, May 28, 1827, AP 1: 1647; Ruiz to Austin, June 2, 1827, AP 1: 1653; Bean to Austin, June 3, 1827, AP 1: 1656; Bustamante to Austin, June 19, 1827, AP 1: 1660; Sánchez, "A Trip to Texas," 287.

35. Antonio Elosúa to Bustamante, July 23, 1827, BA 105; Bustamante to Elosúa, July 27, 1827, BA 105; Bustamante to Elosúa, September 12, 1827, BA 107; Austin to Ramón Músquiz, February 12, 1828, AP 2: 15–16; José Ventura Ramón to Elosúa, October 1828, BA 117; León to Elosúa, October 23, 1828, BA 117; Juan José Galán, Diary of Peace Talks with Comanches, July 18, 1829, BA 124; Elosúa to Nicolas Flores, March 6, 1830, BA 128; Terán to Elosúa, April 11, 1830, BA 129; Guonique, Passport to visit Mexico City, April 3, 1830, BA 130; Kavanagh, *Comanche Political History,* 200.

36. Weber, *Mexican Frontier*, 167–74 Jackson, ed., *Texas by Terán*, 1–5; Almonte, "Statistical Report of Texas," 186, 198, 206.

37. Weber, *Mexican Frontier*, 4, 166; Jackson, ed., *Texas by Terán*, 208, 235, 241; Almonte, "Statistical Report of Texas," 186, 198, 206; Smith, *Caddo Indians*, 125–26; Sjoberg, "Bidai Indians of Southeastern Texas," 40–41.

38. Jackson, ed., *Texas by Terán*, 91–93, 128; Petition of Miller County Citizens, March 20, 1828, TP 21: 629; Wharton Rector to Governor Izard, May 8, 1828, TP 21: 677; Russell B. Hyde to Arbuckle, May 6, 1828, TP 21: 786; Hyde to Adjutant General, November 17, 1828, TP 21: 784–85; Certificate of Jesse Shelton, November 1828, TP 21: 788; Benard to Gaines, July 19, 1836, WSL.

39. José Francisco to José María Letona, June 25, 1831, FC 4; Letona to Músquiz, June 25, 1831, FC 4; Mier Concession of Lands to Coushattas and Alabamas, July 14, 1831, FC 4; Letona to Músquiz, July 19, 1831, FC 4; Letona to Músquiz, September 1, 1831, TIP 1: 2.

40. Weber, *Mexican Frontier*, 172; Everett, *Texas Cherokees*, 62–65.

41. Cherokee Petition, July 16, 1833, SA; Everett, *Texas Cherokees*, 65–66.

42. Austin to Músquiz, February 12, 1828, AP 2: 15–16; José Guadalupe Ruiz to Elosúa, June 2, 1828, BA 114; Sánchez, "A Trip to Texas," 286–88.

43. DeShields, *Border Wars of Texas*, 33–41; Berlandier, *Journey to Mexico*, 386–89; Wilbarger, *Indian Depredations in Texas*, 174–77; Martin Allen to Austin, July 5, 1829, AP 2: 225–26; DeShields, *Border Wars of Texas*, 34–41; Schilz, *Lipan Apaches in Texas*, 43.

44. Bean to Elosúa, June 22, 1830, BA 131; Elosúa to Ruiz, August 16, 1830, BA 133; Elosúa to Nicasio Sánchez, August 17, 1830, BA 133; Sánchez to Elosúa, September 19, 1830, BA 133; Sánchez to Elosúa, September 22, 1830, BA 133; Diary of Sánchez, August 17–September 22, 1830, BA 133; Diary of Gaspar Flores, August 17–September 22, 1830, BA 133; DeShields, *Border Wars of Texas*, 34–37; Wilbarger, *Indian Depredations in Texas*, 177–79.

45. Ruiz to Elosúa, June 10, 1832, BA 150; Smith, *Wichita Indians*, 128, 136.

46. José de los Piedras to Elosúa, September 28, 1830, BA 134; Francisco de Porras to Elosúa, October 4, 1830, BA 135; Manuel de Porras, December 25, 1830, BA 137; Músquiz to Agustín Viesca, January 3, 1831, BA 137; Austin to Manuel Carrillo, January 24, 1831, AP 2: 590; Elosúa to Lafuente, October 15, 1831, BA 145; Lafuente to Elosúa, November 24, 1831, BA 146; Lafuente, Diary of expedition against the Tahuacano Indians, November 30, 1831, BA 146.

47. Elosúa to Terán, January 8, 1831, BA 137; Ruiz to Elosúa, June 1, 1831, BA 141; Ruiz to Elosúa, June 11, 1831, BA 141; José María Moreno to Elosua, July 27, 1831, BA 143; Mariana Cosio to Elosúa, August 16, 1831, BA 143; Elosúa to Cosio, August 18, 1831, BA 143; Elosúa to Ruiz, September 1, 1831, BA 143; Elosúa to Ruiz, October 13, 1831, BA 145; Músquiz to José María Letona, October 23, 1831, BA 145; Elosúa to Terán, December 3, 1831, BA 146; José Mariano Guerra to Elosúa, December 11, 1831, BA 146; Kavanagh, *Comanche Political History*, 231–32; Schilz and Schilz, *Buffalo Hump*, 13.

48. Ruiz to Elosúa, February 4, 1832, BA 147; Elosúa to Terán, February 18, 1832, BA 148.

49. Manuel Barragán to Elosúa, February 27, 1832, BA 148; Juan José Hernández to Músquiz, June 1, 1832, BA 150; Manuel de Dios, Diary, September 2, 1832, BA 152; Saenz, Diary, September 7, 1832, BA 153; Elosúa to Commandant of Matamoros, September 10, 1832, BA 153; Barragán to Elosúa, November 1, 1832, BA 153; Berlandier, *Journey to Mexico*, 561; Elosúa to Filisola, April 23, 1833, BA 156; Kavanagh, *Comanche Political History*, 233; Schilz, *Lipan Apaches in Texas*, 44.

50. Juan José Elguézabal to Elosúa, April 4, 1833, BA 155; Antonio Treviño to Cosio, November 5, 1833, BA 159; Treviño to Filisola, December 29, 1833, BA 159; Juan Nepumenco Seguín to Músquiz, April 6, 1834, BA 161; Placido to Benavides, August 22, 1834, BA 164; Domingo Ugartachea to Juan González, February 8, 1835, BA 164; Ugartachea to Commandant of Agua Verde, May 11, 1835, BA 165; Ugartachea to Martín Perfecto de Cos, August 8, 1835, TRP 1: 321; Kavanagh, *Comanche Political History*, 233–34.

51. Elosua to Músquiz, April 23, 1830, BA 127; Mariano Cosio to Elosua, February

26, 1830, BA 128; Martin de Leon to Músquiz, December 10, 1830, BA 136; Cosio to Elosua, December 22, 1830, BA 137; Cosio to Elosua, March 11, 1831, BA 139; Tiburcio de la Garza to Rafael Manchola, September 30, 1831, BA 144; Cosio to Elosua, October 7, 1831, BA 145; Músquiz to Manchola, October 12, 1831, BA 145; de la Garza to Manchola, November 9, 1831, BA 145; Elosua to Mier Y Teran, November 17, 1831, BA 146.

52. Aldrete to Arciniega, December 6, 1833, BA 159; Teal, "Reminiscences of Mrs. Annie Fagan Teal," 317–28; Holley, Texas, 160; Wilbarger, Indian Depredations, 214; Himmel, Conquest of the Karankawas and the Tonkawas, 53–54.

53. Músquiz to de Leon, February 27, 1833, BA 155; Aldrete to de la Garza, July 15, 1833, BA 157; Minutes of Goliad ayuntamiento, July 16, 1833, BA 157; Elosua to Cosio, September 12, 1833, BA 158; Cosio, Diary of Campaign against Karankawas, November 26, 1833, BA 159; Benavides to Músquiz, May 28, 1834, BA 161; Almonte, "Statistical Report," 194.

54. Sánchez, "A Trip to Texas," 269; Jackson, ed., Texas by Téran, 51; Berlandier, Journey to Mexico, 313; DeWitt to Músquiz, April 23, 1829, BA 122; Statement of Rabb, undated, LP 4: 215–16; Statement of William Pettus, undated, LP 4: 248–49; Report of Standing Committee on Indian Affairs, October 12, 1837, TIP 1: 24.

55. Smith, Wichita Indians, 127.

56. United States Census of 1830, Microfilm Copy, University of North Texas Library; George Gray to William L. Brent, December 15, 1823, TP 19: 578–79; Statement showing the names and numbers of different tribes . . . January 10, 1825, ASP, Indian Affairs, 2: 545–47.

57. Gray to Calhoun, February 28, 1824, TP 19: 703–4; Gray to McKenney, October 1, 1824, TP 19: 739–40; Gray to the secretary of war, May 26, 1825, TP 20: 52–53.

58. Hunter, "Their Final Years," 22; Gray to the secretary of war, May 26, 1825, TP 20: 52–53; McKenney to Gray, July 9, 1825, TP 20: 90–92; Gray to McKenney, September 30, 1825, TP 20: 117; Gray to the secretary of war, October 1, 1825, ASP, Indian Affairs, 706; McKenney to Gray, November 16, 1825, ASP, 152–53.

59. Hunter, "Their Final Years," 22, 29–31; Jehiel Brooks to John Eaton, August 16, 1830, TP 21: 256–58.

60. Thomas Dillard to the secretary of war, August 12, 1828, TP 21: 728–29.

61. Brooks to Bean, July 7, 1830, TP 21: 258–59; Brooks to the secretary of war, August 16, 1830, TP 21: 256; Smith, Caddo Indians, 119.

62. Brooks to John Eaton, September 17, 1830, CAL; Brooks to Eaton, January 14, 1831, CAL; Brooks to Eaton, February 16, 1831, CAL.

63. Brooks to Judge E. Herring, April 9, 1833, CAL; Brooks to Herring, March 20, 1834, HR 1035: 113.

64. Filisola to Treviño, September 24, 1833, BA 158; Treviño to Filisola, October 28, 1833, BA 158; Flores, "Red River Branch of the Alabama-Coushatta Indians," 71–72.

65. Brooks to Herring, April 4, 1833, CAL; Brooks to Henry Leavenworth, April 6, 1833, CAL; Brooks to Herring, June 8, 1833, CAL.

66. Brook to Herring, March 20, 1834, HR 1035: 113; Memorial of the chiefs and head men of the Caddo to the President, undated, HR 1035: 99–100.

67. Journal of the proceedings at the agency-house, Caddo Nation, HR 1035: 116.

68. The Caddo Indian Treaty, HR 1035: 74–77; Smith, Caddo Indians, 122.

69. Soon after Brooks's actions were made public, both Henry Shreve and Kadohadacho members sent memorials to the president informing him of the chicanery within the Caddo Treaty. Nonetheless, the House Committee on Indian Affairs did not investigate the matter until 1841. The committee then recommended that the question of fraud should be decided in court. In 1850, the United States Supreme Court confirmed Brooks's title to the land he had acquired from the Grappes on strictly legal grounds. Whether illegal or not, Brooks' actions concerning the Caddo Treaty demonstrated a total disregard for the best interests of the Kadohadachos. Testimony of Jacques Grappe, HR 1035: 65–67; Smith, Caddo Indians, 123.

6. Defeat

1. Weber, Mexican Frontier, 243–51.

2. Philip Dimmitt to Austin, October 27, 1835, AP 2: 213–14; James Kerr to Committee of Safety and Correspondence, October 28, 1835, TRP 2: 249–50; Himmel, Conquest of the Karankawas and Tonkawas, 77–82, 100–105.

3. Mosely Baker and F. W. Johnson to the Chairman of the General Council of Texas, October 23, 1835, TRP 2: 199–201.

4. Everett, Texas Cherokees, 70–73; Appointment of Sam Houston, John Forbes, and John Cameron as Indian Commissioners, December 22, 1835, TIP 1: 10; Treaty between Texas and the Cherokee Indians, February 23, 1836, TIP 1: 14–17.

5. Santa Ana to José María Tornel, February 16, 1836, TRP 4: 361; Deposition of Miguel Cortinez, April 12, 1836, TRP 4: 5: 446–47; Deposition of C. H. Sims, April 11, 1836, TRP 4: 429; Everett, Texas Cherokees, 76–77.

6. Lt. J. Bonnell to Edmund P. Gaines, April 20, 1836, TRP 5: 506–8; Larkin Edwards to Gaines, May 13, 1836, TRP 6: 254; Bonnell to Gaines, June 4, 1836, TRP 7: 9–10; Bonnell Deposition, June 14, 1836, TRP 148.

7. Smither, "Alabama Indians of Texas," 92; Martin, "Alabama-Coushatta Indians," 79.

8. John T. Mason to Major Nelson, March 20, 1836, TRP 5: 149; Edmund P. Gaines to the governors of Louisiana, Mississippi, Alabama, and Tennessee, April 8, 1836, TRP 5: 375–76; Deposition of C. H. Sims, April 11, 1836, TRP 5: 429; Robert A. Irion to Mason, April 12, 1836, TRP 5: 448; Bonnell to Gaines, June 4, 1836, TRP 5: 7: 9–10.

9. Gaines to Lewis Cass, June 7, 1836, TRP 7: 50–51; Depositions of James Dunn and Montgomery Shackleford, June 15, 1836, TRP 155–56; Smith, The Caddo Indians, 130.

10. M. B. Menard to Sam Houston, August 9, 1836, TRP 8: 177–79; Menard Narrative, August 9, 1836, TRP 8: 179–81; Deposition of Juan Francisco Basques, September 7, 1836, TRP 8: 409–10; Everett, Texas Cherokees, 80–82.

11. Houston to Gaines, August 29, 1836, TRP 8: 346; Houston to the Citizens of Texas,

August 29, 1836, TRP 8: 345–46; Everett, *Texas Cherokees*, 82–83; Smith, *Caddo Indians*, 130–31.

12. Major B. Riley to Gaines, August 24, 1836, TRP 8: 308–9; Smith, *Caddo Indians*, 131–32.

13. Caddo Chiefs to the secretary of war, January 9, 1837, CAL; Colonel James B. Many to Joel Poinsett, April 19, 1839, CAL; Deposition of Charles Sewall, December 15, 1840, HR 1035: 35–36; Deposition of Larkin Edwards, December 16, 1840, HR 1035: 36; Smith, *Caddo Indians*, 132–33.

14. Hogan, ed., "State Census of 1847," 117–18.

15. Haley, *Sam Houston*, 64–97; Houston's Inaugural Address, October 22, 1836, WSH 1: 449.

16. Webb, *Texas Rangers*, 29–30; Muckleroy, "Indian Policy of the Republic of Texas," SWHQ 26 (July 1922): 11–12.

17. Houston to the Chiefs of Six Tribes, November 11, 1836, WSH 1: 479–80; Appointment of commissioners to make Indian treaties, November 12, 1836, WSH 480; Houston to Nathaniel Robbins, December 6, 1836, WSH 495; Everett, *Texas Cherokees*, 84–85; Smith, *Wichita Indians*, 140; Kavanagh, *Comanche Political History*, 252.

18. Report of Standing Committee on Indian Affairs, October 12, 1837, TIP 1: 27; Smith, *Caddo Indians*, 134; Treaty between Texas and the Tonkawa Indians, November 22, 1837, TIP 1: 28–29; Treaty between Texas and the Lipan Indians, January 8, 1838, TIP 1: 30–32; Treaty between Texas and the Tonkawa Indians, April 10, 1838, TIP 1: 46–48. Actually, the terms of the Hainai and Nadaco treaty have been lost, but it certainly contained the same provisions as all of the other treaties negotiated by the Republic of Texas at this time.

19. Paul Ligueste Chouteau to William Armstrong, March 1, 1837, WSL; Auguste Chouteau to C. A. Harris, December 8, 1837, WSL; Smith, *Wichita Indians*, 135–40.

20. Deposition of Edwards, December 16, 1840, HR 1035: 36–37; Smith, *Caddo Indians*, 134–36.

21. *Telegraph and Texas Register*, March 17, 1838; Kavanagh, *Comanche Political History*, 253–55; Schilz and Schilz, *Buffalo Hump*, 16; Richardson, *Comanche Barrier*, 42–43.

22. Smithwick, *Evolution of a State or Recollections of Old Texas Days*, 123–38; Treaty between Texas and the Comanche Indians, May 29, 1838, TIP 1: 50–52; Kavanagh, *Comanche Political History*, 256–61; Schilz and Schilz, *Buffalo Hump*, 16–17.

23. Kavanagh, *Comanche Political History*, 260–61; Brown, *Indian Wars*, 50–51.

24. Report of Standing Committee of Indian Affairs, October 12, 1837, TIP 1: 24–27; Everett, *Texas Cherokees*, 86–88.

25. Vicente Filisola, Private instructions for the captains of the friendly Indians of Texas, n.d., SED, 32 Cong., 2 sess., doc. 14, 13–14; Vicente Córdova to Manuel Flores, July 19, 1838, SED, 32 Cong., 2 sess., doc. 14, 36.

26. Pedro Julian Miracle, Memorandum book, SED, 32 Cong., 2 sess., doc. 14, 14–16; Smith, *Wichita Indians*, 142–43.

27. SED, 32 Cong., 2 sess., doc. 14, 16.

28. Abstract of correspondence, SED, 32 Cong., 2 sess., doc. 14, 60–61; Houston to Big

Mush, August 10, 1838, wsh 2: 269–70; Houston to Bowl, August 14, 1838, wsh 2: 277; Everett, *Texas Cherokees*, 91–95.

29. Herring, "Córdova Rebellion," 323–24; Everett, *Texas Cherokees*, 94–95.

30. Lamar had served as private secretary to Georgia governor George M. Troup during the struggle with the federal government over jurisdiction of Creek lands in the 1820s. By threatening to mobilize the state militia, Governor Troup had succeeded in carrying out the fraudulent Treaty of Indian Springs, in which the Creeks gave up 4.7 million acres of land. Christian, "Mirabeau Buonaparte Lamar," 50–51; Roland, *Albert Sidney Johnston*, 81–86; Muckleroy, "Indian Policy of the Republic of Texas," swhq 25 (October 1922): 128–29; Lamar, Inaugural Address, December 10, 1838, lp 2: 308.

31. Long, "Killough Massacre," 1095–96; H. Henderson, "Battle Creek Fight," 419; Brown, *Indian Wars*, 47–50, 56–57; Rusk to Bowl, October 20, 1838, lp 2: 255; John H. Dyer to James S. Mayfield, October 21, 1838, lp 2: 256–57; Hugh McLeod to Lamar, October 22, 1838, lp 2: 265–67; McLeod to Lamar, October 25, 1838, lp 2: 270; Statement of Elias Vansickle, January 23, 1839, sed, 32 Cong., 2 sess., doc.14, 25–26; Gibson, *Kickapoos*, 155–65.

32. Appointment of Charles A. Sewall by Caddo Chiefs, October 11, 1838, cal; Statement of merchandise received by Caddo Indians from Sewall, hr 1035: 125–29; McLeod to Lamar, November 21, 1838, lp 2: 298–99; Sewall Deposition, January 8, 1839, cal.

33. McLeod to Lamar, November 23, 1838, lp 2: 302–3; Agreement between the Caddo Indians and Rusk, November 29, 1838, sed, 32 Cong., 2 sess., doc. 14, 26–27; McLeod to Lamar, December 1, 1838, lp 2: 308.

34. McLeod to Lamar, January 9, 1839, lp 2: 406; Smith, *Caddo Indians*, 141.

35. Smith, *Caddo Indians*, 144–45.

36. Smith, *Caddo Indians*, 145–46.

37. Webb, *Texas Rangers*, 31–32; Muckleroy, "Indian Policy of the Republic of Texas," swhq 26 (October 1922): 131–33.

38. Valentin Canalizo to Manuel Flores, February 27, 1839, sed, 32 Cong., 2 sess., doc. 14, 31–32; Canalizo to Córdova, March 1, 1839, sed, 32 Cong., 2 sess., doc. 14, 33–34; Canalizo to the chiefs of the tribes, February 27, 1839, sed, 32 Cong., 2 sess., doc. 14, 35.

39. Brown, *Indian Wars*, 62–65; Lamar to Colonel Bowl and other headman, May 26, 1839, lp 2: 590–94; Everett, *Texas Cherokees*, 103–4.

40. Reagan, "Expulsion of the Cherokees from East Texas," 39–42; Brown, *Indian Wars*, 66–69; Lamar to Burnet, Johnston, Rusk . . . June 27, 1839, tip 1: 67–70; Everett, *Texas Cherokees*, 105–7.

41. Kelsey H. Douglass to Johnston, July 16, 1839, lp 3: 45–46; Douglass to Johnston, July 17, 1839, lp 3: 46–47; Reagan, "Expulsion of the Cherokees," 44–46; Everett, *Texas Cherokees*, 108–9.

42. Treaty between Texas and the Shawnee Indians, August 2, 1839, tip 1: 80–82; Valuation of Shawnee Property, September 6, 1839, tip 1: 87–88; Valuation of Shawnee

Indian Property, August–September 1839, TIP 1: 92–95; Account of Rusk and May-field, Commissioners to the Shawnee Indians, August–September 1839, TIP 1: 96; H. Anderson, "Delaware and Shawnee Indians and the Republic of Texas," 245–46.

43. John E. Ross to Lamar, June 10, 1839, LP 3: 16–17; Lamar to the citizens of Liberty County, July 9, 1839, LP 3: 39–40; Citizens of Liberty County to Lamar, August 1, 1839, TIP 1: 79–80; Act authorizing the survey of land for the Coushatta and Alabama Indians, January 14, 1840, TIP 1: 102–4; Martin, "Polk County Indians," 7–10.

44. James H. Starr to Lamar, April 15, 1840, LP 3: 372–74; Starr to Lamar, April 16, 1840, LP 3: 374–75; Mayfield to Lamar, April 25, 1840, LP 3: 378; Thomas G. Stubblefield to Abner L. Lipscomb, November 2, 1840, TIP 1: 117–18; Joseph L. Ellis to Thomas G. Western, December 8, 1844, TIP 2: 146–47.

45. Smithwick, Evolution of a State, 154–57; Captain John H. Moore to Johnston, March 10, 1839, TIP 1: 57–59; Schilz and Schilz, Buffalo Hump, 17–18; Schilz, Lipan Apaches in Texas, 47–48.

46. Henry W. Karnes to Johnston, January 10, 1840, TIP 1: 101–2; Johnston to William S. Fisher, January 30, 1840, TIP 1: 105–6.

47. Brown, Indian Wars, 76–77; Green, ed., Samuel Maverick, Texan, 119; Schilz and Schilz, Buffalo Hump, 18–20.

48. Brown, Indian Wars, 78–82; Schilz and Schilz, Buffalo Hump, 21–23.

49. Telegraph and Texas Register, November 7, 1840; Brown, Indian Wars, 82–84; John C. Hays to Secretary of War, July 1, 1841, in Journals of the Sixth Congress of the Republic of Texas, 1841–1842, Smither, ed., 422; Hays to B. T. Archer, August 13, 1841, in Journals of the Sixth Congress of the Republic of Texas, 1841–1842, Smither, ed., 423–24.

50. Telegraph and Texas Register, September 1, 1841; Brown, Indian Wars, 85–88; Smith, Wichita Indians, 145–46.

51. Houston, First message to Congress, Second Administration, WSH 2: 402; Houston, Appointment of Henry E. Scott, Indian commissioner, July 5, 1842, TIP 1: 136–137; Muckleroy, "Indian Policy of the Republic of Texas," SWHQ 26 (October 1923): 146; Muckleroy, "Indian Policy of the Republic of Texas," SWHQ 26 (January 1924): 184–85.

52. James Logan to Houston, June 1, 1842, TIP 1: 135–136; Red Bear to the Chief of the Muskogees, July 10, 1842, CAL; Letter to the Chiefs of the Caddo from Jim Marthler Mieed, Hopochthli Yoholo, Tuscoomah Hargo, and Jim Boy, July 20, 1842, TIP 1: 137–38; Ethan Stroud, Leonard Williams, and Joseph Durst to Houston, September 4, 1842, TIP 1: 139; Smith, Caddo Indians, 147–48.

53. Stroud, Williams, and Durst to Houston, September 4, 1842, TIP 1: 139; Smith, Wichita Indians, 147.

54. Minutes of Indian Council at Tehuacana Creek, March 28–31, 1843, TIP 1: 149–63; H. Anderson, "Delaware and Shawnee Indians and the Republic of Texas," 247–49.

55. Statement of Luis Sánchez as Taken by Walter Winn, May 1844, TIP 2: 64–65; L. H. Williams to Thomas G. Western, July 16, 1845, TIP 2: 291–92; Roemer, Texas, with Particular Reference to German Immigration and the Physical Appearance of the Country, 200–201; Smith, Caddo Indians, 149, 161.

56. Smith, *Caddo Indians*, 144, 163.

57. Smith, *Wichita Indians*, 144–46.

58. Eldredge to Houston, June 2, 1843, TIP 2: 210–14; Eldredge to Houston, June 11, 1843, TIP 2: 214–18; Eldredge to Houston, December 8, 1843, TIP 2: 251–65.

59. Eldredge to Houston, December 8, 1843, TIP 2: 265–73; Schilz and Schilz, *Buffalo Hump*, 24–25; Richardson, *Comanche Barrier*, 54; Kavanagh, *Comanche Political History*, 264–65.

60. Proclamation by Houston, September 29, 1843, TIP 2: 243–46.

61. Mopechucope to Houston, March 21, 1844, TIP 2: 6–9.

62. Statement of Luis Sánchez as taken by Walter Winn, May 1844, TIP 2: 64–66.

63. Winn to Houston, May 4, 1844, TIP 2: 24–26; Thomas G. Western to Houston, May 15, 1844, TIP 2: 26–27; Minutes of a Council at Tehuacana Creek, May 12–15, TIP 2: 31–56.

64. Minutes of a Council at Tehuacana Creek, May 12–15, TIP 2: 31–56.

65. Western to Houston, July 27, 1844, TIP 2: 84–85; Western to Stephen T. Slater, September 5, 1844, TIP 2: 94–95; John Conner and James Shaw to Houston, October 2, 1844, TIP 2: 101–3; Smith, *Wichita Indians*, 151,

66. John Conner and James Shaw to Houston, October 2, 1844, TIP 2: 101–3; L. H. Williams, Jesse Chisolm, and D. G. Watson to Houston, October 9, 1844, TIP 2: 119–21; Minutes of council at the falls of the Brazos, October 7–9, 1844, iTIP 2: 103–6.

67. Minutes of a council, October 7–9, 1844, TIP 2: 108–9.

68. Minutes of a council, October 7–9, 1844, TIP 2: 109–14; A treaty signed in council at Tehuacana Creek, October 9, 1844, TIP 2: 114–19; Schilz and Schilz, *Buffalo Hump*, 27; Richardson, *Comanche Barrier*, 58–59.

69. Smith, *Wichita Indians*, 152; Talk of Pah-hah-yuco and Roasting Ear, January 19, 1845, TIP 2: 172–73.

70. Western to Robert S. Neighbors, April 9, 1845, TIP 2: 216; Western to Benjamin Sloat and L. H. Williams, April 9, 1845, TIP 2: 217–18; Sloat Report, July 12, 1845, TIP 2: 283–86; Williams to Western, July 16, 1845, TIP 2: 290–91; Sloat to Western, August 18, 1845, TIP 2: 325–26; Western to Thomas I. Smith, October 22, 1845, TIP 2: 393–94; Western to Paul Richardson, October 22, 1845, TIP 2: 394; Minutes of a council with the Waco, Tawakoni, Keechi, and Wichita Indians, November 13–15, 1845, TIP 2: 399–405; Smith, *Wichita Indians*, 153.

71. Western to Neighbors, May 11, 1845, TIP 2: 235–36; Western to A. Coleman, May 11, 1845, TIP 2: 236–37; Western to Williams, May 12, 1845, TIP 2: 237–38; Western to Sloat, TIP 2: May 12, 1845, TIP 2: 238–40; *Telegraph and Texas Register*, May 21, 1845; Sloat to Western, July 24, 1845, TIP 2: 298–99; Sloat to Western, August 18, 1845, TIP 2: 325–26; Report of a council with the Comanche Indians, TIP 2: 410–12; Schilz and Schilz, *Buffalo Hump*, 29.

72. Houston to Thomas J. Smith, March 25, 1842, WSH 2: 535.

73. Smithwick, *Evolution of a State*, 160–61; *Telegraph and Texas Register*, March 20, 1843, and May 10, 1843; General Flacco to Houston, March 24, 1843, WSH 3: 343; Houston

to the Lipans, in memory of their chief, Flacco, March 28, 1843, WSH 3: 341–42; Houston, Testimonial of John Castro's Friendship for the People of Texas, March 28, 1843, WSH 3: 343–44; Schilz, *Lipan Apaches in Texas*, 49–50.

74. *Telegraph and Texas Register*, October 18, 1843, November 1, 1843, April 24, 1844, and May 28, 1845; Western to Neighbors, March 2,1845, TIP 2: 205–7; Neighbors to Western, February 4, 1846, TIP 3: 13–14; Biesele, "Relations between the German Settlers and the Indians in Texas," 116–19.

75. Cambridge Green to Western, December 12, 1844, TIP 2: 150–51; Western to Neighbors, February 12, 1845, TIP 2: 197–98; Western to Neighbors, TIP 2: 216; Western to Neighbors, May 2, 1845, TIP 2: 227–28; Neighbors to Western, September 15, 1845, TIP 2: 361–62; Minutes of a council held at Tehuacana Creek, September 12–27, 1845, TIP 2: 334–44; William G. Cooke to Anson Jones, December 12, 1845, TIP 2: 422–23; Neighbors to Western, February 4, 1846, TIP 2: 3: 13–14.

7. Desperation

1. Three studies include information on the unique situation in Texas. The two best are Harmon, "United States Indian Policy in Texas, 1845–1860," 377–403; Trennert, Jr., *Alternative to Extinction*. Of lesser quality is Koch, "Federal Indian Policy in Texas, 1845–1860," SWHQ 28 (January 1925): 223–34; 28 (April 1925): 259–86; 29 (July 1925): 19–35; 29 (October 1925): 98–127.

2. William Medill to Neighbors, March 19, 1847, SR, 30 Cong., 1 sess., doc. 171, 5.

3. Foreman, "Texas Comanche Treaty of 1846," 314–25; Foreman, ed., "Journal of Elijah Hicks," 68–82.

4. Treaty with the Comanche and other tribes, May 15, 1846, TIP 3: 43–52.

5. Butler and Lewis to Medill, August 8, 1846, HED, 29 Cong., 2 sess., doc. 76, 8–9; Proclamation by Albert C. Horton, June 1, 1846, TIP 3: 62; Treaty between United States and José María and the Anadarko Indians, July 25, 1846, TIP 3: 68; G. W. Hill to Neighbors, October 1, 1853, TAL; Quaife, ed., *Diaries of James K. Polk during His Presidency*, 2: 3–4; Smith, *The Wichitas, the Caddos, and the United States*, 20–21.

6. A. C. Horton to James K. Polk, October 21, 1846, TIP 3: 77–79; Thomas Torrey to Medill, November 1, 1846, TAL; Torrey to Medill, November 28, 1846, TAL; Medill to William Marcy, December 15, 1846, TAL; Neighbors to Medill, January 6, 1847, HED, 29 Cong., 2 sess., doc. 100, 3–4; *Telegraph and Texas Register*, January 11, 1847; Kavanagh, *Comanche Political History*, 301.

7. Biesele, "Relations between German Settlers and Indians," 121–23; Boeck, ed., "They Contributed Very Much to the Success of our Colony," 85–87.

8. Biesele, "Relations between German Settlers and Indians," 124–26; Hoerig, "Relationship between German Immigrants and the Native Peoples in Western Texas," 430–33; Roemer, *Texas*, 235–73; Kavanagh, *Comanche Political History*, 303–5.

9. Neighbors to Medill, June 22, 1847, HED, 30 Cong., 1 sess., doc. 8, 892–93; Richardson, *Comanche Barrier*, 72–73.

10. *Telegraph and Texas Register*, May 27, 1846, September 20, 1846, and November 9, 1846; Neighbors to Medill, June 22, 1847, HED, 30 Cong., 1 sess., doc. 8, 894–96.

11. Neighbors to Medill, August 5, 1847, HED, 30 Cong., 1 sess., doc. 8, 897–98; Governor J. Pinckney Henderson to William Marcy, August 22, 1847, TAL; Neighbors to Medill, September 14, 1847, HED, 30 Cong., 1 sess., doc. 8, 899–903; Neighbors to Medill, October 12, 1847, HED, 30 Cong., 1 sess., doc. 8, 903–6; Neighbors to Medill, March 2, 1848, HED, 30 Cong., 2 sess., doc. 1, 576–78; Neighbors to Medill, April 28, 1848, HED, 30 Cong., 2 sess., doc. 1, 586–87; Schilz, *Lipan Apaches in Texas*, 52.

12. Neighbors to Medill, September 14, 1847, HED, 30 Cong., 1 sess., doc. 8, 899–901.

13. Neighbors to Medill, June 22, 1847, HED, 30 Cong., 2 sess., doc. 1, 892–93; Neighbors to Medill, October 12, 1847, HED, 30 Cong., 2 sess., doc. 1, 903–6; Neighbors to Medill, November 18, 1847, SR, 30 Cong., 1 sess., doc. 171, 9–10.

14. Neighbors to Henderson, December 10, 1847, SR, 30 Cong., 1 sess., doc. 171, 10–11; Henderson to Neighbors, December 10, 1847, SR, 30 Cong., 1 sess., doc. 171, 11–12; Neighbors to Medill, December 13, 1847, SR, 30 Cong., 1 sess., doc. 171, 12–13; Neighbors to Medill, March 2, 1848, HED, 30 Cong., 2 sess., doc. 1, 583.

15. Neighbors to Medill, March 2, 1848, HED, 30 Cong., 2 sess., doc. 1, 580–81; Smith, *The Caddos, the Wichitas, and the United States*, 25–26.

16. Neighbors to Medill, April 28, 1848, HED, 30 Cong., 2 sess., doc. 1, 586–87; Charles E. Barnard to Neighbors, undated, HED, 30 Cong., 2 sess., doc. 1, 588–90.

17. Neighbors to Medill, June 15, 1848, HED, 30 Cong., 2 sess., doc. 1, 591; Neighbors to Medill, August 10, 1848, HED, 30 Cong., 2 sess., doc. 1, 593–95; Agreement between R. S. Neighbors and Colonel P. H. Bell and principal chiefs of the Caddo, José María, Toweash, and Haddabah, September 14, 1848, TAL; Neighbors to Medill, February 14, 1849, HED, 30 Cong., 2 sess., doc. 1, 593–95; H. G. Catlett to Medill, May 12, 1849, SED, 31 Cong., 1 sess., doc. 1, 969–70; Smith, *Caddo Indians*, 159–60.

18. Neighbors to Medill, March 2, 1848, HED, 30 Cong., 2 sess., doc. 1, 584–85; Neighbors to Medill, June 15, 1848, HED, 30 Cong., 2 sess., doc. 1, 590–91.

19. Neighbors to Medill, March 2, 1848, HED, 30 Cong., 2 sess., doc. 1, 577–80.

20. Neighbors to Medill, September 14, 1848, HED, 30 Cong., 2 sess., doc. 1, 595; Neighbors to Medill, October 23, 1848, HED, 30 Cong., 2 sess., doc. 1, 597–98.

21. Neighbors to Medill, April 28, 1848, HED, 30 Cong., 2 sess., doc. 1, 586–87; Neighbors to Medill, October 23, 1848, HED, 30 Cong., 2 sess., doc. 1, 598; Neighbors to Medill, November 7, 1848, HED, 30 Cong., 2 sess., doc. 1, 599–600.

22. Neighbors to William J. Worth, March 7, 1849, SED, 31 Cong., 1 sess., doc. 1, 963–65.

23. Trennert, *Alternative to Extinction*, 77–82; Neighbours, *Indian Exodus*, 70; *Telegraph and Texas Register*, November 2, 1848; Neighbors to Orlando Brown, October 18, 1849, TAL; John Rollins to Brown, May 8, 1850, TAL; Rollins to George Brooke, September 25, 1850, TIP 3: 124.

24. L. W. Williams to Neighbors, October 9, 1849, TAL; Jesse Stem to Luke Lea, 1851, SED, 32 Cong., 1 sess., doc. 1, 523; Ritchie, ed., "Copy of Report of Colonel Samuel Cooper, Assistant Adjutant General of the United States, of Inspection Trip from Fort Graham to the Indian Villages on the Upper Brazos Made in June, 1851," 328–33; Smith, *The Caddos, the Wichitas, and the United States*, 30–33.

25. Neighbors to Medill, June 18, 1849, TAL; William Steele to George Davis, September

22, 1849, TAL; L. H. Williams to Neighbors, October 9, 1849, TAL; Stephen B. Oates, ed., *Rip Ford's Texas*, 113–23; Kavanagh, *Comanche Political History*, 331–32; Schilz and Schilz, *Buffalo Hump*, 33–36.

26. Trennert, *Alternative to Extinction*, 84–87; Harmon, "United States Indian Policy in Texas," 384.

27. Rollins to Brooke, September 25, 1850, TIP 3: 124–25; Rollins to Luke Lea, November 2, 1850, SED, 31 Cong., 2 sess., doc. 1, 143–45; Treaty between United States and the Comanche, Caddo, Lipan, Quapaw, Tawakoni, and Waco Tribes of Indians, December 10, 1850, TIP 3: 130–37.

28. Neighbours, *Indian Exodus*, 87–91.

29. 1850 United States Census Data, http://fisher.lib.virginia.educ/cgi-local/censusbin/census, accessed September 2002; Richardson, *Comanche Barrier*, 86–87.

30. Richardson, *Comanche Barrier*, 107; Negotiations between the United States and the Comanche, Lipan, and Mescalero Tribes of Indians, October 26, 1851, TIP 3: 142–46.

31. George T. Howard to Lea, June 10, 1852, TIP 3: 142–46; Horace Capron to Lea, September 30, 1852, TIP 3: 142–46; Stem to Lea, March 31, 1853; Neighbors to Manypenny, November 21, 1853, TIP 3: 142–46.

32. *Telegraph and Texas Register*, November 29, 1850 and June 13, 1851; John Conner to John Rogers, September 12, 1851, TAL; Stem to Lea, February 20, 1852, TAL; Stem to Lea, October 8, 1852, HED, 32 Cong., 2 sess., doc. 1, 436; Capron to Manypenny, September 30, 1853, TAL; Neighbors to Manypenny, May 2, 1854, TAL; Crimmins, ed., "W. G. Freeman's Report on the Eighth Military Department," SWHQ 53 (October 1949): 208; Marcy, *Thirty Years of Army Life on the Border*, 150.

33. Capron to Lea, June 10, 1852, TAL; Capron to Howard, August 12, 1852, HED, 32 Cong., 2 sess., doc. 1, 430–33; Capron to Lea, August 25, 1852, TAL; Capron to Lea, January 23, 1853, TAL; Howard to Lea, March 18, 1853, TAL.

34. Capron to Lea, January 23, 1853, TAL; Capron to Lea, February 18, 1853, TAL; Howard to Lea, March 18, 1853, TAL; Neighbors to Manypenny, August 6, 1853, TAL.

35. Ritchie, ed., "Report of Colonel Samuel Cooper, June, 1851," 328–33; Stem to Lea, 1851, SED, 32 Cong., 1 sess., doc. 1, 520–24.

36. Stem to Lea, November 1, 1851, SED, 32 Cong., 1 sess., doc. 1, 525–26; Stem to Lea, October 8, 1852, HED, 32 Cong., 2 sess., doc. 1, 435; G. W. Hill to Neighbors, August 10, 1853, HED, 32 Cong., 2 sess., doc. 1, 435.

37. Stem to Lea, October 8, 1852, HED, 32 Cong., 2 sess., doc. 1, 434–36; Stem to H. G. Loomis, January 9, 1853, TAL; Stem Talk with Koweaka, Wichita Chief, February 22, 1853, TAL; Stem to Loomis, March 30, 1853, TAL.

38. Stem to Loomis, March 30, 1853, TAL.

39. George W. Hill to Neighbors, August 10, 1853, TAL; Hill to Neighbors, October 1, 1853, TAL.

40. Neighbours, *Robert Simpson Neighbors*, 102–9, 132; Harmon, "United States Indian Policy in Texas," 392–93.

8. Disappearance

1. Trennert, *Alternative to Extinction*, 41–60; Neighbors to Charles E. Mix, September 10, 1855, HED, 34 Cong., 1 sess., doc. 1, 501.

2. Hill to Neighbors, March 26, 1854, TAL; Neighbors to Manypenny, September 16, 1854, SED, 33 Cong., 1 sess., doc. 1, 367; Hill to Neighbors, September 20, 1854, SED, 33 Cong., 1 sess., doc. 1, 372; Hill to Neighbors, December 15, 1854, TAL; Smith, *The Caddos, the Wichitas, and the United States*, 40–42.

3. Report of an expedition to the sources of the Brazos and Big Wichita rivers, during the summer of 1854, by Captain R. B. Marcy, SED, 34 Cong., 1 sess., doc. 60, 2–3, 22–23; Marcy and Neighbors to Governor P. H. Bell, September 30, 1854, TIP 3: 188; Parker, *Through Unexplored Texas*, 110–17, 213–14; A. H. McKisick to Elias Rector, October 21, 1857, WAL.

4. Report of an expedition to the sources of the Brazos and Big Wichita Rivers, SED, 34 Cong., 1 sess., doc. 60, 17, 28–29; Parker, *Through Unexplored Texas*, 178–83.

5. Report of an expedition to the sources of the Brazos and Big Wichita Rivers, SED, 34 Cong., 1 sess., doc. 60, 20–22; Marcy and Neighbors to Bell, September 30, 1854, TIP 3: 188–89; Parker, *Through Unexplored Texas*, 192–201; Marcy, *Prairie Traveler*, 218.

6. Neighbors to Manypenny, April 18, 1854, TAL; Statement of Christopher Luntzel, July 14, 1854, TAL.

7. Neighbors to Manypenny, April 18, 1854, TAL; Neighbors to Manypenny, May 2, 1854, TAL; Neighbors to Manypenny, May 3, 1854, TAL; Howard to Manypenny, May 4, 1854, TAL; Howard to Manypenny, June 9, 1854, TAL; Statement of Luntzel, July 14, 1854, TAL; Howard to Manypenny, November 20, 1854, TAL; Howard to Manypenny, November 30, 1854, TAL; Tonkawa census, March 25, 1855, TAL; Schilz, *Lipan Apaches in Texas*, 56–59.

8. Hill to Neighbors, April 3, 1855, TAL; Smith, *The Caddos, the Wichitas, and the United States*, 43.

9. Neighbors to Manypenny, April 2, 1855, TAL; Neighbors to Manypenny, April 17, 1855, TAL; Hill to Neighbors, May 31, 1855, TAL; Brazos Reserve census, June 30, 1855 TAL; Neighbours, *Robert Simpson Neighbors*, 155–57; Smith, *The Caddos, the Wichitas, and the United States*, 44–45.

10. Neighbors to Manypenny, January 8, 1855, TAL; Hill to Neighbors, January 25, 1855, TAL; Neighbors to Manypenny, March 20, 1855, TAL; Hill to Neighbors, May 31, 1855, TAL, Hill to Neighbors, August 31, 1855, HED, 34 Cong., 1 sess., doc. 1, 502–3; Matthew Leeper to Neighbors, June 1, 1857, TAL; Thomas T. Hawkins to Mix, October 16, 1858, TAL.

11. Hill to Neighbors, August 31, 1855, HED, 34 Cong., 1 sess., doc. 1, 504–5; Neighbors to Mix, September 10, 1855, HED, 34 Cong., 1 sess., doc. 1, 500; Neighbors to Manypenny, September 18, 1856, SED, 34 Cong., 3 sess., doc. 5, 724, 727; Ross to Neighbors, September 30, 1856, SED, 34 Cong., 3 sess., doc. 5, 730–31.

12. Ross to Neighbors, September 11, 1857, SED, 35 Cong., 1 sess., doc. 2, 557–58; Church to Ross, September 9, 1857, SED, 35 Cong., 1 sess., doc. 2, 558–59; Neigh-

bors to J. W. Denver, September 16, 1857, SED, 35 Cong., 1 sess., doc. 2, 550–51; Murray to Ross, September 10, 1857, SED, 35 Cong., 1 sess., doc. 2, 559–60.

13. Ross to Neighbors, September 6, 1858, SED, 35 Cong., 2 sess., doc. 2, 533; Neighbors to Mix, September 16, 1858, SED, 35 Cong., 2 sess., doc. 2, 525; Invoice of hogs sold for Brazos Reserve Indians, July 27, 1859, TAL; Invoice of property belonging to the tribes of the Brazos Reserve, July 30, 1859, TAL.

14. Ross to Neighbors, September 30, 1856, SED, 34 Cong., 3 sess., doc. 5, 730–31; Samuel Church to Ross, September 9, 1857, SED, 35 Cong., 1 sess., doc. 2, 559; Jonathan Murray to Ross, September 10, 1857, SED, 35 Cong., 1 sess., doc. 2, 559–60; General Statement of houses formerly occupied by each of the several tribes at Brazos Agency, Texas, July 30, 1859, TAL.

15. Brazos and Comanche Reserve census, March 31, 1855, TAL; Brazos Reserve census, June 30, 1855, TAL; Comanche Reserve census, June 30, 1855, TAL; Brazos Reserve census, October 31, 1855, TAL; Comanche Reserve census, October 31, 1855, TAL; Brazos Reserve census, June 30, 1856, TAL; Comanche Reserve census, June 30, 1856, TAL; Brazos Reserve census, December 31, 1857, TAL; Comanche Reserve census, January 30, 1858, TAL; Matthew Leeper to Neighbors, August 20, 1858, SED, 35 Cong., 2 sess., doc. 1, 525; Neighbors to Rector, May 2, 1859, SED, 36 Cong., 1 sess., doc. 2, 635–36; Brazos and Comanche Reserve census, August 1, 1859, TAL.

16. Neighbors to Denver, September 16, 1857, SED, 35 Cong., 1 sess., doc. 2, 551.

17. John Baylor to Neighbors, January 1, 1856, TAL; Shapely P. Ross to Neighbors, January 9, 1856, TAL; Ross to Neighbors, January 15, 1856, TAL; Neighbors to Manypenny, February 20, 1856, TAL; Neighbors to Manypenny, March 19, 1856, TAL; Baylor to Neighbors, May 1, 1856, TAL; Baylor to Neighbors, June 30, 1856, TAL; Comanche Reserve census, June 30, 1856, TAL; Neighbors to Manypenny, September 18, 1856, SED, 34 Cong., 3 sess., doc. 5, 724; Matthew Leeper to Neighbors, February 12, 1858, TAL.

18. Crimmins, ed. "Colonel J. K. F. Mansfield's Report of the Inspection of the Department of Texas, SWHQ 42 (October 1939): 126–27; Baylor to Neighbors, July 21, 1856, TAL; Baylor to Neighbors, August 10, 1856, TAL; Baylor to Neighbors, August 17, 1856, TAL; Baylor to Neighbors, August 30, 1856, TAL; Baylor to Neighbors, September 12, 1856, SED, 34 Cong., 3 sess., doc. 5, 725–26; Baylor to Neighbors, December 31, 1856, TAL.

19. Baylor to Neighbors, March 21, 1857, TAL; Baylor to Neighbors, March 28, 1857, TAL; Neighbors to Mix, May 15, 1857, TAL; Leeper to Neighbors, June 30, 1857, TAL; Neighbors to Major General D. E. Twiggs, July 17, 1856, SED, 35 Cong., 1 sess., doc. 2, 553; Leeper to Neighbors, September 13, 1857, SED, 35 Cong., 1 sess., doc. 2, 556; Neighbors to J. W. Denver, September 16, 1857, SED, 35 Cong., 1 sess., doc. 2, 556; Neighbours, *Robert Simpson Neighbors*, 180–81.

20. Leeper to Neighbors, September 13, 1857, SED, 35 Cong., 1 sess., doc. 2, 554; Leeper to Neighbors, March 31, 1858, TAL; Leeper to Neighbors, April 15, 1858, TAL; Leeper to Neighbors, June 30, 1858, TAL; Leeper to Neighbors, August 20, 1858, SED, 35 Cong., 2 sess., doc. 1, 527–30; Horace P. Jones to Leeper, August 20, 1858, SED,

35 Cong., 2 sess., doc. 1, 532; Jones to Leeper, October 29, 1858, TAL; Comanche Reserve census, July 26, 1859, TAL.

21. Neighbors to Mix, September 10, 1855, HED, 34 Cong., 1 sess., doc. 1, 501; Ross to Neighbors, September 30, 1856, SED, 34 Cong., 3 sess., doc. 5, 730–31; Leeper to Neighbors, September 13, 1857, SED, 35 Cong., 1 sess., doc. 2, 556.

22. Leeper to Neighbors, January 28, 1858, TAL; Leeper to Neighbors, February 12, 1858, TAL; Leeper to Neighbors, June 30, 1858, TAL; Richard Sloan to Leeper, August 18, 1858, SED, 35 Cong., 2 sess., doc. 1, 530–31; Leeper to Neighbors, August 20, 1858, SED, 35 Cong., 2 sess., doc. 1, 529; Leeper to Neighbors, August 31, 1858, TAL.

23. Zachariach E. Coombes to Ross, September 7, 1858, SED, 35 Cong., 2 sess., doc. 1, 535; Coombes, Diary of a Frontiersman; Coombes to Ross, November 30, 1858, TAL.

24. Coombes, Diary of a Frontiersman, 34; Coombes to Ross, February 28, 1859, SED, 36 Cong., 1 sess., doc. 2, 627–28; Coombes to Ross, March 30, 1859, TAL; Leeper to Neighbors, March 31, 1859, TAL; Coombes to Ross, April 30, 1859, TAL.

25. Richardson, Comanche Barrier, 183–92; Schilz and Schilz, Buffalo Hump, 40–44.

26. Ross to Neighbors, September 30, 1855, HED, 34 Cong., 1 sess., doc. 1, 505–6; Ross to Neighbors, October 7, 1855, TAL; Baylor to Neighbors, October 7, 1855, TAL.

27. Baylor to Neighbors, June 30, 1856, TAL; Ross to Neighbors, June 30, 1856, TAL; Baylor to Neighbors, July 12, 1856, TAL; Ross to Neighbors, July 17, 1856, TAL; Neighbors to Manypenny, September 18, 1856, SED, 34 Cong., 3 sess., doc. 5, 725; Smith, The Caddos, the Wichitas, and the United States, 51–52.

28. Ross to Neighbors, July 23, 1856, TAL.

29. Ross to Neighbors, November 30, 1856, TAL; Ross to Neighbors, January 10, 1857, TAL; Ross to Neighbors, April 26, 1858, TAL. For the most recent study on settler attitudes toward the two reserves, see Klos, " 'Our people could not distinguish one tribe from another': The 1859 Expulsion of the Reserve Indians from Texas," 598–619.

30. Neighbors to Denver, December 8, 1857, TAL; Neighbors to Mix, January 17, 1858, TAL; Neighbors to Mix, April 2, 1858, TAL; Petitions from Williamson and Lampasas Counties, December 15, 1857, TAL; Bender, March of Empire, 213–14.

31. W. G. Evans to Joseph Withers, January 14, 1858, TAL; Neighbors to Mix, January 17, 1858, TAL.

32. Ross to Neighbors, February 17, 1858, TAL.

33. Ross to Neighbors, March 31, 1858, TAL; Ross to Neighbors, June 30, 1858, TAL; Ford, List of Indians, actual settlers of Brazos Agency engaged April 23 to May 22, 1858, July 15, 1858, TAL; Ford, Rip Ford's Texas, 223–36; Smith, The Caddos, the Wichitas, and the United States, 55–56.

34. Ross to Neighbors, April 26, 1858, TAL; Address by H. R. Runnels to Captain Ford's Company of Texas Rangers, May 28, 1858, TIP 3: 287; Ross to Neighbors, June 30, 1858, TAL; Ford, Rip Ford's Texas, 237–38.

35. Affadavit of Ford, November 22, 1858, TAL; Smith, The Caddos, the Wichitas, and the United States, 57.

36. Ross to Neighbors, September 30, 1858, TAL; Chalfant, Without Quarter, 37–40.

37. Smith, *The Caddos, the Wichitas, and the United States*, 58.

38. Chalfant, *Without Quarter*, 41–44; Coombes, *Diary of a Frontiersman*, 7–8.

39. Elias Rector to Mix, October 22, 1858, SED, 36 Cong., 1 sess., doc. 2, 583–84; Rector to Mix, October 23, 1858, SED, 36 Cong., 1 sess., doc. 2, 585–86; Census Roll of Wichita Camp on Caddo Creek, January 30, 1859, WAL; Smith, *The Caddos, the Wichitas, and the United States*, 59.

40. J. J. Sturm to Ross, December 30, 1858, SED, 36 Cong., 1 sess., doc. 2, 589–90; Sturm to Ross, January 15, 1859, SED, 36 Cong., 1 sess., doc. 2, 599; Ross to Neighbors, January 26, 1859, SED, 36 Cong., 1 sess., doc. 2, 596.

41. Sturm to Ross, December 28, 1858, SED, 36 Cong., 1 sess., doc. 2, 589; Sturm to Ross, December 30, 1858, SED, 36 Cong., 1 sess., doc. 2, 589–90; Sturm to Ross, January 15, 1859, SED, 36 Cong., 1 sess., doc. 2, 599–600.

42. Palo Pinto Citizens' Committee to Neighbors and Ross, December 27, 1858, SED, 36 Cong., 1 sess., doc. 2, 602–3; Sturm to Ross, January 15, 1859, SED, 36 Cong., 1 sess., doc. 2, 600.

43. Captain T. N. Palmer to Lieutenant W. W. Lowe, January 10, 1859, SED, 36 Cong., 1 sess., doc. 2, 601–2; Ross to Neighbors, January 26, 1859, SED, 36 Cong., 1 sess., doc. 2, 596–97.

44. Letter to the People of Texas, January 4, 1859, SED, 36 Cong., 1 sess., doc. 2, 606–9; Minutes of Assembly, January 6, 1859, SED, 36 Cong., 1 sess., doc. 2, 613–14; Report of the Commissioners, January 12, 1859, SED, 36 Cong., 1 sess., doc. 2, 614–15.

45. Proclamation by H. R. Runnels, January 10, 1859, TIP 3: 312–13; Neighbors to Denver, January 15, 1859, SED, 36 Cong., 1 sess., doc. 2, 590–91; Ross to Neighbors, January 26, 1859, SED, 36 Cong., 1 sess., doc. 2, 596–97; Neighbors to Denver, January 30, 1859, SED, 36 Cong., 1 sess., doc. 2, 594–95.

46. Ford to E. J. Gurley, January 22, 1859, SED, 36 Cong., 1 sess., doc. 2, 606; Ross to Neighbors, February 12, 1859, SED, 36 Cong., 1 sess., doc. 2, 621–22; Neighbors to Denver, February 14, 1859, SED, 36 Cong., 1 sess., doc. 2, 603–4; Neighbors to Denver, February 24, 1859, SED, 36 Cong., 1 sess., doc. 2, 620–21.

47. Ross to Neighbors, February 12, 1859, SED, 36 Cong., 1 sess., doc. 2, 621–22; Ross to Neighbors, February 24, 1859, SED, 36 Cong., 1 sess., doc. 2, 625–26; Sturm to Ross, February 28, 1859, ibid., 627; Coombes, *Diary of a Frontiersman*, 49.

48. F. M. Harris to Ross, March 1, 1859, SED, 36 Cong., 1 sess., doc. 2, 629; Ross to Neighbors, March 2, 1859, SED, 36 Cong., 1 sess., doc. 2, 628; Ross to Runnels, March 4, 1859, SED, 36 Cong., 1 sess., doc. 2, 630–31; Ross to Neighbors, March 25, 1859, TAL; Neighbors to Denver, March 25, 1859, TAL; Coombes, *Diary of a Frontiersman*, 53–59.

49. Mix to Neighbors, March 30, 1859, SED, 36 Cong., 1 sess., doc. 2, 631–32; Mix to Elias Rector, March 30, 1859, SED, 36 Cong., 1 sess., doc. 2, 632–34; Smith, *The Caddos, the Wichitas, and the United States*, 42–43.

50. Petition of Citizens, April 25, 1859, SED, 36 Cong., 1 sess., doc. 2, 641–42; Ross to Neighbors, May 1, 1859, SED, 36 Cong., 1 sess., doc. 2, 639; Gurley to Neighbors,

May 5, 1859, SED, 36 Cong., 1 sess., doc. 2, 642–43; Neighbors to Mix, May 12, 1859, SED, 36 Cong., 1 sess., doc. 2, 636–37.

51. Ross to Neighbors, May 1, 1859, SED, 36 Cong., 1 sess., doc. 2, 640; Chalfant, *Without Quarter*, 64–95; Richardson, *Comanche Barrier*, 242.

52. Sturm to Ross, May 8, 1859, TAL; Estep, ed., *Removal of the Texas Indians and the Founding of Fort Cobb*, 27–30.

53. Estep, ed., *Removal of the Texas Indians and the Founding of Fort Cobb*, 31.

54. J. B. Plummer to the Assistant Adjutant General, May 23, 1859, SED, 36 Cong., 1 sess., doc. 2, 644; Ross to Neighbors, May 23, 1859, SED, 36 Cong., 1 sess., doc. 2, 645; Estep, ed., *Removal of the Texas Indians and the Founding of Fort Cobb*, 33–34.

55. Plummer to the Assistant Adjutant General, May 23, 1859, SED, 36 Cong., 1 sess., doc. 2, 644; Ross to Neighbors, May 26, 1859, SED, 36 Cong., 1 sess., doc. 2, 645; Estep, ed., *Removal of the Texas Indians and the Founding of Fort Cobb*, 34–35.

56. Plummer to the Assistant Adjutant General, May 23, 1859, SED, 36 Cong., 1 sess., doc. 2, 645; Ross to Neighbors, May 26, 1859, SED, 36 Cong., 1 sess., doc. 2, 645–46; Ross to Neighbors, May 30, 1859, TAL; Estep, ed., *Removal of the Texas Indians and the Founding of Fort Cobb*, 34–37.

57. Charles Barnard to Neighbors, May 30, 1859, TAL; Neighbors to A. B. Greenwood, June 10, 1859, SED, 36 Cong., 1 sess., doc. 2, 649–50; Greenwood to Neighbors, June 11, 1859, SED, 36 Cong., 1 sess., doc. 2, 650–51; Estep, ed., *Removal of the Texas Indians and the Founding of Fort Cobb*, 37.

58. Instructions to the peace commissioners, June 6, 1859, SED, 36 Cong., 1 sess., doc. 2, 657–58; G. B. Erath to Neighbors and Ross, June 20, 1859, SED, 36 Cong., 1 sess., doc. 2, 663; Report of the peace commission, June 27, 1859, SED, 36 Cong., 1 sess., doc. 2, 665; Meeting of the citizens of Parker County, June 24, 1859, SED, 36 Cong., 1 sess., doc. 2, 684–85; To the citizens and friends of the frontier counties of the State of Texas, June 24, SED, 36 Cong., 1 sess., doc. 2, 685–86; Neighbors to Greenwood, SED, 36 Cong., 1 sess., doc. 2, 686–87.

59. Rector to Greenwood, July 2, 1859, SED, 36 Cong., 1 sess., doc. 2, 673–77; Smith, *The Caddos, the Wichitas, and the United States*, 73.

60. General statement of houses formerly occupied by each of the several tribes at Brazos Agency, Texas, July 30, 1859, TAL; Invoice of Indian hogs sold, July 27, 1859, TAL; Leeper to Neighbors, July 24, 1859, SED, 36 Cong., 1 sess., doc. 2, 692–93; Neighbors to Greenwood, July 25, 1859, SED, 36 Cong., 1 sess., doc. 2, 688; Smith, *The Caddos, the Wichitas, and the United States*, 73–74.

61. Smith, *The Caddos, the Wichitas, and the United States*, 74–75.

62. Comanche Reserve census, July 26, 1859, TAL; Census Roll of Indians, Brazos Reserve, July 28, 1859, TAL; Abstract of articles for Indians of Texas issued as presents, July 31, 1859, TAL; Invoice of property belonging to Brazos Reserve tribes on their removal, July 30, 1859, TAL; Memorandum of travel from Brazos Agency, Texas to False Washita Agency, August 30, 1859, WAL; Smith, *The Caddos, the Wichitas, and the United States*, 75–76.

63. Memorandum of travel, August 30, 1859, WAL; Smith, *The Caddos, the Wichitas, and the United States*, 75–76.

64. Memorandum of travel, August 30, 1859, WAL; Smith, *The Caddos, the Wichitas, and the United States*, 76–77.

65. Neighbors to Greenwood, September 3, 1859, SED, 36 Cong., 1 sess., doc. 2, 700–701; Smith, *The Caddos, the Wichitas, and the United States*, 76–77.

66. Statement of Leeper, September 15, 1859, SED, 36 Cong., 1 sess., doc. 2, 701–2; Smith, *The Caddos, the Wichitas, and the United States*, 77–78.

67. Smither, "Alabama Indians of Texas," 97–98; Martin, "Alabama-Coushatta Indians," 79.

68. Smither, "Alabama Indians of Texas," 98–99.

69. Martin, "Alabama-Coushatta Indians," 79–80; Smither, "Alabama Indians of Texas," 101–3; Lowe and Campbell, *Planters and Plain Folk*, 31.

Epilogue

1. Smith, *The Caddos, the Wichitas, and the United States*, 70–87; Schilz, "People of the Cross Timbers," 175–215.

2. Smith, *The Caddos, the Wichitas, and the United States*, 87–116.

3. Smith, *The Caddos, the Wichitas, and the United States*, 117–30.

4. La Vere, *Life among the Texas Indians*, 46–47.

5. Smith, *The Caddos, the Wichitas, and the United States*, 142–51; Himmel, *Conquest of the Karankawas and the Tonkawas*, 121–22; Carlisle, "Tonkawa Indians," 526; Hagan, *United States–Comanche Relations*, 262–86.

6. Smith, *The Caddos, the Wichitas, and the United States*, 153; La Vere, *Life among the Texas Indians*, 47–48.

7. Meredith, *Dancing on Common Ground*, 115.

8. Smith, *The Caddos, the Wichitas, and the United States*, 154; Meredith, *Dancing on Common Ground*, 134–35.

9. Smith, *The Caddos, the Wichitas, and the United States*, 154; Meredith, *Dancing on Common Ground*, 132–35; Lipscomb, "Comanche Indians," 245.

10. La Vere, *Texas Indians*, 216; Martin, "Alabama-Coushatta Indians," 79–80.

11. La Vere, *Texas Indians*, 232–33.

12. La Vere, *Texas Indians*, 234.

Bibliography

Manuscript Sources

Archivo General de Indias. Papeles Procedentes de Cuba. Seville, Spain.

Béxar Archives. Microfilm Copy. University of North Texas, Denton.

Béxar Archives Translations. Series One. Microfilm Copy. University of North Texas, Denton.

Béxar Archives Translations. Series Two. Microfilm Copy. University of North Texas, Denton.

Natchitoches Parish Conveyance Records. Microfilm Copy. Mormon Genealogy Society. Family History Center, The Church of Jesus Christ of Latter Day Saints. Dallas, Texas.

Nacogdoches Archives. Microfilm Copy. Center for American History. University of Texas, Austin.

Provincias Internas. Transcript Copy. Center for American History. University of Texas, Austin.

Records of the Bureau of Indian Affairs. Letterbook of the Natchitoches–Sulphur Fork Factory, 1809–1821. Microfilm Copy. National Archives, Fort Worth, Texas.

———. Letters Received by the Office of Indian Affairs. Caddo Indian Agency, 1824–1842. Microfilm Copy. National Archives, Fort Worth, Texas.

———. Letters Received by the Office of Indian Affairs. Texas Agency, 1846–1859. Microfilm Copy. National Archives, Fort Worth, Texas.

———. Letters Received by the Office of Indian Affairs. Western Superintendency, 1832–1851. Microfilm Copy. National Archives, Fort Worth, Texas.

———. Letters Received by the Office of Indian Affairs. Wichita Agency, 1857–1878. Microfilm Copy. National Archives, Fort Worth, Texas.

Records of the Diocese of Louisiana and Florida. Microfilm Copy. Williams Research Center. The Historic New Orleans Collection. New Orleans, Louisiana.

Saltillo Archives. Transcript Copy. Center for American History. University of Texas, Austin.

Secretaria de Fomento-Colonizacíon. Transcript Copy. Center for American History. University of Texas, Austin.

Published Sources

Almonte, Juan N. "Statistical Report on Texas." Carlos E. Castañeda, trans. *Southwestern Historical Quarterly* 28 (January 1925): 177–222.

Alonzo, Armando C. *Tejano Legacy: Rancheros and Settlers in SouthTexas, 1734–1900.* Albuquerque: University of New Mexico Press, 1998.

American State Papers, Indian Affairs. 2 vols. Washington DC: Gales and Seaton, 1832–1834.

American State Papers, Public Lands. 4 vols. Washington DC: Gales and Seaton, 1832–1859.

Anderson, Gary Clayton. *The Indian Southwest, 1580–1830: Ethnogenesis and Reinvention.* Norman: University of Oklahoma Press, 1999.

Anderson, H. Allen. "The Delaware and Shawnee Indians and the Republic of Texas, 1820–1845." *Southwestern Historical Quarterly* 94 (October 1990): 231–260.

Aten, Lawrence E. *The Indians of the Upper Texas Coast.* New York: Academic Press, 1983.

Barker, Eugene C., ed. *The Austin Papers.* 3 vols. Washington DC: Government Printing Office, 1924–1927.

————. "Descriptions of Texas by Stephen F. Austin, 1828." *Southwestern Historical Quarterly* 28 (October 1924): 98–121.

————. "Journal of Stephen F. Austin on His First Trip to Texas, 1821." *Southwestern Historical Quarterly* 7 (April 1904): 286–307.

Bender, Averam. *The March of Empire: Frontier Defense in the Southwest, 1846–1960.* Lawrence: University Press of Kansas, 1952.

Benson, Nettie Lee, ed. "A Governor's Report on Texas in 1809." *Southwestern Historical Quarterly* 71 (April 1968): 603–15.

Berlandier, Jean Louis. *The Indians of Texas in 1830.* Edited by John C. Ewers. Washington DC: Smithsonian Institution Press, 1969.

————. *Journey to Mexico during the Years 1826 to 1834.* 2 vols. Edited by S. M. Ohlendorf, J. M. Bigelow, and M. M. Standifer. Austin: Texas State Historical Association, 1980.

Biesele, R. L. "The Relations between the German Settlers and the Indians in Texas, 1844–1860." *Southwestern Historical Quarterly* 31 (October 1927): 116–29.

Boeck, Brian J., ed. " 'They Contributed Very Much to the Success of Our Colony': A New Source on Early Relations between Germans and Indians at Fredericksburg." *Southwestern Historical Quarterly* 105 (July 2001): 81–91.

Bolton, Herbert Eugene, ed. *Athanase de Mézières and the Louisiana-Texas Frontier, 1768–1780.* 2 vols. Cleveland: Arthur H. Clark, 1914.

Bridges, Kathleen, and Winston De Ville. "Natchitoches in 1766." *Louisiana History* 4 (Spring 1963): 145–58.

Brooks, James F. *Captives and Cousins: Slavery, Kinship, and Community in the Southwest Borderlands.* Chapel Hill: University of North Carolina Press, 2002.

Brown, John Henry. *Indian Wars and Pioneers of Texas.* Austin: L. E. Daniell, 189?.

Burch, Marvin C. "The Indigenous Indians of the Lower Trinity Area of Texas." *Southwestern Historical Quarterly* 60 (July 1956): 36–52.

Burnam, Jesse. "Reminiscences of Captain Jesse Burnam." *Southwestern Historical Quarterly* 5 (July 1901): 12–18.

Burton, H. Sophie. "Family and Economy in Frontier Louisiana: Colonial Natchitoches, 1714–1803." PhD diss., Texas Christian University, 2002.

Campbell, Thomas N. "Deadose Indians." In vol. 2 of *The New Handbook of Texas*. Edited by Ron Tyler. Austin: Texas State Historical Association, 1996.

———. "Ervipiame Indians." In vol. 2 of *The New Handbook of Texas*. Edited by Ron Tyler. Austin: Texas State Historical Association, 1996.

Cantrell, Gregg. *Stephen F. Austin: Empresario of Texas*. New Haven CT: Yale University Press, 1999.

Carlisle, Jeffrey D. "Apache Indians." In vol. 1 of *The New Handbook of Texas*. Edited by Ron Tyler. Austin: Texas State Historical Association, 1996.

———. "The Lipan Apaches and the Anglo-Texans, 1820–1845." Unpublished paper.

———. "Spanish Relations with the Apache Nations East of the Rio Grande." PhD diss., University of North Texas, 2001.

———. "Tonkawa Indians." In vol. 6 of *The New Handbook of Texas*. Edited by Ron Tyler. Austin: Texas State Historical Association, 1996.

Carter, Cecile Elkins. *Caddo Indians: Where We Come From*. Norman: University of Oklahoma Press, 1995.

Carter, Clarence E., ed. *The Territorial Papers of the United States*. Vol. 9, *The Territory of Orleans, 1803–1812*. Vol. 15, *The Territory of Louisiana-Missouri, 1815–1821*. Vol. 19, *The Territory of Arkansas, 1819–1825*. Vol. 21, *The Territory of Arkansas, 1829–1836*. 28 Vols. Washington DC: Government Printing Office, published continuously since 1933.

Castañeda, Carlos E. *Our Catholic Heritage in Texas, 1519–1936*. 7 vols. Austin: Von Boeckmann-Jones, 1936–1958.

Chalfant, William Y. *Without Quarter: The Wichita Expedition and the Fight on Crooked Creek*. Norman: University of Oklahoma Press, 1991.

Chipman, Donald E. *Spanish Texas, 1519–1821*. Austin: University of Texas Press, 1992.

Chipman, Donald E., and Harriet Denise Joseph. *Notable Men and Women of Spanish Texas*. Austin: University of Texas Press, 1999.

Christian, A. K. "Mirabeau Buonaparte Lamar." *Southwestern Historical Quarterly* 24 (July 1920): 39–80.

Couser, Dorothy. "Atakapa Indians." In vol. 1 of *The New Handbook of Texas*. Edited by Ron Tyler. Austin: Texas State Historical Association, 1996.

Coutts, Brian E. "Boom and Bust: The Rise and Fall of the Tobacco Industry in Spanish Lousiana, 1770–1790." *The Americas* 42 (1986): 289–309.

Coombes, Zachariach E. *Diary of a Frontiersman, 1858–1859*. Edited by Barbara Ledbetter. Newcastle TX: n.p., 1961.

Crimmins, M. L., ed. "Colonel J. K. F. Mansfield's Report of the Inspection of the Department of Texas." *Southwestern Historical Quarterly* 42 (October 1938): 122–47; (January 1939): 215–57; (April 1939): 351–87.

———. "W. G. Freeman's Report on the Eighth Military Department." *Southwestern Historical Quarterly* 51–53 (1947–1950).

De la Teja, Jésus F. *San Antonio de Béxar: A Community on New Spain's Northern Frontier*. Albuquerque: University of New Mexico Press, 1995.

DeShields, James T. *Border Wars of Texas: Being an Authentic and Popular Account, in Chrono-logical Order, of the Long and Bitter Conflict Waged between Savage Indian Tribes and the Pioneer Settlers of Texas. Wresting a Fair Land from Savage Rule, a Red Record of Fierce Strife.* Tioga TX: Herald, 1912.

Din, Gilbert C. *Spaniards, Planters, and Slaves: The Spanish Regulation of Slavery in Louisiana, 1763–1803.* College Station: Texas A&M University Press, 1999.

Din, Gilbert C., and Abraham P. Nasatir. *The Imperial Osages: Spanish Diplomacy in the Mississippi Valley.* Norman: University of Oklahoma Press, 1983.

Estep, Raymond, ed. *The Removal of the Texas Indians and the Founding of Fort Cobb: Lieutenant William E. Burnet Letters.* Oklahoma City: Oklahoma Historical Society, 1961.

Everett, Diana. *The Texas Cherokees: A People between Two Fires, 1819–1840.* Norman: University of Oklahoma Press, 1990.

Ewers, John C. "The Influence of Epidemics on the Indian Populations and Cultures of Texas." *Plains Anthropologist* 18 (1973): 104–18.

Flores, Dan L. "The Red River Branch of the Alabama-Coushatta Indians," *Southern Studies* 16 (Spring 1977): 55–72.

Flores, Dan L., ed. *Jefferson and Southwestern Exploration: The Freeman and Custis Accounts of the Red River Expedition of 1806.* Norman: University of Oklahoma Press, 1984.

————. *Journal of an Indian Trader: Anthony Glass and the Texas Trading Frontier, 1790–1810.* College Station: Texas A&M University Press, 1985.

Foreman, Grant. "The Texas Comanche Treaty of 1846." *Southwestern Historical Quarterly* 51 (April 1948): 314–32.

Foreman, Grant, ed. "The Journal of Elijah Hicks." *Chronicles of Oklahoma* 13 (March 1935): 68–99.

Frank, Ross. *From Settler to Citizen: New Mexican Economic Development and the Creation of Vecino Society, 1750–1820.* Berkeley: University of California Press, 2000.

Gannett, William B. "The American Invasion of Texas, 1820–1845: Patterns of Conflict between Settlers and Indians." PhD diss., Cornell University Press, 1984.

Garrett, Julia Kathryn, ed. "Doctor John Sibley and the Louisiana-Texas Frontier, 1803–1814." *Southwestern Historical Quarterly* 45–49 (1942–1946).

Gatschet, Albert S. *The Karankawa Indians: The Coast People of Texas.* Cambridge MA: Harvard University Press, 1891.

Gibson, Ariel. *The Kickapoo Indians: Lords of the Middle Border.* Norman: University of Oklahoma Press, 1963.

Gilmore, Kathleen. "The Indians of Mission Rosario: From the Books and from the Ground." In vol. 1 of *Columbian Consequences: The Spanish Borderlands in Pan American Perspective.* Edited by D. H. Thomas. Washington DC: Smithsonian Institution Press, 1991.

Green, Rena Maverick, ed. *Samuel Maverick, Texan, 1803–1870: A Collection of Letters, Journals, and Memoirs.* San Antonio: n.p., 1952.

Gulick, Charles A., Jr., Katherine Elliott, and Harriet Smither, eds. *The Papers of Mirabeau Buonaparte Lamar.* 6 vols. Austin: Von Boeckmann-Jones, 1921–27.

Gutierrez, Ramón A. *When Jesus Came, the Corn Mothers Went Away: Marriage, Sexuality, and Power in New Mexico, 1500–1846*. Stanford: Stanford University Press, 1991.

Hagan, William T. *United States–Comanche Relations: The Reservation Years*. New Haven CT: Yale University Press, 1976.

Haggard, J. Villasana. "The House of Barr and Davenport." *Southwestern Historical Quarterly* 49 (July 1945): 65–88.

————. "The Neutral Ground Agreement between Louisiana and Texas, 1806–1821." *Louisiana Historical Quarterly* 28 (October 1945): 1001–128.

Haley, James L. *Sam Houston*. Norman: University of Oklahoma Press, 2002.

Hall, Gwendolyn Midlo. *Africans in Colonial Louisiana: The Development of Afro-Creole Culture in the Eighteenth Century*. Baton Rouge: Louisiana State University Press, 1992.

Harmon, George D. "The United States Indian Policy in Texas, 1845–1860." *Mississippi Valley Historical Review* 17 (December 1930): 377–403.

Hatcher, Mattie Austin, trans. "Joaquín de Arredondo's Report of the Battle of the Medina, August 18, 1813." *Southwestern Historical Quarterly* 11 (October 1907): 220–36.

Henderson, Harry McCorry, "Battle Creek Fight," in vol. 1 of *The New Handbook of Texas*. Edited by Ron Tyler. Austin: Texas State Historical Association, 1996.

Henderson, Mary Virginia. "Minor Empresario Contracts for the Colonization of Texas." *Southwestern Historical Quarterly* 31 (April 1928): 295–324; 32 (July 1928): 1–28.

Herring, Rebecca H. "Córdova Rebellion." In vol. 2 of *The New Handbook of Texas*. Edited by Ron Tyler. Austin: Texas State Historical Association, 1996.

Himmel, Kelly F. *The Conquest of the Karankawas and the Tonkawas, 1821–1859*. College Station: Texas A&M University Press, 1999.

Hoerig, Karl A. "The Relationship between German Immigrants and the Native Peoples in Western Texas." *Southwestern Historical Quarterly* 97 (January 1994): 422–51.

Hogan, William R., ed., "State Census of 1847." *Southwestern Historical Quarterly* 50 (July 1946): 117–18.

Holley, Mary Austin. *Texas*. Facsimile copy. Austin: Steck, 1935.

Hook, Jonathan B. *The Alabama-Coushatta Indians*. College Station: Texas A&M University Press, 1997.

Hunter, Donald G. "Their Final Years: The Apalachee and Other Immigrant Tribes on the Red River, 1763–1834." *Florida Anthropologist* 47 (March 1994): 3–45.

Jackson, Jack. *Los Mesteños: Spanish Ranching in Texas, 1721–1821*. College Station: Texas A&M University Press, 1986.

Jackson, Jack, ed. *Texas by Terán: The Diary Kept by General Manuel de Mier y Terán on His 1828 Inspection of Texas*. Austin: University of Texas Press, 2000.

Jenkins, John, ed. *The Papers of the Texas Revolution, 1835–1836*. 8 vols. Austin: Texas State Library, 1959–1961.

John, Elizabeth A. H. *Storms Brewed in Other Men's Worlds: The Confrontation of Indians, Spanish, and French in the Southwest, 1540–1795*. Norman: University of Oklahoma Press, 1975.

————. "Nurturing the Peace: Spanish and Comanche Cooperation in the Early Nineteenth Century." *New Mexico Historical Review* 59 (December 1984): 345–69.

John, Elizabeth A. H., ed. "Inside the Comanchería, 1785: The Diary of Pedro Vial and Francisco Xavier Chaves." *Southwestern Historical Quarterly* 98 (July 1994): 27–56.

Kavanagh, Thomas W. *Comanche Political History: An Ethnohistorical Perspective.* Lincoln: University of Nebraska Press, 1996.

Kinnaird, Lawrence, ed. *Spain in the Mississippi Valley, 1765–1794.* 3 vols. Washington DC: Government Printing Office, 1946–49.

Kinnaird, Lawrence, and Lucia B. Kinnaird. "Choctaws West of the Mississippi, 1766–1800." *Southwestern Historical Quarterly* 83 (April 1980): 350–70.

Kinnaird, Lawrence, and Lucia B.Kinnaird, eds. "The Red River Valley in 1796." *Louisiana History* 24 (Spring 1983): 184–94.

Klos, George. " 'Our people could not distinguish one tribe from another': The 1859 Expulsion of the Reserve Indians from Texas." *Southwestern Historical Quarterly* 97 (April 1994): 598–619.

Kniffen, Fred B., Hiram F. Gregory, and George A. Stokes. *The Historic Tribes of Louisiana: From 1542 to the Present.* Baton Rouge: Louisiana State University Press, 1987.

Koch, Lena Clara. "The Federal Indian Policy in Texas, 1845–1860." *Southwestern Historical Quarterly* 28 (January 1925): 223–34; 28 (April 1925): 259–86; 29 (July 1925): 19–35; 29 (October 1925): 98–127.

Kuykendall, J. H. "Reminscences of Early Texans." *Southwestern Historical Quarterly* 7 (July 1903): 236–53.

La Vere, David. "Between Kinship and Capitalism: French and Spanish Rivalry in the Colonial Louisiana-Texas Indian Trade." *Journal of Southern History* 64 (May 1998): 198–206.

————. *The Caddo Chiefdoms: Caddo Economics and Politics, 700–1835.* Lincoln: University of Nebraska Press, 1998.

————. *Life among the Texas Indians: The WPA Narratives.* College Station: Texas A&M University Press, 1998.

————. *The Texas Indians.* College Station: Texas A&M University Press, 2004.

Lee, Aubry Lane. "Fusils, Paint, and Pelts: An Examination of Natchitoches-Based Indian Trade in the Spanish Period, 1766–1791." Master's thesis, Northwestern State University, 1990.

Lee, Dana Bowker. "Indian Slavery in Lower Louisiana during the Colonial Period, 1699–1803." Master's thesis, Northwestern State University, 1989.

Lipscomb, Carol A. "Karankawa Indians." In vol. 3 of *The New Handbook of Texas.* Edited by Ron Tyler. Austin: Texas State Historical Association, 1996.

Long, Christopher. "Killough Massacre." In vol. 3 of *The New Handbook of Texas.* Edited by Ron Tyler. Austin: Texas State Historical Association, 1996.

Loomis, Noel M., and Abraham P. Nasatir, eds. *Pedro Vial and the Roads to Santa Fe.* Norman: University of Oklahoma Press, 1967.

————. "Philip Nolan's Entry in Texas in 1800." In *The Spanish in the Mississippi Valley, 1762–1804.* Edited by John Francis McDermott. Urbana: University of Illinois Press, 1974.

Lowe, Richard G., and Randolph B. Campbell. *Planters and Plain Folk: Agriculture in Antebellum Texas.* Dallas: Southern Methodist University Press, 1987.

Magnaghi, Russell M., ed. "The Red River Valley, North of Natchitoches, 1817–1818: The Letters of John Fowler." *Louisiana Studies* 15 (Fall 1976): 287–93.

Marcy, Randolph B. *The Prairie Traveler: A Handbook for Overland Expeditions.* New York: Time-Life Books, 1981.

————. *Thirty Years of Army Life on the Border.* New York: Harper Brothers, 1866.

Martin, Howard N. "Polk County Indians: Alabamas, Coushattas, Pakana Muskogees." *East Texas Historical Association* 17 (Spring 1979): 3–23.

————. "Alabama-Coushatta Indians." In vol. 1 of *The New Handbook of Texas.* Edited by Ron Tyler. Austin: Texas State Historical Association, 1996.

McDonald, Archie P. "Fredonian Rebellion." In vol. 2 of *The New Handbook of Texas.* Edited by Ron Tyler. Austin: Texas State Historical Association, 1996.

McElhannon, Joseph Carl. "Imperial Mexico and Texas, 1821–1823." *Southwestern Historical Quarterly* 53 (October 1949): 117–50.

Meredith, Howard. *Dancing on Common Ground: Tribal Cultures and Alliances on the Southern Plains.* Lawrence: University Press of Kansas, 1995.

Mills, Elizabeth Shown, ed. *Natchitoches, 1729–1803: Abstracts of the Catholic Church Registers of the French and Spanish Post of St. Jean Baptiste des Natchitoches in Louisiana.* New Orleans: Polyanthos, 1977.

————. *Natchitoches, 1800–1826: Translated Abstracts of Register Number Five of the Catholic Church Parish of St. François des Natchitoches in Louisiana.* New Orleans: Polyanthos, 1980.

————. *Natchitoches Colonials: Censuses, Military Rolls, and Tax Lists, 1722–1803.* Chicago: Adams Press, 1981.

Morfi, Juan Agustín de. *History of Texas, 1673–1779.* 2 vols. Edited by Carlos E. Castañeda. Albuquerque: Quivira Society, 1935.

Morse, Jedediah, ed. *A Report to the Secretary of War of the United States on Indian Affairs.* New Haven CT: Howe and Spalding, 1822.

Muckleroy, Anna. "The Indian Policy of the Republic of Texas." *Southwestern Historical Quarterly* 25 (April 1922): 229–60; 26 (July 1922): 1–29; (October 1922): 128–48; (January 1923): 184–206.

Nasatir, Abraham P. *Borderland in Retreat: From Spanish Louisiana to the Far Southwest.* Albuquerque: University of New Mexico Press, 1976.

Neighbours, Kenneth F. *Indian Exodus: Texas Indian Affairs, 1835–1859.* N.p.: Nortex, 1973.

————. *Robert Simpson Neighbors and the Texas Frontier, 1836–1859.* Waco: Texian Press, 1975.

Newcomb, W. W., Jr. *The Indians of Texas.* Austin: University of Texas Press, 1961.

———. "Coahuiltecan Indians." In vol. 2 of *The New Handbook of Texas*. Edited by Ron Tyler. Austin: Texas State Historical Association, 1996.

Noyes, Stanley. *Los Comanches: The Horse People*. Albuquerque: University of New Mexico Press, 1995.

Oates, Stephen B., ed. *Rip Ford's Texas*. Austin: University of Texas Press, 1963.

Obereste, William H. *History of the Refugio Mission*. Refugio TX: Refugio Timely Remarks, 1942.

Padilla, Juan Antonio. "Texas in 1820: Report on the Barbarous Indians of the Province of Texas by Juan Antonio Padilla, Made December 27, 1819." Translated by Mattie Austin Hatcher. *Southwestern Historical Quarterly* 23 (July 1919): 47–68.

Parker, W. B. *Through Unexplored Texas*. Austin: Texas State Historical Association, 1990.

Parson, Edward Morris. "The Fredonian Rebellion." *Texana* 5 (Spring 1967): 10–52.

Perttula, Timothy K. "European Contact and Its Effect on Aboriginal Caddoan Populations between AD 1520 and AD 1680." In vol. 3 of *Columbian Consequences: The Spanish Borderlands in Pan American Perspective*. Edited by D. H. Thomas. Washington DC: Smithsonian Institution Press, 1991.

———. *The Caddo Nation: Archaeological and Ethnohistoric Perspectives*. Austin: University of Texas Press, 1992.

Quaife, Milo Milton, ed. *The Diaries of James K. Polk during His Presidency, 1845–1849*. 4 vols. Chicago: Chicago Historical Society, 1910.

Reagan, John H. "The Expulsion of the Cherokees from East Texas." *Southwestern Historical Quarterly* 1 (July 1897): 38–46.

Richardson, Rupert N. *The Comanche Barrier to South Plains Settlement: A Century and a Half of Savage Resistance to the Advancing White Frontier*. Glendale CA: Arthur H. Clark, 1933.

Ricklis, Robert A. *The Karankawa Indians of Texas: An Ecological Study of Cultural Tradition and Change*. Austin: University of Texas Press, 1996.

Ritchie, E. B., ed. "Copy of Report of Colonel Samuel Cooper, Assistant Adjutant General of the United States, of Inspection Trip from Fort Graham to the Indian Villages on the Upper Brazos Made in June, 1851." *Southwestern Historical Quarterly* 42 (April 1939): 327–33.

Roell, Craig H. "Nuestra Señora del Espíritu Santo de Zuñiga Mission." In vol. 4 of *The New Handbook of Texas*. Edited by Ron Tyler. Austin: Texas State Historical Association, 1996.

Roemer, Ferdinand. *Texas, with Particular Reference to German Immigration and the Physical Appearance of the Country*. San Antonio: Standard Printing Company, 1935.

Roland, Charles P. *Albert Sidney Johnston: Soldier of Three Republics*. Austin: University of Texas Press, 1964.

Rollings, Willard H. *The Osage: An Ethnohistorical Study of Hegemony on the Prairie-Plains*. Columbia: University of Missouri Press, 1992.

Rowland, Dunbar, ed. *Official Letter Books of W. C. C. Claiborne, 1801–1816*. 6 vols. Jackson: Press of the Mississippi Historical Society, 1930.

Sánchez, José María. "A Trip to Texas in 1828." Edited by Carlos E. Castañeda. *Southwestern Historical Quarterly* 29 (April 1926): 249–88.

Schilz, Jodye Lynn Dickson, and Thomas F. Schilz. *Buffalo Hump and the Penateka Comanches*. El Paso: Texas Western Press, 1989.

Schilz, Thomas F. "People of the Cross Timbers: A History of the Tonkawa Indians." PhD diss., Texas Christian University, 1983.

———. *Lipan Apaches in Texas*. El Paso: Texas Western Press, 1987.

Sibley, John. "Historical Sketches of the Several Indian tribes in Louisiana, south of the Arkansas river, and between the Mississippi and river Grande. *American State Papers, Indian Affairs*. Washington DC: Gales and Seaton, 1832.

———. *A Report from Natchitoches in 1807*. Edited by Annie Heloise Abel. New York: Museum of the American Indian Foundation, 1922.

Sjoberg, Andree F. "The Bidai Indians of Southeastern Texas." Master's thesis, University of Texas, 1951.

Smith, F. Todd. *The Caddo Indians: Tribes at the Convergence of Empires, 1542–1854*. College Station: Texas A&M University Press, 1995.

———. *The Caddos, the Wichitas, and the United States, 1846–1901*. College Station: Texas A&M University Press, 1996.

———. *The Wichita Indians: Traders of Texas and the Southern Plains, 1540–1845*. College Station: Texas A&M University Press, 2000.

Smither, Harriet. "The Alabama Indians of Texas." *Southwestern Historical Quarterly* 36 (October 1932): 83–108.

Smither, Harriet, ed. *Journals of the Sixth Congress of the Republic of Texas, 1841–1842*. Austin: Capital Printing, 1945.

Smithwick, Noah. *The Evolution of a State or Recollections of Old Texas Days*. Austin: University of Texas Press, 1983.

Taylor, Virginia H., trans. and ed. *The Letters of Antonio Martínez, Last Governor of Texas, 1817–1822*. Austin: Texas State Library, 1957.

Taylor, Virginia H., ed. *Letters from Antonio Martínez to the Viceroy Juan Ruiz de Apodaca*. San Antonio: Research Center for the Arts and Humanities. University of Texas at San Antonio, 1983.

Teal, Annie Fagan. "Reminiscences of Annie Fagan Teal." *Southwestern Historical Quarterly* 34 (April 1930): 317–28.

Thomas, Alfred Barnaby, ed. *Forgotten Frontiers: A Study of the Spanish Indian Policy of Don Juan Bautista de Anza, Governor of New Mexico, 1777–1787*. Norman: University of Oklahoma Press, 1932.

Tjarks, Alicia Vidaurreta. "Comparative Demographic Analysis of Texas, 1777–1793." *Southwestern Historical Quarterly* 77 (January 1974): 291–338.

Trennert, Robert A., Jr. *Alternative to Extinction: Federal Indian Policy and the Beginnings of the Reservation System, 1846–1851*. Philadelphia: Temple University Press, 1975.

Usner, Daniel H., Jr. *Indians, Settlers, and Slaves in a Frontier Exchange Economy: The Lower Mississippi Valley before 1783*. Chapel Hill: University of North Carolina Press, 1992.

Vehik, Susan H. "Problems and Potential in Plains Indian Demography." In *Plains Indian Historical Demography and Health: Perspectives, Interpretations, and Critiques*. Edited by G. R. Campbell. *Plains Anthropologist* Memoir 23, 1989.

Vigness, David M. "Nuevo Santander in 1795: A Provisional Inspection by Félix Calleja." *Southwestern Historical Quarterly* 75 (April 1972): 461–506.

Wallace, Ernest, and E. Adamson Hoebel. *The Comanches: Lords of the Southern Plains*. Norman: University of Oklahoma Press, 1952.

Webb, Walter Prescott. *The Texas Rangers: A Century of Frontier Defense*. Austin: University of Texas Press, 1935.

Weber, David J. *The Mexican Frontier, 1821–1846: The American Southwest under Mexico*. Albuquerque: University of New Mexico Press, 1982.

———. *The Spanish Frontier in North America*. New Haven CT: Yale University Press, 1992.

Weddle, Robert S. *The San Sabá Mission: Spanish Pivot in Texas*. Austin: University of Texas Press, 1964.

———. *The French Thorn: Rival Explorers in the Spanish Sea, 1682–1762*. College Station: Texas A&M University Press, 1991.

White, Richard. *The Middle Ground: Indians, Empires, and Republics in the Great Lakes Region, 1650–1850*. New York: Cambridge University Press, 1991.

Williams, Amelia W., and Eugene C. Barker, eds. *The Writings of Sam Houston*. 8 vols. Austin: University of Texas Press, 1938–43.

Wilbarger, J. W. *Indian Depredations in Texas: Reliable Accounts of Battles, Wars, Adventures, Forays, Murders, Massacres, etc., Together with Biographical Sketches of Many of the Most Noted Indian Fighters and Frontiersmen of Texas*. Austin: Hutchings Printing House, 1889.

Wilson, Maurine T., and Jack Jackson. *Philip Nolan and Texas: Expeditions into the Unknown Lands, 1791–1801*. Waco: Texian Press, 1987.

Winfrey, Dorman, ed. *The Indian Papers of Texas and the Southwest, 1825–1916*. 5 vols. Austin: Texas State Library, 1959–61.

Wolff, Thomas. "The Karankawa Indians: Their Conflict with the White Man in Texas." *Ethnohistory* 16 (1969): 1–32.

Index